W9-ACK-963

Studying
Public Policy
Policy Cycles & Policy Subsystems

Studying
Public Policy

Policy Cycles & Policy Subsystems

Third Edition

Michael Howlett
M. Ramesh
Anthony Perl

OXFORD
UNIVERSITY PRESS

OXFORD
UNIVERSITY PRESS

70 Wynford Drive, Don Mills, Ontario M3C 1J9
www.oupcanada.com

Oxford University Press is a department of the University of Oxford.
It furthers the University's objective of excellence in research, scholarship,
and education by publishing worldwide in

Oxford   New York

Auckland   Cape Town   Dar es Salaam   Hong Kong   Karachi
Kuala Lumpur   Madrid   Melbourne   Mexico City   Nairobi
New Delhi   Shanghai   Taipei   Toronto

With offices in

Argentina   Austria   Brazil   Chile   Czech Republic   France   Greece
Guatemala   Hungary   Italy   Japan   Poland   Portugal   Singapore
South Korea   Switzerland   Thailand   Turkey   Ukraine   Vietnam

Oxford is a trade mark of Oxford University Press
in the UK and in certain other countries

Published in Canada
by Oxford University Press

Copyright © Oxford University Press Canada 2009
The moral rights of the author have been asserted
Database right Oxford University Press (maker)

First published 2009

All rights reserved. No part of this publication may be reproduced,
stored in a retrieval system, or transmitted, in any form or by any means,
without the prior permission in writing of Oxford University Press,
or as expressly permitted by law, or under terms agreed with the appropriate
reprographics rights organization. Enquiries concerning reproduction
outside the scope of the above should be sent to the Rights Department,
Oxford University Press, at the address above.

You must not circulate this book in any other binding or cover
and you must impose this same condition on any acquirer.

Library and Archives Canada Cataloguing in Publication Data

Howlett, Michael, 1955–
Studying public policy : policy cycles and policy subsystems / Michael Howlett,
M. Ramesh and Anthony Perl.—3rd ed.

Includes bibliographical references and index.
ISBN 978-0-19-542802-5

1. Policy sciences.   I. Ramesh, M., 1960– .   II. Perl, Anthony, 1962– .   III. Title.

H97.H69   2009   320.6   C2008-906168-3

This book is printed on permanent (acid-free) paper ∞.
Printed and bound in Canada

Cover credit: Günay Mutlu/Istockphoto

1 2 3 4 – 12 11 10 09

Contents

List of Figures

Acknowledgements

Many individuals contributed to this book. In addition to the many authors and investigators whose empirical and conceptual work provides the foundation for the summaries and discussions contained herein, we are also grateful for the comments and criticisms received from the reviewers of the book's first two editions and from the many students and instructors who used it and took the time to tell us about their experiences.

This edition includes a considerable amount of new material, elements of which have appeared in conference papers, journal articles, and book chapters. We would like to thank all of the publication teams, reviewers, and conference participants who have constructively engaged with this material and helped us refine our thoughts and arguments.

While the list of those to thank is far too numerous to include here, we would like to express our gratitude to some of our closest colleagues and collaborators, whose personal interventions at critical junctures very much helped to shape the direction of our thinking on the subject of 'studying public policy'. They include Jeremy Rayner, Colin Bennett, Jim Bruton, Melody Hessing, Ben Cashore, Tracy Summerville, Adam Wellstead, Paddy Smith, Iris Geva-May, Aidan Vining, Jeremy Wilson, George Hoberg, Evert Lindquist, Ted Parson, Laurent Dobuzinskis, David Laycock, Luc Bernier, Keith Brownsey, Wu Xun, Giliberto Capano, John Fossum, James A. Dunn Jr, and Kennedy Stewart, among others. At OUP we would like to thank Peter Chambers, Kate Skene, and especially Phyllis Wilson and Richard Tallman for their professionalism and many efforts on our behalf in producing the book. Finally, we owe much to our families for their sympathy and understanding over the years. Special thanks to Rebecca Raglon, Alex and Anna Howlett, and Andrea Banks for keeping us grounded during the writing process. Watching Nikisha grow has been a welcome respite from studying public policy; thanks to her and her mother Mandy.

Part I

Methodology, Theory, and Context in Public Policy Research

Chapter 1

Introduction: Why Study Public Policy?

Overview of the Book

Governments make public policy. Behind this simple formulation lies a world of analysis, authority, and organization that can appear quite opaque, and thus daunting, to the untrained observer. Why are particular policy decisions taken at certain times and not others? How do individual decisions add up and work together in policy regimes or mixes, or are they incompatible and contradictory? Do multiple decisions result in recognizable patterns of policy-making and policy content, or just in random or quasi-random accumulations of past decisions, like building new cities atop the ruins of old ones? And how do we go about analyzing public policies and policy-making? Do we examine individual decisions or overall patterns? And what level do we choose to start examining for meaning: individual decision-making behaviour? group action? institutional structures? And how should we best examine the extensive information that is often available about a policy's history, its function and its impacts and how it relates to its legacy and impact?

These and other questions are addressed as part of the approach to studying public policy presented in this book. We begin, in Part I, with an overview of past efforts to understand public policy-making and outline the different stages of the policy-making cycle that can be examined for valuable insights into policy process. We then move to consider the principal elements and patterns of policy dynamics that influence organizational and political behaviour and lead to policy change before discussing the factors that entrench elements of inertia that yield policy stability. As we will demonstrate, the greatest insights into policy contents and processes are produced through studying the interplay of three dimensions of engaging and resolving public problems. We look to the *policy actor*s who interact to determine the content and process of public policy-making. We also explore the structures and *institutions* that serve to constrain and influence these actors' efforts. And finally, we consider the sets of *ideas* and knowledge that inform their deliberations and actions.

As Chapter 2 will demonstrate, policy theory has always focused on these three analytical dimensions—actors, institutions, and ideas—although at various times different theories have tended to emphasize one element over the other. While understandable, the existence of such separate approaches to investigating public policy has led to a plethora of studies that sometimes yield confusion through conflicting conclusions drawn about public policy-making. This fragmentation has burdened the policy sciences with a level of complexity that can be daunting at first, but is largely unnecessary.

Efforts to simplify this profusion of perspectives have created general models or 'frameworks of analysis' that attempt to synthesize the diverse approaches to studying policy into a single point of view (Dunn, 1988). In this volume we draw on the recent study of policy subsystems, institutional regimes, and policy paradigms to develop a more coherent perspective on policy-making than has typically emerged from theories prioritizing ideas, actors, or institutions over the others. These three conceptual elements—*subsystems, regimes, and paradigms*—are developed in Chapter 3, where we see how their use can unify the apparent diversity of actors, structures, and ideas comprising the policy-making 'universe'. This allows an integrated and coherent framework to be developed that can account for both the constant change in policy components observed by even the most superficial observer of contemporary events and for the apparent stability in overall policy development patterns identified by experts steeped in the details of policy sectors and their history.

Analyzing policy dynamics is the focus of Part II, which uses the model of a staged, sequential policy cycle to set out the basic steps through which policy processes unfold. This form of *policy cycle* analysis sees public policy-making as a socio-political process involving successive stages from the articulation of public problems to the adoption and implementation of expected solutions to them (Schmidt, 2008). It allows us to highlight the operative factors and forces at each distinct stage of the cycle, from *agenda-setting, formulation, decision-making, and implementation to evaluation* and then back through the same process once again in successive iterations of the cycle in an effort to improve upon policy outcomes. This representation of policy-making as a cycle of problem-solving attempts, which result in '*policy learning*' through the repeated analysis of problems and experimentation with solutions, is a central approach of the book.

The cycle framework provides insights into policy-making dynamics by focusing on two interrelated temporal dimensions of that process. First, by differentiating each stage of the cycle, the distinctive impacts of actors, organizational structures, and dominant ideas on deliberation and action can be more clearly identified at any given point in time. Second, when these different 'snapshots' of activity in a particular policy stage are brought into focus, the relationship between actors, organizations, and ideas can become apparent across different stages of the policy cycle. Distinctive ways of making policy—known as a *policy style or mode*—and established patterns of outcomes, or *policy regimes*, can thus be identified.

These broad patterns of policy-making are the substance of Part III, our final section, which examines why established styles of policy deliberation and regimes of delivering policy outcomes are often difficult to change. The strong inertia of a typical overall pattern of policy dynamics is one in which policy stability exists despite the permutations and (re)combination of actors, structures, and ideas that occur at each stage and iteration of the policy process.

Public Policy Defined

Before we begin the discussion of policy theories in Chapter 2 and consider the significance of actors, structures, and ideas in Chapters 2 and 3, however, it is important to propose a working definition of public policy. As we have suggested, (policy-making is fundamentally about constrained actors attempting to match policy goals with policy means in a process that can be characterized as 'applied problem-solving'. Identifying problems and (however imperfectly) matching solutions to them (captured by the phrase 'naming, blaming, framing, and claiming') (Felstiner et al., 1980–1; Druckman, 2001; Steinberg, 1998) involves articulating policy goals through policy deliberations and discourses and using *policy tools* in an attempt to attain those goals.

This process of matching goals and means has two dimensions. The *technical* dimension seeks to identify the optimal relationship between goals and tools, since some tools are better suited to address particular problems than others. The second dimension is a *political* one since not all actors typically agree on what constitutes a policy problem or an appropriate 'solution'. Moreover, the analysis of both problems and solutions is further constrained by the existing state of knowledge about social and economic problems, as well as policy actors' ideas, norms, and principles with respect to what they consider to be appropriate courses of action to follow. These ideational assumptions shape both their notions about what constitutes a 'problem' as well as the kinds of policy actions that they feel are 'feasible' and 'acceptable' (May, 2005; Majone, 1975; Melstner, 1972; Huitt, 1968).

Numerous definitions of public policy attempt to capture the idea that policy-making is a techno-political process of defining and matching goals and means among constrained social actors. These definitions all posit policies as being the outcome of such reconciliation processes; that is, that policies are intentional government actions containing both some articulated goal or goals—however poorly the goals may in fact have been identified, justified, and formulated—and some means to achieve them—again, notwithstanding how well or poorly the means have in fact been connected to the goal(s).

While there are substantial areas of agreement among the competing definitions of public policy, however, they also differ considerably in detail (Birkland, 2001: ch. 1). Two examples of widely used definitions illustrate the diverse meanings ascribed to public policy by different authors, even when they agree on the general pragmatic nature of policy-making and policy-making processes.

In probably the best-known definition, Thomas Dye offers a particularly succinct formulation, describing public policy as 'Anything a government chooses to do or not to do' (Dye, 1972: 2). This is, of course, too simple for many analytical purposes, for it would treat equally as public policy every aspect of governmental behaviour, from purchasing or failing to purchase specific types of paper clips to waging or failing to wage nuclear war, and provides no means of differentiating the trivial from the significant aspects of government activities. Nevertheless, this definition has merits.

⌕ First, Dye's definition specifies that the primary agent of public policy-making is a government. This means that private business decisions, decisions by charitable organizations, interest groups, other social groups, or individuals are not in themselves public policies., Governments enjoy a special role in public policy-making due to their unique ability to make *authoritative* decisions on behalf of citizens, that is, ones backed up by sanctions for transgressors in the event of non-compliance. Hence, when we talk about public policies we are always speaking about initiatives sanctioned by governments. Although the activities of non-governmental actors may and very often do influence governments' policy decisions, and governments sometimes leave the implementation of policy to non-governmental organizations (NGOs), the efforts and initiatives of such actors do not in themselves constitute public policy. Thus, for example, how the medical profession interprets the causes of lung cancer and the solutions it proposes for prevention and cure may have a bearing on what a government eventually does about the problem in terms of health-care policy. However, the profession's proposed solution to the problem is not itself a public policy; only measures that a government adopts or endorses—such as a ban on the sale or use of tobacco— would actually constitute *public* policy.

Second, Dye highlights the fact that public policy-making involves a fundamental choice on the part of governments to do something or to do nothing about a problem and that this decision is made by elected politicians and other government officials. As Dye notes, public policy is, at its simplest, a choice made by government to undertake some course of action. A 'negative' or 'non-decision', that is, a government's decision to do nothing and simply maintain the current course of action or status quo (Crenson, 1971; R.A. Smith, 1979) is just as much a policy decision as a choice to attempt to alter some part of the status quo. Such 'negative' decisions, however, like more 'positive' ones, must be *deliberate*, such as when a government decides not to increase taxes or declines to make additional funds available for arts, health care, or some other policy area. The fact we have the freedom to paint our homes any colour we choose, for example, does not mean that this is a public policy, because the government never deliberately decided to uphold our autonomy in this area.

Third, and closely related to this, Dye's definition also highlights the fact that a public policy is a *conscious* choice of a government. That is, government actions and decisions often yield *unintended consequences*, such as when an effort to regulate tobacco consumption or some other vice results in the activity 'going underground' and operating illegally as a 'black market'. Unless this subsequent activity or consequence was specifically anticipated and intended by government (such as occurs when governments increase gasoline taxes to discourage automobile use and thus promote the use of public transit), the unintended consequence of policy is not public policy but merely its unexpected by-product, which sometimes may be beneficial and sometimes not.

Dye's three points are central to understanding public policy as an applied problem-solving process, and his definition brings the idea of conscious, deliberate government decisions to the fore in its analysis. Other definitions become more complex, as they attempt to integrate additional dimensions of public policy into their framework in order to separate out the trivial from the significant elements of the phenomenon. William Jenkins, for example, offered a much more precise conceptualization of public policy than Dye's definition provides, but one that illustrates many of the same themes.

Jenkins (1978) defined public policy as['a set of interrelated decisions taken by a political actor or group of actors concerning the selection of goals and the means of achieving them within a specified situation where those decisions should, in principle, be within the power of those actors to achieve'.\This definition is very helpful in specifying the *content* of a policy as being composed of the 'selection of goals and means', as we noted above. Moreover, it usefully clarifies some of the implicit components of Dye's definition, which could be construed as limiting policy-making to only those situations where there is a single 'choice opportunity' and where only a single decision results from that opportunity. Although even this narrow interpretation of Dye's definition presumes the existence of an underlying process behind decision-making, it does not state so explicitly. Jenkins, however, presents policy-making as a *dynamic* process and explicitly acknowledges that public policy is usually the result of 'a set of interrelated decisions'. In other words, governments rarely address problems with a single decision, as Dye's definition might suggest. Instead, most policies involve a *series of decisions* that cumulatively contribute to an outcome. Thus, a health policy, for example, consists of a series of decisions on building health facilities, certifying personnel and treatment, and financing health-care provision, among many other related items (Tuohy, 1999). These various interrelated decisions are often made by different individuals and agencies within government, such as a Department of Health as well as Ministries of Finance or Social Welfare and by various divisions and sections within them, resulting in a much more complex policy-making process than a quick reading of Dye's definition might suggest. These varied actors and their behaviour and interaction within 'policy sub-systems' structure many elements of the policy-making process and are the first major theme of this book, discussed in Chapters 2 and 3.

Jenkins also improves upon Dye's work by adding the idea that a government's *capacity* to implement its decisions is also a significant component of public policy and a major consideration affecting the types of action that government will consider. Jenkins's definition recognizes that limitations on a government's ability to act can constrain the range of options considered in particular decision-making circumstances or can contribute to the success or lack of success of policy-making efforts. A government's choice of a policy may be limited, for instance, by lack of financial, personnel, or informational resources, by international treaty obligations, or by domestic resistance to certain options. Thus, for example, we will not understand health policy in many countries without realizing the powerful, self-serving opposition that the medical profession can mount against any government's effort to control health-care costs by reducing professionals' income (Alford, 1972). Similarly, understanding domestic government actions increasingly requires detailed awareness of the limits and opportunities provided by international agreements, treaties, and conventions (Milner and Keohane, 1996; Doern et al., 1996a). Again, these external and internal structural constraints on policy-making make its analysis much more complicated than might be assumed from Dye's definition. The role of organizational structures within and beyond government in terms of their impact on government policy capacity forms the second major theme of the book and is also explored in some depth in Chapters 2 and 3 and in subsequent chapters.

Jenkins also introduces the idea of public policy-making as goal-oriented behaviour since, in his definition, public policies are decisions taken by governments that define a goal and set out a means to achieve it. Although this says nothing about the nature of the goals (or the means involved), viewing policy as the pursuit of conscious goals raises the importance of the ideas and knowledge held by policy actors, and especially government actors, to public policy-making and its analysis. These shape actors' understanding of policy problems and the 'appropriateness' of potential solutions. The role of ideas—and especially the proposition that 'policy paradigms' inform and constrain problem definition and policy content—is the final major theme of this book and informs the discussion throughout the volume.

Methodological Implications for Studying Public Policy

Definitions like those of Dye and Jenkins provide the general outline of what a public policy is. Their underlying reliance on appreciating the contribution of actors, structures, and ideas to making policy, however, also suggests some methodological obligations that arise when studying public policy. They illustrate, for example, that the study of public policy is a demanding task that cannot be pursued simply by accessing the official records of government decision-making found in laws, acts, regulations, and official reports. Although these are a vital source of information, public policies extend beyond the record of formal investigation and official decisions to encompass the realm of potential choices, or choices not made (Howlett, 1986). The analysis of such choices necessarily involves considering the array of state and societal actors involved in decision-making processes and their capacities for influence and action. Policy decisions do not reflect the unencumbered will of government decision-makers so much as the evidence of how that will interacted with the constraints generated by actors, structure, and ideas present at a given political and social conjuncture (Sharkansky, 1971).

Moreover, if we looked at only policy decisions per se, then describing government policy would be both straightforward and easy compared to the effort required to understand in more general terms *why* a state adopted the policy it did. Sometimes a government may announce the reasons behind a decision, and these reasons may even be true. However, it is also common for a government not to give any reason for making a decision; or for the publicly stated reason not to be the actual reason a decision was taken. In such situations it is left to analysts to determine why a particular alternative was chosen and, very often, why some other seemingly more attractive option was not.

How analysts explain specific public policy outcomes is influenced by the frameworks they employ and the aspects of policy-making these frameworks emphasize or downplay (Danziger, 1995; Yanow, 1992; Phillips, 1996). These models and techniques orient analysts towards either of two broad approaches. On the one hand, there are those who believe that reasonably *objective* analysis of policy goals and outcomes is possible and that these subjects can be explored with standard social science methodologies for collecting data and analyzing them (Bobrow and Dryzek, 1987; Radin, 2000; Lynn, 1999). In this 'positivist' view, students of public policy must be skilled in evaluating policy outcomes and understanding, for example, why a policy was not implemented as intended and failed, or why it may have succeeded despite poor implementation (Bovens et al., 2001; Bovens and t'Hart, 1995, 1996).

Other analysts, however, embrace more subjective interpretive or 'post-positivist' techniques to help them discern and critique government aims, intentions, and actions. An example of this approach would be examining the way decision-makers' assumptions about human behaviour influence their decisions to use certain policy implementation techniques (Torgerson, 1996; Thompson, 2001; Yanow, 1999; Dryzek, 2005). Although the differences between positive and post-positive approaches should not be overstated (Howlett and Ramesh, 1998), they serve to underscore how orientations towards policy-making as a social phenomenon can affect analytical techniques and outcomes.

This difference in methods and approaches to policy-making underlies the oft-noted distinction drawn between *policy analysis* and *policy studies. Policy analysis* tends to concentrate on the formal evaluation or estimation of 'policy impacts' or outcomes, usually by using quantitative techniques such as cost–benefit analysis (CBA) or risk assessment and management (Weimer and Vining, 1992). It involves the assessment of the direct and indirect effects of specific policies, using techniques of statistical inference to analyze the links between, for example, specific government programs and various measures of policy 'outcomes', such as indicators of social change and progress. Among economists, such studies have examined a wide range of topics in easily quantifiable realms, investigating in great detail topics such as the relations between government expenditures and corporate investment activity or labour migration. This approach focuses almost exclusively on the effects of policy outputs, however, and says very little about the policy processes that created those outputs (Lynn, 1987).

Policy studies, on the other hand, are broader in scope, examining not just individual programs and their effects, but also their causes and presuppositions, and the processes that led to their adoption. One common type of policy study, for example, has attempted to associate particular types of policies with the nature of political regimes—defined loosely as the organization of the political system (Wolfe, 1989; Przeworski and Limongi, 1997). It has often been argued, by B. Guy Peters (Peters et al., 1977) and Frances Castles (1998; Castles and McKinlay, 1997), for example, that both the policy content and form of public policy-making vary according to the nature of a political system and the types of links decision-makers have with society. Much effort has gone into classifying and differentiating between regime types, with the expectation that properly identifying the regime will generate insights into the policies they adopt (Steinberger, 1980).

Another element of the policy studies literature has sought to identify causal variables in public policy-making, which are sometimes referred to as 'policy determinants' (Munns, 1975; Hancock, 1983). Analyses in this tradition, such as those carried out by Harold Wilensky (1975; Wilensky et al., 1985; Wilensky and Turner, 1987) in the mid-1970s, attempted to resolve the question of whether public policies are determined by macro-level socio-economic factors or by micro-level behaviour through the cross-national comparative analysis of policy-making in sectors such as health and welfare (Rakoff and Schaefer, 1970).

Yet another strand of the policy studies literature focuses on the analysis of 'policy content' as a predictor of policy processes. This approach is associated closely with the idea that the nature of a policy problem and especially the solutions devised to address it often determine how it will be processed by the political system. In this approach, problems are expected to be dealt with in different fashion depending on whether they are primarily regulatory, distributive, redistributive, or constitutive in character. Hence, as Theodore Lowi (1972) put it, ultimately 'policy may determine politics' and not the other way around, as most analysts commonly suppose. In a similar vein, James Q. Wilson (1974) argued that the degree of concentration of costs and benefits imposed on political actors by a particular policy shapes the type of policy processes that will accompany it. Lester Salamon (1981), taking this insight to heart, argued that focusing on the nature of the policy tools or instruments governments have at their disposal to implement public policies is therefore the best mode of analysis for understanding public policy.

These different literatures and analytical traditions have existed, in part, as a result of the diverse analytical communities working on public policy. Governments themselves, of course, have always been involved in policy analysis, both within (Meltsner, 1976; Rogers et al., 1981) and beyond their borders (Rose, 1991). However, many analysts work for non-governmental organizations such as corporations, churches, labour unions, and think-tanks or research institutes, as well as in the university system (Pal, 1992; Cohn, 2004; Gormley, 2007). Analysts working for governments and for groups directly affected by public policies tend to focus their research on policy evaluation. They often have a direct interest in condemning or condoning specific policies on the basis of their projected or actual impact on their client organization. Private think-tanks and research institutes usually enjoy more autonomy, though some may be influenced by the preferences of their funding organizations. Nevertheless, they remain interested in the 'practical' side of policy and tend to concentrate either on policy outcomes or on the instruments and techniques that generate those outcomes.

Academics, on the other hand, have greater independence and usually have no direct personal stake in the outcome of specific policies, except to the extent they are working within or are committed to a particular ideological stance. Academics can therefore examine public policies more abstractly than can other analysts and tend to grapple with the theoretical, conceptual, and methodological issues surrounding public policy-making through the lens of policy studies. Academic studies also tend to look at the entire policy process and take into account many factors, including policy regimes, policy determinants, policy instruments, and policy content in their analyses (Gordon et al., 1977).

The Policy Cycle Framework: An Applied Problem-Solving Model of the Policy Process

All of the definitions provided above posited that public policy is a complex phenomenon consisting of numerous decisions made by many individuals and organizations inside government, and that these decisions are influenced by others operating within and outside of the state. Policy outcomes are seen as being shaped by the structures within which these actors operate and the ideas they hold—forces that also have affected earlier policies and related decisions in previous iterations of policy-making processes. As such, the complexity of studying public policy is considerable, posing many analytical difficulties for students of public policy.

Historically, as we have seen, one of the most popular means of simplifying public policy-making for analytical purposes has been to think of it as a process, that is, as a set of interrelated stages through which policy issues and deliberations flow in a more or less sequential fashion from 'inputs' (problems) to 'outputs' (policies). The idea of simplifying public policy-making by breaking the process down into a number of discrete stages was first broached in the early policy studies of Harold Lasswell (1956), one of the pioneers and promoters of what he termed 'the policy science' (Farr et al., 2006). The resulting sequence of stages is often referred to as the '*policy cycle*' (Werner and Wegrich, 2007).

This simplification has its origins in the earliest works on public policy analysis, but has received disparate treatment in the hands of different authors. This model views policy-making in essentially pragmatic terms, as the embodiment of efforts to improve the human condition through harnessing reason to guide human activities, in this case, in the process of governing (Hawkesworth, 1992; Clemons and McBeth, 2001). Improvements are not, however, a matter of forcing reality to fit within the confines of a theory. Rather, theory and practice reinforce each other as theory is fine-tuned in the light of practice, while practice is altered by the application of theory. This relationship, of course, is one of *learning*, and a pragmatic approach to policy-making views that process as being one of policy learning, in which policy-makers struggle through an incremental trial-and-error process of choosing a policy, monitoring its results, and then amending their action in subsequent policy-making rounds while pursuing their original goals or modified ones. The policy cycle, therefore, goes beyond merely input and output stages, but also extends to monitoring and evaluative activities once outputs have emerged.

In his own work, Lasswell (1971) divided the policy process into seven stages, which, in his view, described not only how public policies were actually made but also how they should be made: (1) intelligence, (2) promotion, (3) prescription,

(4) invocation, (5) application, (6) termination, (7) appraisal. In this construct, the policy process begins with intelligence-gathering, that is, the collection, processing, and dissemination of information by policy-makers. It then moves to the promotion of particular options by those involved in making the policy decision. In the third stage the decision-makers prescribe a course of action. In the fourth stage the prescribed course of action is invoked alongside a set of sanctions to penalize those who fail to comply with these prescriptions. The policy is then applied by the courts and the bureaucracy and runs its course until it is terminated or cancelled. Finally, the results of the policy are appraised or evaluated against the original aims and goals.

Lasswell's analysis of the policy-making process focused, like Dye's, on decision-making within government and had little to say about external influences on the state. It simply assumed that policy-making was limited to a small number of officials within the government. Another shortcoming of this early model was its placing of policy appraisal after termination, since policies would logically be evaluated prior to being wound down rather than afterwards. Nevertheless, this model was highly influential in the development of policy studies (DeLeon, 1999). Although not entirely accurate, it reduced the complexity of studying public policy by allowing each stage to be isolated and examined before putting the process back together to ascertain the whole picture.

Lasswell's formulation formed the basis for many other models (Lyden et al., 1968; Simmons et al., 1974). Typical of these was a simpler version of the policy cycle developed by Gary Brewer (1974). According to Brewer, the policy process is composed of only six stages: (1) invention/initiation, (2) estimation, (3) selection, (4) implementation, (5) evaluation, and (6) termination. In Brewer's view, invention or initiation referred to the earliest stage in the sequence when a problem would be initially sensed. This stage, he argued, would be characterized by an ill-conceived definition of the problem and suggested solutions to it. The second stage of estimation concerns calculation of the risks, costs, and benefits associated with each of the various solutions raised in the earlier stage. This would involve both technical evaluation and normative choices. The object of this stage is to narrow the range of plausible choices by excluding the unfeasible ones and, somehow, to rank the remaining options in terms of desirability. The third stage consists of adopting or rejecting some combination of the solutions remaining at the end of the estimation stage. The remaining three stages comprise implementing the selected option, evaluating the results of the entire process, and terminating the policy according to the conclusions reached by its evaluation.

Brewer's version of the policy process improved on Lasswell's pioneering work by expanding beyond the confines of government in exploring how problems are recognized. It also clarified the terminology for describing the various stages of the process. Moreover, it introduced the notion of the policy process as an ongoing cycle. It recognized that most policies do not have a fixed life cycle—moving from birth to death—but rather seem to recur, in slightly different guises, as one policy succeeds another with minor or major modification (Brewer and DeLeon, 1983). Brewer's insights inspired several other versions of the policy cycle to be developed in the 1970s and 1980s, the best known of which were set out in textbooks by Charles O. Jones (1984) and James Anderson (1984). Each contained slightly different interpretations of the names, number, and order of stages in the cycle.

Clarifying the logic behind the cycle model helps avoid the plethora of similar yet slightly different models of policy stages (Hupe and Hill, 2006). In the works of Brewer, Jones, and others the operative principle behind the notion of the policy cycle is the logic of applied problem-solving, even though this logic remains implicit. The stages in applied problem-solving and the corresponding stages in the policy process are depicted in Figure 1.1.

In this model, *agenda-setting* refers to the process by which problems come to the attention of governments; *policy formulation* refers to how policy options are formulated within government; *decision-making* is the process by which governments adopt a particular course of action or non-action; *policy implementation* relates to how governments put policies into effect; and *policy evaluation* refers to the processes by which the results of policies are monitored by both state and societal actors, the outcome of which may be reconceptualization of policy problems and solutions. This model will be used throughout the book and forms the basis for separate chapters on each stage found in Chapters 4–8.

This model is useful not only because of the way it separates out distinct tasks conducted in the process of public policy-making, but also because it helps clarify the different, though interactive, roles played in the process by policy actors, institutions, and ideas (Sobeck, 2003; Parag, 2006, 2008). In this view, agenda-setting is a stage in which virtually any (and all) policy actors might be involved in decrying problems and demanding government action. These policy actors—whether all, many, or few—can be termed the *policy universe*. At the next stage, formulation, only a subset of the policy universe—the *policy subsystem*—is involved in discussing options to deal with problems recognized as requiring some government action. The subsystem is composed of only those actors with sufficient knowledge of a problem area, or a resource at stake, to allow them to participate in the process of developing possible alternative courses of action to address the issues raised at the agenda-setting stage. When a decision is being taken on one or more, or none, of these options to implement, the number of actors is reduced even further, to only the subset of the policy subsystem composed of *authoritative*

Figure 1.1   Five Stages of the Policy Cycle and Their Relationship to Applied Problem-Solving

Applied Problem-Solving	*Stages in Policy Cycle*
1. Problem Recognition	1. Agenda-Setting
2. Proposal of Solution	2. Policy Formulation
3. Choice of Solution	3. Decision-Making
4. Putting Solution into Effect	4. Policy Implementation
5. Monitoring Results	5. Policy Evaluation

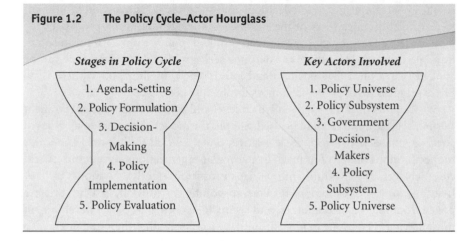

Figure 1.2   The Policy Cycle–Actor Hourglass

Stages in Policy Cycle	Key Actors Involved
1. Agenda-Setting	1. Policy Universe
2. Policy Formulation	2. Policy Subsystem
3. Decision-Making	3. Government Decision-Makers
4. Policy Implementation	4. Policy Subsystem
5. Policy Evaluation	5. Policy Universe

government decision-makers, whether elected officials, judges, or bureaucrats. Once implementation begins, however, the number of actors increases once again to the relevant *subsystem* and then, finally, with the evaluation of the results of that implementation, expands once again to encompass the entire *policy universe* (see Figure 1.2).

The policy cycle model as a framework for analysis of public policy processes has both advantages and disadvantages. The most important advantage is that it facilitates an understanding of a multi-dimensional process by disaggregating the complexity of the process into any number of stages and sub-stages, each of which can be investigated alone or in terms of its relationship to any or all the other stages of the cycle. This aids theory-building by allowing the results of numerous case studies and comparative studies of different stages to be synthesized. Second, the approach can be used at all socio-legal or spatial levels of policy-making, from that of local governments to those operating in the international sphere (Fowler and Siegel, 2002; Bogason, 2000; Billings and Hermann, 1998). Also, as discussed above, this model permits examination of the intertwined role of all actors, ideas, and institutions involved in policy creation, not just those governmental agencies formally charged with the task.

The principal disadvantage of this model is that it can be misinterpreted as suggesting that policy-makers go about solving public problems in a very systematic and more or less linear fashion (Jenkins-Smith and Sabatier, 1993; Howard, 2005). This, obviously, is not the case in reality, as the identification of problems and the development and implementation of solutions are often very ad hoc and idiosyncratic processes. Frequently, decision-makers merely react to circumstances, and do so in terms of their interests and pre-set ideological dispositions (Stone, 1988; Tribe, 1972). Similarly, while the logic of systematic problem-solving may be elegant in principle, in practice the stages are often compressed or skipped, or are followed in an order unlike that specified by the model (Timmermans and Bleiklie, 1999). The cycle may not be a single iterative loop, for example, but rather a series of smaller loops in which, to cite just one possibility, the

results of past implementation decisions may have a major impact on future policy formulation, regardless of the specifics of the agenda-setting process in the
case concerned. Or, as some analysts have noted, policy formulation can sometimes precede agenda-setting as 'solutions seek problems' to which they can be
applied (Kingdon, 1984; Salamon and Lund, 1989). In short, often there is no
linear progression of policy-making as implied by the model.

Second, it is unclear exactly at which level and with what unit of government
the policy cycle model should be used. Should the model be applied to all types of
governmental activity, from the legislative to the judicial? Or is it only applicable
to specific kinds of decisions taken by particular organizations such as bureaucracies (Schlager, 1999)? Third, and perhaps most importantly, the model in itself
lacks any notion of causation. It offers no pointers as to what, or who, drives a
policy from one stage to another, and seems to assume that policy development
must inevitably continue to move from stage to stage, rather than stall or end at a
particular point in the cycle, without explaining why this should be the case
(Sabatier, 1992). Fourth, it does not say anything at all about the content of a
policy (Everett, 2003).

The weaknesses of the framework underscore the need to develop better intellectual devices to advance its understanding. While the simple five-stage cycle
model helps analysis by disaggregating the policy process into a series of distinct
stages, it does not illuminate the nuances and complexities of public policy-
making within each stage or over the cycle as a whole. A better model is needed that
delineates in greater detail the actors and institutions involved in the policy
process, helps identify the instruments available to policy-makers, and points out
the factors that lead to certain policy outcomes rather than others (Mazmanian
and Sabatier, 1980). This improved model of the policy process is set out in Part II
of this book.

Structure of the Book

This book develops an analytical framework that will enable students to study public policy more effectively. It pursues this objective first by examining different
approaches to the subject matter and by providing inventories of the relevant types
of policy actors, structures, and ideas involved in public policy-making. It then
breaks down the policy process into the five sub-processes or sub-stages set out in
the policy cycle model identified above and analyzes the variables affecting each
stage. It concludes with a general commentary on the nature of policy change
and stability.

The book draws on many strands in the literature and enables students to
cover a broad range of material, while maintaining analytical coherence by using
the policy cycle framework. It is not intended to predispose students towards particular conclusions concerning the merits and demerits of particular policy
options or outcomes in particular sectors, but rather to help them identify and
analyze the key variables that affect each stage of public policy-making.

Chapter 1 has briefly charted the development of public policy as an academic discipline and explained what is generally meant by the term. It has outlined a five-stage model of the policy cycle and framed research questions relevant to the analysis of each stage and to the workings of the overall model. Chapter 2 examines in more detail several of the most commonly used approaches to studying public policy, emphasizing those employed by economists, political scientists, sociologists, and others who focus on the nature of public policy processes. The potential and limitations of each approach are discussed, as is the particular manner in which theorizing about policy-making has developed over the past several decades. Chapter 3 then describes the institutional parameters within which policies are made, the nature of the actors who make them, and the ideas that guide the actors. It uses the concept of a policy subsystem to capture the intricate links between actors and structures involved in public policy-making.

Each of Chapters 4 to 8 then examines a critical component or stage of the public policy process. How and why do public concerns make their way onto the government's agenda and what consequences ensue for future policy-making? How and why do some individuals and groups enjoy privileged input into the formulation of governmental policy options and what impact does this have? How and why do governments typically decide on a specific course of action and with what results? Why do governments use the types of policy instruments they do and how do these choices affect policy outcomes? How are government actions and choices typically evaluated, and to what extent does this contribute to policy learning and improved policy-making? These and other questions are posed and answered in each chapter in this section.

Finally, Chapter 9 sets out conclusions about studying policy change, drawing on the general relationships among actors, structures, and ideas outlined in the book. It presents the general pattern of the evolution of policy-making in many policy sectors, and discusses the reasons why policies tend to develop through a highly constrained or 'path-dependent' process resulting in a common pattern of policy change through periodic upheavals in established policy orders (Gersick, 1991; Baumgartner and Jones, 1993).

Study Questions

1. How do the simplifying frameworks adopted by students of public policy affect the outcomes of their studies?
2. What are the common elements found in different definitions of public policy-making?
3. What are the strengths and weaknesses of the policy cycle model of the public policy process?
4. How do actors, structures, and ideas, individually and collectively, affect public policy-making?
5. How is public policy-making related to governance?

Further Readings

Fischer, Frank. 2007. 'Policy Analysis in Critical Perspective: The Epistemics of Discursive Practices', *Critical Policy Analysis* 1, 1: 97–109.

Garson, G. David. 1986. 'From Policy Science to Policy Analysis: A Quarter Century of Progress', in W.N. Dunn, ed., *Policy Analysis: Perspectives, Concepts, and Methods*. Greenwich, Conn.: JAI Press, 3–22.

Lasswell, Harold D. 1951. 'The Policy Orientation', in D. Lerner and H.D. Lasswell, eds, *The Policy Sciences: Recent Developments in Scope and Method*. Stanford, Calif.: Stanford University Press, 3–15.

May, Peter J. 2005. 'Policy Maps and Political Feasibility', in I. Geva-May, ed., *Thinking Like a Policy Analyst: Policy Analysis as a Clinical Profession*. London: Palgrave Macmillan, 127–51.

Sabatier, Paul A. 1999. 'The Need for Better Theories', in P.A. Sabatier, ed., *Theories of the Policy Process*. Boulder, Colo.: Westview Press, 3–17.

Chapter 2

Understanding Public Policy: Theoretical Approaches

As Peter DeLeon has noted, policy studies have a long history and a short past. That is, the actions of government have been a focus of much examination over the centuries, but their systematic analysis using the conceptual framework of policy science dates back less than six decades (DeLeon, 1994; Peters, 1999). Even in the short time period that the discipline has existed, however, the policy sciences have been characterized by a surprisingly large number of overlapping, yet distinct, perspectives (Sabatier, 1999b; Schlager, 1999). In this chapter we outline the main approaches to studying public policy found in the literature, point out their strengths and weaknesses, and suggest how they may be synthesized for a better understanding of the subject.

Evolution of the Policy Sciences

Policy science emerged in North America and Europe following World War II as students of politics searched for new understandings of the relationship between governments and citizens that could better explain the tremendous growth of public-sector activity involved in creating increasingly ambitious economic and social programs (DeLeon and Martell, 2006; DeLeon, 2006). Before the era of big and active governments, studies of political life tended to focus either on the normative and moral dimensions of governing, or on the minutiae of how specific legal and political institutions functioned.

At one end of the analytical spectrum, scholars concerned with the normative or moral dimensions of government studied the great texts of political philosophy, seeking insights into the purpose of governing and the activities that those in power should undertake if their citizens were to attain the good life. These inquiries generated a rich discussion of the nature of society, the role of the state, and the rights and responsibilities of citizens and governments. However, the gap between prescriptive political theory and the political practices of modern states that emerged between the two world wars and during the ensuing Cold War led many to search for another method of examining politics, one that would reconcile political theory and practice not through the analysis of what government officials said was being done in the public sector, but rather by the systematic evaluation of outputs and outcomes generated by actual government programs (Torgerson, 1990; Smith 1982).

At the other end of the spectrum, scholars interested in the institutions of government had been conducting detailed empirical examinations of legislatures, courts, and bureaucracies while generally ignoring the normative aspects of these institutions. Such studies of formal political institutions excelled in attention to detail and procedure but for the most part remained very descriptive, failing to generate the basis for evaluating the strengths and weaknesses of such structures in the new era of large public programs, or their effects on policy deliberations and choices. In the immediate post-war decades of decolonization, when the reconstruction and restructuring of defeated states such as Germany and Japan occurred and new institutions of international governance were established, students of politics sought an approach that would connect their examination of governmental processes and structures more directly with substantive questions of justice, equity, and the pursuit of social, economic, and political development (Mead, 1985).

In this context of change and reassessment, several new approaches to studying politics appeared. Some focused on the micro level of human behaviour and the psychology of citizens, electors, leaders, and followers; others concentrated on the characteristics of national societies and cultures; still others focused on the nature of national and global political systems. Most of these approaches—behaviouralism, elite studies, studies of political culture, and political cybernetics—have come and gone out of intellectual and academic fashion as many scholars experimented with each before grasping its limitations and moving on to search for something more satisfying (Cairns, 1974; Schaefer, 1974). Of course, some researchers remained devotees of each of these post-war perspectives, but only the policy science perspective can claim an unbroken chain of theoretical development that has not been vigorously challenged by dissenters who were previously enamoured of the approach.

Contemporary studies in public policy certainly retain the intellectual vitality of those who originated the approach. Its focus is not so much on the structure of governments or the behaviour of political actors, or on what governments should or ought to do, but on what governments actually do. This approach focuses on the development of generalizations and laws about public policies and public policy-making, or, as its originators deemed it, *policy science*. Pioneered by Harold Lasswell and others in the United States and the United Kingdom, policy science was expected to replace traditional political studies, integrating the study of political theory and political practice without falling into the sterility of formal, legal studies (Lasswell, 1951; Torgerson, 1990).

Lasswell proposed that policy science had three distinct characteristics that would set it apart from earlier approaches: it would be *multi-disciplinary, problem-solving, and explicitly normative*. By multi-disciplinary, Lasswell meant that policy science should break away from the narrow study of political institutions and structures and embrace the work and findings of such fields as sociology and economics, law and politics. By problem-solving, he envisioned a policy science adhering strictly to the canon of relevance, orienting itself towards the solution of real-world problems and not engaging in the purely academic debates that, for example, characterized interpretation of classical and obscure political texts. By explicitly normative, Lasswell meant that policy science should not be cloaked in the guise of 'scientific objectivity', but should recognize the impossibility of separating goals and means, or values and techniques, in the study of government actions (Torgerson, 1983). He expected policy analysts to say clearly which solution would be better than others when two options were compared.

This general orientation towards government activities and the consequences of those actions suggested by Lasswell remains with us and forms the subject matter of this book. However, the passage of time has led to some changes in the three specific components of the policy orientation he first identified (Garson, 1986; DeLeon, 1986, 1988; Hansen, 1983). For one, over the past 40 years the virtually exclusive concern of many policy scholars with concrete problem-solving has waned. At the outset, it was hoped that the study of public policy-making and its outcomes would yield conclusions and recommendations directly applicable to existing social problems. Although laudable, this hope foundered on the complexity of the policy process itself, in which governments often proved resistant to 'expert' advice on subjects with which they were dealing (Wildavsky, 1979; Ascher, 1986; Sharpe, 1975). In the real world of public policy, technically superior analysis was often subordinated to political necessity (Fischer, 2007; Weiss, 1983).

Second, and relatedly, while the emphasis on multi-disciplinarity remains, a large body of literature now focuses on public policy in general. Policy science has become very much a 'discipline' itself, with a unique set of concepts and concerns and a vocabulary and terminology of its own (Fishman, 1991). Although many of these concepts have been borrowed from other disciplines, they have a somewhat particular meaning when used in the context of studying public policy. Furthermore, the concept of multi-disciplinarity has changed in the sense that policy scholars now take it for granted that they must borrow from other disciplines and must be experts in at least two fields: the concepts and concerns of policy science, and the history and issues present in the substantive area of policy, or the 'policy field', under examination (Anderson, 1979a).

Finally, the calls for the policy sciences to remain explicitly normative also changed over time, although rather less than have the other founding principles. For the most part, policy scholars have refused to exclude values from their analyses and have insisted on evaluating both the goals and the means of policy, as well as the process of policy-making itself. However, analysts' desire to prescribe specific goals and norms declined with an increasing realization of the intractability of many public problems. Hence, many investigators now either evaluate policies in terms of simple measures such as efficiency or effectiveness, or use the record of policy efforts to establish whether governments have in practice been directing their activities towards the achievement of their stated goals, in either case without considering the desirability or rationality of these goals themselves (Greenberg et al., 1977; DeLeon, 1994; Yanow, 2007).

As these changes occurred, some observers began to castigate the notion of a policy 'science' and to equate its promotion with that of other similar endeavours in an era of unrealized hopes and expectations for social engineering and government planning (Tribe, 1972; Pielke, 2004; Wedel et al., 2005). Although sometimes justified by the inflated claims of individual studies, this criticism should serve as a warning against premature or ill-founded prescriptions or excessive conceptual sophistry, rather than as a rejection of the need to undertake the systematic study of government actions. To the extent that the policy sciences have developed a significant body of empirical and theoretical studies of the activities of numerous governments around the globe, the early efforts and dicta of Lasswell remain valuable and continue to provide the foundation upon which the study of public policy is conducted (Wagner et al., 1991; Torgerson, 1983; Levin-Waldman, 2005).

In general, contemporary policy studies rely on one of two broad *methods of analysis*: deductive and inductive. Some analysts rely on a *deductive* method in which understanding is developed largely on the basis of applying general presuppositions, concepts, or principles to specific phenomena. Other approaches are less grounded in predetermined principles and apply *inductive* methods that develop generalizations only on the basis of careful observation of empirical phenomena and subsequent testing of these generalizations against other cases (Lundquist, 1987; Przeworski, 1987; Hawkesworth, 1992).

Public choice, Marxist, and some economic institutionalist theories are examples of deductive theories whereas group theories like pluralism and corporatism, historical and sociological neo-institutionalism, and statist theories are examples of inductive theories. Although neither analytical method guarantees a clearer insight into the contingent and idiosyncratic circumstances of policy development, the deductive and inductive methods depict different attributes and highlight distinctive policy dynamics (see Almond and Genco, 1977). Each of these approaches is discussed in some detail below. First, however, the general issue of whether or not it is possible to arrive at law-like scientific findings in the area of policy studies should be broached.

Approaches to Public Policy Analysis: Positivism and Post-Positivism

Unlike physics or chemistry, there is no universally recognized methodology for analyzing policy problems. Instead, a range of skills and techniques can be found in the policy analysis toolkit (e.g., law, economics, quantitative methods, organizational analysis, budgeting, etc.). A combination of analytical tools is applied by policy analysts inside and outside government to understand policy problems. The education of policy analysts trained during the post-war decades, and who now populate most bureaucracies and private research organizations (i.e., consultancies), was oriented towards familiarizing them with generic analytical tools, along with cases, workshops, simulations, or real-world projects designed to illustrate how to choose analytical tools appropriate to specific circumstances and contexts. The idea was to demonstrate how the 'art and craft' of policy analysis owed much to inductive as opposed to deductive reasoning: matching tools and context, and producing time-sensitive advice that policy-makers could absorb (Wildavsky, 1979; Vining and Weimer, 2002; Guess and Franham, 1989; Weimer, 1992; Bardach, 2000; Geva-May, 1997).

While practitioners and those who train them concentrated on acquiring the insight into which analytical approaches and applications will work in a given context, other policy scholars have sought to discern more general overall patterns of policy analysis, influence, and effectiveness from among the potentially infinite variation of analytical practices (Thissen and Twaalfhoven, 2001). Empirical studies of the ways in which policy analysis is generated, interpreted, and utilized have revealed how these processes are affected by the needs and beliefs of ultimate users, the delicacy of the political relations, coalitions and conflicts among decision-makers, the history of previous policy reform efforts, individual personalities and agendas, organizational routines, and other factors (Weiss, 1977a, 1977b; Sabatier, 1987; Shulock, 1999). These studies have shown, on the one hand, that 'one size does not fit all' because analytic opportunities are often idiosyncratic, requiring pragmatic judgement of the appropriate techniques to apply in specific circumstances. On the other hand, they have demonstrated that governments tend to develop preferences for specific types of analysis, leading to an ongoing conflict within the analytical process.

Policy researchers have created frameworks that deepen the understanding of how different methods of policy analysis are matched to the tools, repertoires, and capabilities of particular governance contexts. Successful modes of policy analysis are not simply a matter of the choice and skill of policy analysts and managers, but are conditioned by contextual elements that favour particular techniques and preferences (Shulock, 1999; Radin, 2000). These preferred analytical styles can include a penchant for the use of traditional 'technical' tools such as cost-benefit analysis, but can also involve the use of alternate or complementary techniques such as the frequent use of public consultation or stakeholder participation, or simply an entrenched preference for the use of specific types of policy instruments (Richardson et al., 1982; Van Waarden, 1995; Howlett, 2000).

These studies have shown how public policy is, above all, a practical discipline whose explicit purpose is to advise policy-makers on how best to address public problems. While various approaches analyze public problems and devise solutions to them, the vast majority of formal analyses rely on ideas and techniques drawn from economics. While the proponents of this approach usually describe themselves as merely 'policy analysts', their critics refer to them as '*positivist*' or 'rationalist', in reference to their scientific leanings. Positivist approaches to studying policy embrace scientific rationality and see policy analysis as part of the quest to uncover objective knowledge. This perceived obsession with quantifiable facts and rational reasoning has fostered a counter-movement whose proponents describe themselves as '*post-positivists*'. Both of these broad or 'meta'-approaches to studying public policy are described below.

Positivist Approaches to Policy Analysis

The mainstream in prescriptive policy analysis consists of applying principles from economics, especially welfare economics, to public problems. Indeed, much of what is identified as policy analysis research is often only applied welfare

Figure 2.1   A General Taxonomy of Goods and Services

		Exhaustiveness	
		High	Low
Exclusivity	High	Private Good	Toll Good
	Low	Common-Pool Good	Public Good

Source: Adapted from E.S. Savas, *Alternatives for Delivering Public Services: Toward Improved Performance* (Boulder, Colo.: Westview Press, 1977).

economics, even though this is rarely stated explicitly (Weimer and Vining, 1999). Welfare economics is based on the notion that individuals, through market mechanisms, should be expected to make most social decisions. Its proponents, similar to other mainstream economists, accept that the market is the most efficient mechanism for allocating society's resources, but they also admit that markets do not work properly under all circumstances. In such instances, referred to as *market failures*, they argue that political institutions can act to supplement or replace markets to produce better outcomes in terms of enhancing overall social welfare.

The principles of welfare economics were first worked out by the British economist Alfred Pigou (1932) during World War I. Although he only identified a small number of specific instances of market failures related to the tendency of some industries to generate monopolies and the inability of both consumers and investors to always receive information necessary for rational or optimal economic decision-making, later analysts argued the existence of many more instances of market failure (Bator, 1958; Zerbe and McCurdy, 1999). The market failures on which there is broad agreement include *public goods, natural monopolies, externalities, imperfect information, the tragedy of the commons*, and *destructive competition*. Others exist, but are not universally accepted, such as moral hazard or informational asymmetries.

Public goods. All goods and services in society can be divided into a relatively small number of types. A popular scheme for doing so identifies four types according to the transactional criteria of 'exclusivity' and 'exhaustiveness' (Ostrom, 2003). 'Exclusivity' (also known as non-rival consumption) refers to transactions involving a good or service limited to the consumption or use by a single consumer, while 'exhaustiveness' refers to goods and services whose consumption diminishes their availability to others. These criteria of exclusivity and exhaustiveness generate four types of goods and services, as listed in Figure 2.1, and are used by welfare economists and many policy analysts to determine the need for government action.

In this view, *pure private goods* make up the bulk of goods and services produced in society. These goods or services, such as food, can be divided up for exclusive sale and are no longer available to others after their consumption and can usually be delivered effectively through the market mechanism. At the other extreme are *pure public goods* or services, such as street lighting, which cannot be parcelled out and are consumed by numerous users without diminishing the sum of the good available. These, it is argued, will not generate profits for suppliers and therefore must be supplied by non-market actors, such as governments, who can fund their supply through the tax system. Between the two are *toll goods* and *common-pool goods*. The former include semi-public goods such as bridges or highways, which do not diminish in quantity after use but for whose use it is possible to charge. These can be provided by either market or non-market means. Common-pool goods are those, like fish in the ocean, whose usage cannot be directly charged to individuals but whose quantity is reduced by consumption. These require a non-market organization, like a government, to ration their supply, which will otherwise be quickly exhausted by competitive market firms.

Natural monopoly refers to the situation in certain industries with large capital requirements and disproportionate returns to scale that tend to promote a single firm over its competitors. In industries such as telecommunications, utilities, electricity, and railways, the first company to establish the necessary infrastructure, if unregulated, enjoys cost advantages that make it difficult for other firms to compete using the same technology. The lack of competition, when it occurs, can lead to a loss of the society's economic welfare if monopoly prices are charged for these goods or services. Governments can correct this problem by regulating prices and other aspects of the good or service provided in order to prevent the exercise of monopoly market power by early-entrant firms.

Imperfect information occurs when consumers and/or producers lack the information necessary to make rational decisions. Unregulated pharmaceutical firms, for instance, have no incentive to reveal adverse side effects of their products, nor do consumers have the expertise required to evaluate such products prior to their use. Once again, decisions may be taken that do not serve the society as a whole, justifying government action to mandate information disclosure.

In the presence of *externalities*, too, the market is deemed to fail. These involve situations in which production costs are not borne by producers ('internalized') but passed on to others outside (external to) the production process. The most often cited example of an externality relates to the costs of air, water, or land pollution that a company in pursuit of reduced costs and increased profits imposes on the society as a whole or on specific segments of it. There may also be positive externalities, as when a person getting immunization improves others' health although those beneficiaries do not incur any price or cost for that benefit. In either case, government action is said to be justified to ensure that producers bear all the costs accruing to, and/or reap all the benefits stemming from, their activities.

The tragedy of the commons is a market failure that occurs when common-pool resources, such as fisheries, pastures, or forests, are exploited without a requirement to maintain the resource for future use. In these circumstances individual users, whether farmers pasturing their cattle on the local common land or multinational seafood or forestry corporations, often benefit from increasing their use of the resource in the short term although all users will suffer in the long term due to increased depletion of the resource. As with common-pool goods in general, this is said to justify government action to ration production among resource users.

Destructive competition is a controversial market failure that is deemed to exist when aggressive competition between firms causes negative side effects on workers and society (Utton, 1986). It is argued that excessive competition can drive down profit margins and lead to the unnecessary reduction of safety and working conditions, adversely affecting overall social welfare. The taxicab industry is often cited as an example of such an industry because of the relative ease with which suppliers can enter the market until a point is reached when there are too many taxis and fares crash, negatively affecting all producers and consumers. Like tragedies of the commons and the situation with common-pool goods, this is said to support government regulation of market entry in order to prevent over-competition.

Sustained criticisms of the vague criteria used to define market failures have led many welfare economists to attempt to reconceptualize the original notion. Recent critics have argued that market failures are, in fact, only one side of an equation and that there are also innate limitations to the government's ability to correct market failures. They posit that in several specific instances—*government failures*—the state cannot improve on the market, despite the latter's failings (Le Grand and Robinson, 1984; Mayntz, 1993a; Dollery and Worthington, 1996; Bozeman, 2002).

Gaps between legislative or political intent and administrative practice were frequently held up as a major reason for the kinds of shortcomings associated with government failure (see Kerr, 1976; Ingram and Mann, 1980b; Mulford, 1978). In the *principal–agent* theory that was subsequently often invoked to explain this phenomenon, these gaps were viewed as the inevitable results of the structure of political and administrative institutions in modern states in which decision-makers must delegate responsibility for implementation to officials they only indirectly control.

The existence of structural discretion on the part of the administrative 'agents' of political 'principals' provided a powerful explanation for inefficient or ineffective administrative implementation of government policy, stemming as it did from the common practice in government whereby laws passed by the political branches of government are put into effect through regulations developed by administrative agencies responsible for implementing the laws. This legal framework establishes a particular kind of principal–agent relationship between politicians and administrators in which there is an inherent problem of securing the latter's compliance (see Cook and Wood, 1989; Gormley, 1989). Administrators have their own understanding, ambitions, and fiscal and knowledge resources that may take policies a long way from the objectives originally conceived by decision-makers.

This structural problem is compounded by the complex relationships among policies and policy actors. For example, many policies demand action by multiple government agencies. This requires another administrative layer of inter-organizational co-ordination by specialized administrative entities, such as inter-departmental or intergovernmental committees, or so-called 'staff' or 'central agencies', which can further exacerbate principal–agent dilemmas by adding additional layers of ideas and interests between the policy objective and its realization (see Smith et al., 1993; Campbell and Szablowski, 1979; Mayntz, 1993b; Rogers and Whetton, 1982). Given this diversity of actors and interests involved in addressing problems, the possibility increases that multiple, and not necessarily commensurable analytical frameworks will have been applied to a policy issue.

Three instances of such government failure are commonly cited: organizational displacement, derived externalities, and the principal–agent problem.

Organizational displacement is the situation in which an administrative agency charged with producing a particular good or service eventually displaces publicly sanctioned goals with its own 'private' or 'organizational' ones. These may extend to maximizing its budget or power or whatever else the organization values. In such circumstances, government action to correct market failure may simply increase inefficiency. Thus, it is argued that they should refrain from doing so over the long term but, rather, might intervene for a shorter period of time, after which the determination of activities are returned to the market where possible.

Rising costs are another instance of government failure. Governments receive tax revenues and, unlike their private counterparts, are not under pressure to generate revenues by competing in the marketplace. Without the fear of going bankrupt, a real possibility for private producers, it is argued that governments do not have the same incentive to control expenses and instead may allow them to continually balloon in size. Again, it is argued that due to this limitation, a government must carefully weigh the costs and benefits of altering market relations, and in some cases allowing 'minor' market failures to persist may be cheaper than engineering a government takeover of that activity.

Derived externalities 'are side effects that are not realized by the agency responsible for creating them, and hence do not affect the agency's calculations or behaviour' (Wolf, 1988: 77). Certain government actions, such as health-care provision, have a broad impact on society and the economy and can have the effect of excluding viable market-produced goods and services, negatively affecting overall levels of social welfare (Wolf, 1979; Le Grand, 1991; Weimer and Vining, 1999: 194). Again, this suggests that government replacement of market-based goods and service production should be carefully assessed, and that the 'opportunity costs' associated with such actions should be factored into the government decision-making calculus.

Although the exact status and causes of government and market failures remain controversial and largely inductively derived, welfare economists advanced a theory of public policy-making built on these concepts. They argued that governments have a responsibility to try to correct market failures because society will be left with sub-optimal social outcomes if they are left to private decisions. In this view, governments facing a demand for action should first determine if a market failure is causing a social problem; only if one is found should the government intervene to correct it (Stokey and Zeckhauser, 1978). However, even then, in order to avoid government failures, policy-makers also must carefully evaluate their own capacity to correct the identified market failure before attempting to do so, taking into account both common government failings and inherent *principal–agent problems* (Vining and Weimer, 1990; Weimer and Vining, 1992).

Elegant and logical as the welfare economist's conception of public policy-making appears, it often does not reflect the reality of policy-making as governments almost never make their policies in the manner assumed by this theory. Even if one could identify the most efficient and effective policy, which is difficult given the limitations innate to the social sciences, the actual policy choice is a political, not a technical, one, bound by political institutions and made by political actors in response to political pressures, ideologies, and self-interests, among other factors.

As such, the technical analyses generated by welfare economists are often merely another political resource used by proponents of one or another option for government action or inaction to further their claims (Weiss, 1977b). Only in very specific circumstances when welfare economists happen to be policy-makers—as happens at times in some countries' policy sectors, such as taxation or fiscal management—would one expect political decisions to be based largely on the criteria defined by welfare economists (Markoff and Montecinos, 1993). The neglect of political variables by welfare economics has led its critics to describe it as 'a myth, a theoretical illusion' that promotes 'a false and naive view of the policy process' (Minogue, 1983: 76; Hogwood and Gunn, 1984: 50–1) and to propose a more politically informed, alternative 'post-positivist' view.

Post-Positivist Approaches

Post-positivism and the associated 'argumentative turn' in public policy emerged in the early 1990s following widespread dissatisfaction with the technocratic direction the discipline had taken in the preceding decades following orthodox, 'positivist' welfare economics maxims. Many of the critics of mainstream public policy analysis (described in the preceding section) banded together as 'post-positivists' with the explicit objective of going beyond technocratic positivism (which is a strong version of the *empiricism* they felt incorrectly informed welfare economic analysis) in their own analyses of policies and policy-making.

Post-positivists are a disparate collection of scholars bound mainly by their common purpose of generating usable policy analysis through reliance on political and social analysis of public problems and policy-making processes and outcomes. Indeed, any effort to draw up a single blueprint for post-positivist analysis would be an anathema for its proponents because of the importance they attribute to contextual socio-political factors, which by definition vary across cases (Dryzek, 1990; Fischer, 2003, 1998; Forester, 1993; Göktug, 2002; Hajer and Wagenaar, 2003; Majone, 1989; Stone, 1988).

Post-positivists do, however, generally argue that mainstream policy analysts informed by welfare economics and other similar approaches are misguided in their obsession with quantitative analysis, objective separation of facts and values, and generalizable findings independent of particular social contexts—all hallmarks of 'positivist' thinking. They posit subjective reflection, normative analysis, and argumentation as more fruitful tools for understanding public policies and policy-making. Although post-positivists are influenced by more general social philosophies and methods such as critical theory, post-structuralism, post-modernism, and social constructivism, which tend to deny the existence of an objective realm of facts independent of the observer, they are not against objectivity and empirical analysis per se. Rather, they believe that (positivist) empirical analysis needs to be combined with (post-positivist) normative analysis because the two are inseparable, a position in fact argued explicitly by founders of the policy sciences such as Harold Lasswell (see above).

Post-positivists believe that the almost exclusive emphasis on empirical evidence found in positivist analyses is seriously misguided on both methodological and ethical grounds. The instrumental, ends–means analyses on which welfare economics-inspired policy analysts spend so much effort, they argue, are mistaken because policies rarely have unambiguous goals and rarely do policy-makers choose the most efficient means of achieving them. Instead, they suggest, policy goals and means are products of constant conflict and negotiation among policy-makers guided by their values and interests and shaped by a variety of contingent circumstances. By ignoring or downplaying partisan politics and value conflicts among policy-makers, post-positivists note, positivists fail to examine the most vital elements that shape policy and provide seriously misleading, if not entirely incorrect, analyses (Dryzek, 2002).

Post-positivists not only find positivist policy analysis to be lacking in comprehending reality, however, but also object to it on ethical grounds, arguing it promotes 'top-down' bureaucratic policy management and stifles democracy and participation (Heineman et al., 1990). By emphasizing efficiency and effectiveness in their assessment and design of the means to achieve goals, positivist analysis, they argue, promotes a 'technocratic form' of governance characterized by disdain for politics. As Fischer (2007a: 97) argued: 'If pluralist politics and competing interests don't fit into the methodological scheme, then politics is the problem. Some have gone so far as to argue that the political system itself must be rearranged to better suit the requirements of policy analysis.'

However, unlike the model of market–governance failure inspired by welfare economics and used by positivist policy analysts, there is no set formula for post-positivist analysis because post-positivism is not a formal theory. Rather, it is more appropriate to describe it as an 'orientation' whose proponents are bound by a number of core common beliefs. They start from the assumption that there is no single incontrovertible or 'objective' understanding of policy problems or solutions, as positivists claim. Instead, they explicitly recognize that all knowledge is contestable (Fischer, 2007b: 224). Post-positivists make no pretense of analytical objectivity and political neutrality but take on the role of 'deliberative practitioners operating within a clear value framework that promotes greater social and political equity' (Burton, 2006: 174).

The need to promote democracy and public participation also occupies a central place in post-positivist thinking (Dryzek, 2002). As we have seen, traditional policy analysis is criticized for its technocratic orientation, which is alleged to exclude ordinary citizens from the policy process (Durning, 1999; Hajer and Wagenaar, 2003). To address the lacunae, post-positivists ascribe central impor-tance to providing 'access and explanation of data to all parties, to empower the public to understand analyses, and to promote serious public discourse' (Fischer, 2003: 15). In this approach, the policy analyst is more a facilitator than a policy-maker or designer. In their role as facilitator, policy analysts should promote pol-icy deliberations by removing inequalities among participants 'so that a consensus around policy is achieved more by the inherent power of argument than by the status of the person advancing it' (Burton, 2006: 182). Understand-ably, then, post-positivists place a great deal of emphasis on giving citizens the information they need to participate meaningfully in the policy process.

From this view, participatory policy analysis is desirable not only because it is more democratic but also because it is alleged to lead to better policies and more effective implementation since it brings a greater number of perspectives to bear on a policy problem than is the case with an exclusive, top-down, technocratic orientation. This is especially germane, it is argued, since many policies are increasingly made not by politicians responding to voters' sentiments but by unelected officials influenced by powerful special interest groups and far removed from the concerns of the general public. Only an organized dialogue between the bureaucracy and the public, it is argued, can allow generation of alternatives that effectively address the latter's needs (Hajer and Wagenaar, 2003).

Arguments, therefore, are the basic unit of analysis in post-positivism and dis-course or discursive analysis its primary methodology. As Majone (1989: 7) explains, 'the job of policy analyst consists in large part of producing evidence and arguments to be used in the course of public debate.' In the post-positivist view, persuasion through argumentation plays a vital role at every stage of the policy process. From agenda-setting to policy evaluation, the policy process is essentially a 'rhetorical and interpretative' exercise in which protagonists engage in dis-courses intended to both define and further their ideas and interests. As Fischer (2007b: 227) puts it: 'In politics, politicians and policy decision-makers put forth proposals about what to do based on normative arguments. Empirical analysis comes into play but only when there are reasons to question or explore the fac-tual aspects of the argument.'

Legal argumentation, in which different protagonists prepare arguments for and against particular policy positions, offers a template for what post-positivist analysis and policy formulation look like. The opposing analyses take the form of a debate in which participants not only present arguments but also disclose their norms, values, and circumstances. Fischer (ibid.) explains:

> In such a policy debate, each party would confront the others with counter-proposals based on varying perceptions of the facts. The participants would organize the established data and fit them into the world views that underline their own arguments. The criteria for rejecting or accepting a proposal would be the same grounds as those for accepting or rejecting a counterproposal.

Rules of evidence as used in courts are proposed as a means of assessing the conflicting arguments and choosing among them. Such a strategy would allow analysts to combine empirical and normative analyses, making their efforts pragmatic yet analytically rigorous.

Fischer (ibid., 230) offers 'practical reasoning' as a way to deal with conflicting arguments. Unlike mathematical or logical proof, which either is true or false:

> practical arguments are only more or less convincing, more or less plausible to a particular audience. What is more, there is no unique way to construct a practical argument: data and evidence can be chosen in a wide variety of ways from the available information, and there are various methods of analysis and ways of ordering values.

All of these allow policy-makers considerable room to use their judgement in making a final choice both among the sorts of problems to be addressed and among the tools and techniques available to address them.

Post-positivist analysis combining empirical and normative analyses proceeds at two levels (ibid., 232–4). At the micro level, study focuses on issues concerning the actual programs in place, the problems they are directed at, and those involved in making and implementing the program. Typical questions at this level include: 'Does the program fulfill its stated objective(s)?' 'Does the program fulfill these objectives more efficiently than alternative means available?' 'Is the program objective(s) relevant to the problem?' At the macro level, post-positivist analysis is concerned with abstract goals and contexts. Does the policy goal 'contribute value for the society as a whole?' 'Does the policy goal result in unanticipated problems with important societal consequences?' Finally, the analyst must address the broader values underpinning the conceptualization of public problems and efforts to address them.

The greatest strength of post-positivist analyses is that they are sensitive towards the messy realities of the public policy process, unlike their positivist counterparts who tend to have an orderly, even mechanistic, conception of the policy realm. For positivists, policy problems are largely technical issues that can be addressed effectively once the right solution is found through rigorous technical analysis. Post-positivists correctly point out that technical analysis needs to be complemented by study of a range of other factors, including conflicts based on different values and interests.

The emphasis on participation and democratic decision-making is another great strength of post-positivism. According to Dryzek (2002: 35):

> A more participatory policy process helps to create more effective and competent citizens, who are also more effective problem solvers, within the policy process and beyond. They are also more capable of constructing productive relationships with others concerned with different facets of complex problems.

Public participation in the policy process has the additional benefit of generating social capital, which not only helps solve immediate problems but also strengthens the government and society's overall capacity for addressing public problems in the future (ibid.).

One of the limitations of post-positivism, however, is the lack of accepted criteria for evaluating competing arguments. The absence of such criteria promotes 'relativism in which a commitment to avoid the privileging of any one viewpoint becomes a tolerance of anything' (Burton, 2006: 186).

Moreover, the deliberative process on which post-positivists place so much emphasis may be hijacked by those who gain from the status quo. The potential losers in any change situation are likely to be the most active participants in such processes, and they will have an overwhelming interest in scuttling any process that negatively affects them through protracted deliberation.

Third, while post-positivists correctly point out the importance of value-based discourse, they unwittingly underestimate the importance of the material interests in which the discourse is grounded. As Burton (ibid., 187) warns: 'in believing that discourse is everything and that material inequalities can be overcome by discourse alone, it may appear not only that words are deeds but that they are sufficient to change society for the better.'

The lack of a clear research method, a guide as it were, also severely handicaps those trying to include post-positivism in their teaching curriculum and may at least partially explain why it receives scant attention in public policy syllabi. Although Dryzek (2002: 32) has argued that 'most of its proponents would say that the whole point is to replace the illusion of certainty with recognition of the reality of contention and so avoid simplistic recipes', it does raise the level of difficulty for those trying to teach or put it into practice a post-positivist mode of policy analysis—unlike the easily codified and understood welfare economics-inspired 'positivist' analysis it condemns.

Reconciling the Positivist and Post-Positivist Debate

Recent empirical work has identified several of the basic parameters of the range of analytical styles found in different locales, which fall between the rational, *modern* positivist analyst of the 1960s and 1970s, focused on the quantification of economic costs and benefits, and the *postmodern* or post-positivist analyst of the 1980s and 1990s, concerned with the social construction of policy problems, policy discourses, and the politics of the policy process (Radin, 2000).

Drawing on European experience, Mayer, Van Daalen, and Bots (2001) have provided a finer-grained dissection of the policy analysis function. They note how both types may coexist within a given polity or policy sector, and argue that policy analysis embraces distinct tasks of research, clarification, design, advice, mediation, and democratization. Using pairs of these activities, Mayer et al. produce six distinct, but not mutually exclusive, styles of policy analysis:

1. *Rational.* In the traditional positivistic style, researchers apply mainly economic and other empirical methods to specific cases. Here, the generation of new knowledge is the main task of the analyst.

2. *Client advice.* The analyst provides political and strategic advice to clients.
3. *Argumentative.* The analyst is actively involved in debate and policy discourse as a distinct independent actor both within and outside governments.
4. *Interactive.* The analyst serves as a facilitator in consultations in which key players and participants define their preferred outcome.
5. *Participative.* The researcher/analyst is an advocate, aggregating and articulating the interests of silent players in the policy process: the poor, the general interest, or any other actor not represented in the policy process.
6. *Process.* The analyst acts a 'network manager', steering the policy process towards a preferred outcome defined as part of the analytic task.

This analysis helps break out of the often sterile debate between positivist and post-positivist policy analysis and emphasizes the extent to which all types of policy analysis are subordinated to larger concerns and analyses in the policy studies tradition (Knoepfel et al., 2007).

Approaches to Public Policy Studies: Multi-Level, Multi-Disciplinary

Theorizing with Different Units of Analysis

This high-level, meta-dispute between positivists and post-positivists over the nature of policy knowledge and methods of 'formal' policy analysis has affected the general approaches taken to explain policy-making and the methods used to evaluate or critique public policies within policy studies. However, these disputes have had little effect on policy studies per se, because virtually all theories developed to explain public policy-making and public policy outcomes from a policy studies perspective already assumed a heavily politicized policy process.

A great many theories, generated in fields as diverse as geography, history, economics, sociology, and political science, inform work in the policy studies tradition. These theories can be differentiated according to the basic *unit of analysis* they use in their investigations. *Public choice* theory, for example, focuses on the micro-level behaviour of individuals. *Group and class* theory looks at the interaction of organized interests that often mediate between individuals and the state. And adopting the broadest perspective on how people come to make policy, *institutional analysis* looks to the structure of political and economic arrangements—from the ways in which finance and industry operate to the respective roles of bureaucracy, legislatures, and courts in the policy process. These three perspectives (see Figure 2.2) are representative of the range of focuses found in policy studies. Like the visual variety found in a good movie, however, superior policy studies combine wide-angle, midrange, and close-up shots of policy-making in action to highlight different elements of the process. In other words, the best policy analyses from a policy studies perspective combine elements of these macro-, meso-, and micro-level approaches.

Figure 2.2   Levels of Analysis and Examples of Relevant Policy-Related Theories

Unit of Analysis	Approach
Individual	• Public choice
Collectivity	• Class analysis • Group analysis: Pluralism and Corporatism
Structures	• Institutionalism and Neo-institutionalism • Statism

In the following discussion, each of these approaches is defined and its key principles and assumptions are set out. We then assess the strengths and weaknesses of each approach, in terms of its ability to help understand policy-making, including formal policy analysis, and explain the nature of policy outcomes.

Public Choice

Public choice theory rests on a firm foundation of rationality and draws on the values of neo-classical economics to try and explain virtually all aspects of human behaviour. The rational choice framework it resides within has informed theoretical applications in political science, psychology (Tversky and Kahneman, 1986), and sociology (Hecter and Kanazawa, 1997; Kiser and Hecter, 1991), as well as being a mainstay of economics. The primary assumption in this perspective is that political actors, like economic ones, act 'rationally', that is, in a calculating fashion, to maximize their 'utility' or 'satisfaction'. In this model, the only political actor that counts is the individual and the primary motivation that arises from that person's rationality is self-interest, as defined by the individual.

Public choice theory is a 'strong' application of the *rational choice framework* and is often used in policy analyses because the deductive application of its general principles easily generates a clear and consistent set of policy prescriptions, whether or not there is merit to its fundamental axioms. As James Buchanan (1980: 5), one of the founders of public choice theory and the first among public choice theorists to win a Nobel Prize (for Economics), put it: 'In one sense, all public choice or the economic theory of politics may be summarized as the "discovering" or "re-discovering" that people should be treated as rational utility maximizers, in all of their behavioural capacities.'

In the public choice approach it is assumed that individual political actors (whether policy-makers, administrative officials, or voters) are guided by self-interest in choosing a course of action that will be to their best advantage (McLean, 1987; Van Winden, 1988). This simple assumption about the basis of human behaviour leads public choice theorists to an extensive series of related propositions used to explain various aspects of politics and public policy-making. In these studies, each political action is analyzed in terms of individual self-interest.

Thus, for example, voters are deemed to vote for parties and candidates that will best serve their interest in terms of the rewards they hope to receive from governments (Downs, 1957). Politicians are seen as constantly vying for election in order to promote their interests in the income, power, and prestige derived from holding office, and thus offer policies that will win them voters' support (Becker, 1958; Coase, 1960). Political parties are seen to operate in much the same way as politicians, devising policy packages that will appeal to voters (Riker, 1962). Bureaucrats' self-interest leads them to maximize their budgets because larger budgets are a source of power, prestige, perks, and higher salaries (Niskanen, 1971). They are largely successful in realizing their interest because, as monopoly suppliers of unpriced goods and services, they face no competition and because citizens and elected officials lack the expertise to monitor their activities. Peter Self (1985: 51) succinctly summarized the theory as follows:

> Following this approach, voters can be likened to consumers; pressure groups can be seen as political consumer associations or sometimes as co-operatives; political parties become entrepreneurs who offer competing packages of services and taxes in exchange for votes; political propaganda equates with commercial advertising; and government agencies are public firms dependent upon receiving or drumming up adequate political support to cover their costs.

Public choice theorists view the policy process as one in which a variety of political actors engage in competitive *rent-seeking* behaviour. That is, each actor attempts to use the state to capture some portion of the social surplus ('rents') that accrues from productive social labour and is amassed through taxation. Each actor would prefer, if possible, to *free ride*, that is, to obtain a share in the surplus resulting from the action of other parties at no cost to themselves (Buchanan, 1980; Kreuger, 1974).

This conception of the motivations and roles of voters, parties, and politicians in the policy process leads to the conclusion that voters will constantly seek more programs from government, constrained only by their willingness to pay or ability to evade taxes, and that politicians, parties, and bureaucrats will be willing to supply the programs because of their own self-interest in power, prestige, and popularity. The result is a constant increase in the level of state intervention in the economy and society, often in the form of a *political business cycle*. That is, democratic governments are seen to operate in a perpetual campaign mode, buying votes with public money according to the timing of the electoral cycle. Popular decisions that dispense benefits will thus be taken before election and unpopular ones, attributing costs, will be made soon afterwards (Boddy and Crotty, 1975; Frey, 1978; Locksley, 1980; Tufte, 1978).

Public policy-making in this view leads to an inexorable process of extending the state's provision of goods and services. Public choice theorists oppose this dynamic, arguing that it distorts the 'natural' operation of market-based societies and reduces overall levels of social welfare by encouraging free riders and other counterproductive forms of rent-seeking behaviour, as well as promoting government deficit financing or tax increases to cover the costs of expanded programs. The general conclusion of public choice theorists is that institutions must be developed to curb destructive utility-maximizing behaviour that serves the interests of particular individuals while adversely affecting the society as a whole. Hence, according to Buchanan, public choice theory does not lead to the conclusion that all collective action, and all government initiative, is necessarily undesirable. It leads, instead, to an understanding that because people will maximize their own utilities, institutions must be designed so that individual behaviour will further the interests of the group, small or large, local or national. The challenge, then, is to design, or reconstruct, a political order that will channel the self-serving behaviour of participants towards the common good along the lines once described by Adam Smith (Buchanan et al., 1978: 17).

Put simply, for public choice theorists, the same individual utility maximization that promotes the general good in the market takes on a decidedly harmful form when combined with the ability to compel action available in the political arena. This leads public choice theorists to reject most policy analyses and prescriptions generated by researchers who tend to see government activity as more benign (Rowley, 1983). Instead, public choice perspectives seek to restrain and redirect government intervention to supplementing the market by enforcing and creating property rights so that economic forces can operate at a safe distance from political authority and allocate resources to benefit the whole society.

The simplicity and logical elegance of public choice, along with the impressive mathematical presentations found in many studies, mask its shortcomings (Jones, 2001; Green and Shapiro, 1994). First of all, the theory is based on an oversimplification of human psychology and behaviour that does not accord with reality. Many political activities, for example, are undertaken for symbolic or ritualistic reasons; to treat them as goal-oriented behaviour directed at utility maximization is to underestimate the complexity of politics that surrounds public policy-making (Zey, 1992). Second, because of this oversimplification, the theory has poor predictive capacity. There is no empirical proof, for example, that government functions will grow inexorably because democratic representation spurs public spending to buy votes. If anything, in most industrialized countries governments have been pruning spending on popular social programs such as health and education, or, at least, have not been expanding them as the theory would predict.

The actual fluctuations in government growth patterns are also not new and bear little relationship to the electoral cycle. How and why this variation in government size and programming occurs is virtually inexplicable within a public choice framework (Dunleavy, 1986). A third reason for empirical shortcomings can be found in the public choice perspective's heavy reliance on US experience. By presuming a pattern of electoral competition between two parties that requires voters to make 'either-or' choices on contending alternatives, the political reality of multi-party democracies is distorted. The legislative coalitions that are common under multi-party representation do not present voters with the clear-cut bidding for support between 'in' and 'out' parties found in the US or the UK since electoral promises may be overridden by post-election legislative deal-making (Warwick, 2000).

And despite the public choice theorists' insistence that their analysis is 'positive' and 'value-free', the theory is explicitly normative. The notions that only social interactions in market-based exchange produce wealth and that the state exists as a kind of parasite extracting rents from the marketplace ignore the important role played by the state not only in establishing the economy's foundation through property rights and public security, but also in organizing such key economic activities as education and technological innovation (Dosi et al., 1988). Thus, public choice theory seeks, in effect, to promote a particular vision of orthodox liberalism (also called neo-conservatism or neo-liberalism) that would advance markets wherever possible and severely restrict the scope for government activity without any empirical justification for so doing (Hood, 1991, 1995, 1998).

More recently, public choice theorists have acknowledged that a gap exists between their deductive models and empirical reality. Although they are loath to drop any of their fundamental assumptions about human behaviour, they have come to realize that some modifications in their fundamental units of analysis are needed. Many public choice adherents recognize that their theory is institutionally constrained. It has little to say, for example, about policy-making in non-democratic systems that do not rely on free and competitive elections, a central assumption of the model.

Moreover, the theory also disregards or underestimates the effects of institutional factors in shaping actors' preferences, despite its pretensions towards institutional design (Ostrom, 1986a, 1986b). Pioneering public choice theorists tended to regard institutions themselves as changeable according to actors' preferences and were unwilling to fully recognize the durability of institutions and the pervasive impact they have on individual behaviour. The realization by many former public choice adherents of the effects of institutional structures on individual choices has moved many rational choice theorists, including many who had previously endorsed variants such as game theory (Harsanyi, 1977; Scharpf, 1990; Elster, 1986), to embrace a more subtle and supple approach to deductive social theory, a form of economistic 'neo-institutionalism' or 'actor-centred institutionalism', which will be discussed in more detail below.

Class Analysis

Class and group theories explore the often messy middle ground between individuals and the governments that formally enact policy along with the public and private agencies that implement it. They accord primacy to collective entities, the organized interests and associations that seek to influence policy agendas, policy options, and policy outputs. The deductive variant of this mid-range perspective is class theory, which ascribes group membership according to certain observable characteristics of individuals, whether or not the individuals involved see themselves in those terms. Class theorists expect behaviour that maximizes group interests to flow from this attributed orientation.

While there are several types of class analysis, we present the 'Marxist' variant, which, because of its influence on the development and spread of European socialism in the nineteenth and twentieth centuries, is by far the best known and theoretically developed. In this approach, class membership is determined by the presence or absence of certain characteristics, usually, but not always, related to the economy (Ossowski 1963).

The mid-nineteenth-century *Manifesto of the Communist Party* (1848), written by German philosopher and political economist Karl Marx and his friend and colleague, Friedrich Engels, is the best-known articulation of class theory. Marx and Engels presented society as being composed of two classes contesting political and economic power throughout history. Society has passed through a number of distinct stages ('modes of production'), each of which had particular technological conditions of production ('means of production') and a distinct manner in which the various actors in the production process relate with each other ('class structure' or 'relations of production') (Cohen, 1978). In the logic of this model, each mode of production develops a dichotomous class system consisting of those who own the means of production and those who must work for the owners, and the relationship between the two groups is inherently adversarial.

Slaves battled their owners in slave-holding societies; serfs contended with landlords in feudal society; and workers struggle with owners in capitalist society. Continued class struggle leads to eventual collapse of modes of production and their replacement by another mode, which in turn is eventually replaced by yet another system. Marxist class theory interprets public policies in capitalist societies as reflecting the interests of the capitalist class. The capitalists' dominance of the base—that is, the economy—affords them control over the state and what it does. Indeed, according to Marx, the state is merely an instrument in the hands of capitalists, who use it for the purposes of maintaining the capitalist system and increasing profits ('surplus value'), necessarily at the expense of labour.

While this instrumentalist view proved a popular approach to studying public policy in many countries and colonies during the 1930s and 1940s, by the late 1960s in Western Europe it was beginning to be seen as problematic by Marxists on two counts. First, even if a policy did serve the interest of capital, it is not necessarily true that the policy had been enacted at the behest of capital. To show this, one would have to demonstrate that capitalists issued instructions that were faithfully carried out by state officials, proof of which is usually lacking. Second, and more importantly, this approach cannot explain policies adopted over the opposition of capitalists. In most capitalist states, for instance, the adoption of social welfare policies was vehemently opposed by many capitalists, something that cannot be explained if the state is merely an instrument of capital. Recognizing this problem forced a reappraisal of the role of the state in Marxist theory (Block, 1980; Foley, 1978; Gough, 1975; Poulantzas, 1978; Therborn, 1977, 1986).

Much as with public choice theory, the traditional Marxist view—that the means of production constitutes the principal force shaping the state, law, and ideology—

has been challenged to address a broader range of causal factors. For example, the state has been shown to play a crucial role in organizing the economy and shaping the mode of production (Cox, 1987). The nineteenth-century promotion of natural resource sector production and the protection of inefficient import substitution industrialization in Canada, Argentina, Australia, Brazil, and Mexico, for example, had a decisive impact on those countries' economic structures and class relations and continue to shape these various classes' interests, the policy outcomes they desire, and the policy responses they elicit (Clarke-Jones, 1987; Duquette, 1999; Hirschman, 1958). Similarly, the proliferation of Keynesian policies in the 1950s and 1960s in many countries (Hall, 1989) occurred over the opposition of entrenched business interests and cannot be understood without reference to ideological factors influencing state behaviour, just as policies promoting privatization and deregulation in many of the same countries in the 1980s (Ikenberry, 1990) cannot be traced entirely or directly to the interests of capitalists (Amariglio et al., 1988).

Like public choice analysis, which came to recognize a much greater role for the independent effects of institutions and social structures on individual behaviour, class analysis in the 1960s and 1970s placed an increased emphasis on institutional or structural factors to account for state activities and behaviour (McLennan, 1989: 117–19). To account for the state devising policies opposed by capital, for example, the notion of the *relative autonomy* of the state was developed (Poulantzas, 1973a; Althusser and Balibar, 1977). Nicos Poulantzas, for example, argued that conflicts among the various fractions of capital, coupled with the existence of a bureaucracy staffed by individuals drawn from non-capitalist classes, permitted the state to have some autonomy from capital. This autonomy, in turn, allowed the state to adopt measures favourable to the subordinate classes if such policies were found to be politically unavoidable or necessary for promoting the long-term interests of capital in social stability.

Hence, in this 'structural' version of neo-Marxism, policy-making was still viewed as serving the interest of capital, but not in the same instrumental sense as conceived by early Marxists (Thompson, 1978). The rise of the welfare state, for example, is explained not as a direct response to the needs of capital, but as the result of political pressures exerted by the working class on the state (Esping-Andersen, 1981, 1985; Esping-Andersen and Korpi, 1984). The structural imperatives of capitalism are not ignored, however, because they impose limits on what the state can do in response to working-class demands. Thus, it is argued, the welfare state, established by capitalist governments in response to working-class demands, was designed in a manner that did not undermine fundamental property rights or profits. By introducing a structural component to class analysis, however, this version of neo-Marxist social theory, as occurred with public choice theory, shifted towards more institutional types of analysis (see below).

Pluralism

One of the most prominent approaches to studying the middle ranges of policy-making is 'pluralism', which originated in the United States in the early twentieth century and continues, in one form or another, to dominate American political science perspectives on studying politics and policy. 'Corporatism', discussed below, is a parallel group theory developed in Europe around the same time.

While pluralist thinking can be found in the principles that James Madison articulated to justify the 1789 United States Constitution (Madison and Hamilton, 1961), the doctrine received its first formal expression by Arthur Bentley in 1908. The theory has been considerably refined since then, but the fundamental tenets remain. Some prominent pluralist thinkers, responsible for a revival of Bentley's work in the US during the post-World War II era, include Robert Dahl (1956, 1961), Nelson Polsby (1963), and especially David Truman (1964).

Pluralism is based on the assumption that interest groups are the political actors that matter most in shaping public policy. In *The Process of Government*, Bentley argued that societal interests found their concrete manifestation in different groups consisting of individuals with similar concerns and, ultimately, that 'society itself is nothing other than the complex of the groups that compose it.' Truman expanded on Bentley's notion of a one-to-one correspondence between interests and groups and argued that two kinds of interests—'latent' and 'manifest'—resulted in the creation of two kinds of groups—potential and organized (Truman, 1964; also see Jordan, 2000). For Truman, latent interests in the process of emerging provided the underpinnings for potential groups, which over time led to the emergence of organized groups, allowing politics to be seen as a more dynamic process than Bentley seemed to depict.

Groups in pluralist theory are not only many and free-forming, they are also characterized by overlapping membership and a lack of representational monopoly (Schmitter, 1977). That is, the same individual may belong to a number of groups for pursuing his or her different interests; a person, for instance, may belong at the same time to Greenpeace, the local Chamber of Commerce, and Ducks Unlimited. Overlapping membership is said to be a key mechanism for reconciling conflicts and promoting co-operation among groups. In addition, the same interest may be represented by more than one group. Environmental causes, for example, are espoused by a large number of groups in every industrialized country. Politics, in the pluralist perspective, is the process by which various competing interests and groups are reconciled. Public policies are thus a result of competition and collaboration among groups working to further their members' collective interests (Self, 1985).

Contrary to many critics of this approach, pluralists do not believe that all groups are equally influential or that they have equal access to government (Smith, 1990: 303–4). In fact, pluralists recognize that groups vary in terms of the financial or organizational (personnel, legitimacy, members' loyalty, or internal unity) resources they possess and their access to government (Lindblom, 1968; Lowi, 1969; McConnell, 1966; Schattschneider, 1960). Nevertheless, as far as the policy process is concerned, as McLennan (1989: 32) has observed, 'It is impossible to read the standard works without getting the sense that resources, information and the means of political communication are openly available to all citizens, that groups form an array of equivalent power centres in society, and that all legitimate voices can and will be heard.' As such, pluralist theories are justifiably criticized for not having a sufficiently developed notion of groups' varying capacity to determine or influence government decision-making.

A more significant problem with the application of pluralism to public policy-making, however, is that government's role in making public policies is quite unclear (Smith, 1990). The early pluralists assumed that the government was a sort of 'transmission belt' that simply registered and implemented the demands of interest groups. The government was often thought of not actually as an entity but as a place, an 'arena' where competing groups met and bargained (Dahl, 1967). A more nuanced reformulation subsequently presented government as a 'referee' or 'umpire' of the group struggle. In this view, the state was still ultimately a place where competing groups met to work out their differences, but this time the government was considered a kind of neutral official setting out the rules of group conflict and ensuring that groups did not violate them with impunity (Berle, 1959).

This is still an overly simplistic view of how government works, however, as public choice scholars such as Mancur Olson (1965) have pointed out, because it assumes that public officials do not seek to realize their own interests and ambitions through the control they exert over governmental machinery. It also neglects the fact that states often maintain special ties with certain groups and may even sponsor establishment of groups where there are none or if those in existence are found to be difficult to co-opt or accommodate (Pal, 1993a).

The pluralist notion of the government responding to group pressure is also misconceived because it assumes both that pressure is not exerted in the opposite direction and that there is a unity of purpose and action by government. Indeed, with respect to the latter point, it has been noted that 'bureaucratic politics' is a pervasive phenomenon that can have a decisive impact on public policies (Allison and Halperin, 1972). That is, different departments and agencies often have different interests and conflicting interpretations of the same problem. How these differences are resolved has an impact on what policies are adopted and how they are implemented.

Recognition of these problems with early forms of pluralism (Connolly, 1969) led to the emergence of what is sometimes described as 'neo-pluralism' within the American political science community (McFarland, 2004, 2007). The reformulation retained the significance attributed to competition among groups, but modified the idea of approximate equality among groups and explicitly acknowledged that some groups are more powerful than others. Charles Lindblom, for example, argued that business is often the most powerful interest group in liberal democratic societies for two closely related reasons. First, these types of governments are invariably located in a capitalist economy and need a prosperous economy in order to have an adequate basis of tax revenues required to spend on programs that enable their own re-election. To avoid a capital strike where businesses scale back their investment and operations, governments must maintain business confidence, which often means paying special heed to the demands of the business community. Second, in capitalist societies there is a division between public and private sectors, the former under the control of the state and the latter dominated by business. The private sector's dominance by business gives it a privileged position in comparison to other groups in that much employment and associated social and economic activity ultimately depend on private-sector investment behaviour (Lindblom, 1977).

Unlike the classical pluralists, who seemed only to acknowledge but not incorporate the observation that some groups may be more powerful than others because of their superior organization and resources, Lindblom argued that the strength of business lay in the nature and structures of capitalism and democracy itself. Business need not, though it may, exert pressure on the government to realize its interests; the government, in accordance with the imperatives of capitalism and the pursuit of its own self-interest, will itself ensure that business interests are not adversely affected by its actions.

Neo-pluralist studies revealed that groups form for a variety of reasons, and pointed to the role patrons played in providing start-up funding and organizational assistance to groups, either directly through the provision of state funds or indirectly through favourable treatment afforded foundations and other funding groups by specific tax, estate, and charities laws (Nownes and Neeley, 1996; Nownes, 1995; Nownes and Cigler, 1995). Such studies highlighted another problem with pluralist theory: its excessive concentration on the role of interest groups themselves and its relative neglect of other equally important factors in the political and policy-making processes that influence their creation, operation, and activities.

While neo-pluralism was a significant improvement on its immediate past predecessor, it did not resolve all the problems inherent in a focus on groups as driving forces behind policy. Neo-pluralism, for example, continued to overlook the role of the international system in shaping public policies and their implementation (Grande, 1996; Schafer, 2006). International economic interdependence makes states' policies increasingly subject to international pressures, regardless of domestic group pressures. It is difficult to understand, for example, the industrial and trade policies of industrialized countries without reference to the international economy and the political pressures it places on policy-makers. The role of ideology was also unjustifiably neglected in the pluralist explanations of politics and public policy. The liberal tradition pre-eminent in Anglo-Saxon countries (including Canada, the US, and Australia), for example, has had a significant impact on their governments' hesitant and often contradictory intervention in the economy.

The applicability of pluralism to countries besides the United States has also been found to be especially problematic because of differences in underlying political institutions and processes that challenge pluralist assumptions and precepts derived only from examination of the US experience (Zeigler, 1964). British parliamentary institutions found in Australia, Canada, the United Kingdom, Japan, and Sweden, for example, do not lend themselves to the kind of open access that groups enjoy in relation to legislatures in the US and other countries with similar republican systems of government (Presthus, 1973). And many authoritarian countries simply lack the kinds of groups conceived by pluralists as being the basic building blocks of political analysis. Even if groups have the freedom to organize, the numbers actually formed are fewer than in the US and tend to be much more permanent and formalized. This finding led some group theorists, such as Phillipe Schmitter, to speculate that pluralism was only one form in which group systems could develop. Schmitter (1977) argued that, depending on a range of variables and historical factors, a *corporatist* form of political organization was much more likely than a pluralist one to emerge in many countries outside the US.

Corporatism

In Europe, theories treating groups as their primary unit of analysis have tended to take a corporatist rather than a pluralist form. The roots of corporatist theory are also much older than pluralist ones, extending back to the Middle Ages when there were concerns about protecting the 'intermediate strata' of autonomous associations between the state and the family (Gierke, 1958a, 1958b). These included, notably, guilds and other forms of trade associations as well as, most importantly, religious organizations and churches.

Corporatist theory argued that these intermediate strata had a life of their own above and beyond their constituting individuals, and that their existence was part of the 'organic' or 'natural order' of society. Much of political life and conflict in Europe in the fifteenth and sixteenth centuries concerned efforts by emerging national states to control the operations of these 'autonomous strata'—especially religious bodies—and the latter's efforts to resist state control (Cawson, 1986; Mann, 1984; Winkler, 1976).

As a group theory, corporatism can be best understood, as Schmitter has observed, in contrast to pluralism. As we have seen, the latter proposes that multiple groups exist to represent their respective members' interests, with membership being voluntary and groups associating freely without state interference in their activities. In contrast, corporatism is:

> [a] system of interest intermediation in which the constituent units are organized into a limited number of singular, compulsory, non-competitive, hierarchically ordered and functionally differentiated categories, recognized or licensed (if not created) by the state and granted a deliberate representational monopoly within their respective categories in exchange for observing certain controls on their selection of leaders and articulation of demands and supports. (Schmitter, 1977: 9)

The groups here are not thought of as free-forming, voluntary, or competitive, as in pluralism. Nor are they considered to be autonomous, for they depend on the state for recognition and support to play their role in policy-making. Corporatism thus explicitly takes into account two problems endemic to pluralism: its neglect of the role of the state in group formation and activities, and its failure to recognize institutionalized patterns of relationships between the state and groups.

In corporatist theory, public policy is shaped by the interaction between the state and the interest group or groups recognized by the state. Interaction among groups is institutionalized within and mediated by the state (McLennan, 1989: 245). Public policy formation towards a declining industry, for instance, would take the form of negotiations and bargaining between and among the state and relevant industry associations and trade unions as to how best to rationalize or streamline the industry and make it competitive. In France and Germany, for example, corporatist bargaining was a key element in passenger train development, providing commercially successful high-speed transportation between cities (Dunn and Perl, 1994). The making of social welfare policies similarly involves negotiations with business associations, social welfare groups, and possibly trade unions—if the proposed policies affect their members. The outcome of these negotiations depends not only on the organizational characteristics of the groups but on the closeness of their relationship with the state. The state itself is viewed as a powerful actor, although it is not seen as a monolith, but rather as an organization with internal fissures that shape its actions.

Although this conception accords fairly well with political practices in many European countries, there are still problems with corporatism as an approach to politics or the study of public policy. First, it is a descriptive category of a particular kind of political arrangement between states and societies (such as in Sweden or Austria), not a general explanation of what governments do, especially those in non-corporatist countries. Thus, it has little to say about why countries such as Australia, Canada, and the United States have the particular public policies that they do, except to point out that the lack of institutionalized co-operation between the state and groups in these countries often leads to fragmented and inconsistent policies (Panitch, 1977, 1979).

Second, the theory does little to further our understanding of public policy processes, even in ostensibly corporatist countries. While it is significant to know that not all countries have open-ended competition among groups as suggested by pluralism, this in itself does not say very much about why a policy is adopted or why it is implemented in a particular manner. The close links between governments and certain groups are certainly important, but these are also only one among many factors shaping policies and policy-making, and these relationships may vary significantly by policy sector or issue area (Castles and Merrill, 1989; Keman and Pennings, 1995).

Third, the theory does not contain a clear notion of even its own fundamental unit of analysis, the 'interest' group. Contemporary societies contain myriad interests, as pluralists have noted, and it is not clear which are or should be represented by the state. In some cases, the relevant groups are defined in terms of ethnicity, language, or religion (Lijphart, 1969), while in others they are defined with reference to their economic activities. The bulk of corporatist literature concentrates somewhat arbitrarily on producer groups, such as industry associations and trade unions, and on their role in specific economic sectors, such as labour market policy and wage bargaining (Siaroff, 1999).

Fourth, the theory is vague about the relative significance of different groups in politics. Are we to treat all groups as equally influential? If not, then what determines their influence? Some argue that corporatism is a manifestation of an autonomous state desiring to manage social change or ensure social stability (Cawson, 1978). Others suggest it is a system sought by the major corporate actors and thus is simply put into place by the state at their behest (Schmitter, 1985).

Despite its shortcomings, corporatist theory has played a significant role in the analysis of public policy, especially in Europe and Latin America, but also to a certain extent in China and in the former socialist countries, many of which were organized along corporatist lines, albeit with a very powerful central state apparatus. By highlighting the autonomous role of the state in politics, it paved the way for more sophisticated explanations of public policy-making than those provided by group theories such as pluralism (Smith, 1997). More significantly, by emphasizing the importance of institutionalized patterns of relationships between states and societies, it fostered the emergence of new institutional approaches such as 'statism', which focus on the macro level of social and political structures to draw their insights about public policy-making and serve to correct some of the oversights not only of pluralism and corporatism, but also of class and public choice theories (Blom-Hansen, 2001).

Neo-institutionalism

The broadest perspective on the forces that drive the policy process can be found in neo-institutionalism and statist theories. These theories seek to overcome the limits of individual and group and class-based theories to explain the full range of social behaviour and organizational activity behind policy-making (Peters, 1999; Hall and Taylor, 1996; Kato, 1996).

Neo-institutionalism avoids the limitations of most earlier theories informing policy studies by explaining why political, economic, and social institutions such as governments, firms, and churches exist at all, as well as what impact these macro-level structures have in fashioning constraints and providing opportunities for policy-makers (March and Olsen, 1984, 1989, 1995). Many variants of this approach have existed over the past 25 years, under titles such as the 'New Economics of Organization' (Moe, 1984; Yarbrough and Yarbrough, 1990; Williamson, 1996) or the 'Institutional Analysis and Development' (IAD) framework (Kiser and Ostrom, 1982; Ostrom et al., 1993). All, however, use a form of what Fritz Scharpf has termed '*actor-centred institutionalism*' to understand social processes, including political and policy-oriented ones (Scharpf, 1997).

Like recent class analysis, actor-centred institutionalism emphasizes the autonomy of political institutions from the society in which they exist. And, like public choice theory, it begins with a simple idea about calculating human behaviour. But unlike these more focused perspectives, neo- or actor-centred institutionalism assumes that a greater influence on human behaviour comes from the socio-political environment surrounding people and organizations than from within an individual or from group-based interactions (Cooney, 2007). Neo-institutionalism thus seeks to identify how rules, norms, and symbols affect political behaviour; how the configuration of governmental institutions affects what the state does; and how unique patterns of historical development can constrain subsequent choices about public problem-solving (Scharpf, 2000). Institutions are defined to include not only formal organizations, such as bureaucracies and markets, but also legal and cultural codes and rules that affect how individuals and groups calculate optimal strategies and courses of action (Ostrom, 1999).[1]

These assumptions orient neo-institutionalist policy research to examining the 'big picture' effects of structure on policy actors and, as James March and Johan Olsen (1984: 738) put it:

> They deemphasize the dependence of the polity on society in favor of an interdependence between relatively autonomous social and political institutions; they deemphasize the simple primacy of micro processes and efficient histories in favor of relatively complex processes and historical inefficiency; they deemphasize metaphors of choice and allocate outcomes in favor of other logics of action and the centrality of meaning and symbolic action.

Transaction cost analysis is an example of a neo-institutionalist approach to policy studies that expands the concerns of welfare economics about how governments and markets can fall short of optimal outcomes into a broader search for the historical legacies, social structures, and political approaches that lie behind these shortcomings (North, 1990; Williamson, 1985). This approach suggests that institutions constitute an essential element of political life, because they can overcome impediments caused by information asymmetries and other barriers to 'perfect' exchange in society. The basic unit of analysis in this approach is related to the 'transaction' among individuals within the confines of an institutional order (Coase, 1937). Institutions of various kinds are significant to the extent that they can increase or lower the costs of transactions. In this perspective institutions are 'the products of human design, the outcomes of purposive actions by instrumentally oriented individuals' (Powell and DiMaggio, 1991: 8) that also influence human behaviour.[2]

In institutionalist approaches to social theory, the argument usually is not that institutions *cause* an action, per se. Rather, they are said to *influence* actions by shaping the interpretation of problems and possible solutions by policy actors, and by constraining the choice of solutions and the way and extent to which they can be implemented. In the political realm, for example, institutions are significant because they 'constitute and legitimize individual and collective political actors and provide them with consistent behavioural rules, conceptions of reality, standards of assessment, affective ties, and endowments, and thereby with a capacity for purposeful action' (March and Olsen, 1994: 5). That is, while individuals, groups, classes, and states have their specific interests, they pursue them in the context of existing formal organizations and rules and norms that shape expectations and affect the possibilities of their realization (Williamson, 1985; Searle, 2005).

This approach is somewhat eclectic in the sense that it directs attention to a wide range of international and domestic norms, rules, and behaviour that affect aspects of policy-making behaviour, such as the calculations and perceptions made by actors of actual and perceived transaction costs (Putnam, 1988; Atkinson, 1978).[3]

A more serious problem for economistic or actor-centred neo-institutionalism, however, lies with its inability to provide a plausible coherent explanation of the origin of institutions, or their alteration, without resorting to functionalism (Blyth, 2007). That is, since this approach argues that individual and collective preferences are shaped by institutions, it is unclear how institutions or rules themselves are created, and once in place, how they would change (Cammack, 1992; March et al., 2000; Peters, 1999; Gorges, 2001; Dimitrakopoulos, 2005). Actor-centred institutionalism, for example, tends to provide an excellent discussion of the constraints placed by structures on policy actors and to show how what is 'rational' for them to do in specific circumstances is affected by such institutions, but says very little about what causes those constraints to move in any particular direction (Bromley, 1989: ch. 1; Ruiter, 2004). Studies that compare policy-making over time, however, have noted an 'institutional durability' in which some social and political structures endure much longer than others (Perl, 1991), an observation that is difficult to explain within the deductive logic of institutions orienting individual behaviour found in neo-institutionalism (Clemens and Cook, 1999; Greif and Laitin, 2004). This has led many students of policy studies to turn away from it and towards a more sociologically or historically informed version of institutionalism, which we shall term 'statism', in order to provide a more thorough and rigorous base for their studies of public policy-making.

Statism

'Statism' is the term sometimes employed to describe a second kind of inductive institutional approach to policy-making that addresses both the neo-institutionalist lacunae regarding institutional origins and change as well as the pluralist, corporatist, class, and public choice neglect of the state.

Many statist policy studies focus solely on formal state structures, seeing government as the leading institution in society and the key agent in the political process. Others, however, also attribute explanatory significance to organized social actors in addition to the state. Continuing earlier work by Zysman (1983) and Hall (1986), for example, Hall and Soskice (2001b) have argued that each political system has an underlying logic and a matching set of interrelated institutions that foster certain choices and hinder others. Thus, the liberal variety of capitalism found in the UK and the US is said to promote choices centred on the market, which in turn promote competition, innovation, and low-cost mass production. The corporatist variety of capitalism found in Germany and Japan, in contrast, is based on co-operation and consensus, which is conducive to high-cost but high-quality production but is ill-equipped for rapid changes. While Hall and Soskice believe that neither is inherently superior because both have successful track records, it is sometimes suggested that the corporatist variety is ill-suited for the globalized world, which requires rapid responses that are not possible in political systems based on consensus (Hay, 2004). Yet, the corporatist variant of capitalism may turn out to be better suited to devising appropriate responses to the vulnerability of global capitalism in the face of looming energy and climate shocks (Ferguson et al., 2007).

Statist interpretations have their origin in the works of late nineteenth- and early twentieth-century German historical sociologists and legal theorists who highlighted how establishing modern state institutions influenced the development of society. Rather than argue that the state reflected the character of a nation's populace or social structure, theorists such as Max Weber and Otto Hintze noted how the state's monopoly on the use of force allowed it to reorder and structure social relations and institutions (Hintze, 1975; Nettl, 1968; Weber, 1978).

The statist perspective on policy-making explicitly acknowledges that policy preferences and capacities are best understood in the context of the society in which the state is embedded (Nettl, 1968; Przeworski, 1990; Therborn, 1986). Like economistic neo-institutionalism, Peter Hall described the statist approach to 'institutionalist' analysis as one that focuses on the impact of large-scale structures on individuals and vice versa. In this approach:

> The concept of institutions . . . refer[s] to the formal rules, compliance procedures, and standard operating practices that structure the relationship between individuals in various units of the polity and economy. As such, they have a more formal status than cultural norms but one that does not necessarily derive from legal, as opposed to conventional, standing. Throughout the emphasis is on the relational character of institutions; that is to say, on the way in which they structure the interactions of individuals. In this sense it is the organizational qualities of institutions that are being emphasized. (Hall, 1986: 19)

However, statist perspectives differ from more economistic neo-institutional approaches in several important aspects. First, no effort is made to reduce institutions to less organized forms of social interaction, such as norms, rules, or conventions. Second, there is no attempt to reduce institutions to the level of individuals and individual activities, such as economic or social transactions, as is the case with more actor-centred neo-institutional thinking. And, third, institutions are simply taken as 'givens', that is, as observable historical social entities in themselves, with little effort made to derive the reasons for their origins from *a priori* principles of human cognition or existence (March and Olsen, 1994).

Using such a line of analysis yields, to use Theda Skocpol's terms, a 'state-centric' as opposed to 'society-centric' explanation of political life, including public policy-making (Skocpol, 1985). In a 'strong' version of the statist approach, as Adam Przeworski (1990: 47–8) put it in a pioneering book:

states create, organize and regulate societies. States dominate other organizations within a particular territory, they mould the culture and shape the economy. Thus the problem of the autonomy of the state with regard to society has no sense within this perspective. It should not even appear. The concept of 'autonomy' is a useful instrument of analysis only if the domination by the state over society is a contingent situation, that is, if the state derives its efficacy from private property, societal values, or some other sources located outside it. Within a true 'state-centric' approach this concept has nothing to contribute.

It is problematic to accept statism in the strong form described above, however, because it has difficulty accounting for the existence of social liberties and freedoms or explaining why states cannot always enforce their will, such as in times of rebellion, revolution, civil war, or civil disobedience. In fact, even the most autocratic governments make some attempt to respond to what they believe to be popular preferences. It is, of course, impossible for a democratic state to be entirely autonomous from a society with voting rights. And, as Lindblom and others pointed out, in addition to efforts to maintain and nurture support for the regime among the population, capitalist states, both democratic and autocratic, need to accommodate the imperatives of the marketplace in their policies. Second, the statist view suggests implicitly that all 'strong' states should respond to the same problem in the same manner because of their similar organizational features. This is obviously not the case, as different states (both 'strong' and 'weak') often have different policies dealing with the same problem. To explain the differences, we need to take into account factors other than the features of the state (Przeworski, 1990).

To be fair, however, few subscribe to statism in the 'strong' form described above. Instead of replacing the pluralist notion of the societal direction of the state with the statist notion of the state's direction of society, most inductively oriented institutionalist theorists merely point out the need to take both sets of factors into consideration in their analyses of political phenomena (Hall and Ikenberry, 1989; McLennan, 1989; Levy, 2006). As Skocpol has conceded:

> In this perspective, the state certainly does not become everything. Other organizations and agents also pattern social relationships and politics, and the analyst must explore the state's structure in relation to them. But this Weberian view of the state does require us to see it as much more than a mere arena in which social groups make demands and engage in political struggles or compromises. (Skocpol, 1985: 7–8)

In this view, the state is seen as an autonomous actor with the capacity to devise and implement its own objectives; it does not necessarily just respond to pressure from dominant social groups or classes. Its autonomy and capacity derive from its staffing by officials with personal ambitions and agency interests, as well as from the fact that it is a sovereign organization with unparalleled financial, personnel, and—in the final instance—coercive resources. Proponents of this perspective claim that emphasizing state centrality as an explanatory variable enables statism to offer more plausible explanations of policy development patterns in many countries than do other political theory perspectives (Krasner, 1984; Skowronek, 1982; Orren and Skowronek, 1998–9).

This milder version of statism thus concentrates on the links between the state and society in the context of the latter's pre-eminence in pluralist group theory. To that extent, statism complements rather than replaces society-centredness and restores some balance to social and political theorizing, which, it can be argued, had lost its equilibrium (Orren and Skowronek, 1993; Almond, 1988; Cortell and Peterson, 2001; Thelen and Steinmo, 1992; March and Olsen, 1996; Keman, 1997). This view and approach to policy studies inform the analysis of policy processes found in the remainder of this volume.

Conclusion

In considering a range of deductive and inductive perspectives on public policy-making across individual, group, and societal scales, we have encountered different and often contradictory ways to approach the study of public policy. An extensive literature exists on policy analysis from both positivist and post-positivist orientations, both promoting and denouncing the origins, assumptions, and application of each approach to the subject. Nevertheless, a few general conclusions can be offered.

In each of the theoretical frameworks that seek to make sense of policy, we can find three essential elements that are addressed, albeit differently. First, understanding policy requires some knowledge about the *actors* who raise issues, assess options, decide on those options, and implement them. These actors can be seen as subjects trying to advance their own interests, or as objects influenced by the circumstances of their surrounding environment. Second, policy insights also call for an appreciation of the *ideas* that shape policy deliberations. These ideas can range from the most particular and self-interested points of view to widely held belief systems that endure through the ages. And third, policy-making takes place within a set of social and political *structures* that affect the deliberations about what is to be done. Those structures can be seen as arenas that set the 'rules of the game' for the competition among different interests and the clash of distinctive ideas. These structures can also be seen as the subjects of political initiative—providing a focus for debate over how to better govern a society, how to better sustain an economy, or how to better express a culture.

Actors, ideas, and structures form the common ground where all policy theories converge—from different directions, and with distinctive points of view. It is in adopting, and adapting, these conceptual particularities that the potential for greater insight into policy-making and policy outcomes can be realized. We turn to elaborating that context in Chapter 3.

Study Questions

1. Are the positivist and post-positivist approaches to policy analysis necessary counterweights to each other's limitations, or can one of these frameworks yield sufficient insight on its own?
2. How should the unit of analysis be selected for understanding policy attributes?
3. Can deductive and inductive approaches to analysis be used in conjunction to study public policy, or must one choose between their competing logic of inquiry?

Further Readings

Fischer, Frank. 2007. 'Deliberative Policy Analysis as Practical Reason: Integrating Empirical and Normative Arguments', in Fischer, Gerald Miller, and Mara Sidney, eds, *Handbook of Public Policy Analysis: Theory, Politics, and Methods*. Boca Raton, Fla: CRC Press, 223–36.

Kiser, Larry, and Elinor Ostrom. 1982. 'The Three Worlds of Action', in Ostrom, ed., *Strategies of Political Inquiry*. Beverly Hills, Calif.: Sage, 179–222.

Le Grand, Julian. 1991. 'The Theory of Government Failure', *British Journal of Political Science* 21, 4: 423–42.

McLennan, Gregor. 1989. *Marxism, Pluralism and Beyond: Classic Debates and New Departures*. Cambridge: Polity Press.

March, James G., and Johan P. Olsen. 1984. 'The New Institutionalism: Organizational Factors in Political Life', *American Political Science Review* 78: 734–49.

Schmitter, Phillipe C. 1977. 'Modes of Interest Intermediation and Models of Societal Change in Western Europe', *Comparative Political Studies* 10, 1: 7–38.

Skocpol, Theda. 1985. 'Bringing the State Back In: Strategies of Analysis in Current Research', in Peter B. Evans, Dietrich Rueschemeyer, and Skocpol, eds, *Bringing the State Back In*. New York: Cambridge University Press, 3–43.

Van Winden, Frans A.A.M. 1988. 'The Economic Theory of Political Decision-Making', in Julien van den Broeck, ed., *Public Choice*. Dordrecht: Kluwer, 9–57.

Chapter 3

The Policy Context

Introduction: Institutions, Ideas, and Actors

Recent research findings about what most influences policy fuel a debate that has lost none of its vitality since the time Harold Lasswell urged researchers to connect technical analysis of policies to their social and political context. Different policy studies—ranging from broad comparisons of economic or social policy to narrowly focused case studies of a particular industrial or resource management policy—provide a rich, though complex, picture of the myriad factors that shape public policy.

Those who seek a universal theory of policy-making might question whether policy science has made much progress from its post-war origins, given the ongoing divergence over what merits attention in explaining policy. But those who accept Lasswell's proposal that the policy researcher needs to make sense of the particular context to gain effective insight will discover that advances have been made in teasing out the intricate relationships between some generally accepted critical factors affecting policy development, namely actors, institutions, and ideas.

With respect to actors, studies of political or administrative leadership, chronicles of policy entrepreneurs' efforts, and examinations of the way that 'street-level' bureaucrats or private contractors and consultants work through the many details of delivering policy highlight the role that both individual and organized actors play in policy development. Such studies indicate one location where we need to look for answers as to why policy turns out one way instead of another. This behavioural orientation, however, is tempered by the fact that what actors seek and do depends on the political, economic, and social structures that surround them. And, finally, growing numbers of studies also seek to explain the content of policy based on the ideas actors hold and their expectations of appropriate government and policy action.

As the survey in Chapter 2 revealed, many of the analytical approaches to studying public policy and itemized in Figure 2.2 fail to adequately take into account all of the different actors, institutions, and ideas that affect public policy. Welfare economics and public choice theory, for example, treat individual and group actors as key explanatory variables and would thus suggest that policy context should be seen mainly from the perspective of these individuals. Theories built on group and class theory, such as pluralism and Marxism, attribute influence to organized groups of actors affected by social, economic, and political structures, but still consider actors to be primary and other factors such as structures and ideas to be secondary or peripheral.

As we also have seen in Chapter 2, the most successful syntheses of the different models and theories of politics and policy-making have been varieties of neo-institutional approaches to political life (Goldmann, 2005; Kato, 1996; Scharpf, 1991, 1997). Arising from critiques of these long-established theories, these more recently elaborated analytical frameworks for studying policy, such as statism and the different variants of neo-institutionalism, attempt to account for both actor-oriented and structural variables. Although their assumptions differ somewhat, these approaches treat state and social institutions as important entities affecting the preferences and activities of other policy actors. Both attempt to explain public policy as the product of interdependent interaction between state capacity and social action.

While ever more accurately describing policy processes, however, none of these analytical frameworks provides much insight into policy substance or *content*. In many early theories of policy-making, for example, the actual content of policy outputs is often simply assumed to be determined by, for instance, the manifestation of the 'self-interest' of policy actors in any given policy choice context (Flathman, 1966; Heclo, 1994; Braun, 1999), tempered by the nature of the conflicts and the compromises they make during policy formation (Sabatier, 1988, 1993). Some neo-institutional theories, however, have a more sophisticated conception of the role of ideas in the policy process. They note that the presence of particular actors in the policy process and the interests they pursue are often largely determined by the nature of the organization within which they operate. Moreover, they also note that many of the ideas that participating policy actors articulate have been shaped by past policy choices and the ideas embodied in those choices (Schmidt, 2008).

As John Campbell has noted, a number of distinct idea sets go into public policy-making: *program ideas, symbolic frames, policy paradigms*, and *public sentiments* (see Figure 3.1). Symbolic frames and public sentiments tend to affect the perception of the legitimacy or 'correctness' of certain courses of action, while policy paradigms represent a 'set of cognitive background assumptions that constrain action by limiting the range of alternatives that policy-making elites are likely to perceive as useful and worth considering' (Campbell, 1998: 385; also Surel, 2000). 'Program ideas', then, largely represent the selection of specific solutions from among the set designated as acceptable within a particular paradigm.

This notion of the filtering of reality through a policy paradigm helps make the analysis of policy content possible. Developed originally to describe enduring sets

Figure 3.1   Ideational Components of Policy Contents

		Level of Policy Debate Affected	
		Foreground	Background
Level of Ideas Affected	Cognitive (Causal)	Program Ideas	Policy Paradigms
	Normative (Value)	Symbolic Frames	Public Sentiments

Source: Adapted from John L. Campbell, 'Institutional Analysis and the Role of Ideas in Political Economy', *Theory and Society* 27, 5 (1998): 385.

of ideas that are present in the natural sciences, the term 'paradigm' was later applied to long-lasting points of view on 'the way the world works' that are found in the social sciences (Kuhn, 1962, 1974; Hall, 1990, 1992, 1993). The concept is closely related to traditional philosophical notions of 'ideologies' as overarching frameworks of ideas influencing action and to more recent sociological notions of 'discourses' or 'frames' (Goffman, 1974; Surel, 2000). The notion of a paradigm is compatible with the basic elements of a neo-institutional approach to policy studies since it captures the idea that established beliefs, values, and attitudes lie behind understandings of public problems and emphasizes how paradigm-inspired notions of the *feasibility* of the proposed solutions, just as much as actor self-interest, are significant determinants of policy content (Hall, 1990: 59; also Edelman, 1988; Hilgartner and Bosk, 1981; Schneider, 1985). The implicit power of embedded ideas is clearly evident in how policy-makers understand problems and view solutions to them.

Much recent theorizing reflects this understanding that both actors and institutions and the ideas they hold play a meaningful role in affecting the unfolding and outcome of policy processes. Individuals, groups, and classes engaged in the policy process certainly have their own interests, but how they interpret and pursue their interests and the outcomes of their efforts are shaped by institutional and ideational factors (Lundquist, 1987; Schmidt, 2008; Menahem, 2008).[1]

As noted in Chapter 2, in this book we adopt the statist tendency to define institutions quite narrowly as comprising only the actual structures or organizations of the state, society, and the international system. Following this approach, we are less preoccupied than many scholars with the origins of these institutions, which are taken as given. While not monolithic, omnipresent, or immutable, institutions can only rarely be avoided, modified, or replaced without a considerable degree of effort. As such, we are concerned with the way institutions are organized internally and in relation to each other and how this affects actor behaviour (March and Olsen, 1998b). In addition to their formal organizational characteristics—membership, rules, and operating procedures—we emphasize the principles, norms, and ideas they embody. These principles, in the shape of formal or informal rules and conventions, as well as ethical, ideological, and epistemic concerns, further help to shape actors' behaviour by conditioning their perception of their interests and the probability that these interests will be realized in policy outcomes (March et al., 2000; Timmermans and Bleiklie, 1999).

The Political-Economic Context

Two meta-institutions— *capitalism* and *democracy*—inform the structures within which the public policy process unfolds in most modern societies. These overarching institutions deserve particular attention, not only because they are influential among policy-makers, but also because they are not intrinsically compatible and hence must be somehow constantly reconciled, leading to unstable compromises that pose major challenges to liberal-democratic countries. In this chapter, these two important contextual aspects of the policy-making process and outcomes are discussed in some depth.

Capitalism

Capitalism refers to both a market-oriented political economy or system of production and exchange and to a society in which control over the property required for production (capital) is concentrated in the hands of a small section of the populace, while most of the rest of the population sells their labour-time in a system of wages.

Under capitalism, production is undertaken not for direct consumption by the producer but for purposes of sale or exchange, so the producer can use the money thus derived to purchase other goods for consumption. This differs from pre-capitalist societies in which producers directly consumed much of what they produced, except for a small portion exchanged through barter or taxed for military protection. In capitalism, exchange takes place through markets among individuals usually unknown to each other.

Capitalism is a socio-economic system that was first produced by the breakdown of agricultural societies, which operated on quite different principles—lacking, for the most part, markets, capital, and wage labour. In Europe, these societies underwent industrialization towards the end of the eighteenth century. This system of organizing social and economic relations in society spread rapidly to North America and most of the rest of the world during the nineteenth century, often through its direct imposition on colonies in Africa, North and South America, Australasia, and Asia by European and other imperial states, but also through its emulation by many developing countries in Europe, Asia, and elsewhere.

In the twentieth century many nations rejected capitalism and adopted socialism—a state-oriented political economy in which 'capital' is publicly owned and allocated—with the expressed intention of working towards the establishment of a communist political economy, in which 'capital' would be communally owned and wage labour abolished. But by the end of the twentieth century, as economic growth stagnated in socialist countries, most embraced capitalism with renewed enthusiasm. Now almost all countries in the world are capitalist, though they vary a great deal in terms of their specific political arrangements (Coates, 2005; Lehne, 2001; Howell, 2003; Hall and Soskice, 2001b).

The hallmark of capitalism is that ownership of production inputs—e.g., raw materials, machinery, factory buildings—is largely in private hands. This implies that the owners of the means of production have the exclusive right to decide on the use of those means of production. This right is guaranteed by the state, with certain restrictions required to ensure the effective reproduction of the capitalist order such as avoiding fraud or the mistreatment of workers. Capitalism thus entitles owners to decide what will be produced, in what manner, and in what quantities, a power that also establishes the capitalists as the dominant social class since other classes and strata in society—workers, peasants, small shop owners, religious authorities, intellectuals, and the like—all rely on capitalists for their incomes and well-being. To earn a livelihood, those who do not own the means of production must work for those who do. In many capitalist societies, their own labour and skill are often the only productive inputs non-capitalists own. In order to survive, this must be sold to capitalists for salaries and wages.

This underpins a critical feature of capitalism: the need for firms to make profits, or accumulate capital, in order for both producers and the economy as a
whole to survive. Profit is to capitalism what motion is to bicycles: capitalism, like
bicycles, cannot properly function by standing still. If an adequate return on
investment is not forthcoming, capitalists will withhold their investment or invest
it somewhere else. The result can be a decline in economic activity in a society and
a general lowering of a society's living standards. This imposes an enormous pressure on states to ensure hospitable conditions for continued, and expanded, capital investment.

Businesses and firms attempt to influence governments directly and, through
their membership in various forms of business associations, indirectly (Coleman,
1988; Jacek, 1986). Business associations, among the many interest groups found
in capitalist societies, enjoy an unmatched capacity to affect public policy, given
the reliance of states in capitalist societies on businesses for their revenues and for
overall levels of social well-being (Lindblom, 1977). The increasing globalization
of production and financial activities has further reinforced this power of capital.
It is now much more possible for investors and managers to respond, if they so
choose, to an unwanted government action by moving capital to another location.
Although this theoretical mobility is limited by various practical considerations,
such as the availability of resources or trained labour, the potential loss of employment and revenues is a threat with which the state must contend in making decisions. Because of their potential to affect state revenues negatively, capitalists—
both domestic and foreign—have the ability to 'punish' the state for any actions of
which they disapprove (Hayes, 1978).

Even in democratic states where power and influence lie in electoral and legislative systems that empower non-capitalists, the financial contributions of businesses to political parties, for example, continue to afford them an important
resource for influencing policy-makers. Modern elections can sometimes turn on
relatively short-term issues and personalities, which necessitate large budgets to
influence voters through extensive media advertising campaigns. In such situations, political parties supported by contributions from business are in a better
position to run such campaigns and thus influence voting behaviour. This can
lead political parties and candidates running for office to accommodate business
interests more than they would those of other groups. Similarly, the financial contributions that businesses often make to public policy research institutions and
individual researchers serve to further entrench their power. The organizations
and individuals receiving funds tend to be sympathetic towards business interests
and can provide business with the intellectual wherewithal often required to prevail in policy debates (McGann and Weaver, 1999; Abelson, 1999; Rich, 2004).
Hence, for all these reasons, business actors and behaviour deserve special consideration in the study of public policy.

Liberalism
Another distinctive feature of capitalism, as it has emerged historically, is its inex-
tricable link with the theory and ideology of liberalism, which refers to a set of

more or less well-organized and institutionalized beliefs and practices that serve to maintain and promote capitalism (Macpherson, 1978). Liberalism emerged in tandem with capitalism in the eighteenth century as a political ideology dedicated to justifying and reinforcing the increasingly important capitalist mode of production. This highly adaptive social theory has changed substantially since its origin in order to accommodate changing economic and political circumstances, without departing very far from its fundamental belief in the righteousness and appropriateness of private ownership of the means of production as the key to the attainment of human progress and freedom (Howlett et al., 1999).

Liberalism is centred on the assumption of the primacy of the individual in society. It views individuals as having inalienable natural rights, including the right to own property and to enter into contracts with other individuals concerning the disposition of that property. These rights have to be protected from intrusion by collective social organizations such as the state, churches, or trade unions. A good society in liberal theory is one that guarantees individuals freedom to pursue their interests and realize their potential. This freedom should be restricted only when one person's freedom erodes that of another, for example, through theft or violence (Macpherson, 1962).

Freedom to pursue the livelihood of one's choice and to accumulate wealth is sacrosanct in liberalism. The preferred mechanism for liberalism through which individuals can pursue their interests in an unencumbered fashion is, of course, the market. Here, all individuals selfishly pursue their own interests according to their own abilities and preferences. Liberals see exchange in the marketplace as benefiting everyone who engages in it, and the net result of this activity is the enhancement of society's welfare as a whole. This tenet links liberalism closely to capitalism, as a system of market-based exchange based on individual property rights.

Liberalism is essentially a theory of the market that has had to include the state on grounds of contingency to perform functions that would not otherwise be performed. Liberal political economy contains two slightly different formulations concerning the state. The first is the idea of the *supplementary* or *residual state*: the notion contained in neo-classical and neo-conservative liberal political economy that the state should only undertake those activities—such as the provision of pure public goods—that markets cannot perform. The second is the notion of the *corrective state*: the idea found in later so-called Keynesian and post-Keynesian analyses, which asserted that the state can act in a variety of other areas of market activity to correct the host micro- or macro-level market failures described in Chapter 2 (Dunleavy and O'Leary, 1987).

Significantly, both variants of liberal thinking under-theorize the state and, in so doing, public policy-making. This is because they treat the state as an inherently anti-liberal entity whose very existence tends to threaten markets and individual freedoms, on the one hand, but as one that ought to follow liberal tenets in doing only whatever it is that the market cannot do. The state is generally not considered to be in any way constrained by the society in which it exists or by its organizational capacity in its pursuit of either of these two contradictory goals

(Schott, 1984: 60). In fact, the capacity of the state to act and the forces that act upon the state are usually not considered at all in liberal theory, which tends to focus on questions of individual rights and freedoms and urges the adoption of a limited state on purely ethical grounds (Sandel, 1984). Or, in slightly more sophisticated analyses, it is usually just assumed that the state can and will act either to provide goods and services or to correct market failures out of a concern for economic growth and efficiency. Neither of these analyses, however, does justice to the complexity of state action and public policy-making in the contemporary world, as the subsequent discussion of these processes in this book will attest.

Democracy

The second major meta-institution affecting states and policy-making is democracy. Democracy is one of the most contentious concepts in the study of politics. One survey in the late 1980s, for example, found 311 definitions of 'democracy' (Cunningham, 1987: 25). It is not our objective to resolve this definitional debate. For our purposes, it is sufficient to regard democracy as a plan of political organization, a political decision-making system, which involves structuring the mechanisms of day-to-day control of the state through representative institutions staffed through periodic elections (Bealey, 1988: 1). Thus, Göran Therborn succinctly defines modern democracy as '(1) a representative government elected by (2) an electorate consisting of the entire adult population, (3) whose votes carry equal weight, and (4) who are allowed to vote for any opinion without intimidation by the state apparatus' (Therborn, 1983: 262).

Democracy confers entitlements on citizens to choose who they want to have represent them in government. The method of election varies among nations, but the primary purpose is always to declare the candidate with the largest number of votes as the winner in periodic competitions to staff legislative and executive branches of governments, as well as the judiciary in certain jurisdictions. This condition establishes that the government is to be formed by the representatives of the largest number of citizens and, depending on the type of system used, that through those representatives it is to be held directly or indirectly accountable to the citizens. Elections as a means of removing a government and replacing it with another were virtually unheard of until the nineteenth century, and even today some governments find ingenious excuses to avoid submitting themselves to the judgement of the electorate.

It was only towards the end of the nineteenth century that Western nations began to establish democratic institutions in the sense that we understand them today (Doorenspleet, 2000), a process not completed until well after World War II when the franchise, or right to vote, was made universal for most adults in most Western nation-states (Therborn, 1983: 264). The intent of earlier restrictions on voting, so that, for example, only white male property owners could vote, as was the case in the US, UK, Canada, and Australia and many other countries, was to limit the privilege of voting to social and economic elites.

The removal of these barriers represented a major milestone in promoting social equality and reducing or offsetting the direct power of capitalists over state actions in capitalist countries. From a political-economic perspective, insofar as democracy is based on the principle of the secret ballot and majority rule, those who do not own the means of production can, in principle, exercise their numerical superiority in elections to vote in governments that will use state authority to alter the adverse effects of capitalist ownership of the means of production, often in the face of stiff opposition from business (Przeworski, 1985).

Democracy, by requiring that governments be elected, permits the weaker sections of the society some degree of control over the state and thus helps to shape not only the internal functioning of the state but also, through the use of state authority, how markets for particular goods and services will function. As Adam Przeworski (1985: 11) points out: 'Political democracy constitutes the opportunity for workers to pursue some of their interests. Electoral politics constitutes the mechanism through which anyone can as a citizen express claims to goods and services. . . . Moreover . . . they can intervene in the very organization of production and allocation of profit.' Influenced by democratic politics, for example, in most countries the state has introduced income redistribution measures, defying one of the basic capitalist tenets that the market alone ought to determine the distribution of income (Przeworski, 1991). Similarly, in many countries, states have replaced private ownership of some means of production with public, or state, ownership: all countries have some state-owned or controlled enterprises producing a variety of goods and services; from those related to national security and defence to finance, shipping, transportation, and telecommunications activities, to the production of various kinds of small-scale consumer items.

Democracy thus offers a political mechanism that can moderate the economic effects of capitalism. The degree of harmony achieved between these two meta-institutions is a major contributor to social cohesion and can reduce the need for coercive authority (e.g., police and prisons) to maintain domestic order. The potential for symbiosis between capitalism and democracy is realized through specific policy options and their outcomes. As will be shown in the following section, attaining an effective balance between capitalism and democracy, however, is a difficult task that is by no means automatic or inevitable.

Policy-Making in the Liberal-Democratic Capitalist State

To the extent liberalism and its corollary, capitalism, are about individual rights while democracy is about collective rights, the two are fundamentally contradictory, notwithstanding the common term 'liberal democracy' often used to describe countries with both systems in place. As the early liberal thinkers understood all too well, democracy poses a fundamental threat to the liberal order because it gives the majority the capacity to erode individual rights, including especially the rights of capitalists to dispose of their property as they see fit. The liberals' worst fears were realized in the twentieth century when left-leaning parties in many parts of the globe formed governments that often used their powers to nationalize industries, raise taxes, and redistribute income. The opportunities for political control that democracy offers economically weak groups thus sit uneasily with the basic tenets of liberalism. While the advent of democracy did not lead to the extermination of capitalism, as some had hoped and others had feared, it did mean that democratic governments could no longer ignore the interests of the majority of non-elites to the extent to which they had in the past (Korpi, 1983).

Democracy complicates policy-making and implementation tasks in a capitalist society because its presence means policy-makers can no longer concentrate on serving only state interests and the interests of their business allies in accordance with the tenets of a pure liberal policy paradigm (Swank, 2000; DeLeon, 1997; Gourevitch, 1993). In democracies policy-makers have to at least appear to be heeding the concerns of farmers and workers, children and seniors, men and women, and other sections of the populace who have different and often contradictory interests that need to be constantly juggled and are inherently unstable. Political violence is particularly detrimental to economic growth (Butkiewicz and Yanikkaya, 2005) and democracy is often needed to diffuse the tensions generated by capitalism so as to avoid revolution and rebellions. Such conflicts make policy-making challenging and often lie at the heart of the sometimes very ad hoc and contradictory policy choices that governments regularly make.

Along with liberalism, capitalism and democracy form an important part of the meta-institutional and macro-ideational, or 'political-economic', context of policy-making in many modern countries. Taken together, they greatly influence the actors and ideas in most policy-making processes. However, a government's capacity to act autonomously or relatively autonomously within this context is shaped not just by the existence of capitalism and democracy and the ideas and interests they generate, but also by the manner in which the government and the various more or less empowered actors under liberal capitalism found in each country or issue area are organized.

Political-Economic Structures and Public Policy

To make and implement policies effectively in a capitalist democracy, the state needs to be well organized and supported by prominent social actors. The extent to which these actors are able to offer the necessary support depends, among other things, on their own internal organization and their relationships with the state and with other similarly powerful social actors.

These are complex relationships. Fragmentation within and among prominent social groups simultaneously strengthens the state's level of *policy autonomy* and undermines its *policy capacity* by limiting its ability to mobilize social actors towards the resolution of societal problems. If the societal conflicts are particularly severe, the state may find its functioning paralyzed. Conversely, unity within and among social groups makes for a stable policy environment that facilitates policy-making and promotes effective implementation (Painter and Pierre, 2005). But strong social cohesion can also constrain the state's ability to change policy in a significant or large-scale way.

Strong organizations can bargain more effectively and need not make unreasonable demands for the sake of maintaining their members' support. And when they agree to a measure, they can enforce it upon their membership, through sanctions if necessary. Mancur Olson has argued that in societies characterized by 'encompassing' groups (that is, umbrella groups consisting of a variety of similar interests) rather than 'narrow' interest groups, the groups 'internalize much of the cost of inefficient policies and accordingly have an incentive to redistribute income to themselves with the least possible social cost, and to give some weight to economic growth and to the interests of society as a whole' (Olson, 1982: 92). The existence of numerous narrow interest groups, in contrast, promotes competition among groups that pressure the state to serve their members' interests only, regardless of the effects on others. The cumulative effect of policy-making led by interest groups often can be contradictory and ineffective policies that leave everyone worse off.

The most desirable situation for the state, insofar as effective policy-making and implementation are concerned, is for both state and society to be strong, with close partnership between the two, thereby maximizing and balancing both state policy capacity and autonomy. Peter Evans (1992) calls this institutional arrangement 'embedded autonomy'. In contrast, policy effectiveness is lowest when the state is weak and the society fragmented. In the former scenario, states in partnership with social groups can be expected to devise cohesive and long-term policies. In the latter, the state can be expected to produce only short-term and, usually, ineffective or difficult to implement policies.

Political Systems and Public Policy

Political systems also have a crucial impact on state policy capacity and on how states make and implement policies and their outcomes (Fabbrini and Sicurelli, 2008). One of the most significant aspects of the political system affecting public policy is whether it is federal or unitary. In *unitary* systems, the existence of a clear chain of command or hierarchy linking the different levels of government together in a superordinate/subordinate relationship reduces the complexity of multi-level governance and policy-making. Thus, in countries like Britain, France, Japan, and Thailand, the national government retains all decision-making powers. It can choose to delegate these powers to lower levels of government or dictate to them, but the role of the central, national government is legally unchallenged.

The salient feature of *federal* political systems with respect to public policy is the existence of at least two autonomous levels or orders of government within a country. The two levels of government found in such countries as Australia, India, Brazil, Nigeria, and the United States (Burgess and Gagnon, 1993; Duchacek, 1970) are not bound together in a superordinate/subordinate relationship but, rather, enjoy more or less complete discretion in matters under their jurisdiction and guaranteed by the constitution. This is distinct from the multi-level systems of government found in unitary systems, where the local bodies (for example, regional districts, counties, or municipalities) owe their existence to the national government rather than to the constitution.

Federalism has been cited as a major reason for the weak policy capacity of governments in many policy sectors in countries such as the US and Canada (Howlett, 1999; McRoberts, 1993). In federal countries, governments find it difficult to develop consistent and coherent policies because national policies in most areas require intergovernmental agreement, which involves complex, extensive, and time-consuming negotiations among governments that do not always succeed (Banting, 1982; Schultz and Alexandroff, 1985; Atkinson and Coleman, 1989b). Furthermore, both levels of government are subject to unpredictable judicial review of their measures, which further restricts governments' ability to realize their objectives.

Federalism thus makes public policy-making a long, drawn-out, and often rancorous affair as the different governments wrangle over jurisdictional issues or are involved in extensive intergovernmental negotiations or constitutional litigation. Different governments within the same country may make contradictory decisions that may weaken or nullify the effects of a policy (see Grande, 1996; McRoberts, 1993).

Another domestic institutional variable affecting public policy concerns the links between the executive, legislature, and judiciary provided under a country's constitution. In *parliamentary* systems, the executive is chosen by the legislature from among its members and remains in office only as long as it enjoys majority support from legislators. In *presidential* systems, the executive is separate from the legislature, is usually elected directly by the voters, and need not enjoy majority support in the legislature (Stewart, 1974). The United States is the archetype of the presidential system, whereas most of the rest of the world has some version of a parliamentary system; other countries, such as France, have a hybrid of the two systems.

The separation between the executive and legislative branches of the government in presidential systems, and the fusion of the two in parliamentary ones, has important consequences for the policy process (Weaver and Rockman, 1993a). The division of powers promotes difficulties for policy-makers in presidential systems. The individual members and committees of the legislature play an active role in designing policies, including those proposed by the president. It matters if the party of the president's affiliation forms the majority in both houses of the legislature, but local concerns often motivate legislators and can override partisan loyalties. To ensure majority support for policy measures requiring legislative approval, it is common for the president to have to bargain with the members of the legislature, offering administrative and budgetary concessions in return for support, and thereby often changing the original intent of a policy proposal. The active involvement of the members of the legislature in drafting bills promotes multiple points of conflict with the executive; it also opens up greater opportunities for interest groups and voters to influence the policy process, the result of which may be diluted or even conflicting policies (Besley and Case, 2003).

In parliamentary systems, in contrast, the executive can more often than not take legislative support for its measures for granted, thanks to the strict party discipline enforced on individual members of the parliament. While there may be some bargaining over a policy within a party caucus, there is little chance of changing a bill once it has been introduced in parliament. The only time when this may not be the case is when the governing party does not have an outright majority in the legislature and governs in coalition with other parties, who often demand modification to the policy in return for their support. In many countries, especially those with proportional systems of representation that allow for a proliferation of minor parties, coalition governments are routine, which complicates policy-making, though not as much as in the presidential system (Warwick, 2000). Generally speaking, however, policy-making in parliamentary systems is centralized in the executive, which usually enables the government to take decisive action if it so chooses (Bernier et al., 2005). While sometimes decried as overly concentrating power and decision-making (Savoie, 1999), this is not entirely undesirable from a policy-making perspective, insofar as a state's policy capability is concerned, because the adversarial politics characteristic of legislatures in presidential systems reduces the likelihood of generating coherent policies.

Domestic Policy Actors

Flowing from the nature of a country's political economy and its political system, the following sets of policy actors exist in most liberal-democratic capitalist countries and exercise some influence over policy processes and outcomes.

Elected Politicians
The elected officials participating in the policy process may be divided into two categories: members of the executive and legislators. The *executive*, also referred to in many countries as the cabinet or, simply, the government, is a key player in any policy subsystem. Its central role derives from its constitutional authority to govern the country. While other actors also are involved in the process, the authority to make and implement policies rests ultimately with the executive. As we have seen, there are indeed few checks on the executive in parliamentary systems (such as Japan, Canada, Australia, and Britain) as long as the government enjoys majority support in the legislature. It is somewhat different in presidential systems (as in the United States or Brazil), where the executive often faces an adversarial legislature with different policy preferences and priorities. But even here, the executive usually has a wide area of discretion beyond legislative control in financial and regulatory matters, as well as in defence, national security, and issues related to international treaty obligations of different kinds.

In addition to its prerogative in policy matters, the executive possesses a range of other resources that strengthen its position. Control over information is one such critical resource. The executive has unmatched information that it withholds, releases, and manipulates with the intention of bolstering its preferences and weakening the opponents' case. Control over fiscal resources is another asset favouring the executive because legislative approval of the budget usually permits wide areas of discretion for the executive. The executive also has unparalleled access to mass media in publicizing its positions—the 'bully pulpit', as it is called in the US—and undermining those of its opponents. Moreover, the executive has the bureaucracy at its disposal to provide advice and to carry out its preferences. It can, and often does, use these resources to control and influence societal actors such as interest groups, mass media, and think-tanks. In many countries, as well, the government has important powers allowing it to control the timing of the introduction and passage of laws in the legislature. This gives the executive a great deal of control over the political agenda (Bakvis and MacDonald, 1993).

Counterbalancing the executive's immense constitutional, informational, financial, and personnel resources are conditions that make their task difficult. The tremendous growth in the size, scope, and complexity of government functions over the years, for example, prevents generalist politicians from controlling, or often even being aware of, the many specific activities of government nominally under their control (Adie and Thomas, 1987; Kernaghan, 1979, 1985a). Moreover, in democratic governments, ministers are constantly bombarded with societal demands, many of which are mutually contradictory but which they often cannot ignore because of the need to maintain voters' support (Canes-Wrone et al., 2001). Finally, and perhaps most importantly, a government may not have the organizational capacity to make coherent policies and implement them effectively.

Members of the *legislature* play a very different role. In parliamentary systems the task of the legislature is to hold governments accountable to the public rather than to make or implement policies. But the performance of this function permits opportunities for influencing policies. Legislatures are crucial forums where social problems are highlighted and policies to address them are demanded. Legislators also get to have their say during the process of approving government bills and governmental budgets to fund policy implementation. In return for their consent, they are sometimes able to demand changes to the policies in question. Legislators may also raise and discuss problems of implementation and request changes. However, a legislature's policy potential often may not be realized in practice. This is because of the dominance enjoyed by the executive and its effects on the internal organization of the legislature and on the role played by legislative committees (Olson and Mezey, 1991).

Most laws are proposed by the executive and more often than not subsequently adopted by the legislature. This is especially so in parliamentary systems, where the majority party forms the government and therefore is generally expected to support the passage of bills proposed by the executive. In presidential systems, on the other hand, the legislature is autonomous of the government constitutionally as well as in practice, which explains why presidents, irrespective of whether their party holds a legislative majority, must strike bargains with the legislature or risk defeat of their policy proposals.

The internal organization of the legislature is also a significant determinant of its role in the policy process. Legislatures where the membership is tightly organized along party lines, and marked by a high degree of cohesion and discipline, permit little opportunity for legislators to take an independent stand. This is particularly true in parliamentary systems where the legislators belonging to the governing party are always expected to support the government except, infrequently, when contentious social issues of a moral nature are brought to a vote. Similarly, the role of individual legislators is lower in parliaments in which one party has a clear majority; the existence of several minor parties in coalition governments permits greater opportunity for legislators to express their opinion and force the government to deal with them.

In many contemporary legislatures, most important policy functions are performed not on the floor of the legislature but in the committees established along functional or sectoral lines to review proposed legislation. Committees often build considerable expertise in the area with which they deal, and the extent to which this happens enables the legislature to exercise influence over making and implementing policies. But to build expertise, the members need to serve on the committees over a relatively long period of time. Committee members must also not necessarily vote along party lines if their influence is to be maintained.

The nature of the problem being considered also affects legislative involvement in the policy process. Technical issues are unlikely to involve legislators because they may not fully understand the problems or solutions, or they may see little political benefit in pursuing the matter. National security issues and foreign policy-making are also usually conducted in a shroud of secrecy and outside the legislature. Similarly, policies dealing with a problem perceived to be a crisis are unlikely to involve the legislature very much because of the time it takes to introduce, debate, and pass a bill. Policies dealing with allocation or redistribution of resources or income among components of the public generate the highest degree of passion and debate in legislatures, but usually do not have much effect on a government's overall policy orientation. However, other policies related to the propagation and maintenance of certain symbolic values—such as the choice of a national flag, immigration, multiculturalism, prayers in schools, or the elimination of racism and sexism—are often so divisive that the executive may be somewhat more willing to take the legislators' views into account in forming legislation.

As a result of these limitations, legislatures generally play only a small role in the policy process in parliamentary systems. While individual legislators, on the basis of their expertise or special interest in a particular issue, can become engaged as individual policy actors, legislatures as a whole are not very significant actors in policy-making or implementation. In congressional or republican systems, on the other hand, where the legislative agenda is less tightly controlled by the executive, individual legislators can and do play a much more influential role in policy processes, and legislative committees and coalitions are often significant members of many policy subsystems (Warwick, 2000; Laver and Hunt, 1992; Laver and Budge, 1992).

The Public
Surprising as it may appear, the *public* plays a rather small direct role in the public policy process. This is not to say that its role is inconsequential, as it provides

the backdrop of norms, attitudes, and values against which the policy process unfolds. However, in most democratic states, policy decisions are taken by representative institutions that empower specialized actors to determine the scope and content of public policies, but these institutions do not, as a matter of course, provide mechanisms through which the public can directly determine policy.

One important role played by members of the public in a democratic polity is as voters. On the one hand, voting offers the most basic and fundamental means of public participation in democratic politics and, by implication, policy processes. It not only affords citizens the opportunity to express their choice of government, but also empowers them to insist that political parties and candidates seeking their votes provide (or at least propose) attractive policy packages. On the other hand, the voters' capacity to direct the course of policy usually cannot be realized, at least not directly, for at least three reasons (Hibbing and Theiss-Morse, 2002).

First, most democracies delegate policy-making to political representatives who, once elected by the voters, are not required to heed constituent preferences on every issue (Birch, 1972). Second, as was discussed above, most legislators participate very little in the policy process, which tends to be dominated by experts in specific sectoral areas rather than by legislative generalists (Edwards and Sharkansky, 1978: 23). Third, candidates and political parties often do not run in elections on the basis of their policy platforms; and even when they do, voters usually do not vote on the basis of proposed policies alone. Having said that, it is true that politicians do pay attention to public opinion in a general sense while devising policies, even though they do not always respond to or accommodate it (Soroka, 2002).

The impact of public opinion on policy processes is more frequent and pervasive, although even less direct than voting. Despite many works over the past decades that have consistently found the relationship between public opinion and public policy-making in democratic societies to be a tenuous, complex one, there persists a tendency to view this relationship as simple, direct, and linear (see Luttbeg, 1981; Shapiro and Jacobs, 1989). From at least the time of the early works on the subject by scholars such as V.O. Key (1967), E.E. Schattschneider (1960), and Bernard Berelson (1952), prominent political scientists and others have repeatedly found little or no direct linkage between public opinion and policy outcomes. Nevertheless, in study after study this finding has been made and remade, as investigators appear dissatisfied with it (Monroe, 1979; Page and Shapiro, 1992). As Schattschneider suggested, this is no doubt due to the sincere but sometimes simplistic notion of democracy that privileges 'government by the people' over 'government for the people'. But the reality is more complex (Soroka, 2002): democracy is more than mob rule (Birch, 1972). While a concern for popular sovereignty is laudable, theoretical speculations must be tempered by empirical reality if the relationship between public opinion and public policy is to be effectively analyzed and understood.[2]

The simplest model of the relationship between public opinion and public policy-making views government as a policy-making machine—directly processing popular sentiments into public policy decisions and implementation strategies. This is a highly problematic perception as it assumes that public opinion has a concrete, quasi-permanent character that can be easily aggregated into coherent policy positions (Erikson et al., 1980; Erikson et al., 1989). Numerous studies have underlined the vague, abstract, and transitory nature of public opinion, and have emphasized the difficulties encountered in aggregating the 'babble of the collective will', as Rousseau put it, into universally endorsed policy prescriptions (Rousseau, 1973; also see Lowell, 1926). Moreover, many opinion researchers and policy scholars have noted how these difficulties have multiplied as scientific and complex legal issues have come to dominate policy-making in contemporary societies, further divorcing policy discourses from public ones (see Pollock et al., 1989; Torgerson, 1996; Hibbing and Theiss-Morse, 2002).

The public's role in policy-making should thus not be taken for granted as either straightforward or decisive. But neither should it be ignored, especially in relation to other elements of the policy context. Even if elections rarely provide focused public input on specific policy options, they can often introduce real change to policy agendas even if these changes are something of a wild card.

Bureaucracy

The appointed officials dealing with public policy and administration are often collectively referred to as the 'bureaucracy'. Their function is to assist the executive in the performance of its tasks, as is suggested by the terms 'civil servants' and 'public servants'. However, the reality of modern government is such that their role goes well beyond what one would expect of a 'servant'. Indeed, bureaucrats are very often the keystone in the policy process and the central figures in many policy subsystems (Kaufman, 2001).

Most of the policy-making and implementation functions once conducted directly by legislatures and the political executive are now performed by the bureaucracy because the responsibilities of modern government are too complex and numerous to be performed by the cabinet alone (see Bourgault and Dion, 1989; Cairns, 1990b; Priest and Wohl, 1980). Certain policies have indeed been 'automated' so that routine actions can be taken without human intervention. Indexing public pensions to the rate of inflation is an example of such 'automatic government' (Weaver, 1988). The most exceptional policy decisions can also be removed from the deliberation of men and women, as with the case of the US 'Mutual Assured Destruction' (MAD) security policy during the height of the Cold War—in this instance, due to the presumption that there would be no time for a deliberative reaction to a nuclear attack from the Soviet Union.

The bureaucracy's power and influence are based on its command of a wide range of important policy resources (see Hill, 1992: 1–11). First, the law itself provides for certain crucial functions to be performed by the bureaucracy, and may confer wide discretion on individual bureaucrats to make decisions on behalf of the state. Second, bureaucracies have unmatched access to material resources for pursuing their own organizational, even personal, objectives if they so wish. The government is the largest single spender in most countries, a situation that gives its officials a powerful voice in many policy areas. Third, the bureaucracy is a repository of a wide range of skills and expertise, resources that make it a premier organization in society. It employs large numbers of just about every kind of professional, hired for their specialized expertise. Dealing with similar issues on a continuing basis endows these experts with unique insights into many problems. Fourth, modern bureaucracies have access to vast quantities of information about society. At times the information is deliberately gathered, but at other times the information comes to it simply as a part of its central location in the government. Fifth, the permanence of the bureaucracy and the long tenure of its members often give it an edge over its nominal superiors, the elected executive. Finally, the fact that policy deliberations for the most part occur in secret within the bureaucracy denies other policy actors the chance to effectively oppose its plans. Bureaucrats can thus exert a prominent influence on the shape of the policy context.

The structure of the bureaucracy has perhaps the strongest effect on public policy processes, especially at the sectoral level (Atkinson and Coleman, 1989a). Concentration of power in only a few agencies reduces occasions for conflict and permits long-term policy planning. Diffusion of power, in contrast, fosters interagency conflicts and lack of co-ordination; decisions may be made on the basis of their acceptability to all concerned agencies rather than their intrinsic merit. The bureaucracy's autonomy from politicians and societal groups also contributes to its strength and effectiveness in policy-making. To be strong, a bureaucracy must have a clear mandate, a professional ethos, and enjoy strong support, but not interference, from politicians in its day-to-day activities. Close ties with client groups are also to be avoided if a bureaucracy is to be effective. An ability to generate and process its own information is also important if reliance on interest groups is to be avoided.

Countries like France, Korea, Singapore, and Japan have historically had bureaucracies that enjoy a somewhat exalted status in government and society (Katzenstein, 1977). They are said to constitute a homogeneous elite grouping that plays the most important role in the policy process. They undergo long professional training and pursue service in the government as a lifelong career. In other societies, such as Russia and Nigeria, bureaucracies enjoy relatively low status and lack the capacity to resist pressures from legislators or social groups, which often promotes incoherence and short-sightedness in policies. At the extreme, bureaucrats can become so marginalized that corruption becomes the norm, either to supplement meagre salaries or because ethics and the rule of law are not deemed to matter.

The effective mobilization of bureaucratic expertise is rarer than commonly believed (Evans, 1992). Despite the massive expansion in bureaucracies throughout the world over the last several decades, weak bureaucracies in the sense understood here are the norm rather than the exception (Evans, 1995). In many countries with corruption, low wages, and poor working conditions, bureaucracies often do not have the capability to deal with the complex problems they are asked to address. If these conditions obtain in a country, then it is quite likely that the state will have difficulty devising effective policies and implementing them in the manner intended (Halligan, 2003; Burns and Bowornwathana, 2001; Bekke and van der Meer, 2000; Verheijen, 1999; Bekke et al., 1996). In many countries, even if bureaucratic expertise exists in a particular area, problems of organization and leadership prevent its effective marshalling (Desveaux et al., 1994).

While it can be tempting to view bureaucrats as the most influential policy actors, either through their grasp of the levers of power or because their ineffectiveness constrains many policy initiatives, we must avoid exaggerating the bureaucracy's role. The political executive is ultimately responsible for all policies, an authority it does assert at times. High-profile political issues are also more likely to involve higher levels of executive control. Executive control is also likely to be higher if the bureaucracy consistently opposes a policy option preferred by politicians. Moreover, the bureaucracy itself is not a homogeneous organization but rather a collection of organizations, each with its own interests, perspectives, and standard operating procedures, which can make arriving at a unified position difficult. Even within the same department, there are often divisions along functional, personal, political, and technical lines. Thus, it is not uncommon for the executive to have to intervene to resolve intra- and inter-bureaucratic conflicts, and bureaucrats in democratic countries require the support of elected officials if they are to exercise their influence in any meaningful way (Sutherland, 1993).

Political Parties

Political parties can connect people and their government in ways that affect policy. Parties operate along the boundary between state and societal actors, sometimes acting as gatekeepers on which actors will gain access to political power. They tend to influence public policy indirectly, primarily through their role in staffing the executive and, to a lesser degree, the legislature. Indeed, once in office, it is not uncommon for party members in government to ignore their official party platform while designing policies (Thomson, 2001).

Political parties' impact on policy outcomes has been the subject of empirical research and commentary (Blais et al., 1996; Castles, 1982; Imbeau and Lachapelle, 1993; McAllister, 1989). Findings concerning the role of parties in public policy-making, for example, have included evidence that, historically, European governments led by Christian democratic and social democratic parties have been related positively to the development of welfare state programs (Wilensky, 1975; Korpi, 1983), and that 'left-wing' and 'right-wing' governments have had different fiscal policy orientations towards, respectively, unemployment and inflation reduction (Hibbs, 1977). Partisan differences have also been linked to different characteristic preferences for certain types of policy tools, such as public enterprises or market-based instruments (Chandler and Chandler, 1979; Chandler, 1982, 1983). However, the contemporary significance of parties has also been challenged by those who argue that government has become too complex for influence by partisan generalists, with day-to-day influence stemming more from policy specialists in government and those in the employ of interest groups and specialized policy research institutes (King and Laver, 1993; Pross, 1992). Similarly, other studies focusing on the extent of policy learning and emulation occurring between states or subnational units (Lutz, 1989; Poel, 1976; Erikson et al., 1989) and those examining the impact of international influences on domestic policy-making have argued the case for the reduced importance of parties in contemporary policy processes (Johnson and Stritch, 1997; Doern et al., 1996a).

The idea that political parties play a major role in public policy processes, of course, stems from their undeniable influence on elections and electoral outcomes in democratic states. While vote-seeking political parties and candidates attempt to offer packages of policies they hope will appeal to voters, the electoral system is not structured to allow voters a choice on specific policies. Likewise, as discussed above, the representational system also limits the public's ability to ensure that electorally salient policy issues actually move onto official government agendas (King, 1981; Butler et al., 1981). The official agenda of governments is, in fact, usually dominated by routine or institutionalized agenda-setting opportunities rather than by partisan political activity (Kingdon, 1984; Walker, 1977; Howlett, 1997a).

Even when parties do manage to raise an issue and move it from the public to the official agenda, they cannot control its evolution past that point. As Richard Rose (1980: 153) has put it:

> A party can create movement on a given issue, but it cannot ensure the direction it will lead. Just as defenders of the status quo may find it difficult to defend their position without adapting it, so too proponents of change face the need to modify their demands. Modifications are necessary to secure the agreement of diverse interests within a party. They will also be important in securing support, or at least grudging acceptance, by affected pressure groups. Finally, a governing party will also need to make changes to meet the weaknesses spotted by civil service advisors and parliamentary draftsmen responsible for turning a statement of intent into a bill to present to Parliament.

While political parties' direct influence on policy may be muted, however, their indirect influence is not. The role played by political parties in staffing political executives and legislatures, of course, allows them considerable influence on the content of policy decisions taken by those individuals, including those related to the staffing of the senior public service. However, this power should not be overestimated. In modern governments, as we have seen, the degree of freedom enjoyed by each decision-maker is circumscribed by a host of factors that limit the conduct of each office and constrain the actions of each office-holder. These range from limitations imposed by the country's constitution to the specific mandate conferred on individual decision-makers by various laws and regulations (Pal, 1988; Axworthy, 1988). Various rules set out not only which decisions can be made by which government agency or official, but also the procedures they must follow in doing so.

Political parties tend to have only a diffuse, indirect effect on policy-making through their role in determining who actually staffs legislative, executive, and judicial institutions. Their role in agenda-setting is very weak, while they play a stronger, but still indirect, role in policy formulation and decision-making due to the strong role played in these two stages of the policy cycle by members of the political executive. Their role in policy implementation is virtually nil, while they can have a more direct effect on policy evaluation undertaken by legislators and legislative committees (Minkenberg, 2001).

The fact that the influence of parties on particular stages of the policy process may be muted, or that any such influence may be waning, does not necessarily lead to the conclusion that 'parties don't matter'. Richard Rose's perspective on the influence of twentieth-century political parties in governing Britain remains valid today:

> Parties do make a difference in the way [a country] is governed—but the differences are not as expected. The differences in office between one party and another are less likely to arise from contrasting intentions than from the exigencies of government. Much of a party's record in office will be stamped upon it from forces outside its control . . . . (Rose, 1980: 141; also see Hockin, 1977)

Interest or Pressure Groups

Another policy actor that has received a great deal of attention, thanks in part to the significant role attributed to it by pluralist and neo-pluralist theorists, is the interest group. While policy decisions are taken by government and implemented by the executive and bureaucracy, organized groups that advocate the economic interests or social values of their members can exert considerable influence on policy (Walker, 1991).

One valuable resource that such interest groups deploy is knowledge, specifically information that may be unavailable or less available to others. The members of specialized groups often have unique knowledge about the policy issue that concerns them. Since policy-making is an information-intensive process, those who possess information hold something of value. Politicians and bureaucrats often find the information provided by interest groups indispensable. Government and opposition politicians are thus inclined to assist such groups to obtain information that can improve policy-making or undermine their opponents. Bureaucrats will also solicit groups' help in developing and implementing many policies (Hayes, 1978; Baumgartner and Leech, 1998).

Interest groups also possess other important organizational and political resources besides information. These groups often make financial contributions to political campaigns. They also campaign for and deliver votes to sympathetic candidates who would support their cause in the government. However, interest groups' political impacts on the formulation and implementation of public policies vary considerably according to their differing levels of organizational resources and whether they represent business interests or any of various 'altruistic' civil society causes (Pross, 1992; Baumgartner and Leech, 2001). First, interest groups come in all sizes. All other things being equal, larger groups can be expected to be taken more seriously by the government. Second, some groups may form a 'peak association' working in concert with business or labour groups that share similar interests (Coleman, 1988). A coherent peak association may exert greater influence on policy than even a large interest group operating on its own. Third, some groups are well funded, which enables them to hire more staff, including those with expertise in the 'black arts' of political campaigning and elections (Nownes, 2004; Nownes and Cigler, 1995).

While the policy impact of interest group campaign expenditures and political engagement on behalf of (or against) political parties and candidates is contentious, there is no doubt that differences in financial resources matter (Nownes and Neeley, 1996; Nownes, 1995, 2000; Nownes and Cigler, 1995). In democratic political systems, these information and power resources make interest groups key members of policy subsystems. While this does not guarantee that their interests will be accommodated, they are unlikely to be ignored except in rare circumstances when government leaders deliberately decide to approve a policy despite opposition from concerned groups (Thatcher and Rein, 2004).

Among interest groups, the role of business is particularly salient, as was mentioned earlier. The structural strength of business has the potential to both promote and erode social welfare. Erosion is more likely when business lacks organizational coherence. If 'successful', the ability of individual firms and capitalists to pressure governments to serve their particular interests can lead to incoherent and short-sighted policies. Endemic conflicts among competing business groups only aggravate such situations. The problem may be offset if business has a central cohesive organization—or *peak association*—able to resolve internal differences and come up with coherent policy proposals.

The strength or weakness of business and the varying patterns of government–industry relations found in a country are usually shaped by historical factors (Wilson, 1990a). Although the example of Japan cited above is somewhat atypical, one political legacy that can yield powerful business organizations is a period of strong, persistent challenges from trade unions or socialist parties. The stronger the unions, the more cohesive will be the private sector's organized advocacy. The threat does not necessarily have to be continuing, so long as workers and socialist parties exerted power in the past. Another political characteristic that encourages strong business organizations is the presence of a strong (e.g., autonomous) state. Business must be well organized to have policy influence in countries with strong states. A strong state may also nurture a strong business association in order to avoid the problems arising from too many groups making conflicting demands on the same issue. Strong business associations can simplify the management of policy-making by presenting government with an aggregation of private-sector demands in place of a cacophony of disparate pleas.

Another factor affecting the organizational strength of business is a nation's economic structure. In national economies characterized by low industrial concentration or high levels of foreign ownership, it is difficult for the disparate business firms to organize and devise a common position. Political culture also has an important bearing on the extent and nature of business involvement in politics. Where cultures are highly supportive of 'free enterprise', such as in the US and Canada, corporations have seen fewer reasons to invest in costly political organizations. Moreover, the degree to which social norms approve of functional representation affects the strength of business. Americans, and to a lesser extent citizens of Britain, Canada, Australia, and other Anglo-American democracies, are distrustful of business representing their interests on a regular basis behind closed doors. In the corporatist countries, on the other hand, functional representation is accepted and, indeed, is seen as an appropriate behaviour of responsible groups (Siaroff, 1999).

Labour, too, occupies a somewhat unique position among interest groups in that it is stronger than most, though considerably weaker than business. Unlike business, which enjoys considerable weight with policy-makers even at the level of the firm, labour needs a collective organization, a trade union, to have much influence on policy-making. In addition to their primary function of bargaining with employers regarding members' wages and working conditions, trade unions engage in political activities to shape government policies (Taylor, 1989: 1). The origin of trade unions' efforts to influence public policy is rooted in late nine-teenth-century democratization, which enabled workers, who form a majority in every industrial society, to have some say in the functioning of the government. Given the clout that their members' votes could produce in democratic elections, it was sometimes easier for unions to pressure government to meet their needs than to bargain with their employers. The organization of labour or social demo-cratic parties, which eventually formed governments in many countries, further reinforced labour's political power (Qualter, 1985).

The nature and effectiveness of trade unions' participation in the policy process depend on a variety of institutional and contextual factors. As with busi-ness, the structure of the state itself is an important determinant of union partic-ipation in policy-making. A weak and fragmented state will not be able to secure effective participation by unions, because the latter would see little certainty that the government would be able to keep its side of any bargain. Weak businesses can also inhibit the organization of a powerful trade union movement because the need appears less immediate.

However, the most important determinant of labour's capacity to influence policy-making is its own internal organization. The level of union membership affects the extent to which states seek or even accept union participation in the policy process. The same is true for the structure of bargaining units: decentral-ized collective bargaining promotes a fragmented articulation of labour demands. Britain, Canada, and the United States, for example, have decentralized bargain-ing structures, whereas in Australia, Austria, and the Scandinavian countries bar-gaining takes place at the industry or even country-wide level (Esping-Andersen and Korpi, 1984; Hibbs, 1987). A union movement that is fragmented along regional, linguistic, ethnic, or religious lines, or by industrial versus craft unions, foreign versus domestic unions, or import-competing versus export-oriented labour organizations will also experience difficulties in influencing policy. Fragmentation within the ranks of labour tends to promote local and sporadic industrial strife and yields an incoherent articulation of labour interests in the policy process (Hibbs, 1978; Lacroix, 1986).

To realize its policy potential, labour needs a central organization even more than does business. Such peak labour associations include the Australian or

British Trade Union Congress (TUC), the Canadian Labour Congress (CLC), and the American Federation of Labor–Congress of Industrial Organizations (AFL–CIO). Collective action is the principal tool that labour has to influence the employers' or the government's behaviour, so the extent to which labour is able to present a united front determines to a great extent its success in the policy arena. To be effective, the trade union central needs to enjoy comprehensive membership and have the organizational capacity to maintain unity by dealing with conflicts among its members. Trade unions' role in policy-making ranges from most influential in corporatist political systems, such as in the Scandinavian countries, Austria, and the Netherlands, where the state encourages the formation and maintenance of strong trade union centrals, to least influential in pluralist political systems such as the United States and Canada, where there is no encouragement of strong central unions.

Think-Tanks and Research Organizations

Another set of societal actors who influence the policy process are the researchers working at universities, institutes, and think-tanks on particular policy issues and issue areas. University researchers often have theoretical and philosophical interests in public problems that can be translated directly into policy analysis. To the extent academics contribute their research to policy debates, they function in the same manner as research experts employed by think-tanks. Indeed, in many instances academics undertaking relevant policy research are sponsored by think-tanks (Ricci, 1993; Stone et al., 1998). The following discussion will therefore concentrate on the role of these private organizations and the way that they interpret policy options through particular ideological and interest-based perspectives.

A think-tank can be defined as 'an independent organization engaged in multidisciplinary research intended to influence public policy' (James, 1993: 492). Such organizations maintain an interest in a broad range of policy problems and employ, either full-time or on a contract basis, experts on various issue areas in order to present thorough recommendations on their areas of concern. Their research tends to be directed at proposing practical solutions to public problems or, in the case of some think-tanks, justifying their ideological or interest-driven positions. This sets them apart somewhat from academic researchers at universities, whose interests are more specialized, who do not necessarily seek practical solutions to policy problems, and who often are not so ideologically motivated. Explicitly partisan research is also generally eschewed in academia.

However, while think-tanks are generally more partisan than their academic counterparts, they, too, must maintain an image of intellectual autonomy from governments, private corporations, or any political party if policy-makers are to take them seriously. Large prominent think-tanks in the United States include the Brookings Institution, the American Enterprise Institute, and the Urban Institute. Similar organizations in Canada include the C.D. Howe Institute, the Fraser Institute, the Canadian Centre for Policy Alternatives, and the Institute for Research on Public Policy. Major think-tanks in Britain include the Policy Studies Institute and the National Institute for Economic and Social Research (McGann,

2008). Literally hundreds of such institutes are active in the Western, developed countries, some with broad policy mandates, others that are more limited in their purview, such as the Canadian Environmental Law Association (Lindquist, 1993; Abelson, 1996). In the developing world, think-tanks tend to be financed by and linked to governments, which raises questions about their autonomy.

Think-tanks target their research and recommendations to those politicians who may be favourably disposed to the ideas being espoused (Abelson, 2002). They also seek originality in their ideas and, unlike government and university-based researchers, they spend a great deal of effort publicizing their findings (Dobuzinskis, 2000; Stone, 1996; Weaver, 1989). The need for a quick response to policy 'crises' has led many think-tanks to develop new 'product lines'. Short, pithy reports and policy briefs that can be quickly read and digested have replaced lengthy studies as the primary output of many think-tanks. A premium now exists on writing articles and op-ed pieces for newspapers and making appearances on radio and television programs. This new brand of research and analysis is dependent on 'the public policy food chain', which includes a range of knowledge- and policy-oriented institutions. Over the last few decades, much of the work of think-tanks has been devoted to promoting economic efficiency, since this has been an important preoccupation of the governments across the industrialized world.

A number of policy trends have influenced the way that think-tanks function in recent years. Some of these dynamics and their effects include think-tanks devoted to actors or issue areas affecting women, families (e.g., in Canada, the Vanier Institute of the Family), and indigenous groups, and non-governmental organizations are now playing a central role in developing and implementing foreign and domestic policies and programs. These new entrants to the policy debates have created many new specialized think-tanks and public policy research organizations, which in turn has fostered enhanced competition among them (see Rich, 2004; Abelson, 2007; Stone, 2007; McGann et al., 2005). Globalization and the associated growth of transnational problems such as pandemics, hunger, and climate change require a global response, and this has affected the activities of think-tanks. Some think-tanks have responded by developing transnational linkages and partnerships, or by becoming multinational organizations themselves, in the effort to bridge the chasm between North/South and East/West. In addition, the emergence of regional or continental economic alliances such as the European Union and NAFTA has created new networks of regionally oriented policy institutions (Stone, 2008).

The proliferation of think-tanks, however, has been accompanied by cutbacks in public funds available for research, which in turn has led to increasing competition among think-tanks for funding (t'Hart and Vromen, 2008). In many countries, the cutback in government funding for policy research happened at the same time as policy units in governments were downsized or eliminated in budget-cutting exercises in the 1990s. At the same time, events occurring elsewhere, such as the end of the Cold War, had a profound impact on the funding of research organizations focused on areas such as international and security affairs since donors and governments no longer saw the need for such research.

As a result, think-tanks have had to devote considerable resources to raising funds at the expense of research and dissemination of findings (McGann and Weaver, 1999). This has led to 'over-specialization' and to destructive competition in this aspect of the political marketplace of ideas (Stone, 2007).

Mass Media

The media constitute another set of policy actors with an important indirect influence on public policy-making. Some suggest that the mass media play a pivotal role in the policy process (Herman and Chomsky, 1988; Parenti, 1986), while others describe it as marginal (Kingdon, 1984). There is no denying that the mass media are crucial links between the state and society, a position that allows for significant influence on public and private preferences regarding the identification of public problems and their solutions. Yet, like political parties, the media's direct role in the various stages of the policy process is often sporadic and often quite marginal.

The role of the media in the policy process originates from the function of reporting on problems, which often leads to analyzing what went wrong and sometimes extends into advocating particular solutions. Journalists frequently go beyond identifying obvious problems to defining their nature and scope, and suggesting or implying solutions. The media's role in agenda-setting is thus particularly significant (Spitzer, 1993; Pritchard, 1992). Media portrayal of public problems and proposed solutions often conditions how they are understood by the public and many members of government, thereby shutting out some alternatives and making the choice of others more likely. Questions in parliamentary question periods or at presidential press conferences are often based on stories in the day's television news or newspapers.

This is particularly significant considering that news reporting is not an objective mirror of reality, undistorted by bias or inaccuracy. News organizations are gatekeepers in the sense that they define what is worthy of reporting and the aspects of a situation that should be highlighted. Thus, policy issues that can be translated into an interesting story tend to be viewed by the public as more important than those that do not lend themselves so easily to narrative structures, first-person accounts, and sound bites. This partially explains why, for example, crime stories receive so much prominence in television news and, as a corollary, the public puts pressure on governments to appear to act tough on crime. Similarly, groups and individuals able to present problems to the media in a packaged form are more likely than their less succinct counterparts to have their views projected (Callaghan and Schnell, 2001; Lutz and Goldenberg, 1980; Herman and Chomsky, 1988; Parenti, 1986).

We must not, however, exaggerate the mass media's role in the policy process. Other policy actors have resources enabling them to counteract media influence, and policy-makers are for the most part intelligent and resourceful individuals who understand their own interests and have their own ideas about appropriate or feasible policy options. As a rule, they are not easily swayed by media portrayals of issues and preferred policy solutions or by the mere fact of media attention. Indeed, they often use the media to their own advantage. It is not uncommon for public officials and successful interest groups to provide selective information to the media to bolster their case (Lee, 2001). Indeed, very often the media are led by government officials' opinion rather than vice versa (Howlett, 1997a, 1997b).

Academic Policy Experts and Consultants

Analysts working in universities or government tend to research policy problems determined by the public's or the government's interest, or by their own personal curiosity about a particular subject. Although academic policy findings tend to receive far less attention than the output from think-tanks, the scholar's opportunity for sustained analysis and critique can make up for the lack of an immediate 'buzz' (Cohn, 2004, 2006; Whitley et al., 2007). Carol Weiss has termed this dynamic of scholarly impact on public policy the 'enlightenment function' to highlight the long-term ability to inform policy actors' understanding (Weiss, 1977a, 1977b; Bryman, 1988).

This role of introducing new findings about policy issues can also be undertaken by consultants, who can carry the ideas and results of policy research directly to governments (Lapsley and Oldfield, 2001). There has been an explosion in the growth and use of consultants for policy analysis and implementation in governments in recent years, a development whose impact and implications are yet to be fully recognized (Speers, 2007; Perl and White, 2002).

The International System and Public Policy

Policy-making is very much a domestic concern involving national governments and their citizens: in liberal-democratic countries with a capitalist economy organized along the lines set out above. However, the international system also is increasingly vital in shaping domestic public policy choices and policy developments. Its effects are manifested through individuals working as advisers or consultants to national governments or as members of international organizations with the authority under international agreements to regulate their members' behaviour.

Assessing the effects of international institutions is more difficult than assessing those in the domestic arena. For one thing, states are sovereign entities with, in theory, the legal authority to close their borders to any and all foreign influences as and when they choose. In reality, however, it is nearly impossible for states to stop foreign influences at the border because of constraints rooted in the international system (Held and McGrew, 1993; Walsh, 1994). The extent to which a state is able to assert its sovereignty depends on the severity of international pressures and the nature of the issue in question, as well as features innate to the state itself (Knill and Lehmkuhl, 2002; March and Olsen, 1998b).

The international system not only influences policy sectors that are obviously international—trade and defence, for example—but also sectors with no immediately apparent international connection, such as health care and old-age pensions (Brooks, 2007, 2005). The sources of influence lie in the overall structure of the international system, and a nation's place in it, and the specific 'regimes' that exist in many policy areas.

International Actors and Regimes

International actors vary considerably in their ability to influence domestic policies, and this, to a significant extent, is the result of differences in their resource
endowments. One of the strongest resources determining their influence is
whether an *international regime* facilitates their involvement (Krasner, 1982;
Haggard and Simmons, 1987). International regimes have been defined by Robert
Keohane and Joseph Nye (1989: 19) as 'sets of governing arrangements' or 'networks of rules, norms, and procedures that regularize behaviour and control its
effects'. Such regimes vary considerably in form, scope of coverage, level of adher-
ence, and the instruments through which they are put into practice (Haggard and
Simmons, 1987). Some are based on explicit treaties whereas others are based simply on conventions that develop as a result of repeated international behaviour.
Some cover a variety of related issues while others are quite narrow in coverage.
Some are closely adhered to and others often are flouted. Some are enforced
through formal or informal penalties whereas others make no such provision.
Some regimes are administered by formal organizations with large budgets and
staffs, while some are more akin to moral codes (see Rittberger and Mayer, 1993).

Like other more formal institutions, international regimes affect public policy
by promoting certain options and constraining others. More than that, they shape
actors' preferences and the ease with which they can be realized (Doern et al.,
1996b). Thus, a government willing to assist domestic producers by offering
export subsidies, for example, may not be able to do so because of formal or informal international constraints. Regimes of varying scope and depth can be found
in most, though not all, prominent policy areas.

International actors find it easier to intervene in policy sectors in which an
international regime sanctioning their intervention already exists (Risse-Kappen,
1995: 6; Coleman and Perl, 1999). The central place occupied by the International
Monetary Fund (IMF) in the international monetary regime, for example, enables
its officers to intervene in the intimate details of public policy-making in many
nations facing serious financial or fiscal problems.

An even more significant resource at the international level is the actor's the-
oretical and practical expertise in a policy sector (Barnett and Finnemore, 1999).
Many international organizations—for example, the World Bank, IMF,
Organization for Economic Co-operation and Development (OECD), and World
Health Organization (WHO)—are vast repositories of established expertise in policy issues, and governments often rely on this expertise when making policies,
thus giving such international actors significant influence in the policy process.
The financial resources that international organizations can dispense to governments are another source of influence. The different levels of expertise and
finance that international organizations can deploy often turn out to be crucial
determinants of the impact that international actors can have on domestic policies (Finnemore and Sikkink, 1998).

However, the nature of the national policy subsystems also affects the international actors' role in the policy process. International actors can be expected to

be influential in sectors with fragmented subsystems, because such fragmentation allows them greater opportunity for intervention. For example, the International Civil Aviation Organization—a UN agency responsible for the air transport sector—develops common design standards for airports that are widely adopted around the world. Since many of the world's airports are locally owned or operated, they would be hard-pressed to develop compatible design among themselves.

Conversely, international actors find it difficult to influence policies where the associated subsystem is coherent and united in opposition to external intervention (Risse-Kappen, 1995: 25; Sabatier and Jenkins-Smith, 1993b). The oil industry's resistance to the Kyoto Protocol's plan for reducing greenhouse gas emissions has undermined United Nations efforts to limit climate change by scaling back greenhouse gas emissions among many affluent nations, including Australia, Canada, and the United States. The most conducive situation for international actors is, of course, when the subsystem is coherent and in favour of external involvement, as occurs, for example, in many free trade negotiations where strong business communities support international trade regimes—in such instances the international actors can be expected to be an integral part of the domestic policy process (Pappi and Henning, 1999).

Not all international actors work for public entities or private agencies, of course. An influential niche has been carved out by international non-governmental organizations (NGOs) that advocate policy issues and options. At one end of the spectrum, advocacy NGOs such as Greenpeace and Amnesty International draw attention to environmental and human rights concerns in particular national contexts. These NGOs can capture public attention, both within and beyond national borders, and exert leverage on policy options through calling for boycotts or other sanctions. At the other extreme, NGOs like the World Business Council on Sustainable Development can support international corporations trying to pre-empt the kinds of criticism launched by advocacy NGOs (Sell and Prakesh, 2004; Woodward, 2004; Mathiason, 2007).

Recognition of the international system's influence on domestic public policy is one of the more exciting recent developments in the discipline. While the international system has probably always affected public policy to some extent, its scope and intensity have increased greatly in recent times. This is the result of what is described as *globalization* or, more precisely, *internationalization* (Hirst and Thompson, 1996). Although initially conceived in somewhat simplistic terms, the recent literature recognizes the highly complex character of internationalization, the different forms it takes across space and time, and the varying effects it has on different policy sectors and states (Bernstein and Cashore, 2000; Bennett, 1997; Brenner, 1999; Hobson and Ramesh, 2002; Weiss, 1999). This recognition has led researchers to investigate more carefully the means, manner, and mechanisms through which domestic policy processes are linked to the international system (Coleman and Perl, 1999; Risse-Kappen, 1995; Finnemore and Sikkink, 1998; Keck and Sikkink, 1998).

Such studies are still at an early stage, and the challenge before scholars is to incorporate changes induced by internationalization into existing conceptions of domestic policy processes and their outcomes (Hollingsworth, 1998; Lee and McBride, 2007; Cohen and McBride, 2003). However, several key trends can still be identified.

First, the internationalization of the world economy has accelerated the speed with which the effects of events elsewhere (natural calamities, wars, terrorist actions, financial crises, stock market gyrations, etc.) spread via the telecommunications media (Rosenau, 1969). This has expanded the scope for *policy spillovers* as previously isolated sectors converge, overlap, and collide.

What were in the past seen as discrete sectors—such as telecommunications and computers, or agriculture and trade—are now increasingly viewed as elements of a single sector. Any international effort to reduce agricultural subsidies, for instance, has an effect on rural development, social welfare, and environment policies and, ultimately, overall government fiscal policy. Traditional social policy areas such as social security and health care have thus become a part of economic and trade policy-making as a result (Unger and van Waarden, 1995; Coleman and Grant, 1998).

Second, internationalization also creates new opportunities for learning from the policy experiences of others. This is the theme of much recent work on policy transfers, which especially highlights the role of transnational epistemic (knowledge-based) communities and non-governmental organizations in promoting learning activities (Haas, 1992; Evans and Davies, 1999; King, 2005; Levi-Faur and Vigoda-Gadot, 2006). The lessons of privatizing telecommunications in Britain and deregulating airlines in the United States in the 1980s rapidly spread around the world and across policy sectors because of the active role played by the associated policy communities (Ikenberry, 1990; Ramesh and Howlett, 2005; Eisner, 1994b). Although these ideas are often reinterpreted in the transfer process and are then adapted to fit into particular policy-making processes (Dobbin et al., 2007), there is no doubt that opportunities for drawing on ideas that originated beyond a nation's boundary have increased in recent years as internationalization has proceeded apace (Coleman and Perl, 1999; de Jong and Edelenbos, 2007; Pedersen, 2007).

Moreover, internationalization promotes new patterns of policy-making (Rittberger and Mayer, 1993). When a domestic policy actor loses out in a domestic setting, it now may seek to have the policy transferred to the arena of international organizations if it expects its position to receive a more favourable reception in that venue. Powerful new international organizations and regimes such as the European Union (EU), the WTO, and the North American Free Trade Agreement (NAFTA) have opened up new action channels for domestic policy actors pursuing their interests (Howlett and Ramesh, 2002; Richardson, 1999; Cortell and Davis, 1996; Demaret, 1997).

Examples of International Regimes in Trade and Finance
Mapping the myriad effects of all international regimes is clearly beyond the scope of this book. Here we will only outline the regimes prominent in the areas of trade, finance, and production to illustrate how they affect domestic public policy-making.

The edifice on which the contemporary international trade regime is based is the General Agreement on Tariffs and Trade (GATT), signed in 1947 and succeeded by the World Trade Organization (WTO) in 1995. Its membership includes almost all states in the world and the vast majority of world exports are governed by its provisions.

The WTO requires members to work towards lowering trade barriers by according 'national treatment'[3] to imports and not subsidizing exports. These requirements are intended to assist internationally competitive producers, at the expense of producers who are not competitive. The agreement restricts governments' ability to support domestic industries, either through protection against imports or subsidy for exports, although tenacious governments do find ways of getting around the restrictions. The difficulties involved in protecting against imports create opportunities and wealth for successful exporters, and by implication the whole economy, but at the same time impose costs on uncompetitive industries and firms. These costs, again, are often borne by the whole society in the form of higher unemployment and greater public expenditure on social welfare (see Hoekman and Kostecki, 1995).

The international monetary regime has an even greater impact on public policy, especially after the adoption of a flexible exchange rate system in 1976. The fact that exchange rates of currencies are determined by financial markets according to the demand and supply of a country's currency—instead of being fixed by international agreement, as was the case under the Bretton Woods agreement of 1944—exposes governments to international financial pressures. Since the financial markets depend on dealers' interpretation of a country's present economic conditions and their expectations for the future, this system often results in unpredictable fluctuations in the value of national currencies. Governments are therefore under constant pressure not to do anything that may, rightly or wrongly, displease the foreign exchange market.

Even more important than the flexible exchange rate system are the effects of financial deregulation and technological improvements that enable the transfer of money around the globe at high speed. By the late 1990s, foreign exchange trading around the world amounted to more than $2 trillion per *day*. With such huge volumes at stake, international money markets have the ability to cause havoc for a country whose policies are viewed unfavourably by international capital. States must now be extremely careful about the effects of their policies, as these affect exchange rates, which in turn affect interest rates and export competitiveness, the repercussions of which are felt by the entire economy. A government's decision to increase expenditure on social welfare, for instance, may be viewed unfavourably by money traders, who may sell off the currency, thereby depreciating it, which may in turn necessitate an increase in interest rates by the government, the result of which will be a slow-down in the economy and higher unemployment. The net result of all these actions and reactions would be negation of the original decision to increase spending. The expected adverse market reaction to budget deficits also limits the scope for using this vital fiscal policy instrument to boost economic activity and lower unemployment (Huber and Stephens, 1998). The rapid fall in the US dollar in 2008 following years of budget and current accounts deficits suggests that even a superpower is not entirely immune to global forces.

Similarly, the liberalization of rules restricting foreign investment, particularly since the 1980s, has led to a massive expansion of foreign direct investment and proliferation of transnational corporations (TNCs), which in turn have affected states' policy options. In 2006, there were 73,000 parent TNCs with more than 780,000 foreign affiliates, whose assets amounted to US$51 trillion and that had 73 million employees and annual sales exceeding US$25 trillion (UNCTAD, 2007). TNCs not only control large pools of capital, but they are also major players in international trade—they account for over two-thirds of world trade—and control much of the world's leading technology and management skills. Since their primary interest is profits, the TNCs have a motive to locate production where they see the greatest opportunity for maximizing profits.

Given their size and strength, TNCs are major players in the world economy and, by implication, in politics and public policy. They can cause serious damage to a country's economy by withholding investment or deciding to take their investment elsewhere, possibilities that policy-makers can ignore only at great economic peril. There is also now a competition among countries to attract TNCs by offering conditions the latter would find appealing. This often takes the form of a state commitment to control labour costs, maintain tax levels comparable to those in other similar nations, and set minimal restrictions on international trade and investment. Such pledges can also be elicited by transnational financial companies such as banks and bond rating agencies, which can downgrade public debt, increasing the costs governments must pay to borrow money abroad. All these pressures create severe restrictions on states' policy options, not just in economic matters but in non-economic matters as well.

However, international regimes do not affect all nations equally. The more powerful nations enjoy greater policy autonomy within the international system than their less powerful counterparts. This is not only because the powerful states have the capacity to force other nations to change their behaviour, but also because others often voluntarily alter their behaviour to match the expectations of the dominant powers (Hobson and Ramesh, 2002). Thus, for example, at the present time any international trade or investment agreement opposed by a predominant trade and investment nation such as the United States is unlikely to be reached, and if it is achieved it is unlikely to be of much significance. The Chinese government is similarly able, for example, to negotiate terms with TNCs desiring access to its gigantic domestic market that are unlikely to be available to most other nations. Depending on their economic and military power, in the international arena some countries are policy-*makers* while others are policy-*takers*. The more powerful countries and actors—for instance, China, the European Union, and the United States—exercise leverage on other nations to conform to their preferred policy options. Policy-takers—which includes most countries in the world—are nations that give up their capacity to pursue preferred policy options in exchange for preferred access to financial and product markets and/or security alliances.

Policy Subsystems and Policy Regimes:
Integrating Institutions, Ideas, and Actors

The actors we have identified above originate in the political economic structure and institutions of contemporary society and exercise their role in policy-making through their interactions. These interactions are imbued with meaning from the ideas that actors invoke in supporting or opposing particular policy options. Given this mutually defining relationship among actors, institutions, and ideas, it is useful to have analytical concepts that can encompass these fundamental elements of policy relationships. We have already discussed the concept of a *policy paradigm*, or a set of high-level ideas that structure policy debates. Identifying the key actors in a policy process, what brings them together, how they interact, and what effect their interaction has on policy-making and policy outcomes has attracted the attention of many students of public policy-making and policy formulation (Timmermans and Bleiklie, 1999). The concept of a *policy subsystem* has emerged from these studies as a concept that helps to capture the interplay of actors, institutions, and ideas in policy-making (McCool, 1998).

Policy Subsystems

The policy universe can be thought of as an encompassing aggregation of all possible international, state, and social actors and institutions that directly or indirectly affect a specific policy area. The actors and institutions found in each sector or issue area can be said to constitute a *policy subsystem* (Freeman, 1955; Cater, 1964; Freeman and Stevens, 1987; McCool, 1998) within the larger political economic system (Knoke, 1993; Laumann and Knoke, 1987; Sabatier and Jenkins-Smith, 1993b).

Over the years scholars have developed a variety of models to try to capture the manner in which ideas, actors, and institutions interact in the policy process. The oldest conception of a policy subsystem was developed in the United States by early critics of pluralism who developed the notion of the '*sub-government*', understood as groupings of societal and state actors in routinized patterns of interaction, and as a key player in policy development (deHaven-Smith and Van Horn, 1984). This concept was based on the observation that interest groups, congressional committees, and government agencies in the United States developed systems of mutual support in the course of constant mutual interaction over legislative and regulatory matters. The three-sided relationships found in areas such as agriculture, transportation, and education were often dubbed *iron triangles* to capture the essence of their structure as well as their iron-clad control over many aspects of the policy process (Cater, 1964).

Such groupings were usually condemned for having 'captured' the policy process, thus subverting the principles of popular democracy by ensuring that their own self-interests prevailed over those of the general public (Bernstein, 1955; Huntington, 1952; Lowi, 1969). However, in the 1960s and 1970s, further research into the American case revealed that many sub-governments were not all-powerful, and that in fact their influence on policy-making varied across issues and over time (Hayes, 1978; Ripley and Franklin, 1980). Soon a more flexible and less rigid notion of a policy subsystem evolved, called the *'issue network'* by Hugh Heclo (1978). He argued that while some areas of American political life were organized in an institutionalized system of interest representation, others were not (Heclo, 1974). The membership and functioning of 'iron triangles', he suggested, were often not as closed or rigid as they were depicted to be. Heclo conceived of policy subsystems as existing on a spectrum, with iron triangles at one end and issue networks at the other. Issue networks were thus larger, much less stable, had a constant turnover of participants, and were much less institutionalized than iron triangles.

Subsequent studies led to the identification of a large variety of subsystems, which in turn necessitated the development of alternate taxonomies to Heclo's simple spectrum of issue networks and iron triangles. Thus, R.A.W. Rhodes (1984) argued that interactions within and among government agencies and social organizations constituted policy networks that were instrumental in formulating and developing policy. He argued that networks varied according to their level of 'integration', which was a function of their stability of membership, restrictiveness of membership, degree of insulation from other networks and the public, and the nature of the resources they controlled. In the US, similar attributes were specified by Hamm (1983), who argued that sub-governments could be differentiated according to their internal complexity, functional autonomy, and levels of internal and external co-operation.

In a major study of European industrial policy-making, Wilks and Wright (1987) endorsed Rhodes's typology, arguing that networks varied along five key dimensions: 'the interests of the members of the network, the membership, the extent of members' interdependence, the extent to which the network is isolated from other networks, and the variations in the distribution of resources between the members'. Refining the iron triangle–issue network spectrum developed by Heclo, they argued that this conception allowed a 'high–low' scale to be developed in which highly integrated networks would be characterized by stability of memberships and inter-membership relations, interdependence within the network, and insulation from other networks. At the other extreme, weakly integrated networks would be large and loosely structured, with multiple and often inchoate links with other groups and actors.

In the US, empirical efforts to clarify and reformulate the concept of policy networks were also undertaken. Salisbury, Heinz, Laumann, and Nelson (1987; see also Heinz et al., 1990), for example, argued that networks tended to have 'hollow cores' in that even the most institutionalized networks appeared to have no clear leadership. Others argued that networks could be classified according to whether or not state and societal members shared the same goals and agreed on the same means to achieve those goals. Still others argued that the number of discernible interests participating in the network was the crucial variable defining different types of networks (McFarland, 1987).

The insight that a policy subsystem might consist of a number of sub-components was developed at length in the 1980s in the works of Paul Sabatier and his colleagues. In their work, an *advocacy coalition* refers to a subset of actors in the policy subsystem (Sabatier and Jenkins-Smith, 1993b).

> An advocacy coalition consists of actors from a variety of public and private institutions at all levels of government who share a set of basic beliefs (policy goals plus causal and other perceptions) and who seek to manipulate the rules, budgets and personnel of governmental institutions in order to achieve these goals over time. (Ibid., 215)

Jenkins-Smith and Sabatier argued that advocacy coalitions include both state and societal actors at all levels of government. Their scheme cleverly combined the role of knowledge and interest in the policy process, as policy actors are seen to come together for reasons of common beliefs, often based on their shared knowledge of a public problem and their common interest in pursuing certain solutions to it. The core of their belief system, consisting of views on the nature of humankind and the ultimate desired state of affairs, is quite stable and holds the coalition together. All those in an advocacy coalition participate in the policy process in order to use the government machinery to pursue their (self-serving) goals.

While belief systems and interests determine the policies an advocacy coalition will seek to have adopted, their chances of success are affected by a host of factors. These include the coalition's resources, such as money, expertise, number of supporters, and legal authority (Sabatier, 1987). External factors also affect what the coalition can achieve by making some objectives easier to accomplish than others (Jenkins-Smith and Sabatier, 1993). Some of these external factors—such as the nature of the problem, natural resource endowments, cultural values, and constitutional provisions—are relatively stable over long periods of time, and are therefore quite predictable. Others are subject to a greater degree of change, including public opinion, technology, level of inflation or unemployment, and change of political party in government (Kim and Roh, 2008).

By the end of the 1980s, it was clear from these works and others in many different countries that a variety of different types of subsystems existed, depending on the structural interrelationships among their component parts. Efforts then turned to developing a more consistent method of classifying these components so that the different types of subsystems could be better understood (Atkinson and Coleman, 1989; McCool, 1989; Ouimet and Lemieux, 2000).

This is not to say that all actors and institutions play the same role in every subsystem. Some actors are engaged mainly in the struggle over ideas, as members of knowledge- or idea-based discourse or 'epistemic' communities (Hajer, 1993; Fischer, 1993; Kisby 2007), while only a subset of that group—a policy network—is engaged in the active and ongoing formulation and consideration of policy options and alternatives (Marier, 2008) In the banking sector, for example, numerous academics, think-tanks, journalists, consultants, and others specialize

Figure 3.2   The Policy Universe and Policy Subsystems

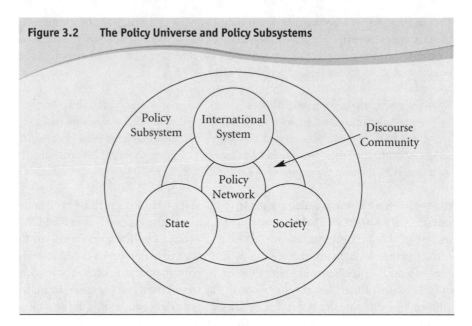

in monitoring the sector and recommending policy alternatives. This subset of the entire possible universe of policy actors constitutes an epistemic or discourse community. The group of government regulators, decision-makers, and bankers who actually make government policy, constitute the policy network (see Figure 3.2).

A useful distinction can be drawn between communities in which there is a dominant knowledge base and those in which there is not. A second critical dimension of policy community structure is the number of relatively distinct 'idea sets' (Schulman, 1988; MacRaw, 1993; Smith, 1993) in the community and if, and to what extent, a consensus exists on any particular set. Using these two dimensions allows us to construct a simple matrix of common discourse community types (see Figure 3.3).

In a situation where one idea set is dominant and unchallenged—such as is presently the case in the area of fiscal policy, where there is virtually no opposition

Figure 3.3   A Taxonomy of Discourse Communities

		Number of Idea Sets	
		Few	Many
Dominant Idea Set	Yes	Hegemonic Community	Fractious Community
	No	Contested Community	Chaotic Community

Source: Adapted from Michael Howlett and M. Ramesh, 'Policy Subsystem Configurations and Policy Change: Operationalizing the Postpositivist Analysis of the Politics of the Policy Process', *Policy Studies Journal* 26, 3 (1998): 466–82.

to balanced budget orthodoxy—a form of monopolistic or 'hegemonic' community may develop. On the other hand, where multiple sets of ideas circulate, with no single idea in a dominant position, a more chaotic community will exist. A good example of this at present is biogenetics policy, where ideas ranging from the 'pure science' of genome research to ethical, religious, and conspiratorial theories coexist in the subsystem. When several major idea sets contest dominance, as Sabatier and Jenkins-Smith noted, a third type of contested community may form; as is the case in many countries' debates over environmental protection where ideas such as biodiversity and sustainable development contest equally well-entrenched concepts of resource exploitation and utilitarianism. Finally, where one idea set is dominant but faces challenges from less popular ideas, a fractious community is likely to be found. This is a type of community found at present in trade and development policy subsystems, for example, where a dominant free-trade globalism faces a challenge from less popular but still compelling sets of ideas promoting more autarkic local or national forms of economic exchange and development.

With respect to policy networks, or more structured forms of subsystem interactions, many observers have highlighted the significance of two key variables in shaping the structure and behaviour of policy networks: the number and type of their membership and the question of whether state or societal members dominate their activities and interactions (Smith, 1993; Coleman and Perl, 1999). With these variables, a reasonable classification of issue networks can be developed (see Figure 3.4) (Coleman and Skogstad, 1990).

In this model, small (state corporatist) networks dominated by government actors, as are commonly found in highly technical issue areas such as nuclear, chemical, or toxic substance regulation, can be distinguished from those (state pluralist) in which many societal actors are included, as might be the case with education or other areas of state-led social policy-making. Other distinct network types exist where a few societal actors dominate a small (social corporatist) network—as in many areas of industrial policy—or where they dominate large networks (social pluralist), as is the case in many countries in areas such as transportation or healthcare delivery.

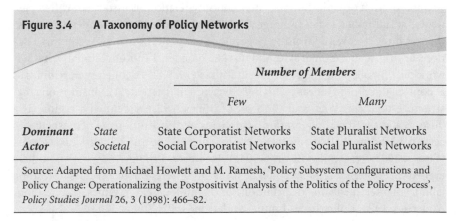

Figure 3.4   A Taxonomy of Policy Networks

		Number of Members	
		Few	*Many*
Dominant Actor	*State*	State Corporatist Networks	State Pluralist Networks
	Societal	Social Corporatist Networks	Social Pluralist Networks

Source: Adapted from Michael Howlett and M. Ramesh, 'Policy Subsystem Configurations and Policy Change: Operationalizing the Postpositivist Analysis of the Politics of the Policy Process', *Policy Studies Journal* 26, 3 (1998): 466–82.

These types of classification schemes help to clarify the possible structure of discourse communities and interest networks in policy subsystems and give us a general mechanism through which to organize the complex reality of multiple actors and institutions found in the policy-making process. Combining policy paradigms and policy subsystems, as discussed below, helps to further clarify policy-making complexity by linking those two components together into specific, relatively long-lasting policy frameworks or *policy regimes* (Richardson, 1995).

Policy Regimes

Whether they start at the domestic or international level, relatively few policy initiatives revisit the first principles of capitalism and democracy each time they consider what government can or cannot do to address a policy problem. These 'big questions' of governance and market organization are inherited through the policy paradigms and policy subsystems that affect how to approach policy-making and what policy options to consider in specific circumstances (see Leman, 1977; Lowi, 1998; Gormley and Peters, 1992). The concept of a *policy regime* has been developed to describe this phenomenon of the persistence of fundamental policy components over fairly long periods of time.

Although the term is sometimes confused with similar, but distinct, concepts such as 'political regime', 'international regime' (Preston and Windsor, 1992; Krasner, 1983; Young, 1980), 'implementation regime' (Stoker, 1989), 'regulatory regime' (Lowi, 1966, 1972; Kelman, 1981), and 'accumulation regime' (Lipietz, 1982; Aglietta, 1979), the idea of a 'policy regime' is a unique and specialized concept that helps to capture the enduring nature of many policy processes and contents found at the sectoral level of policy-making (Doern, 1998; Doern et al., 1999). The term 'policy regime' attempts to capture how policy institutions, actors, and ideas tend to congeal into relatively long-term, institutionalized patterns of interaction that combine to keep public policy contents and processes more or less constant over time.

In his work on social policy, for example, Gosta Esping-Andersen found 'specific institutional arrangements adopted by societies in the pursuit of work and welfare. A given organization of state–economy relations is associated with a particular social policy logic' (Rein et al., 1987). Initially, Esping-Andersen argued that such regimes were linked to larger national patterns of state–economy relations or the organization of state and market-based institutions. Similarly, in their work on US policy-making, Harris and Milkis (1989: 25) defined such regimes as a 'constellation' of (1) ideas justifying governmental activity, (2) institutions that structure policy-making, and (3) a set of policies. Eisner defined a regime as a 'historically specific configuration of policies and institutions which establishes certain broad goals that transcend the problems' specific to particular sectors (Eisner, 1993: xv; see also Eisner, 1994a). However, Esping-Andersen and others argued that different regimes could be found in different policy sectors, including labour market, pension, distribution, and employment regimes (see Esping-Andersen, 1990; Kolberg and Esping-Andersen, 1992; Kasza, 2002).

A policy regime, hence, can be seen to embody each of the salient characteristics of a policy context at a given point in time. It can be thought of as combining a common set of policy ideas (a policy paradigm) and a common or typical set of policy actors and institutions organized around those ideas (a policy subsystem).

As such, the 'policy regime' is a useful term for identifying what lies behind the long-standing patterns found in both the substance and process of public policy-making in specific sectors and issue areas. The general idea is that sectoral policy-making will develop in such a way that the same actors, institutions, and governing ideas tend to prescribe what happens over extended periods of time, infusing a policy sector with both a consistent content and a set of typical procedures through which policies are developed. Understanding how subsystems, paradigms, and regimes form, how they are maintained, and how they change, therefore, is a crucial aspect of the study of public policy.

Conclusion

Policy context forms the setting in which the drama of responding to public problems unfolds. While this stage for policy-making can extend to cover issues ranging from local to global, it is not a uniform backdrop. The policy universe is filled with distinctive constellations of actors, ideas, and institutions that constitute the space where actual problems are engaged and responses get crafted.

Policy processes tend to draw upon actors from a subset of the policy universe, increasingly at both the domestic and international levels. Policy subsystems involve both state and societal actors in complex systems of mutual interaction. Political-economic, constitutional, and legal provisions are important determinants of subsystem participation, while the power and knowledge resources of subsystem actors critically affect the nature of their activities and interactions. The ideas invoked to justify some actions and to disparage others are both introduced by these actors, as well as embedded in the institutions that structure subsystem creation.

In most subsystems in liberal-democratic capitalist societies, given their central location and access to abundant organizational resources, the minister(s) and bureaucrats in charge of a policy sector are usually the key governmental actors in a policy process, with the legislators (particularly in parliamentary systems) playing a secondary role. Their societal counterparts are drawn mainly from among interest groups, research organizations, and business and labour. These non-state participants bring expertise, information, and interest in the issues under consideration, and seek influence over the policy outcomes through their subsystem membership and participation in the policy process. The media often play an intermediating role in publicizing issues connected to the subsystem and identifying possible solutions to those issues.

The policy regime concept introduced in this chapter represents one cornerstone of the analytical framework on which Lasswell's promised insight for the policy sciences can be realized. The rest of that framework comprises the distinctive problem-solving dynamics that will be elaborated in subsequent chapters focusing on the *policy cycle*. When policy subsystems and paradigms are connected to appropriate stages of the policy cycle, it is possible to uncover how policy issues get on the agenda; how choices for addressing those issues are selected; how decisions on pursuing courses of action are taken; how efforts to implement the policy are organized and managed; and how assessments of what is working and what is not are produced and fed back into subsequent rounds or cycles of policy-making.

Studying regime interactions within different stages of the policy cycle thus enables researchers to reveal not only a static 'snapshot' of the policy-making process in particular areas of government activity, but also the *dynamics* of policy stability and policy change. This analytical framework offers much greater depth than the intuition, hearsay, and educated guessing of many of the 'informed sources' and media pundits that bolster many generally held beliefs about policy-making processes in liberal-democratic and other states. Mastering the configuration and application of policy subsystems and policy paradigms within different stages of the policy cycle is what this book intends to teach its readers.

Study Questions

1. How are key policy actors empowered (or not) in a liberal-democratic capitalist system?
2. Is the policy universe expanding or contracting with the advent of inter-nationalization? What difference would this make for policy-makers?
3. Identify examples of 'strong', well-organized policy subsystems and 'weak', disorganized ones.
4. In the context of a particular policy sector, identify the range of policy actors that comprise the policy universe and the policy subsystem. Why are some actors found in one group and not the other?
5. What are the salient features of policy regimes? How can these be identified in practice?

Further Readings

Haggard, Stephen, and Beth A. Simmons. 1987. 'Theories of International Regimes', *International Organization* 41, 3: 491–517.

Held, David. 1991. 'Democracy, the Nation-State and the Global System', in Held, ed., *Political Theory Today*. Oxford: Polity Press, 197–235.

James, Simon. 1993. 'The Idea Brokers: The Impact of Think Tanks on British Government', *Public Administration* 71: 471–90.

Kaufman, Herbert. 2001 'Major Players: Bureaucracies in American Government', *Public Administration Review* 61, 1: 18–42.

King, Anthony. 1981. 'What Do Elections Decide?', in D. Butler, H.R. Penniman, and A. Ranney, eds, *Democracy at the Polls: A Comparative Study of Competitive National Elections*. Washington: American Enterprise Institute for Public Policy Research.

Olson, David M., and Michael L. Mezey, eds. 1991. *Legislatures in the Policy Process: The Dilemmas of Economic Policy.* Cambridge: Cambridge University Press.

Spitzer, Robert J., ed. 1993. *Media and Public Policy.* Westport, Conn.: Praeger.

Weaver, R. Kent, and Bert A. Rockman. 1993. 'Assessing the Effects of Institutions', in Weaver and Rockman, eds, *Do Institutions Matter? Government Capabilities in the United States and Abroad.* Washington: Brookings Institution, 1–41.

Part II

The Five Stages of the Policy Cycle

Chapter 4

Agenda-Setting

Why do some issues get addressed by governments while others are ignored? Although sometimes taken for granted, the means and mechanisms by which issues and concerns are recognized as requiring government action are by no means simple. Some demands for government resolution of public problems come from the international and domestic actors discussed in Chapter 3, whereas others are initiated by governments themselves. These issues originate in a variety of ways and must undergo intense scrutiny before they are seriously considered for resolution by government.

Agenda-setting, the first and perhaps the most critical stage of the policy cycle, is concerned with the way problems emerge, or not, as candidates for government's attention. What happens at this early stage of the policy process has a decisive impact on the entire subsequent policy cycle and its outcomes. The manner and form in which problems are recognized, if they are recognized at all, are important determinants of whether, and how, they will ultimately be addressed by policy-makers. As Cobb and Elder (1972: 12) put it:

> Pre-political, or at least pre-decisional processes often play the most critical role in determining what issues and alternatives are to be considered by the polity and the probable choices that will be made. What happens in the decision-making councils of the formal institutions of government may do little more than recognize, document and legalize, if not legitimize, the momentary results of a continuing struggle of forces in the larger social matrix.

John Kingdon, in his path-breaking 1984 inquiry into agenda-setting practices in the United States, provided the following concise definition of this crucial first stage of the policy cycle:

> The agenda, as I conceive of it, is the list of subjects or problems to which governmental officials, and people outside of government closely associated with those officials, are paying some serious attention at any given time. . . . Out of the set of all conceivable subjects or problems to which officials could be paying attention, they do in fact seriously attend to some rather than others. So the agenda-setting process narrows this set of conceivable subjects to the set that actually becomes the focus of attention. (Kingdon, 1984: 3–4)

At its most basic, agenda-setting is about the recognition of some subject as a problem requiring further government attention (Baumgartner and Jones, 2005).

This does not in any way guarantee that the problem will ultimately be addressed, or resolved, by further government activity, but merely that it has been singled out for the government's consideration from among the mass of problems existing in a society at any given time. That is, it has been raised from its status as a subject of concern to that of a private or social problem and finally to that of a *public issue*, potentially amenable to government action. While threats and challenges are more frequently the forces that motivate issue definition in policy agenda-setting, there are also times when policy agendas are set by the attraction of an opportunity— such as the US space program's race to land a man on the moon during the 1960s.

How a subject of concern comes to be interpreted as a public issue susceptible to further government action raises deeper questions about the nature of human knowledge and the social construction of that knowledge (Berger and Luckmann, 1966; Holzner and Marx, 1979), and the policy sciences literature has gone through significant changes in its understanding of what constitutes such problems. Early works in the policy sciences often assumed that problems had an 'objective' existence and were, in a sense, waiting to be 'recognized' by governments who would do so as their understanding and capacity for action progressed. Later works in the post-positivist tradition, however, acknowledged that problem recognition is very much a socially constructed process since it involves the creation of accepted definitions of normalcy and what constitutes an undesirable deviation from that status (McRobbie and Thornton, 1995). Hence, in this view, problem recognition is not a simple mechanical process of recognizing challenges and opportunities, but a sociological one in which the 'frames' or sets of ideas within which governments and non-governmental actors operate and think are of critical significance (Goffman, 1974; Haider-Markel and Joslyn, 2001; Schon and Rein, 1994). Each of these perspectives will be discussed in turn below.

The Objective Construction of Policy Problems: The Role of Social Conditions and Structures

Most early works on the subject of agenda-setting began with the assumption that socio-economic conditions led to the emergence of particular sets of problems to which governments eventually responded. These include both models that posited that the issues facing all modern governments are converging towards a common set, and those postulating that the interplay of economic and political cycles will affect the nature of issues that make it onto the agenda.

The idea that public policy problems and issues originate in the level of 'development' of a society, and that particular sets of problems are common to states at similar levels of development, was first broached by early observers of comparative public policy-making. By the mid-1960s, Thomas Dye and other observers of differences and similarities in the policies across 50 American states had concluded that cultural, political, and other factors were less significant for explaining the mix of public policies than were factors related to the level of economic development of the society. In his study of US state-level policy development, for example, Ira Sharkansky concluded that 'high levels of economic development—

measured by such variables as urban per capita income, median educational level and industrial employment—are generally associated with high levels of expenditure and service outputs in the fields of education, welfare and health.' This conclusion led him to argue that 'political characteristics long thought to affect policy—voter participation, the strength of each major party, the degree of interparty competition, and the equity of legislative apportionment—have little influence which is independent of economic development' (Sharkansky, 1971: 277).

This observation about the nature of public policy formation in the American states was soon expanded to the field of comparative, cross-national studies dealing with the different mixes of policies across countries. Authors such as Harold Wilensky (1975), Philip Cutright (1965), Henry Aaron (1967), and Frederick Pryor (1968) all developed the idea that the structure of a nation's economy determined the types of public policies adopted by the government.

Taken to the extreme, this line of analysis led scholars to develop the *convergence thesis*. The convergence thesis suggests that as countries industrialize, they tend to converge towards the same policy mix (Bennett, 1991; Kerr, 1983; Seeliger, 1996). The emergence of similar welfare states in industrialized countries, its proponents argue, is a direct result of their similar levels of economic wealth and technological development. Although early scholars indicated only a positive correlation between welfare policies and economic development, this relationship assumed causal status in the works of some later scholars. In this 'strong' view, high levels of economic development and wealth created similar problems and opportunities, which were dealt with in broadly the same manner in different countries, regardless of the differences in their social or political structures. Wilensky (1975: 658–9), for example, noted that 'social security effort'—defined as the percentage of a nation's gross national product (GNP) devoted to social security expenditures—was positively related to the level of GNP per capita, a correlation leading him to argue that economic criteria were more significant than political ones in understanding why those public policies had emerged.

In this view, agenda-setting is a virtually automatic process occurring as a result of the stresses and strains placed on governments by industrialization and economic modernization. It matters little, for example, whether issues are actually generated by social actors and placed on government agendas, or whether states and state officials take the lead in policy development. Instead, what is significant is the fact that similar policies emerged in different countries irrespective of the differences in their social and political structures.

The convergence thesis was quickly disputed by critics who argued that it oversimplified the policy development process and inaccurately portrayed the nature of the actual welfare policies found in different jurisdictions, where policies were characterized by significant divergences as well as convergences (Heidenheimer et al., 1975). It was noted, for example, that in comparative studies of policy development in the American states, economic measures explained over one-half of the interstate variations in policies in only 4 per cent of the policy sectors examined. Second, it was intimated that the desire to make a strong economic argument had led investigators to overlook the manner in which economic factors varied in significance over time and by issue area (Sharkansky, 1971; Heichel et al., 2006).

By the mid-1980s, a second, less deterministic explanation of agenda-setting behaviour had emerged, which treated political and economic factors as an integral whole. This *resource-dependency model* argued that industrialization creates a need for programs such as social security (because of the aging of the population and processes of urbanization that usually accompany economic modernization) as well as generating the economic resources (because of increased productivity) to allow states to address this need (through programs such as public pension plans, unemployment insurance, and the like). More importantly, in this view, industrialization also creates a working class with a need for social security and the political resources (because of the number of working-class voters and the ability to disrupt production through work stoppages) to exert pressure on the state to meet those needs. The ideology of the government in power and the political threats it faces are also important factors affecting the extent to which the state is willing to meet the demand for social welfare and the types of programs it is willing to utilize to do so.

While some issues, such as the role of international economic forces in domestic policy formation, were still debated (Cameron, 1984; Katzenstein, 1985), this resource-dependency view offered a reasonable alternative to convergence theory-inspired explanations of public policy. However, it remained at a fairly high level of abstraction and was difficult to apply to specific instances of agenda-setting (see Uusitalo, 1984).

One way that scholars sought to overcome this problem was by reintegrating political and economic variables in a new 'political economy of public policy' (Hancock, 1983). Here it was argued that both political and economic factors are important determinants of agenda-setting and should therefore be studied together, especially insofar as political-economic events can affect the *timing and content* of specific policy initiatives.

One of the most important versions of this line of argument posited the idea of a *political business cycle*. The economy, it was suggested, has its own internal dynamics, which on occasion are altered by political 'interference'. In many countries the timing of this interference could be predicted by looking at key political events such as elections and budgets, which tend to occur with some degree of regularity in democratic states.

The notion of a political business cycle grew out of the literature on business cycles, which found that the economy grew in fits and starts according to periodic flurries of investment and consumption behaviour (see Schneider and Frey, 1988; Frey, 1978; Locksley, 1980). When applied to public policy-making, it was argued that in the modern era governments often intervened in markets to smooth out fluctuations in the business cycle. In democratic states, it followed that the nature of these interventions could be predicted on the basis of the political ideology of the governing party—either pro-state or pro-market—while the actual timing of interventions would depend on the proximity to elections. Policies that caused difficulties for the voting public and hence could affect the electoral prospects of political parties in government, it was argued, were more likely to be developed when an election did not loom on the immediate horizon. As Edward Tufte (1978: 71) put it:

> Although the synchronization of economic fluctuations with the electoral cycle often preoccupies political leaders, the real force of political influence on macroeconomic performance comes in the determination of economic priorities. Here the ideology and platform of the political party in power dominate. Just as the electoral calendar helps set the timing of policy, so the ideology of political leaders shapes the substance of economic policy.

While few disagreed that partisan ideology could have an impact on the nature of the types and extent of government efforts to influence the economy, this approach was criticized for its limited application to democratic countries, and only to a subset of these such as the United States, where electoral cycles were fixed. In many other countries, elections either do not exist, are not competitive, or their timing is indeterminate and depends on events in parliaments or other branches of government, making it difficult if not impossible for governments to make such precise policy timing calculations (Foot, 1979; Johnston, 1986). It was also argued that the concept of the business cycle itself was fundamentally flawed and that the model simply pointed out the interdependence of politics and economics already acknowledged by most analysts (see McCallum, 1978; Nordhaus, 1975; Schneider and Frey, 1988; Boddy and Crotty, 1975).

The Subjective Construction of Policy Problems: The Role of Policy Actors and Paradigms

In the alternative post-positivist view, the 'problems' that are the subject of agenda-setting are considered to be constructed purely in the realm of public and private ideas, detached from economic conditions or other macro-social processes such as industrialization and unionization (Berger and Luckmann, 1966; Hilgartner and Bosk, 1981; Holzner and Marx, 1979; Rochefort and Cobb, 1993; Spector and Kitsuse, 1987).

It had long been noted in policy studies that the ideas policy actors hold have a significant effect on the decisions they make. Although efforts have been made by economists, psychologists, and others to reduce these sets of ideas to rational calculations of self-interest, it is apparent that, even in this limiting case, traditions, beliefs, and attitudes about the world and society affect how individuals interpret their interests (Flathman, 1966).

As we have discussed in Chapters 2 and 3, sets of ideas or ideologies can have a significant impact on public policy-making, for it is through these ideational prisms that individuals conceive of social or other problems that inspire their demands for government action and through which they design proposed solutions to these problems (Chadwick, 2000; George, 1969). However, different types of ideas will have different effects on policy-making, and especially on agenda-setting. As Goldstein and Keohane (1993b) have noted, at least three types of ideas are relevant to policy: world views, principled beliefs, and causal ideas (see Braun, 1999; Campbell, 1998). These ideas can influence policy-making by serving as 'road maps' for action, defining problems, affecting the strategic interactions between policy actors, and constraining the range of policy options that are proposed.

World views or *ideologies* have long been recognized as helping people make sense of complex realities by identifying general policy problems and the motivations of actors involved in politics and policy. These sets of ideas, however, tend to be very diffuse and do not easily translate into specific views on particular policy problems. While scholars recognized that the general *policy mood* or *policy sentiment* found in a jurisdiction can be an important component of a general macro-policy environment, for example by influencing voting for representatives and yielding a certain political orientation in government (Durr, 1993; Stimson, 1991; Stimson et al., 1995; Lewis-Beck, 1988; Suzuki, 1992; Adams, 1997), the links of these kind of beliefs to agenda-setting remain quite indirect (Stevenson, 2001; Elliott and Ewoh, 2000).

Principled beliefs and causal stories, on the other hand, can exercise a much more direct influence on the recognition of policy problems and on subsequent policy content (see George, 1969). In the policy realm, this notion of ideas creating claims or demands on governments was taken up by Frank Fischer and John Forester (1993) and Paul Sabatier (1987, 1988), among others writing in the 1980s and 1990s. The concept of causal stories, in particular, was applied to agenda-setting by Deborah Stone (1988, 1989). In Stone's view, agenda-setting usually involved constructing a 'story' of what caused the policy problem in question. As she has argued:

> Causal theories, if they are successful, do more than convincingly demonstrate the possibility of human control over bad conditions. First, they can either challenge or protect an existing social order. Second, by identifying causal agents, they can assign responsibility to particular political actors so that someone will have to stop an activity, do it differently, compensate its victims, or possibly face punishment. Third, they can legitimate and empower particular actors as 'fixers' of the problem. And fourth, they can create new political alliances among people who are shown to stand in the same victim relationship to the causal agent. (Stone, 1989: 295)

As Murray Edelman (1988: 12–13) argued, in this view policy issues arise largely on their own within social discourses, often as functions of pre-existing ideological constructs applied to specific day-to-day circumstances:

> Problems come into discourse and therefore into existence as reinforcements of ideologies, not simply because they are there or because they are important for well-being. They signify who are virtuous and useful and who are dangerous and inadequate, which actions will be rewarded and which

penalized. They constitute people as subjects with particular kinds of aspirations, self-concepts, and fears, and they create beliefs about the relative importance of events and objects. They are critical in determining who exercise authority and who accept it.

As originally presented by the French social philosopher Michel Foucault (1972), the concept of a political discourse was a tool for understanding the historical evolution of society. Foucault believed that historical analysis should contribute to social theory by explaining the origin, evolution, and influence of discourses over time, and by situating current discourses into this framework. In a policy context this means that policy issues can be seen as arising from pre-existing social and political discourses that establish both what a problem or policy opportunity is and who is capable of articulating it.

In this view, the idea that agenda-setting proceeds in a mechanistic fashion or through rational analysis of objective conditions by social and political actors is considered to be deceptive, if not completely misleading. Rather, policy-makers are a part of the same discourses as the public and, in Edelman's metaphor of the 'political spectacle', are involved in manipulating the signs, sets, and scenes of a political drama. According to the script of these discourses, which is written as the play is underway, different groups of policy actors are involved, and different outcomes prescribed, in agenda-setting (Muntigl, 2002; Schmidt and Radaelli, 2005; Johnson, 2007).

The discursive frames from which actors define policy challenges, of course, are not always widely, or as strongly, held by all policy actors, meaning that the agenda-setting process very often features a clash of frames and a struggle among policy actors over the 'naming' of problems, the 'blaming' of conditions and actors for their existence, and the 'claiming' of specific vantage points or perspectives for their resolution (Felstiner et al., 1980–1; Bleich, 2002). The resolution of this conflict and the elevation of a private or social grievance to the status of a public problem, therefore, are often related more to the abilities and resources of competing actors than to the elegance or purity of their ideas, but these ideas are critical in determining its content (Surel, 2000; Snow and Benford, 1992; Steinberg, 1998, Dostal, 2004).

In this view, then, the policy-making agenda is created out of the history, traditions, attitudes, and beliefs encapsulated and codified in the discourses constructed by social and political actors (Jenson, 1991; Stark, 1992). Symbols and statistics, both real and fabricated, are used to back up one's preferred understanding of the causes and solutions of a problem. Symbols are discovered from the past or created anew to make one's case. When using statistics, policy-makers and analysts know how to find what they are looking for.

Thus, in the post-positivist view, understanding agenda-setting requires understanding how individuals and/or groups make demands for a policy that is responded to by government, and vice versa. In short, policy researchers need to identify the conditions under which these demands emerge and are articulated in prevailing policy discourses (Spector and Kitsuse, 1987: 75–6; McBeth et al.,

2005). How the material interests of social and state actors are filtered through, and reflect, their institutional and ideological contexts is a required component of the study of agenda-setting (Thompson, 1990).

Combining Ideas, Actors, and Structures in Multi-Variable Models of Agenda-Setting

Alone, neither the pure positivist approach, with its emphasis on structures and institutions, nor the pure post-positivist approach, with its emphasis on ideas, has withstood subsequent testing and examination. Their difficulty in identifying a single source of factors driving public policy agenda-setting led to the development of multivariate models, which attempt to systematically combine some of the central variables identified in these early studies into a more comprehensive, and empirically accurate, theory of agenda-setting.

Funnel of Causality

One such multivariate model was advanced in parallel efforts by Anthony King (1973) in Great Britain, Richard Hofferbert (1974) in the United States, and Richard Simeon (1976a) in Canada. Each author developed a model of policy formation that sought to capture the relationships among social, institutional, ideational, political, and economic conditions in the agenda-setting process. These models considered *all* these variables to be important but situated them within a *funnel of causality*, in which each factor was 'nested' among other variables.

Rather than considering structural, ideational, and actor-related variables as contradictory or zero-sum relationships, the funnel of causality conception suggested that the substance of government's agenda is shaped by socio-economic and physical environment, the distribution of power in society, the prevailing ideas and ideologies, the institutional frameworks of government, and the process of decision-making within governments (King, 1973). These variables were intertwined in a nested pattern of interaction where policy-making occurs within institutions, institutions exist within prevailing sets of ideas, ideas operate within relations of power in society, and relations of power arise from the overall social and material environment.

This synthetic model pointed to the relations between the material and ideational variables that had been identified by previous positivist and post-positivist studies without bogging down in attempts to specify their exact relationship or causal significance. Such causal diversity is the model's greatest strength because it allows different views on agenda influences to be explored empirically so that specific relationships among the variables can be established. This approach is also a weakness, though, because it does not explain the reasons for these factors influencing agendas in different ways. Why the place of one issue on the public agenda might be influenced by ideas and that of another, for example, by environmental factors is not broached, let alone resolved. The funnel-of-causality model also says very little about how multi-dimensional influences on policy agendas, such as the environmental context, ideas, and economic interests, create any particular effect on policy actors in the agenda-setting process (Mazmanian and Sabatier, 1980; Green-Pedersen, 2004).

Issue-Attention Cycles

Another early example of an agenda-setting model built on the premise that this stage of the policy process involved the interaction of institutions, actors, and ideas was put forward by Anthony Downs in 1972. Downs proposed that agenda-setting often followed what he termed an *'issue-attention cycle'*, much like the media 'news cycle'. In an article focusing on the emergence of environmental policy in the United States in the early 1960s, Downs argued that public policy-making often focused on issues that momentarily capture public attention and trigger demands for government action. However, he also noted that many of these problems soon fade from view as their complexity or intractability becomes apparent. As he put it:

> public attention rarely remains sharply focused upon any one domestic issue for very long—even if it involves a continuing problem of crucial impor-tance to society. Instead, a systematic issue-attention cycle seems strongly to influence public attitudes and behaviour concerning most key domestic problems. Each of these problems suddenly leaps into prominence, remains there for a short time, and then—though still largely unresolved—gradually fades from the center of public attention. (Downs, 1972: 38)

The idea of the existence of a systematic issue-attention cycle in public policy-making gained a great deal of attention in subsequent years and Downs's work is often cited as an improved model for explaining the linkages between political institutions, actors, and beliefs, especially public opinion, and public policy agenda-setting (see, e.g., Dearing and Rogers, 1996). In a democracy, where politicians ignore public demands at their electoral peril, Downs argued, waxing and waning public attention to policy problems results in a characteristic cyclical pattern of agenda-setting, but without necessarily producing policy action on the part of governments.

Despite its frequent citation in the policy literature over the past three decades, however, the idea of Downsian-type issue-attention cycles was rarely subject to empirical evaluation. In 1985, Peters and Hogwood made an effort to opera-tionalize their own version of Downs's cycle, attempting to assess the relationship between waves of public interest as measured in Gallup polls and periodic waves of organizational change or institution-building in the US federal government. Although they found evidence of major periods of administrative consolidation and change over the course of recent US history, they noted that only seven of 12 instances of administrative reorganization met the expectations of the Downsian model, when dramatic administrative changes occurred during the same decade as the peak of public interest as measured by Gallup survey questions.

On the basis of these results, Peters and Hogwood argued: 'Our evidence supports Downs' contention that problems which have been through the issue-attention cycle will receive a higher level of attention after rather than before the peak' (ibid., 251). However, they were also careful to note that there appeared to be at least two other patterns or cycles at work in the issue-attention process beyond what Downs first identified. In the first type, cycles were initiated by external or exogenous events such as war or an energy crisis and then were mediated by public attention. In this type of 'crisis' cycle, the problem would not 'fade away' as Downs hypothesized. In the second type of 'political' cycle, issue initiation originated in the political leadership and then caught public attention (ibid., 252; see also Hogwood, 1992).

Peters and Hogwood's work emphasized the key role played by state actors in socially constructed agenda-setting processes (Sharp, 1994b; Yishai, 1993). Officially scheduled political events, such as annual budgets, speeches from the throne, or presidential press conferences, can spark media attention, reversing the purely reactive causal linkages attributed to these actors by Downs (Cook et al., 1983; Howlett, 1997; Erbring and Goldenberg, 1980; Flemming et al., 1999). Evidence from other case studies revealed that interest group success and failure in gaining agenda access tended to be linked to state institutional structures and the availability of access points, or policy venues, from which these groups could gain the attention of government officials and decision-makers (Baumgartner and Jones, 1993; Brockmann, 1998; Pross, 1992; Newig, 2004). These insights and others were soon put together in new models that attempted to more accurately reconcile policy theory with agenda-setting reality.

Modes of Agenda-Setting

A major breakthrough in agenda-setting studies occurred in the early 1970s when Cobb, Ross, and Ross identified several typical patterns or 'modes' of agenda-setting. In so doing, they followed the insight of Cobb and Elder, who distinguished between the *systemic* or informal public agenda and the *institutional* or formal state agenda. The systemic agenda 'consists of all issues that are commonly perceived by members of the political community as meriting public attention and as involving matters within the legitimate jurisdiction of existing governmental authority' (Cobb and Elder, 1972: 85). This is essentially a society's agenda for discussion of *individual and social* problems, such as crime and health care. Each society, of course, has literally thousands of issues that some citizens find to be matters of concern and would have the government do something about.

As we have noted, however, only a small proportion of the problems on the systemic or informal agenda are taken up by the government for serious consideration as *public* problems. Only after a government has accepted that something needs to be done about a problem can the issue be said to have entered the institutional agenda. These are issues to which the government has agreed to give serious attention. In other words, the informal agenda is for *discussion* while the institutional agenda is for *action*.

Cobb, Ross, and Ross identified four major phases of agenda-setting that occur as issues move between the informal and institutional agendas. Issues are first *initiated*, their solutions are *specified*, support for the issue is *expanded*, and, if successful, the issue *enters* the institutional agenda (Cobb et al., 1976: 127). Cobb, Ross, and Ross then proposed three basic patterns or modes of agenda-setting based on the previous comparative work of Cobb and Elder (1972). Each of these modes is associated with the different manner and sequence in which issue initiation, specification, expansion, and entrance occurs. In a further step, they identified or linked each mode with a specific type of political regime.

They identified the *outside initiation model* with liberal pluralist societies. In this model, 'issues arise in nongovernmental groups and are then expanded sufficiently to reach, first, the public [systemic] agenda and, finally, the formal [institutional] agenda.' Here, social groups play the key role by articulating a grievance and demanding its resolution by the government. These groups lobby, contest, and join with others in attempting to get the expanded issue onto the formal agenda. If they have the requisite political resources and skills and can out-manoeuvre their opponents or advocates of other issues and actions, they will succeed in having their issue enter the formal agenda (Cobb et al., 1976). Successful entry on the formal agenda does not necessarily mean a favourable government decision will ultimately result. It simply means that the item has been singled out from among many others for more detailed consideration.

The *mobilization model* is quite different and was attributed by Cobb and his colleagues to 'totalitarian' regimes. This model describes 'decision-makers trying to expand an issue from a formal [institutional] to a public [systemic] agenda' (ibid, 134.) In the mobilization model, issues are simply placed on the formal agenda by the government with no necessary preliminary expansion from a publicly recognized grievance. There may be considerable debate within government over the issue, but the public may well be kept in the dark until an official announcement. Gaining support for the new policy is important, since successful implementation will depend on public acceptance. Towards this end, government leaders hold meetings and engage in public relations campaigns. As the authors put it, 'The mobilization model describes the process of agenda building in situations where political leaders initiate a policy but require the support of the mass public for its implementation . . . the crucial problem is to move the issue from the formal agenda to the public agenda' (ibid., 135).

Finally, in the *inside initiation model*, influential groups with special access to decision-makers launch a policy and often do not want public attention. This can be due to technical as well as political reasons and is an agenda-setting pattern one would expect to find in corporatist regimes. In this model, initiation and specification occur simultaneously as a group or government agency enunciates a grievance and specifies some potential solution. Deliberation is restricted to specialized groups or agencies with some knowledge or interest in the subject. Entrance on the agenda is virtually automatic due to the privileged place of those desiring a decision (ibid., 136)

This line of analysis identified several typical agenda-setting modes that combined actor behaviour with regime type, and also identified key sources of policy ideas and discourses associated with each mode. In its original formulation, Cobb, Ross, and Ross suggested that the type of agenda-setting process is ultimately determined by the nature of the political system, with outside initiation being typical of liberal democracies, mobilization characteristic of one-party states, and inside initiation reflective of authoritarian bureaucratic regimes. However, it was soon recognized that these different styles of agenda-setting varied not so much by political regime as by policy sector, as examples of each type of agenda-setting behaviour could be found within each regime type (Princen, 2007). Subsequent investigations sought to specify exactly what processes were followed within political regimes, especially in complex democratic polities like the United States with multiple quasi-autonomous policy subsystems. Their results have led to a more nuanced understanding of how agenda-setting modes are linked to actors, structures, and ideas and, ultimately, as set out below, to the actual content of the problems and issues likely to emerge in specific instances of agenda-setting.

Linking Agenda-Setting Modes to Content: Policy Windows and Policy Monopolies

In the 1980s, John Kingdon (1984) developed an analytical framework for agenda-setting that drew upon his investigations of policy initiation in the US Congress. His model examined state and non-state influences on agenda-setting by exploring the role played by *policy entrepreneurs* both inside and outside of government in constructing and utilizing agenda-setting opportunities—labelled *policy windows*—to bring issues onto government agendas. His model suggested that policy windows open and close based on the dynamic interaction of political institutions, policy actors, and the articulation of ideas in the form of proposed policy solutions. These forces can open, or close, policy windows, thus creating the chance for policy entrepreneurs to construct or leverage these opportunities to shape the policy agenda.

In Kingdon's study of agenda-setting in the United States, three sets of variables—*streams* of problems, policies, and politics—are said to interact. The *problem stream* refers to the perceptions of problems as public issues requiring government action. Problems typically come to the attention of policy-makers either because of sudden events, such as crises, or through feedback from the operation of existing programs (ibid., 20). The *policy stream* consists of experts and analysts examining problems and proposing solutions to them. In this stream, the various possibilities are explored and narrowed down. Finally, the *political stream* 'is composed of such factors as swings of national mood, administrative or legislative turnover, and interest group pressure campaigns' (ibid., 21). In Kingdon's view, these three streams operate on different paths and pursue courses more or less independent of one another until specific points in time, or during *policy windows*, when their paths intersect or are brought together by the activities of entrepreneurs linking problems, solutions, and opportunities.

Thus, in the right circumstances, policy windows can be seized upon by key players in the political process to place issues on the agenda. Policy entrepreneurs play the chief role in this process by linking or 'coupling' policy solutions and policy problems together with political opportunities (ibid., chs 7–8; Roberts and King, 1991; Mintrom 1997; Tepper, 2004).

As Kingdon argues, 'The separate streams of problems, policies, and politics come together at certain critical times. Solutions become joined to problems, and both of them are connected to favourable political forces.' At that point an item enters the official (or institutional) agenda and the public policy process begins.[1]

Kingdon suggests that window openings can result from fortuitous happenings, including seemingly unrelated external 'focusing events', crises, or accidents; scandals; or the presence or absence of policy entrepreneurs both within and outside of governments. At other times, policy windows can be opened by institutionalized events such as periodic elections or budgetary cycles (Birkland, 1997, 1998; Tumber and Waisbord, 2004; Nohrstedt, 2005; Mertha and Lowry, 2006).

Kingdon (1984: 213) characterizes the different types of windows and their dynamics as follows:

> Sometimes, windows open quite predictably. Legislation comes up for renewal on schedule, for instance, creating opportunities to change, expand or abolish certain programs. At other times, windows open quite unpredictably, as when an airliner crashes or a fluky election produces unexpected turnover in key decision-makers. Predictable or unpredictable, open windows are small and scarce. Opportunities come, but they also pass. Windows do not stay open long. If a chance is missed, another must be awaited.

Kingdon differentiates the 'problem' from the 'political' window as follows:

> Basically a window opens because of change in the political stream (e.g. a change of administration, a shift in the partisan or ideological distribution of seats . . . or a shift in national mood); or it opens because a new problem captures the attention of governmental officials and those close to them. (Ibid., 176)

He then notes that windows also vary in terms of their predictability. While arguing that random events are occasionally significant, he stresses the manner in which institutionalized windows dominate the US agenda-setting process (Birkland, 2004). As he puts it, 'There remains some degree of unpredictability. Yet it would be a grave mistake to conclude that the processes . . . are essentially random. Some degree of pattern is evident' (ibid., 216).

The model established by Kingdon suggests at least four possible window types based on the relationship between the origin of the window—political or problem—and their degree of institutionalization or routinization. Although he does

not describe these four window types specifically, the general outline of each type is discernible from examining his work and several of his sources. The four principal window types are:

- *routinized political windows*, in which institutionalized procedural events trigger predictable window openings;
- *discretionary political windows*, in which the behaviour of individual political actors leads to less predictable window openings;
- *spillover problem windows*, in which related issues are drawn into an already open window (May et al., 2007); and
- *random problem windows*, in which random events or crises open unpredictable windows (Cobb and Primo, 2003).

In this model, the level of institutionalization of a window type determines its frequency of appearance and hence its predictability (Boin and Otten, 1996; Howlett, 1997b).

Kingdon's model has been used to assess the nature of US foreign policy agenda-setting (Woods and Peake, 1998); the politics of privatization in Britain, France, and Germany (Zahariadis, 1995; Zahariadis and Allen, 1995); the nature of US domestic anti-drug policy (Sharp, 1994a); the collaborative behaviour of business and environmental groups in certain anti-pollution initiatives in the US and Europe (Lober, 1997; Clark, 2004); and the overall nature of the reform process in Eastern Europe (Keeler, 1993). While a major improvement on earlier models, it has been criticized for presenting a view of the agenda-setting process that is too contingent on unforeseen circumstances, ignoring the fact that in most policy sectors, as Downs had noted, action tends to produce bursts of change that are followed by lengthy periods of inertia (Dodge and Hood, 2002).

One way that policies 'congeal' into lengthy periods of program stability, for example, is that policy windows can be designed to stay closed for extended periods—as occurs, for example, in the multi-year funding authorizations of transportation and military programs which reduce the opportunities available to discuss issues and adjust priorities. Windows can even be locked through fiscal devices such as trust funds and revenue bonding that commit spending and taxing for many years into the future (French and Phillips, 2004).

A key mechanism that provides stability in agenda-setting, through its control over the policy discourse, is the construction of a stable policy subsystem or '*policy monopoly*'. Such a subsystem entrenches the basic idea set, many of the actors, and the institutional order in which policy development occurs, 'locking in' a policy discourse or frame in which policy issues are named and claimed. Frank Baumgartner and Bryan Jones (1991, 1993, 1994, 2005), in a landmark series of studies, developed this idea, which modifies Kingdon's work and helps to explain the likely content of the typical patterns or modes of agenda-setting behaviour identified earlier by Cobb and his colleagues.

The key element that differentiates modes of agenda-setting, Baumgartner and Jones argue, revolves around the manner in which specific subsystems gain the ability to control the interpretation of a problem and thus how it is conceived and discussed. For Baumgartner and Jones, the 'image' of a policy problem is significant because:

> When they are portrayed as technical problems rather than as social questions, experts can dominate the decision-making process. When the ethical, social or political implications of such policies assume center stage, a much broader range of participants can suddenly become involved. (Baumgartner and Jones, 1991: 1047)

The primary relationship that affects agenda-setting dynamics in Baumgartner and Jones's view is that between individuals and groups who have power inside existing subsystems and those who are seeking to impact those subsystems by leveraging outside influences. In their model, policy monopolies attempt to construct hegemonic images of policy problems that allow influential actors in a subsystem to practise *agenda denial*—that is, preventing alternate images and ideas to penetrate and thus influence governments (on agenda denial, see Yanow, 1992; Bachrach and Baratz, 1962; Debnam, 1975; Frey, 1971; R.A. Smith, 1979; Cobb and Ross, 1997b). Subsystem members opposed to prevailing conditions and government responses seek to alter policy images through a number of tactics related to altering the venue of policy debate, or other aspects of the prevailing policy discourse, thus undermining the complacency or stability of an existing policy subsystem (Sheingate, 2000).

Baumgartner and Jones posit that actors attempting to alter the official agenda of government will adopt either of two strategies to make subsystems more 'competitive'. In the Downsian strategy, groups can publicize a problem in order to alter its venue through mobilizing public demands for government to resolve it (Baumgartner and Jones, 1993: 88). In a second typical approach, which they term a 'Schattschneider' mobilization (after the early American scholar of pressure group behaviour), groups involved in the policy subsystem dissatisfied with the policies being developed or discussed seek to alter the institutional arrangements within which the subsystem operates in order to expand or contract its membership (ibid., 89; for examples of these strategies in practice, see Maurier and Parkes, 2007; Daugbjerg and Studsgaard, 2005; Hansford, 2004; Pralle, 2003).

The key change that results if either strategy succeeds is the transformation of a policy monopoly into a more competitive subsystem where new actors and new discourses, and thus new issues, can enter into policy debates. A good example of this occurring in recent years can be found in the transformation of smoking from a highly stable issue framed as a personal consumption issue to one that, through venue shifts to courts and other bodies on the part of policy entrepreneurs, was redefined as a social health and welfare issue. This led, ultimately, to the articulation and subsequent implementation of alternative options for tobacco control related to sales, advertising, and workplace bans and other restrictions, which were unthinkable under the previous regime (Studlar, 2002).

Figure 4.1   Typical Agenda-Setting Modes

		Subsystem Type	
		Monopolistic	Competitive
Ideas	Old	**Status Quo** Character: static/hegemonic (agenda denial)	**Contested** Character: contested variations on the status quo
	New	**Redefining** Character: internal discursive reframing	**Innovative** Character: unpredictable/ chaotic

The four typical modes of agenda-setting that flow from the analysis of Baumgartner and Jones are shown in Figure 4.1. In this model, the chance for new problems or options to emerge on government agendas depends on whether policy subsystems are monopolistic or competitive and whether new ideas about the nature of a policy problem and its solution can be found in the subsystem. Where a well-established monopoly exists with no new ideas present, agenda denial and a status quo orientation are likely to result: that is, the hegemony of the existing subsystem over the definition and construction of problems and solutions will be maintained. When that same monopoly has some new ideas, these are likely to result in some reframing of issues within the subsystem.

When a more competitive subsystem exists but no new ideas have been developed, contested variations on the status quo are likely to be features of agenda-setting. When the ideas remain old, however, nothing more than proposals for modest changes to the status quo are likely to be raised to the institutional agenda. Only when both situations exist—that is, both a competitive subsystem and the presence of new ideas—are more profound (and potentially paradigmatic) innovative changes in problem definition and identification likely to proceed onto the formal agenda of governments and move forward for consideration in the next stage of the policy cycle: policy formulation.

Conclusion: Revisiting Agenda-Setting Modes through a Policy Subsystem Lens

This overview of agenda-setting studies has shown how investigations have moved from simple univariate models focused on 'objective' or 'subjective' constructions of policy problems to more sophisticated examinations that link many variables in complex multivariate relationships. It has also shown how contemporary studies have developed a set of agenda-setting patterns or modes that reveal how this stage of the policy process is influenced by key actors in prevailing policy subsystems, the dominant sets of ideas about policy problems they espouse, and the kinds of institutions within which they operate.

The most significant variables influencing modes of agenda-setting turn out to have less to do with automatically responding to changes in the nature of the economy, as Dye, Wilensky, and Sharkansky argued, or with the nature of the political regime involved, as Cobb, Ross, and Ross had claimed. Instead, as Kingdon points out, agenda-setting processes are contingent, but very often are still predictable, involving the complex interrelationships of ideas, actors, and structures. And, as Baumgartner and Jones have suggested, the nature of the actors initiating policy discussions and whether the structures in which they operate allow new ideas to come forward are the most important determinants of the movement of public problems from the informal agenda to the state's institutional agenda (Daugbjerg and Perdersen, 2004).

While the exact timing of the emergence of an issue onto the systemic or formal policy agenda depends, as Kingdon showed, on the existence of a policy window and of the capacity and ability of policy entrepreneurs to take advantage of it, the content of the problems identified in the agenda-setting process depend very much on the nature of the policy subsystem found in the area concerned and the kinds of ideas its members have. Whether subsystem members are capable of creating and retaining an interpretive monopoly on understanding a policy issue, as understood by Baumgartner and Jones, largely determines if the matching of problems with solutions found in the agenda-setting and subsequent policy formulation stages of the policy process will yield consideration of the issue within an existing policy paradigm or in a new ideational framework (Haider-Markel and Joslyn, 2001; Jeon and Haider-Markel, 2001).

Study Questions

1. What is the difference between the informal and formal, or systemic and official, policy agendas?
2. How do problems get recognized as public problems and make it onto the official policy agenda?
3. How do different agenda-setting modes reflect different configurations of institutions, ideas, and actors?
4. Why and how is access to the policy agenda denied to certain problems? What are the implications?
5. What is a policy discourse? Why is it important in understanding agenda-setting?

Further Readings

Baumgartner, Frank R., and Bryan D. Jones. 1993. *Agendas and Instability in American Politics*. Chicago: University of Chicago Press.
Cobb, Roger W., J.K. Ross, and M.H. Ross. 1976. 'Agenda Building as a Comparative Political Process', *American Political Science Review* 70, 1: 126–38.

Cobb, Roger W., and Marc Howard Ross, eds. 1997. *Cultural Strategies of Agenda Denial: Avoidance, Attack and Redefinition.* Lawrence: University Press of Kansas.

Downs, Anthony. 1972. 'Up and Down with Ecology—the "Issue-Attention Cycle" ', *The Public Interest* 28: 38–50.

Kingdon, John W. 1995 [1984]. *Agendas, Alternatives and Public Policies.* Boston: HarperCollins.

Simeon, Richard. 1976. 'Studying Public Policy', *Canadian Journal of Political Science* 9: 548–80.

Spector, Malcolm, and John I. Kitsuse. 1987. *Constructing Social Problems.* New York: Aldine de Gruyter.

Yanow, Dvora. 1992. 'Silences in Public Policy Discourse: Organizational and Policy Myths', *Journal of Public Administration Research and Theory* 2, 4: 399–423.

Chapter 5

Policy Formulation: Policy Instruments and Policy Design

Policy formulation refers to the process of generating options on what to do about a public problem. In this second stage of the policy process, policy options that might help resolve issues and problems recognized at the agenda-setting stage are identified, refined, and formalized. An initial feasibility assessment of policy options is conducted at this stage of policy development, but these formulation efforts and dynamics are distinct from the next stage, decision-making (discussed in Chapter 6), where some course of action is approved by authoritative decision-makers in government.

What Is Policy Formulation?

Once a government has acknowledged the existence of a public problem and the need to do something about it, that is, once it has entered onto the formal agenda of government, policy-makers are expected to decide on a course of action. Formulating what this course of action will entail is the second major stage in the policy cycle.

As Charles Jones (1984: 7) has observed, the distinguishing characteristic of policy formulation is simply that means are proposed to resolve perceived societal needs. Policy formulation, therefore, involves identifying and assessing possible solutions to policy problems or, to put it another way, exploring the various options or alternative courses of action available for addressing a problem. The proposals may originate in the agenda-setting process itself, as a problem and its possible solution are placed simultaneously on the government agenda (Kingdon, 1984), or options may be developed after an item has moved onto the official agenda. In all cases, the range of available options considered at this stage is always narrowed down to those that policy-makers could accept before these alternatives move on to the formal deliberations of decision-makers. Defining and weighing the merits and risks of various options hence forms the substance of this second stage of the policy cycle, and some degree of formal 'policy analysis' is typically a critical component of policy formulation activity.

Jones (1984: 78) describes other broad characteristics of policy formulation:

- Formulation need not be limited to one set of actors. Thus there may well be two or more formulation groups producing competing (or complementary) proposals.
- Formulation may proceed without clear definition of the problem, or without formulators ever having much contact with the affected groups. . . .

- There is no necessary coincidence between formulation and particular institutions, though it is a frequent activity of bureaucratic agencies.
- Formulation and reformulation may occur over a long period of time without ever building sufficient support for any one proposal.
- There are often several appeal points for those who lose in the formulation process at any one level.
- The process itself never has neutral effects. Somebody wins and somebody loses even in the workings of science.

This picture presents policy formulation as a highly diffuse and disjointed process that varies by case. However, it is possible to say something about the general nature of the formulation process and the activities it involves.

The Phases of Policy Formulation

The formulation stage of policy-making can be subdivided into phases to clarify how various options are considered and to highlight how some options are carried forward while others are set aside. Harold Thomas (2001) identifies four such phases to policy formulation: appraisal, dialogue, formulation, and consolidation.

In the *appraisal* phase, data and evidence are identified and considered. These may take the form of research reports, expert testimony, stakeholder input, or public consultation on the policy problem that has been identified. Here, government both generates and receives input about policy problems and solutions.

The *dialogue* phase seeks to facilitate communication between policy actors with different perspectives on the issue and potential solutions. Sometimes, open meetings are held where presenters can discuss and debate proposed policy options. In other cases, the dialogue is more structured, with experts and societal representatives from business and labour organizations invited to speak for or against potential solutions. Hajer (2005) notes that the structure of engaging input about policy options can make a considerable difference in the effects of that participation, both on the policy process and on the participants themselves. Formal consultations and public hearings tend to privilege expert input and frustrate new participants, while techniques that engage participants from less established organizations and points of view can add energy and enthusiasm to the dialogue over policy options.

At the core of deliberations, the aptly named *formulation* phase sees public officials weighing the evidence on various policy options and drafting some form of proposal that identifies which of these options, if any, will advance to the ratification stage. Such feedback can take the form of draft legislation or regulations, or it could identify the framework for subsequent public and private policy actors to negotiate a more specific plan of action.

Making recommendations about which policy options to pursue will often yield dissent by those who have seen their preferred strategies and instruments set aside during formulation. These objections can be addressed during the *consolidation* phase, when policy actors have an opportunity to provide more or less formal feedback on the recommended option(s). Some actors who advocated alternative options may come around to joining the consensus so that they can stay connected to official policy development efforts. Supporting the policy solutions that are being recommended for further action may provide the opportunity to subsequently influence the ratification and implementation stages from within. Other policy actors will register their continued dissent from specific policy options, hoping to leverage future developments from outside the consensus that has emerged over what is to be done.

Note once again that the limitations that lead policy-makers to reject certain types of options need not be based on facts (Merton, 1948). If significant actors in the policy subsystem believe that something is unworkable or unacceptable, this is sufficient for its exclusion from further consideration in the policy process (Carlsson, 2000). As we have seen with the discussion of agenda-setting in the previous chapter, perception is just as real as reality itself in this second stage of the policy process.

The General Content of Policy Formulation

Like agenda-setting, the nuances of policy formulation in particular instances can be fully understood only through empirical case studies. Nevertheless, most policy formulation processes do share certain characteristics.

Policy formulation involves identifying the technical and political constraints on state action. It involves recognizing limitations, which uncovers what is infeasible and, by implication, what is feasible. This may seem obvious, but it is not reflected in many proposals made about what policy-makers ought to be doing, which often fail to acknowledge the limitations that constrain a proposed course of action. For instance, the public choice theorists' key assumption—that politicians choose policies that best promote their electoral appeal—presumes more room for manoeuvre than is actually available (Majone, 1989: 76). Politicians simply cannot do everything they think might appeal to voters. Other constraints can arise from the state's administrative and financial capacity. For example, governments that have an ownership stake in economic sectors such as energy, finance, and transportation may have more policy options open to them than states where the private sector exclusively delivers these goods and services.

Policy-makers typically face numerous substantive or procedural constraints when considering policy options. *Substantive* constraints are innate to the nature of the problem itself. Thus, policy-makers wishing to eliminate poverty do not have the option of printing money and distributing it to the poor because inflation will offset any gains, and so they must necessarily address the problem in more indirect ways. Similarly, the goal of promoting excellence in arts or sports cannot be accomplished simply by ordering people to be the best artists or sportswomen in the world; the pursuit of these goals requires far more delicate, expensive, and time-consuming measures. The problem of global warming, for instance, cannot be entirely eliminated because there is no known effective solution that can be employed without causing tremendous economic and social dislocations, which leaves policy-makers to tinker with options that barely scratch the surface of the problem. Substantive problems with policy alternatives are thus 'objective' in the sense that redefining them does not make them go away, and their resolution or partial resolution requires the use of state resources and capacities such as money, information, personnel, and/or the exercise of state authority.

Procedural constraints have to do with procedures involved in adopting an option or carrying it out. These constraints may be either institutional or tactical. Institutional constraints, as discussed in Chapter 3, can include constitutional provisions, the nature of the organization of the state and society, and established patterns of ideas and beliefs that can prevent consideration of some options or promote others (Yee, 1996). Efforts to control handguns in the United States, for example, run up against constraints imposed by the constitutional right to bear arms. Federalism imposes similar constraints on German, American, Mexican, and Australian policy-makers in areas of public policy where two levels of government must agree before anything can be done (Montpetit, 2002; Falkner, 2000). How the main social groups are organized internally and are linked with the state also affects what can or cannot be done, especially the nature of political party and electoral systems, which can create 'policy horizons' or limited sets of acceptable choices for specific actors in the policy process (Warwick, 2000; Bradford, 1999). In a similar vein, the predominance of specific sets of philosophical or religious ideas in many societies can lead to difficulties with potential policy solutions that might seem routine in others (DeLeon, 1992). The actual options that will be weighed and measured for potential adoption in policy thus depend a great deal on the people who consider them, their ideas about the world and the issue involved, and the nature of the structures within which they work.

The essence of the search for solutions to a policy problem entails discovering not only which actions are considered to be technically capable of addressing or correcting a problem but also which among these is considered to be politically acceptable and administratively feasible (Majone, 1975, 1989; Huitt, 1968; Meltsner, 1972; Dror, 1969; Webber, 1986). Choosing a solution to a public problem or fulfilling a societal need does not even remotely resemble the orderly process of detached, 'objective' analytical scrutiny of all policy alternatives often proposed by subscribers to rationalist analytical models. As we saw in the preceding chapter, defining and interpreting a problem is often a nebulous process that does not lead to clear or agreed-upon problem definitions, making the identification of solutions equally problematic. Even if policy-makers agree that a problem exists, they may not share an understanding of its causes or ramifications.

Hence, the search for a policy solution will usually be contentious and subject to a wide range of conflicting pressures and alternative perspectives and approaches, frustrating efforts to systematically consider policy options in a rational or maximizing manner. Among other things, certain players in the policy process can be advantaged over others if they are granted some authority in diagnosing a policy ill or in establishing the feasibility of a proposed solution. This is the case, for example, with scientists or government specialists in many policy areas, but such privileged positions can be eroded if these experts are challenged on their neutrality or competence (see Afonso, 2007; Carpenter, 2007; Nathanson, 2000; Heikkila, 1999; Doern and Reed, 2001; Harrison, 2001; Callaghan and Schnell, 2001).

Understanding the ideas and experiences that these actors bring to policy formulation, and the contexts within which they operate, can help explain why some options gain considerable attention while others are ignored. Before delving into the details of the formulation process and the types of policy instrument typically considered at this stage, it is worth highlighting key characteristics of the actors involved in the analysis of alternatives and the kinds of activities they undertake.

The Substance of Policy Formulation: Policy Instruments

When policy-makers are exploring policy options, they consider not only what to do but also how to do it. Thus, while formulating a policy to tackle traffic congestion, for example, policy-makers must simultaneously consider whether to build more roads, improve public transit, restrict automobile usage, or some combination of these, as well as the tools by which the policy will actually be implemented. These *policy tools*, also known as *policy instruments* and *governing instruments*, are the actual means or devices that governments make use of in implementing policies. Proposals that emanate from the formulation stage, therefore, will specify not only whether or not to act on a policy issue, but also how to best address the problem and implement a solution. For example, in a case such as that of deteriorating water quality, policy options could emphasize public educational campaigns that urge people to refrain from polluting activities, they could embrace regulations that prohibit all activities causing the pollution, they could propose a subsidy to the polluting firms encouraging them to switch to safer technologies, or they could advance some combination of these or other means (Gunningham et al., 1998; Gunningham and Young, 1997).

Taxonomies of Policy Instruments

The variety of instruments available to policy-makers is limited only by their imaginations. However, scholars have made numerous attempts to identify such instruments and classify them into meaningful categories (see Salamon and Lund, 1989: 32–3; Lowi, 1985; Bemelmans et al., 1998).

Most efforts to construct such a typology stem from Lasswell's insight that governments use a variety of policy instruments to achieve a relatively limited number of political ends. Lasswell (1958: 204) argued that governments had developed a limited number of 'strategies' that involved 'the management of value assets in order to influence outcomes'. Understanding these basic strategies and the instrument types that go with them required identifying the resources that governments work with (see also French and Raven, 1959). Cushman (1941) introduced a simple taxonomy of policy instruments based on whether government chose to regulate societal activities or not, and whether those regulations were coercive or not. Dahl and Lindblom (1953) went on to categorize policy tools by their degree of intrusiveness and dependence on state agencies or markets. Theodore Lowi (1966, 1972) blended these insights to create the first encompassing model of how preferences for particular types of policy tools were involved in characterizing epochs or periods of government activity.

Lowi observed in the US case that American governments had tended to favour certain types of instruments for prolonged periods, providing the opportunity to identify major transitions in government activities between these periods. To distinguish the major types and eras of government activity, he proposed a four-cell matrix based on the specificity of the target of coercion and the likelihood of its actual application. The original three policy types he identified included the weakly sanctioned and individually targeted 'distributive' policies; the individually targeted and strongly sanctioned 'regulatory' policy; and the strongly sanctioned and generally targeted 'redistributive' policy. To these three, Lowi later added the weakly sanctioned and generally targeted category of 'constituent' policy.

Although widely read, Lowi's typology was rarely applied because it was not only difficult to operationalize but also somewhat internally inconsistent. Nevertheless, Lowi's central premise of 'policy determining politics' proved alluring and encouraged further efforts to classify and comprehend policy instruments. Anderson's (1971) suggestion that public policy analysis shift from the study of policy problems and inputs to the study of policy implements and outputs was endorsed by scholars such as Bardach (1980) and Salamon (1981), both of whom suggested that policy studies had 'gone wrong' right at the start by defining policy in terms of 'areas' or 'fields' rather than in terms of tools. As Salamon (1981: 256) argued: 'rather than focusing on individual programs, as is now done, or even collections of programs grouped according to major "purpose", as is frequently proposed, the suggestion here is that we should concentrate instead on the generic tools of government action, on the "techniques" of social intervention.' This challenge was taken up in the 1980s and 1990s by the 'policy design' literature (Bobrow and Dryzek, 1987; Dryzek and Ripley, 1988; Linder and Peters, 1984).

Rather than attempt to construct exhaustive lists, which had already produced arcane inventories (such as the scheme for at least 64 general types of instruments in European economic policy produced by Kirschen and his colleagues [1964]), policy design researchers sought ways to group roughly similar types of instruments into a few categories that could then be analyzed to determine the answers to Salamon's questions. Scholars returned to Lasswell's early work on instrument 'strategies' and tried to identify the basic 'governing resources' that different instruments relied on for their effectiveness (Balch, 1980).[1]

A simple and powerful taxonomy known as the 'NATO model' was developed by Christopher Hood (1986a), who proposed that all policy tools used one of four broad categories of governing resources. He argued that governments confront public problems through the use of the information in their possession as a central policy actor ('nodality'), their legal powers ('authority'), their money ('treasure'), or the formal organizations available to them ('organization') or 'NATO'. Governments can use these resources to manipulate policy actors, for example, by

---

Figure 5.1   Policy Instruments, by Principal Governing Resource

Nodality	Authority	Treasure	Organization
Information collection and release	Command-and-control regulation	Grants and loans	Direct provision of goods and services and public enterprises
Advice and exhortation	Self-regulation	User charges	Use of family, community, and voluntary organizations
Advertising	Standard-setting and delegated regulation	Taxes and tax expenditures	Market creation
Commissions and inquiries	Advisory committees and consultations	Interest group creation and funding	Government reorganization

Note: Cells provide examples of instruments in each category.
Source: Adapted from Christopher Hood, *The Tools of Government* (Chatham, NJ: Chatham House, 1986), 124–5.

---

withdrawing or making available information or money, by using their coercive powers to force other actors to undertake activities they desire, or simply by undertaking the activity themselves using their own personnel and expertise. Using Hood's idea of governing resources, a basic taxonomy of instrument categories can be set out. Figure 5.1 presents such a classification scheme with illustrative examples of the types of policy tools found in each category.

In the post-Salamon era, studies of instrument choice tended to look at instances of single-instrument selection and, on the basis of such cases, to discern the general reasons why governments would choose one category of instrument over another. These studies, heavily influenced by economists, tended to focus on *substantive* instruments—that is, those tools (such as classical command-and-control regulation, public enterprises, and subsidies) that more or less directly affect the type, quantity, price, or other characteristics of goods and services being produced in society, either by the public or private sector (Salamon, 1989, 2002a; Bemelmans-Videc et al., 1998; Peters and van Nispen, 1998).

Much less attention was paid by analysts of this period to the systematic analysis of their *procedural* counterparts—that is, instruments designed mainly to affect or alter aspects of policy processes rather than social or economic behaviour per se. In these early works, policy instruments had often been defined broadly to include a wider range of tools, or techniques, of governance than in the post-Salamon era. By 2000, however, this neglect had been noted, prompting the emergence of systematic treatments of procedural instruments (Riker, 1983, 1986; Dunsire, 1986, 1993a, 1993b), such that we now have knowledge of both substantive and procedural instruments, their effects, and the reasons they are chosen.

Common Policy Tools by Category

Policy formulation to a very great extent involves the effort to match potential policy tools to policy problems. This can be undertaken in a highly systematic, analytical fashion or as a much more trial-and-error exercise based simply on the experiences and preferences of policy formulators. Although it is often represented in the literature as a highly technical exercise, most instrument uses involve trade-offs of various kinds, meaning it is very difficult to make a clear, maximizing tool selection. In what follows, examples of the most common kinds of both procedural and substantive policy tools are provided along with a description of their principal strengths and weaknesses.

Nodality or Information-based Instruments

The first category of policy tools that Hood drew together involves the use of information resources at the disposal of governments. These resources are quite considerable, as the possibilities outlined below will demonstrate.

Public Information Campaigns

Government chronicles a great deal about societal activities through both routine reporting and special studies. It is not uncommon, therefore, for government to disseminate information with the expectation that individuals and firms will change their behaviour in response to it. This information is often fairly general, intended to make societal actors more knowledgeable so that they can make informed choices. For instance, information on tourism, trade, and economic and social trends can be disseminated by the government through public service advertising, leaving it to the population to draw conclusions and respond accordingly (Salmon, 1989a).

Public information may also be more precisely targeted to elicit a particular response, as in the case of publicizing information on the ill effects of smoking (Weiss and Tschirhart, 1994; Vedung and van der Doelen, 1998). In either case, there is no obligation on the public to respond in a particular manner (Adler and Pittle, 1984). In many countries this passive release of information may be mandated or facilitated by freedom of information or access to information laws. These laws allow access to specific types of government information by members of the public (Relyea, 1977; Bennett, 1990, 1992). Such legislation is usually accompanied by privacy acts and official secrets acts, which balance open access with restrictions on the release of some types of information, the exact content of which varies from country to country (Qualter, 1985).

Findings on the impact of public information campaigns suggest that disclosure will not automatically lead to policy change. Other conditions must be present, such as an ability to calculate the impact of data on (and by) societal actors (Cohen and Santhakumar, 2007). The public's capacity to interpret information has been shown to vary by socio-economic status, by the quantity of information presented, and by the ways in which this information is presented (Howells, 2005).

Exhortation

Exhortation, or 'suasion' as it is also called, involves slightly more government activity than pure dissemination of information (Stanbury and Fulton, 1984). Here, public effort is devoted to influencing the preferences and actions of societal members, rather than just informing the public about a situation with the hope that behaviour will spontaneously change in a desired manner (Salmon, 1989a, 1989b). Public advertisements that urge people to keep fit and healthy, not to waste water or energy, and to use public transportation are classic forms of exhortation (Firestone, 1970). Agency spokespersons can play an important role in both delivering and shaping these messages (Lee, 2001). Consultations between government officials and financial, industry, or labour representatives reveal another form of exhortation because government officials often use these meetings to try to alter target group behaviour.

Ultimately, government exhortation can only go so far. As Stanbury and Fulton (1984) conclude, 'In the absence of positive or negative inducements (or more bluntly, leverage), most efforts at suasion probably have either a low probability of success or have a relatively short shelf life.' At best, it should be used in conjunction with other instruments when they are available. Complex problems, such as influencing private corporations to make their industrial production more sustainable, require policy packages that also include other components of the NATO tool kit (Norberg-Bohm, 1999).

Benchmarking and Performance Indicators

Benchmarking is increasingly used as a process-oriented information-gathering technique in the public sector (Papaioannou et al., 2006). In theory, it enables structured comparison and, when successful, enhances the opportunity for policy learning by presenting relevant information in ways that can generate policy insight (Johnsen, 2005). The standardization of benchmarks promotes co-ordination of policy across jurisdictions, as seen in the European Union's use of an 'open method of co-ordination' in sharing information on employment and labour market policies (de la Porte et al., 2001). Performance management schemes can also work to redefine the problems addressed by public agencies such as hospitals or universities (Adcroft and Willis, 2005).

Commissions and Inquiries

Governments often employ temporary bodies to gather information about an issue or sometimes just to procrastinate in making a decision, hoping that public pressure for action will fade by the time a report is prepared. Foremost among the techniques they utilize to do so is the ad hoc inquiry, commission, or task force. These agencies exist in many forms and are often established to deal with new or particularly troubling policy problems. They attempt to provide a forum that combines specialized academic research and general public input into the definition of and potential solution to policy problems, generating information that becomes available to all participants in the policy process and altering their knowledge base as a result (Sheriff, 1983; Wraith and Lamb, 1971: 302–23; Chapman,

1973; Elliott and McGuinness, 2001; Resodihardjo, 2006; McDowall and Robinson, 1969; Cairns, 1990a; d'Ombrain, 1997).

In many jurisdictions, a system of formal reviews of ongoing policy areas is also evident. These reviews serve as 'institutionalized' task forces or investigations into ongoing issues and the efforts made by government bodies to deal with them (Bellehumeur, 1997; de la Mothe, 1996; Raboy, 1995; Banting, 1995). These reviews are usually done 'in-house' but sometimes also involve the use of outside experts (Owens and Rayner, 1999).

Authority-based Policy Instruments

Command-and-Control Regulation

Regulation is a prescription by the government that must be complied with by the intended targets; failure to do so usually involves a penalty. This type of instrument is often referred to as 'rule-making' or 'command-and-control' regulation (Kerwin, 1994, 1999).

Regulations take various forms and include rules, standards, permits, prohibitions, laws, and executive orders (Keyes, 1996). Some regulations, such as proscribing criminal behaviour, take the form of laws enforced by police and the judicial system (Rosenbloom, 2007). Most regulations, however, are written and promulgated by civil servants working under the delegated authority of enabling legislation. These regulations are then administered by a government department or a specialized, quasi-judicial government agency (first called independent regulatory commissions in the US) that is more or less autonomous of government control in its day-to-day operations.

The nature of regulations varies somewhat depending on whether they are targeted at economic or social issues. Economic regulations have been the traditional form of regulation and their purpose has been to control specific aspects of the market economy, such as the prices and volumes of production, or return on investment, or the entry into or exit of firms from an industry (Salamon, 2002b). A good example of this type of regulation is that carried out by various kinds of marketing boards, regulatory bodies that are particularly prominent in the agricultural sector. The intent of such boards is to restrict the supply of agricultural output to keep farm commodity prices at or above a certain threshold of income deemed acceptable for farmers. Their objective is to correct perceived imbalances or inequities in economic relationships that may emerge as a result of the operation of market forces.

Social regulations are of more recent origin and refer to controls in matters of health, safety, and societal behaviour such as civil rights and discrimination of various sorts. They have more to do with our physical and moral well-being than with our pocketbooks, though the costs to business of certain regulatory measures, such as environmental protection, often are passed on to the consumer. Examples of social regulation include rules regarding liquor consumption and sales, gambling, consumer product safety, occupational hazards, water-related hazards, air and noise pollution, discrimination on the basis of religion, race, gender, or ethnicity, and pornography (Padberg, 1992). With a proliferation of industry-developed norms and standards for ethical and environmentally sustainable business practices, government's regulatory role can sometimes involve enforcing compliance with these private codes of practice (Baksi and Bose, 2007).

There are several advantages of regulation as a policy instrument (see Mitnick, 1980: 401–4). First, the information needed to establish regulation is often less compared to other tools. Second, where the concerned activity is deemed entirely undesirable, as is the case with films and videos depicting pedophilia, it is easier to establish regulations prohibiting the possession of such products than to devise ways of encouraging the production and distribution of other types of more benign materials. Third, regulations allow for better co-ordination of government efforts and planning because of the greater predictability they entail. Fourth, their predictability makes them a more suitable instrument in times of crisis when an immediate response is needed or desired. Fifth, regulations may be less costly than other instruments, such as subsidies or tax incentives.

The disadvantages of regulation are equally telling (see Anderson, 1976). First, regulations, whether technical or not, are set politically and hence quite often distort voluntary or private-sector activities and can promote economic inefficiencies (Wilson, 1974). Price regulations and direct allocation restrict the operation of the forces of demand and supply and affect the price mechanism in capitalist societies, raising the potential for economic windfalls through distortions in the market. These tendencies create powerful forces for regulated firms to try and 'capture' the organizations that supervise them, to yield ongoing economic advantages through regulation. To avoid such capture, the regulatory body can nurture working relationships with other societal actors who will keep up the pressure to regulate in the public interest (Sabatier, 1975, 1977). Second, regulations can, at times, inhibit innovation and technological progress because of the market security they afford existing firms and the limited opportunities for experimentation they permit. Third, regulations are often inflexible and do not permit the consideration of individual circumstances, resulting in decisions and outcomes not intended by the regulation (Dyerson and Mueller, 1993). Such instances annoy the subject population and are often easy targets for the government's critics.

The early 1980s saw a turning point in the debate on regulations, as the idea that regulations were conceived and executed solely in the public interest came under heavy attack from a wide range of critics.[2] Understanding why *deregulation* occurred has proven to be a challenge to regulatory theorists, however. In Libecap's view, five conjectures regarding the forces underlying deregulation are offered: (i) dissatisfied incumbent firms join with consumers in lobbying for deregulation and seek to capture quasi-rents during the transition to a more competitive environment; (ii) stockholders, dismayed at poor firm performance, pressure management to jettison regulation; (iii) management chafes at government restrictions; (iv) regulators lose enthusiasm for regulatory controls; and (v) exogenous forces, such as changes in regulatory policies in other jurisdictions, force adoption of more competitive arrangements (Libecap, 1986: 72). Often, all five reasons underlie deregulation efforts.

Delegated or Self-Regulation

Another form of regulatory instrument is delegated regulation. Unlike command-and-control regulation, in this instance governments allow non-governmental actors to regulate themselves. This is sometimes referred to as 'self-regulation', although this term tends to portray the resulting regulatory arrangements as more 'voluntary' than is actually the case (Gunningham and Rees, 1997). That is, while non-governmental entities may, in effect, regulate themselves, they typically do so with the implicit or explicit permission of governments, which consciously refrain from regulating activities in a more directly coercive fashion (Donahue and Nye, 2001).

These delegations can be explicit and direct, for example, when governments allow professions such as doctors, lawyers, or teachers to regulate themselves through the grant of a licensing monopoly to a bar association, a college of physicians and surgeons, or a teachers' federation (see Sinclair, 1997; Tuohy and Wolfson, 1978). However, they can also be less explicit, as occurs in situations where manufacturing companies develop standards for products or where independent certification firms or associations certify that certain standards have been met in various kinds of private practices (see Andrews, 1998; Gunningham and Rees, 1997; Iannuzzi, 2001). While many standards are invoked by government command-and-control regulation, others can be developed in the private sphere. As long as these are not replaced by government-enforced standards, they represent the acquiescence of a government to the private rules, a form of delegated regulation (see Haufler, 2000, 2001; Knill, 2001).

A major advantage of the use of voluntary standard-setting should be in cost savings, since governments do not have to pay for the creation, administration, and renewal of such standards, as would be the case with traditional command-and-control regulation. While these attributes offer a powerful general incentive towards delegated regulation, empirical findings of negotiated environmental rule-making in the US show that both time and cost savings turned out to be minimal compared to command-and-control processes (Coglianese, 1997). The potential cost savings of delegation can be highest in professional areas such as medicine or law, where information asymmetries between those being regulated and regulators mean that public administration of standards is especially expensive and time-consuming. Such programs can also be effective in international settings, where establishing effective governmental regimes, such as sustainable forestry practices, can be especially difficult (Elliott and Schlaepfer, 2001). However, possible administrative cost savings must again be balanced against additional costs to society that might result from ineffective or inefficient administration of voluntary standards, especially those related to non-compliance.

Advisory Committees

A long-established procedural tool in this category is the *advisory committee* (Smith, 1977; Gill, 1940). Some of these are formalized and more or less permanent, while others tend to be more informal and temporary (Brown, 1955, 1972; Balla and Wright, 2001). Both involve governments selecting representatives to sit on these committees and the extension to those representatives of some special rights within the policy process. Many countries have created permanent bodies to provide advice to governments on particular ongoing issue areas, such as the economy, science and technology, and the environment (for Canada, see Phidd, 1975; Doern, 1971; Howlett, 1990). However, many other ad hoc bodies can be found in almost every policy area. These range from general advisory committees and specialized clientele advisory committees to specific task-oriented committees and others (see Peters and Barker, 1993; Barker and Peters, 1993).

Advisory bodies are often situated closer to societal actors than the formal governments they report to. They are usually quite specific in their focus and conduct different types of hearings and 'stakeholder' consultations to receive input and, at times, to engage in dialogues that seek to build consensus with, and among, societal actors (van de Kerkof, 2006; Flitner, 1986; Chapman, 1973). These advisory bodies should not be confused with the more open-ended, research-oriented organizations created under these same titles (Sheriff, 1983). Ad hoc task forces and similar bodies are not intended to develop new knowledge or promulgate old, but rather to provide a venue for organized and unorganized interests to present their views and analyses on pressing contemporary problems, or to frame or reframe issues in such a way that they can be dealt with by governments (Owens and Rayner, 1999; Jenson, 1994; Barker et al., 1993; Peters and Barker, 1993).

Treasure-based Policy Instruments

A third general category of policy instrument relies not so much on government personnel or governmental authority for its effectiveness, but rather on government financial resources and the government's ability to raise and disburse funds. This refers to all forms of financial transfers to individuals, firms, and organizations from governments or from other individuals, firms, or organizations under government direction. These transfers can serve as incentives or disincentives for private actors to follow government's wishes. The transfer rewards or penalizes and thus encourages or discourages a desired activity, thereby affecting social actors' estimates of costs and benefits of the various alternatives. While the final choice is left to individuals and firms, the likelihood of the desired choice being made is enhanced because of the financial subsidy it draws (Beam and Conlan, 2002; Cordes, 2002).

Subsidies: Grants, Tax Incentives, and Loans

One of the most prominent forms of treasure-based instrument is *grants*, which are 'expenditures made in support of some end worthy in itself, almost as a form of recognition, reward or encouragement, but not closely calibrated to the costs of achieving that end' (Pal, 1992: 152; Haider, 1989). Grants are usually offered to producers, with the objective of making them provide more of a desired good or service than they would otherwise. The expenditure comes out of the government's general revenues, which requires legislative approval. Examples of grants include government funds provided to schools, universities, and public transportation agencies.

Another prominent form of subsidy is the *tax incentive* involving 'remission of taxes in some form, such as deferrals, deductions, credits, exclusions, or preferred rates, contingent on some act (or the omission of some act)' (Mitnick, 1980: 365). Tax incentives or tax expenditures involve taxes or other forms of government revenues, such as royalties or licence fees, which are forgone. That is, a subsidy is provided since revenues that would normally have been collected are not. Governments find tax incentives appealing, not least because they are hidden in complex tax codes and so escape outside scrutiny, which makes their establishment and continuation relatively easy (McDaniel, 1989; Leeuw, 1998; Howard, 1997). Moreover, in most countries they do not need legislative budgetary approval, for no money is actually spent; rather, revenues are forgone (Maslove, 1994). Nor is their use constrained by availability of funds, because they involve no direct expenditure. They are also easier to administer and enforce because no special bureaucracy needs to be created to administer them, as would be the case with many other instruments (Brunori, 1997). The existing taxation bureaucracy is usually entrusted with the task. The amounts 'spent' in this manner are huge. For example, Christopher Howard has estimated that US federal tax expenditures alone accounted for $744.5 billion or 42 per cent of total federal direct expenditures in the year 2000 (Howard, 2002: 417).

Loans from the government at an interest rate below the market rate are also a form of subsidy. However, the entire amount of the loan should not be treated as a subsidy, only the difference between the interest charged and the market rate (Lund, 1989).[3]

Subsidies offer numerous advantages as policy instruments (see Mitnick, 1980: 350–3; Howard, 1993, 1995). First, they are easy to establish if government and an organization share a preference for doing a particular activity. Second, subsidies are flexible to administer because participants decide for themselves how to respond to the subsidy in the light of changing circumstances. Likewise, they take local and sectoral circumstances into account, since only individuals and firms seeing a benefit would take up the subsidy. Third, by allowing individuals and firms to devise appropriate responses, subsidies may encourage innovation. Fourth, the costs of administering and enforcing subsidies may be low because it is up to potential recipients to claim benefits. Finally, subsidies are often politically more acceptable because the benefits are concentrated on a few whereas the costs are spread across the population, with the result that they tend to be supported strongly by the beneficiaries and opposed less intensely by their opponents, if they are noticed at all (Wilson, 1974).

There are also disadvantages to using subsidies. Since subsidies (except tax incentives) need financing, which must come from new or existing sources of revenues, their establishment through the formal budgetary process is often difficult. They must compete for funding with other government programs, each backed by its own network of societal groups, politicians, and bureaucrats. Second, the cost of gathering information on how much subsidy would be required to induce a desired behaviour may also be high. Arriving at a correct amount of subsidy by trial and error can be an expensive way of implementing a policy. Third, since subsidies work indirectly, there is also often a time lag before the desired effects are discernible. This makes them an inappropriate instrument to use in a time of crisis. Fourth, subsidies may be redundant in cases where the activity would have occurred even without the subsidy, thus causing a windfall for the recipients. At the same time, they are hard to eliminate because of the opposition from existing beneficiaries. Fifth, subsidies may be banned by international agreements, as they are in trading industries because of the pernicious effects that subsidized imports can have on local industries and employment.

Financial Disincentives: Taxes and User Charges

A *tax* is a legally prescribed compulsory payment to government by a person or firm (Trebilcock et al., 1982: 53). The main purpose of a tax is normally to raise revenues for the government expenditures. However, it can also be used as a policy instrument to induce a desired behaviour[4] or discourage an undesirable behaviour.

In contrast to a subsidy, which is a positive incentive and works by rewarding a desired behaviour, taxes can be applied as a negative incentive (or sanction) that penalizes an undesired behaviour. By taxing a good, service, or activity, the government indirectly discourages its consumption or performance by making it more expensive to purchase or produce. Many governments' policy objectives of reducing smoking, drinking, and gambling because of their ill effects, for example, can be partially achieved through exceptionally high taxes on cigarettes, alcohol, and gambling revenues (Cnossen, 2005; Studlar, 2002; OECD, 2006).

A particularly innovative use of a tax as a policy instrument is a *user charge*. Instead of motivating behaviour by rewarding it through subsidy or requiring it through regulations, the government imposes a 'price' on certain behaviours that those undertaking them must pay. The price may be seen as a financial penalty intended to discourage the targeted behaviour. User charges are most commonly used to control negative externalities. An example from the area of pollution control is that of user charges on pollution, known as effluent charges (Sproule-Jones, 1994; Zeckhauser, 1981). Reducing pollution has costs, the marginal rate of which tends to increase with each additional unit of reduction. If a charge is levied on effluent discharge, the polluter will keep reducing its level of pollution to the point at which it becomes more expensive to reduce pollution than simply to pay the effluent charge. In theory at least, the polluter will thus be constantly seeking ways to minimize its charges by cutting back on the level of pollution it discharges.[5]

Taxes and user charges offer numerous advantages as policy instruments. First, they are easy to establish from an administrative standpoint. Second, taxes and user charges provide continuing financial incentives to reduce undesirable activities. Third, user charges promote innovation by motivating a search for cheaper alternatives. Fourth, they are flexible, since the government can adjust rates until the desired amount of the target activity occurs. Finally, they are desirable on administrative grounds because the responsibility for reducing the target activity is left to individuals and firms, which reduces the need for large bureaucratic enforcement machinery.

These opportunities must be weighed against the disadvantages of employing taxes and user charges, however. First, they require precise and accurate information in order to set the correct level of taxes or charges to elicit desired behaviour. Second, during the process of experimentation to arrive at optimum charges, resources may be misallocated. Third, they are not effective in times of crisis when an immediate response is required. Finally, they can involve cumbersome and possibly damaging administration costs if their rates are not set properly and they encourage evasive behaviour on the part of their targets, as occurred in the smoking example cited above.

Advocacy, Interest Group, and Think-Tank Funding

A prominent procedural tool in this category is *advocacy funding*. As public choice theorists have pointed out, interest groups do not arise automatically to press for certain policy solutions to ongoing problems, but rather require active personnel, organizational competence, and, above all, funding if they are to become a policy force. While different countries have different patterns and sources of advocacy funding, governments play a large role in this activity in all democratic states (Maloney et al., 1994).

In some countries, including the US, funding for interest group creation and ongoing expenses tends to come from private-sector actors, especially philanthropic trust funds and private companies, but governments facilitate this through favourable tax treatment for estates, charitable trusts, and corporate donations (Nownes and Neeley, 1996; Nownes, 1995). These private foundations then partner with governments in certain policy areas, such as social service delivery (Knott and McCarthy, 2007). The magnitude of public funding can influence non-profit organization governance, insulating their policies from societal preferences when these diverge from those of government (Guo, 2007). Similar dynamics have been noted for research and communication grants made by governments to interest groups and think-tanks (Rich, 2004; Lowry, 1999).

In other countries, including Canada and Australia, the state plays a much greater role in providing direct financing for interest groups in specific areas where the government wishes to see such groups become, or become more, active (Pal, 1993a; Phillips, 1991a; Pross and Stewart, 1993; Finkle et al., 1994). And, of course, in corporatist countries in continental Europe, states not only facilitate interest group activities through financial means, but also through the extension of special recognition and associational rights to specific industry and labour groups, providing them with a monopoly or near-monopoly on representation. This brings with it a greater ability to raise revenues through memberships (Jordan and Maloney, 1998; Schmitter, 1977, 1985).

Like many other procedural instruments, alteration of the advocacy system through the use of financial or treasure-based instruments involves some risks. Although it may be useful for government to build social capacity in these areas of interest group activity in order to obtain better information on social needs and wants, this kind of 'boundary-spanning' activity also can result in the co-optation or even emasculation of bona fide interests (Young and Everitt, 2004). In addition, it can bring about a significant distortion of the overall system of interest articulation if only certain groups receive funding (Saward, 1990, 1992; Cardozo, 1996).

Organization-based Policy Instruments

Direct Provision

In analyzing the more exotic instruments employed by governments, we tend to forget the basic and widely used public policy instrument of direct action by the public sector. Most public policy involves bureaucratic action, a reality that can be overshadowed by the rhetoric on government reinvention whereby governments are expected to rely on private initiative and public–private partnerships (Olsen, 2005; Mayntz, 1979). Instead of waiting for the private sector to do something or regulating non-governmental performance, government often performs the task itself, delivering goods and services directly through government employees, funded from the public treasury (Leman, 1989: 54; Leman, 2002; Mayntz, 1979; Devas et al., 2001). Much of the policy output of government is delivered by government and its bureaucracy, including national defence, diplomatic relations, policing, firefighting, social security, education, management of public lands, maintenance of parks and roads, public health services, and census and geological surveys.

Direct provision offers three main advantages (Leman, 1989: 60). First, direct provision is easy to establish because of its low information requirements—there is no need to ascertain the preferences of non-government actors. Second, the large size of public agencies usually involved in direct provision enables them to enlist established resources, skills, and information to offer cost-effective project delivery. Adding a new task to a bureaucracy with existing know-how can often be done for far less than contracting outside provision. Third, direct provision avoids many problems associated with indirect provision—discussion, negotiations, and regulatory concerns with non-compliance—that can lead governments to pay more attention to enforcing terms of grants and contracts than to results.

The disadvantages of direct provision also can be significant. While in theory a government can do everything that the private sector can, in practice this may not be the case. Bureaucratic program delivery is often characterized by inflexibility, something that is unavoidable in liberal democracies, which value accountability and the rule of law, meaning that governments must follow time-consuming budgeting and appointment requirements. Second, political control over the agencies and officials involved in providing goods and services may, and often does, promote political meddling to strengthen a government's re-election prospects or address other political needs of the moment rather than to serve the public as a whole. Political control also may lead to incoherent directives to agencies delivering goods and services because of the contradictory pressures that beset governments. Third, since bureaucratic agencies are not subject to competition, they are often not sufficiently cost-conscious, for which the taxpayers ultimately pay. Fourth, the delivery of programs may suffer because of inter- and intra-agency conflicts within the government (Bovens et al., 2001).

Public Enterprises
Also known as state-owned enterprises, Crown corporations, or parastatal organizations, public enterprises are entities totally or partially owned by the state but yet enjoying some degree of autonomy from the government. There is no universally accepted definition of a public enterprise, which explains why governments often do not maintain a list of the enterprises they own. The main problem is determining how public an enterprise must be in order to qualify as a 'public' enterprise. At one extreme, with only a small government share of ownership, a firm may resemble a private enterprise, and at the other, with close to 100 per cent government equity ownership, an enterprise may appear no different from a bureaucratic agency (Stanton and Moe, 2002). Examples of such confusion can be found in Amtrak, the United States national passenger rail service provider, which was incorporated as a 'for-profit' corporation in the District of Columbia but has received over $30 billion in federal grants to cover the difference between its revenues and costs since 1971 (Perl and Dunn, 1997). The US Corporation for Public Broadcasting's motto, 'A private corporation funded by the American people', echoes this ambiguity.

However, three broad generalizations can be made about public enterprises (Ahroni, 1986: 6). First, they involve a large degree of public ownership. Analysts often use a minimum 51 per cent government ownership threshold to classify a firm as being a public enterprise, since this ensures government control of the company's board of directors. However, in large corporations with widely held stock, a much smaller percentage would be sufficient to appoint the controlling interest on a board. The term 'mixed enterprise' is used to describe a category of firms owned jointly by government and the private sector. Second, public enterprises entail some control over management by the government. Passive public ownership of an enterprise that operates entirely free from government control does not constitute a public enterprise. Hybrid 'special operating agencies' or 'public authorities' created in many countries in recent years to operate specific services such as airports, harbours, and water or electrical power utilities are not traditional public enterprises in that governments usually do not directly control their boards of directors (Advani and Borins, 2001; Kickert, 2001; Walsh, 1978). Third, public enterprises produce goods and services that are sold, unlike public goods such as defence or street lighting for which those receiving the services do not pay directly but rather through taxation.

Public enterprises provide governments with four advantages among organization-based policy instruments (Mitnick, 1980: 407). First, they are an efficient economic development tool in situations where a good or service necessary to productive activity is not being provided by the private sector because of high capital costs or low expected profits. Examples include rural electrification and Internet access to smaller communities. Second, as with direct provision, the information threshold required to launch public enterprises is often lower than that required by other means, such as voluntary instruments or regulation. It does not require information on the target activity or the goals and preferences of the targeted firms, because the government can act directly through the enterprise it owns. Third, public enterprises can simplify public management of a policy domain if extensive regulation already exists. Instead of building additional layers of regulation to enforce compliance with government aims, for instance, it might be desirable simply to establish a company that does so without the costs of further regulation. Finally, profits from public enterprises may accrue to the public treasury, supporting public expenditures in other areas. A significant proportion of government revenue in Singapore, for example, comes from the profits of its public enterprises.

The disadvantages of public enterprises are no less significant. First, governments often find them difficult to control because managers can evade government directives. Moreover, the ultimate shareholders (the voters themselves) are too diffuse, and their personal interest too distant, to exercise effective control over the company. Second, public enterprise can be inefficient in operation because continued losses do not lead to bankruptcy, as would occur in the private sector. Indeed, a large number consistently lose money, which is a major reason underlying efforts to privatize them in many countries in recent years (see Howlett and Ramesh, 1993; Ikenberry, 1988). Without this market discipline, politicians find it hard to resist pressure from beneficiaries to keep public enterprise subsidies (and the below-cost goods and services they yield) flowing. Finally, many public enterprises, such as those delivering electricity and water, exercise a monopoly that enables passing the costs of their inefficiency on to consumers, just as a private firm would do under such circumstances (Musolf, 1989).

Quangos

In recent years governments have been leery of creating new 'traditional' forms of public enterprises and instead have turned to a variety of forms of what are known in Britain as 'quasi-autonomous non-government organizations' or *quangos* (Flinders and McConnel, 1999; Hood, 1986). Quangos share many of the same characteristics as public enterprises but usually are more at arm's length from government, functioning as quasi-independent, self-organizing actors (Christensen and Laegreid, 2003). They are only quasi-independent, however, because they often enjoy a government-granted monopoly—for example, over an airport or scholarship program (Advani and Borins, 2001; Aucoin, 2006)—and their 'licence' to do so can be revoked by the government at any time.

Quangos have advantages for governments by making it possible to off-load expensive or controversial areas of government activity to 'local' authorities. This is also a disadvantage in that the ability of governments to control their activities are very indirect, even though their failure may cause significant expenses—politically as well as financially—for governments (Kickert, 2001; Koppell, 2003).

Partnerships

A hybrid form of market and governmental reorganization, the public–private partnership (PPP) has recently gained momentum despite, and in some cases spurred by, political conflicts over privatization and outsourcing of public services (Linder, 1999). There are numerous different types of such partnerships. One trajectory for PPPs takes the form of contracting out the delivery of goods and services. However, some of these partnerships exist primarily to enhance the capacity and stability of private-sector actors, usually non-governmental organizations (NGOs), which are delegated minor government tasks in order to receive funding, the main purpose of which is to maintain these organizations' availability for consultations (Armstrong and Lenihan, 1999; Kernaghan, 1993).

Using partnerships to promote engagement between state and societal organizations raises questions of procedural and substantive equity. The criteria for including or excluding organizations for partnership, the breadth of interests represented by those organizations, and how specific individuals are designated as 'representative' can each effect the nature of the partnership and its policy implications (Edelenbos and Klijn, 2006; Cook, 2002).

Family, Community, and Voluntary Organizations

In all societies, relatives, friends, and neighbours, or family and community organizations, such as churches and charities, provide numerous goods and services, and the government may take measures to expand their role in ways that serve its policy goals. The characteristic feature of this instrument type is that it entails no or little government involvement. Instead, the desired task is performed on a voluntary basis by non-governmental actors. In some cases, however, governments must create the conditions under which voluntary actors operate (Phillips et al., 2001). In others, governments deliberately decide to do nothing ('non-decision') about a recognized public problem because they believe a solution is already being provided, or will be, by some other societal actor. These services are often provided by NGOs operating on a voluntary basis in that their members are not compelled to perform a task by the government. If they do something that serves public policy goals, it is for reasons of self-interest, ethics, or emotional gratification (Salamon, 1995, 1987, 2002c; Dollery et al., 2003).[6]

Voluntary organizations produce 'activities that are indeed voluntary in the dual sense of being free of [state] coercion and being free of the economic constraints of profitability and the distribution of profits' (Wuthnow, 1991: 7). Voluntary organizations providing health services, education, and food to the poor and temporary shelter for battered women and runaway children are prime examples of policy delivery that relies on voluntary choice. Voluntary groups that form to clean up beaches, riverbanks, and highways are other examples. Charitable, not-for-profit groups, often church-based, used to be the primary means of fulfilling the basic needs of those who could not provide for themselves, but over the last century the expansion of the welfare state gradually diminished their importance.

Even so, they are still a widely used means of addressing social problems today. In fact, in the US, often seen as the archetype of an individualist materialistic society, the non-profit voluntary sector delivers more services than the government itself (Salamon, 1987: 31). In recent years, the US government has encouraged 'faith-based' organizations to play a larger role in program delivery, with implications for the relationship between governments, markets, and religion that are yet to be well understood (Hula et al., 2007).[7]

In theory, voluntary organizations are an efficient means of delivering most economic and social services. If it were feasible, it would obviously be cost-efficient to provide social security or health and education services or build dams and roads on the basis of voluntary efforts of individuals. For example, local communities supplied volunteer labour to maintain the roads of eighteenth-century France and nineteenth-century America (Cavaillès, 1946: 70–1; Lane, 1950). Voluntary organizations also offer flexibility, speedy response time, and the opportunity for experimentation that are rarely matched by government departments (Johnson, 1987: 114). They often beat government to the scene of natural disasters, providing initial assistance to the victims (Mitchell, 2001). Another beneficial spillover is their positive contribution to promoting community spirit, social solidarity or cohesion, and political participation (Putnam, 1995a, 1995b, 1996, 2000, 2001).

However, practical circumstances severely limit the usefulness of voluntary organizations. Because they often lack the hierarchy of a formal bureaucracy, voluntary organizations demand considerable time and energy to keep their deliberative processes functioning. Oscar Wilde famously pinpointed the drawback of such arrangements when he said that 'The only problem with socialism is that it takes up too many evenings' (Sampson, 1991: 16). But when voluntary groups emulate bureaucracy's administrative specialization and chain of command, they can easily lose their democratic character and function as unaccountable oligarchies (Jonsson and Zakrisson, 2005). Furthermore, voluntary efforts are largely inapplicable to many economic problems, such as the promotion of technological innovation and enhanced productivity. Financing arrangements can exacerbate the administrative challenges faced by voluntary associations. Government contracts impose heavy performance and reporting burdens that strain administrative capacity, and can erode program delivery as resources are reallocated to meet these managerial imperatives (Phillips and Levasseur, 2004).

Using the family as a policy tool has some additional disadvantages. It may be inequitable because many individuals do not have anyone, or anyone with the financial resources or emotional commitment, to look after them. It is similarly inequitable for the caregivers. In most societies, for example, women tend to be the main care providers, a role increasingly difficult to perform because of increasing female participation in the labour force. As such, family and community instruments can often be relied on only as adjuncts to other instruments needed to address the pressing social problems of our times,

Market Creation

By far the most important, and contentious, type of policy instrument is the market organization. The voluntary interaction between consumers and producers, with the former seeking to buy as much as they can with their limited funds and the latter searching for highest possible profits, can usually be expected to yield outcomes that satisfy both. In theory at least, while the primary motive on the part of both sides is self-interest, the society as a whole gains from their interaction because whatever is wanted (backed by the ability to pay) by the society is provided at the lowest price. Theoretically, then, those wanting even such critical goods as health care or education can simply buy the services from hospitals and schools operating for profit.

Markets exist when there is scarcity and a demand for particular goods or services. But government action is required both to create and to support market exchange. This is accomplished by securing the rights of buyers and sellers to receive and exchange property through the establishment and maintenance of property rights and contracts through the courts, police, and quasi-judicial systems of consumer and investor protection. Even so-called 'black', 'grey', or other types of illegal or quasi-legal markets for commodities or services, such as illegal drugs or prostitution, owe their existence to governments that ban the production and sale of these goods or services, thereby creating shortages that produce high rates of return for those willing to risk punishment for their provision. Governments can use a variety of regulatory, financial, and information-based tools to affect market activities. However, they use their organizational resources to create markets (Averch, 1990; Cantor et al., 1992).

One way this can be done is by creating property rights through government licensing schemes. Based on the assumption that the market is often the most efficient means of allocating resources, property-rights auctions by the government establish markets in situations where they do not exist. The market is created by setting a fixed quantity of transferable rights to consume a designated resource, which has the effect of creating an artificial scarcity of a public good and enabling the price mechanism to work. The resource can be communal radio, television, or cellphone frequencies, oil wells, or fish stocks—anything that would not be scarce in the short term unless the government took action (Sunnevag, 2000).

Many countries have proposed controlling dangerous pollutants in this manner (Bolom, 2000), and market creation has been a feature of international environmental agreements, such as the Kyoto Protocol on greenhouse gases. In these schemes, the government is expected to set the total amount of the pollutant that will be permitted and then, through periodic auctions, sell rights to discharge amounts below this level. This means that firms intending to use or generate a pollutant in their activities must buy the right to do so. Those with cheaper alternatives will avoid using or generating the pollutant because of the extra cost. Manufacturers for whom there is no cheap alternative will pay for pollution rights. However, they remain under pressure to search for alternatives in order to reduce their costs.

The advantage of using an auction of rights in such cases is that it restricts the use of specific goods while still making them available to those without alternatives. If the same goal were pursued through regulation, the government would have to determine access rules, a difficult task because of the high information costs involved. In the case of auctions, in theory the decision will be made by the market according to the forces of demand and (government-controlled) supply.

One advantage of auctions of property rights to establish markets is that they are easy to conduct (Cantor et al., 1992). The government, based on what it considers the maximum amount of a good or service that should be permitted, fixes the ceiling and then lets the market do the rest. Second, they are flexible, allowing the government discretion to vary the ceiling whenever it wants. Property-rights auctions also allow the subjects to adjust their behaviour according to changes in their circumstances, such as with respect to development of cost-saving technology, without requiring a corresponding change in the government's policy or instrument. Third, auctions offer the certainty that only a fixed amount of a particular activity occurs, something not possible with other voluntary or mixed instruments. Moreover, auctions are, of course, a highly lucrative source of revenue for the government.

One of the disadvantages of auctions is that they may encourage speculation, with speculators inflating prices and hoarding all rights by bidding high, thereby erecting entry barriers to small firms or consumers. Second, it is often the case that those who cannot buy the rights, because none may be available for sale, will be forced to cheat, whereas in the case of user charges or subsidies they would have an alternative, albeit often at a high price. This can result in high enforcement costs if grey or black markets are to be avoided (Marion and Muehlegger, 2007). Third, auctions are inequitable to the extent that they allocate resources according to ability to pay, rather than need, and can generate fierce opposition from those affected because of the extra costs they must bear in buying the right (Woerdman, 2000; Kagel and Levin, 2002). Thus, rich families in Singapore buy more than one car, while those who really need one, for example, to start up a business or take children to school, may not be able to buy a vehicle if they do not have the additional money required to purchase the Certificate of Entitlement.

Another way that governments can create or enhance markets is through the privatization of public enterprises, especially if those enterprises had previously exercised a state-sponsored monopoly or near-monopoly on the production or distribution, or both, of a particular good or service. Privatization can be carried out in numerous ways, from issuing shares to all citizens, to the simple transfer of state shares to community organizations or their sale on public exchanges. In all cases, this amounts to the transfer of a public enterprise to the private sector and the transformation of the goal of the enterprise from public service provision to maximization of shareholder value. In addition, it usually involves the signal, either overt or covert, that new firms will be able to enter into the market formerly served by the state-owned company, allowing for the creation of a competitive market for that particular good or service (Starr, 1989).

Although some scholars see privatization as a panacea, capable at one stroke of eliminating corrupt or inefficient public-sector providers and replacing them with more efficient private-sector ones, others point out that this is not always the case (Donahue, 1989). In many Eastern European post-socialist countries, for example, large-scale and largely uncontrolled privatizations resulted in many instances of massive layoffs and plant closures, with severe economic consequences for affected families, communities, and regions. In others, such as Russia, where securities markets were not well developed, plants were simply transferred to their managers, who in many cases were able to reap windfall profits from their sale. It is also the case, as welfare economists have argued, that some industries have economies of scale that allow large firms to maintain their monopolistic position, regardless of whether they are owned by governments or private investors. Privatization of such firms merely transfers monopoly profits from the public sector, where they can be used to finance additional public services, to the private sector, where they are often used for personal luxury consumption (Beesley, 1992; Bos, 1991; Donahue, 1989; Le Grand and Robinson, 1984; MacAvoy et al., 1989; Starr, 1990a).

In Western countries with much smaller numbers of public enterprises, a more common form of privatization has involved *contracting out government services*, that is, the transfer of various kinds of goods and services formerly provided 'in-house' by government employees to 'outsourced' private firms (Kelman, 2002; DeHoog and Salamon, 2002). Again, while some see any transfer of service provision from the state to the private sector as an inherent welfare gain, others note that in many cases the same employees end up being hired by the new service provider to provide the same service, but at less pay, while others have noted that the costs to administrators of establishing, monitoring, and enforcing contracts often cancels out any cost savings (see Lane, 2001; Ascher, 1987; Grimshaw et al., 2001; Donahue and Zeckhauser, 2006; Zarco-Jasso, 2005).

A much discussed but little used form of government market creation relies on *vouchers*. These government-issued certificates have a monetary face value that consumers can use to acquire a particular good or service from their preferred supplier, who in turn presents the voucher for redemption. Vouchers allow consumers to exercise relatively free choice in the marketplace, but only for specific types or quantities of goods. They are common in wartime as a means to ration supplies of various goods, and have also been used in peacetime in schemes such as food stamps for the poor. This promotes competition among suppliers, which arguably improves quality and reduces costs to the government. However, vouchers can also disrupt established patterns of public service provision. Their proposed use in education, for example, may force schools to compete against each other for students, which can lead to greater inequities in service provision between wealthy and impoverished school districts (Valkama and Bailey, 2001; Steuerle and Twombly, 2002). Vouchers can also be issued to producers to ration access to limited natural resources (e.g., fish stocks) by market mechanisms (Townsend et al., 2006). Other similar instruments exist, such as the provision of government insurance, which allows some activities to take place that otherwise might not due to the costs associated with failure or because of their risky nature (Feldman, 2002; Katzman, 1988; Moss, 2002; Stanton, 2002).

Establishing markets can be a highly recommended instrument in certain circumstances (Averch, 1990; OECD, 1993; Hula, 1988). It is an effective and efficient means of providing most private goods and can ensure that resources are devoted only to those goods and services valued by the society, as reflected in the individual's willingness to pay. It also ensures that if there is meaningful competition among suppliers, then valued goods and services are supplied at the lowest possible price. Since most goods and services sought by the population are of a private nature, governments in capitalist societies rely extensively on the market instrument.

In many situations, however, the market may be an inappropriate instrument (Kuttner, 1997). As we saw in Chapter 2, markets cannot adequately provide public goods, precisely the sort of things most public policies involve. Thus, markets cannot be used for providing defence, policing, street lights, and other similar goods and services valued by society. Markets also experience difficulties in providing various kinds of toll goods and common-pool goods[8] due to difficulties involved in charging consumers for these kinds of products. The market is also a highly inequitable instrument because it meets the needs of only those with the ability to pay. In a purely market-based system of health-care delivery, for example, a rich person with money can have a wish for cosmetic surgery fulfilled, while a poor person suffering from kidney failure will not receive treatment. It is not surprising that the market, in such situations, faces tough political opposition in democratic societies otherwise structured along more egalitarian principles.

A 'free market' in the true sense of the term is therefore almost never used as a policy instrument in practice. When a government does resort to this instrument to address a public problem, it is usually accompanied by other instruments, such as regulation to protect consumers, investors, and workers; it is also accompanied frequently by subsidies intended to further promote the desired activity (Cantor et al., 1992). Thus, the voluntarism of markets is relative rather than absolute.

Government (Re)organizations

The foremost example of such an instrument in a procedural sense is institutional reorganization whereby governments seek to affect policy processes by reorganizing the structures or processes through which they perform a function (Peters, 1992b; Carver, 2001).

Reorganizations can involve the creation of new agencies or the reconfiguration of old ones. One popular technique for such purposes is ministerial reorganization. Some of these alterations can occur accidentally or as a by-product of organizational changes in government machinery brought about for other reasons, such as electoral or partisan ones. Since 'there is no agreed normative basis for organizing government', the political, policy, and administrative priorities and pressures of the day provide disparate points of departure for prime ministers and presidents considering what, if anything, to do about their government's organization (Davis et al., 1999: 42).

Intentional organizational change to the basic structures or personnel of government departments and agencies has become an increasingly significant aspect of modern policy-making (Lindquist, 1992; Aucoin, 1997; Bertelli and Feldmann, 2007; March and Olson, 1993). This can involve changes in the relationships between departments and central co-ordinating agencies, or between departments, or within ministries. In the first instance, ministries can be given greater autonomy and capacity to set their own direction, or they can be brought into tighter control by central executive agencies (Smith et al., 1993). Proposals over how far, and in what direction, to go with government reorganization can depend on how those pursuing a particular policy agenda judge the existing organizational arrangements will serve their substantive preferences, as compared to some organizational alternative (McCubbins et al., 1987, 1989).

However, there are limits to such reorganizations. First, they can be expensive and time-consuming. Second, if they occur too frequently, their impact can be much dissipated. Third, constitutional or jurisdictional factors may limit the kinds of activities that specific governments can take and the fashion in which they can do so (Gilmore and Krantz, 1991).

The Nature of Policy Alternatives

Policy formulation is about choosing from among these types of policy instruments those that can be used to address particular policy problems and then analyzing these choices in terms of both their technical and political feasibility, with an eye to reducing their number to a small set of alternative courses of action that can be laid out for decision-makers at the next stage of the policy process. Exactly which instruments will be selected, of course, depends on the nature of the problem context, who is conducting the analysis, how it is conducted, and what ideas about appropriate and possible government actions the analysts bring to the discussion. Policy formulation is thus a complex matter featuring a wide range of possible choices and mixes of policy instruments into potential policy options or alternatives.

A useful way to think about the nature of the policy options developed in the policy formulation process is in terms of the extent to which they propose solutions to problems that depart from the policy status quo. Some options call for new, substantial, or dramatic policy change, while others involve only minor tinkering with existing policies and programs (Majone, 1991).

In his work on economic policy change in Britain, Peter Hall identified three different possible types of change: *first-order* change in which only the settings (or calibrations) of policy instruments varied; *second-order* change in which change occurred in the basic types or categories of instruments used to effect policy; and *third-order* change in which the goals of policy were altered (Hall, 1993).[9] While useful, some of this terminology is confusing and should be altered, and the logic of the model also suggests that there should be four basic types of change, not three. These can be described as changes related to abstract *policy goals* or more concrete *program specifications*, referring to the ends of policy-making; and to basic policy *instrument type* or genus, as opposed to alterations of existing *instrument components*, when discussing changes in policy means.[10]

Options that address policy goals and instrument types require the injection of new ideas and thinking into policy deliberations. More specific options dealing with program specifications and instrument 'settings' or components, on the other hand, are much more status quo-oriented, involving relatively minor alterations

Figure 5.2   A Model of the Effects of the Presence or Absence of New Actors
and Ideas on Types of Policy Options Considered

	Presence of New Actors	Continuity of Old Actors
Presence of New Ideas	Options relating to changes in policy goals	Options relating to changes in program specifications
Continuity of Old Ideas	Options relating to changes in instrument types	Options relating to changes in instrument components

in existing policies. Proposals for policy and program changes tend to arise from new actors in existing policy processes, while changes relating to instrument types and components tend to develop among existing actors as their preferences change (Krause, 1997; Berridge, 2005; Chair and McMahon, 2003; Boyer and Cremieux, 1999). This general situation is set out in Figure 5.2.

In practice, there is often a strong tendency towards consideration of incremental options in policy formulation; that is, towards changes in instrument components. This is because, as we saw in Chapters 3 and 4, policy regimes tend to form in most policy areas and these regimes entrench policy subsystems and policy paradigms, limiting the ability of new actors and new ideas to penetrate into existing policy monopolies.

The Role of Policy Subsystems in Policy Formulation

Observers have often noted how policy-makers, in the course of interaction among themselves and in their day-to-day dealings with a public problem, tend to develop a common way of looking at and dealing with a problem (Kenis, 1991; Haas, 1992; Sabatier, 1988). This suggests that policy subsystems play a significant role in the process of policy formulation (Zijlstra, 1978–9; Rhodes and Marsh, 1992; Raab and Kenis, 2007). Sabatier (1988), for example, has argued that the nature of the policy subsystem responsible for policy formulation is an important element in the analysis of policy change as coalition members mediate the exchange of interests and ideas in public policy-making. More specifically, analysts have suggested that the 'cohesiveness' or 'closedness' of policy subsystems is an important factor affecting the propensity for new or innovative policy solutions to emerge from the policy formulation process (Marsh and Rhodes, 1992b; Bressers and O'Toole, 1998; Zahariadis and Allen, 1995; Jordana and Sancho, 2005).[11] As Hanspeter Kriesi and Maya Jegen (2001: 251) put it, 'to know the actor constellation is to know the parameters determining the choices among the substantive policy options.'[12]

This suggests that, as was the case with agenda-setting, a principal factor affecting the propensity of a policy subsystem to generate policy options involving substantial changes is a subsystem structure that allows new actors and new ideas to enter into policy deliberations (Schmidt, 2001). The relevant general

Figure 5.3   Basic Policy Subsystem Configurations Affecting Policy Formulation Processes

		Receptive to New Actors	
		No	Yes
Receptive to New Ideas	No	Closed subsystem	Resistant subsystem
	Yes	Contested open subsystem	Open policy subsystem

Source: Adapted from Michael Howlett and M. Ramesh, 'Policy Subsystem Configurations and Policy Change: Operationalizing the Postpositivist Analysis of the Politics of the Policy Process', *Policy Studies Journal* 26, 3 (1998): 466–82.

types of policy subsystems that determine the outcomes of the policy formulation process are set out in Figure 5.3.

The expected links between policy subsystem structure and the kinds of policy options developed in the policy formulation process are shown in Figure 5.4.

Conclusion: Understanding Policy Formulation Styles as a Function of Policy Regimes

What type of regime exists in a given sector or issue area is of major significance in understanding the dynamics of policy formulation within that area (Thompson, 2003). Which policy options on the institutional agenda will be considered seriously for adoption, the types of solutions or options thought to be feasible for resolving policy problems, and the kinds of instruments selected to address them are largely a function of the nature and motivation of key actors arrayed in policy subsystems and the ideas that they hold (Howlett, 2002).

Figure 5.4   A Model of Policy Formulation Modes

		Entrance of New Actors	
		No	Yes
Availability of New Ideas	No	Closed policy subsystem: program instrument tinkering, with instrument settings within existing paradigm	Resistant policy subsystem: policy experimentation, working with new instruments within existing paradigm
	Yes	Contested policy subsystem: program reform within existing range of policy instruments	Open policy subsystem: policy renewal; inclusion of alternative instruments

Study Questions

1. What difference would it make to use different categories of policy instruments in trying to address a particular economic problem?
2. Are certain types of policy instruments better suited to solving social problems than others?
3. How does understanding the nature of a policy subsystem help us understand the potential for policy change in the kinds of alternatives considered at the policy formulation stage of the policy process?
4. Why is there a bias towards incrementalism in the development of policy alternatives?
5. Where do considerations of the feasibility of policy alternatives emerge from? Why is this important in understanding the nature of policy formulation activities?

Further Readings

Adcroft, A., and R. Willis. 2005. 'The (Un)Intended Outcome of Public Sector Performance Measurement', *International Journal of Public Sector Management* 18, 5: 386–400.

Agranoff, R., and M. McGuire. 1999. 'Managing in Network Settings', *Policy Studies Review* 16, 1: 18–41.

DeLeon, Peter. 1992. 'Policy Formulation: Where Ignorant Armies Clash By Night', *Policy Studies Review* 11, 3 and 4: 389–405.

Hajer, M.A. 2005. 'Setting the Stage: A Dramaturgy of Policy Deliberation', *Administration and Society* 36, 6: 624–47.

Hall, Peter A. 1993. 'Policy Paradigms, Social Learning and the State: The Case of Economic Policy Making in Britain', *Comparative Politics* 25, 3: 275–96.

Hula, Richard, Cynthia Jackson-Elmoore, and Laura Reese. 2007. 'Mixing God's Work and the Public Business: A Framework for the Analysis of Faith-based Service Delivery', *Review of Policy Research* 24, 1: 67–89.

Lindquist, Evert A. 1992. 'Public Managers and Policy Communities: Learning to Meet New Challenges', *Canadian Public Administration* 35, 2: 127–59.

Majone, Giandomenico. 1975. 'On the Notion of Political Feasibility', *European Journal of Political Research* 3: 259–74.

Mayer, I., P. Bots, and E. van Daalen. 2004. 'Perspectives on Policy Analysis: A Framework for Understanding and Design', *International Journal of Technology, Policy and Management* 4, 1: 169–91.

Milward, H. Brinton, and Gary L. Walmsley. 1984. 'Policy Subsystems, Networks and the Tools of Public Management', in Robert Eyestone, ed., *Public Policy Formation*. Greenwich, Conn.: JAI Press, 3–25.

Olsen, J.P. 2005. 'Maybe It Is Time to Rediscover Bureaucracy', *Journal of Public Administration Research and Theory* 16, 1: 1–24.

Chapter 6

Public Policy Decision-Making

The decision-making stage of the policy process is where one or more, or none, of the many options that have been debated and examined during the previous two stages of the policy cycle is approved as an official course of action. Policy decisions usually produce some kind of a formal or informal statement of intent on the part of authorized public actors to take, or not to take, some action such as a law or regulation (O'Sullivan and Down, 2001). Acting on this decision is the subject of the next stage of the policy cycle, policy implementation, discussed in the following chapter.

Gary Brewer and Peter DeLeon (1983: 179) characterized the decision-making stage of the public policy process as:

> the choice among policy alternatives that have been generated and their likely effects on the problem estimated . . . . It is the most overtly political stage in so far as the many potential solutions to a given problem must somehow be winnowed down and but one or a select few picked and readied for use. Obviously most possible choices will not be realized and deciding not to take particular courses of action is as much a part of selection as finally settling on the best course.

This definition makes several important points about the decision-making stage of the policy cycle. First, decision-making is not a self-contained stage, nor is it synonymous with the entire public policy-making process. Rather, it is a specific stage rooted firmly in the previous stages of the policy cycle. It involves choosing from among a relatively small number of alternative policy options identified in the process of policy formulation in order to resolve a public problem. Second, this definition highlights the fact that different kinds of decisions can result from a decision-making process. That is, decisions can be '*positive*' in the sense that they are intended, once implemented, to alter the status quo in some way, or they can be '*negative*' in the sense that the government declares that it will do nothing new about a public problem but will retain the status quo. Third, this definition underlines the point that public policy decision-making is not a technical exercise but an inherently political process. It recognizes that public policy decisions create 'winners' and 'losers', even if the decision is a negative one.

Brewer and DeLeon's definition, of course, says nothing about the actors involved in this process, or the desirability, likely direction, or scope of public decision-making. To deal with these issues, different theories and models have been developed to describe how decisions are made in government as well as to prescribe how decisions ought to be made. The nature of public policy decision-makers, the different types of decisions that they make, and the development and evolution of decision-making models designed to help understand the relationship between the two are described below.

Actors in the Decision-Making Process

With the exception of usually infrequent exercises in direct democracy such as referendums (Wagschal, 1997; Butler and Ranney, 1994), the number of relevant policy actors decreases substantially when the public policy process reaches the decision-making stage. Such concentrated engagement is not found at the agenda-setting stage, where virtually any actor in the policy universe could, theoretically at least, become active and involved. The policy formulation stage is also open to numerous actors, though in practice only those who are members of specific policy subsystems tend to participate. But when it comes time to decide on adopting a particular option, the relevant group of policy actors is almost invariably restricted to those with the authority to make binding public decisions. In other words, the public policy decision-making stage normally centres on those occupying formal offices in government. Excluded are virtually all non-state actors, including those from other levels of governments, both domestically and internationally. Only those politicians, judges, and government officials actually empowered to make authoritative decisions in the area in question can participate with both 'voice' and 'vote' at this stage of the policy cycle (Aberbach et al., 1981).

This is not to say that other actors, including non-state ones as well as those belonging to other governments, are not active and even influential during policy decision-making. These actors can and do engage in various kinds of lobbying activities aimed at persuading, encouraging, and sometimes even coercing authoritative office-holders to adopt preferred options and avoid undesirable ones (Woll, 2007). However, unlike office-holders, those other actors have, at best, a 'voice' in the decision-making process, not a 'vote' (see Pal, 1993b; Richardson et al., 1978; Sarpkaya, 1988).

This does not mean that decision-makers, since they occupy positions of formal authority, can adopt whatever policy they wish. As discussed in earlier chapters, the degree of freedom enjoyed by decision-makers is in fact circumscribed by a host of constraining rules and structures governing political and administrative offices, as well as by the sets of ideas or paradigms and the social, economic, and political circumstances within which they work. As we have seen, key rules and structures that affect configurations of political power and resources in both state and non-state actors range from the country's constitution to the specific mandates conferred on individual decision-makers. Specific decision-makers, such as judges and civil servants, must act within specific sets of laws and regulations governing their behaviour and fields of competence (Markoff, 1975; Page, 1985a; Atkinson and Coleman, 1989a), while the different actors with which they must contend in so doing were discussed in Chapter 3.

Countries have different constitutional arrangements and distinct sets of rules governing the structure of public agencies and the conduct of government officials. Some political systems concentrate decision-making authority in the elected executive and the bureaucracy, while others permit the legislature and judiciary to play a greater role. Parliamentary systems tend to fall in the former category and presidential systems in the latter. Thus, in Australia, Britain, and Canada and other parliamentary democracies, the cabinet and bureaucracy are often solely responsible for making many policy decisions. They may at times have decisions imposed on them by the legislature in situations when the government does not enjoy a parliamentary majority, or by the judiciary in its role as interpreter of the constitution, but these are not routine occurrences. In the United States and other presidential systems, although the authority to make most policy decisions rests with the executive (and the cabinet and bureaucracy acting on the president's or governor's behalf), those decisions requiring legislative approval often involve intense negotiation with the legislators, while some are modified or overturned on a regular basis by the judiciary on constitutional or other grounds (Weaver and Rockman, 1993b).

At the micro level, various rules usually set out not only which decisions can be made by which government agency or official, but also the procedures that must be followed. As Allison and Halperin (1972) have noted, over time such rules and operating procedures often provide decision-makers with 'action channels'—a regularized set of *standard operating procedures* for producing certain types of decisions. These rules and standard operating procedures help explain why so much of the decision-making in government is of a routine and repetitive nature. Nevertheless, while rules and normal procedures circumscribe the freedom available to some decision-makers (especially those in administrative or judicial positions), others (especially political decision-makers) retain considerable discretion to judge the 'best' course of action to follow in specific circumstances. Since decision-makers themselves vary greatly in terms of background, knowledge, and the beliefs that affect how they interpret a problem and its potential solutions (Huitt, 1968), different decision-makers operating in similar institutional environments can respond differently even when dealing with the same or similar problems. Hence, even with standard operating procedures in place, exactly what process is followed and which decision is considered 'best' will vary according to the structural and institutional context of a decision-making situation.

Choices: Negative, Positive, and Non-Decisions

Regardless of which actor or actors make a policy decision, whether a relatively large group of legislators in a partisan political arena or a single civil servant in a more insulated bureaucratic setting, the results of this process will fit into just a few categories. That is, although the substance of decisions can be infinitely varied, their fundamental effect will be to either perpetuate the policy status quo or alter it.

Traditional *'positive' decisions* that alter the status quo receive considerable attention in the decision-making literature and are therefore accorded most attention in this chapter. However, it is important to note that other kinds of decisions uphold the status quo. Here we can distinguish between *'negative'* decisions, in which a deliberate choice is made to preserve the status quo, and what are sometimes termed '*non-decisions*' (discussed earlier in the book) in which options to deviate from the status quo are not considered at the policy formulation or agenda-setting stages (see Zelditch et al., 1983; R.A. Smith, 1979).

Non-decisions have been the subject of many inquiries and studies by scholars interested in tracing the effects of ideologies, religions, and other similar factors that blind decision-makers to the need to act on a public problem; similarly, power allows decision-makers to ignore certain issues despite public clamour for change (see Bachrach and Baratz, 1962, 1970: ch. 3; Debnam, 1975; Bachrach and Baratz, 1975; Zelditch and Ford, 1994; Spranca et al., 1991; Oliviera et al., 2005).

Very little research into negative decisions, however, exists. This is partly due to the difficulties associated with identifying instances in which policy options to alter the status quo are explicitly rejected in favour of its maintenance (see Howlett, 1986). Nevertheless, these decisions can be examined in terms of their affect on the functioning of the policy cycle. That is, negative decisions are instances of *arrested* policy cycles. Unlike non-decisions, in which certain options are filtered out at earlier stages of the policy process and may thus never be identified in policy deliberations, negative decision-making does go through agenda-setting and policy formulation efforts that place alternative courses of action before those with the authority to decide. However, when a negative decision is made, the policy process does not move onto the implementation stage but simply confirms that the status quo is appropriate and halts at that point (van der Eijk and Kok, 1975).

The outcome likely to emerge from the decision-making stage thus depends both on the operation of earlier stages in the cycle, which serve to filter out some policy options while allowing others to proceed, and on the exact configuration of decision-making actors, their beliefs, and the context in which they work. The nature of the relevant subsystem and the kinds of constraints under which decision-makers operate will have a significant effect on the type of decision that will emerge in different situations and, especially, will affect the particular weight accorded to the option of simply retaining the status quo (Bardach, 2006; Kay, 2006; Genschel, 1997).

Early Models of Decision-Making: Rationalism and Incrementalism

Whether a public policy decision is negative or positive, it involves the development and expression of a statement of intent by authoritative decision-makers to undertake or implement some course of action (or inaction). In this section we will review the different models that have been developed to help describe, conceptualize, and analyze such decision-making processes. We set out the elements of these models and discuss their success and failure in describing governmental decision-making processes. Although many decision-making models can be found in the extensive literatures across fields as diverse as psychology and business management, we shall see that they all suggest that a variety of different decision-making process styles exist, and that the likelihood of one being followed can be ascertained with some certainty by examining the nature of the actors making the decision and the constraints under which they operate.[1]

The policy cycle's decision-making stage received considerable attention in the early years of the evolution of policy sciences. At that time, analysts borrowed heavily from models and studies of decision-making in complex organizations developed by students of public administration and business organization. By the mid-1960s, these discussions about public policy decision-making had ossified into two purportedly incompatible models: rational and incremental.

The first to emerge was the *rational model*, which asserted that public policy decision-making was inherently a search for maximizing solutions to complex problems in which policy-relevant information was gathered and then used in a scientific mode of assessing policy options. The other model—often termed *the incremental model*—identified public policy decision-making as a less technical and more political activity, in which analysis played a much smaller role in determining outcomes than did bargaining and other forms of interaction and negotiation between key decision-makers (see Mossberger, 2000: ch. 2). The mainstream position throughout much of this period was that while the 'rational' model was more preferable for showing how decisions ought to be taken to assure 'maximum' results, the 'incremental' model best described the *actual* practice of decision-making in governments (Dror, 1968; Etzioni, 1967; Howard, 1971).

However, by the mid-1970s it was apparent that neither model accurately represented all instances of decision-making; that different decision-making opportunities featured different methods and modes of decision-making; and that the range of decision-making styles varied beyond the two 'ideal types' represented by the rational and incremental models (Smith and May, 1980; Allison, 1969, 1971). This led to efforts to develop alternative models of the decision-making processes followed by complex organizations. Some attempted to synthesize the rational and incremental models (Etzioni, 1967). Others—including the so-called '*garbage-can*' model of decision-making—focused on the irrational elements of organizational behaviour in order to arrive at a third path beyond rationalism and incrementalism (Cohen et al., 1972; March and Olsen, 1979a). Only recently have efforts been made to move beyond these debates among rationalists, irrationalists, and incrementalists and develop a more nuanced understanding of the complex processes associated with public policy decision-making and the role that policy subsystems play in influencing these dynamics.

The Rational Model

First developed to aid economic analysis, and especially the analysis of producer and consumer choices, the 'rational' theory of decision-making postulated that in developing and expressing a preference for one course of action over another, decision-makers would attempt to pursue a strategy that, in theory, would maximize the expected outcomes of the choices they could make (Edwards, 1954). Decision-making in the public policy arena was seen to parallel the marketplace behaviour of buyers and sellers seeking to obtain top 'utility' from their limited resources by minimizing costs and maximizing benefits.

This idealized model of rational decision-making presumed that decision-makers would consistently and predictably undertake the following series of sequential activities leading to decision:

1. A goal for solving a problem is established.
2. All alternative strategies of achieving the goal are explored and listed.
3. All significant consequences of each alternative strategy are predicted and the probability of those consequences occurring is estimated.
4. Finally, the strategy that most nearly solves the problem or solves it at least cost is selected. (Carley, 1980: 11)

Ideally, the process would involve attributing costs and benefits to each option, comparing these across widely divergent options, and estimating the probability of failure and success for each option (Edwards, 1954; March, 1994).

The rational model is 'rational' in the sense that it prescribes procedures for decision-making that, in theory, will lead every time to the choice of the most efficient possible means of achieving policy goals. Rooted in Enlightenment notions of rationality and positivist schools of thought that sought to develop detached, scientific knowledge to improve human conditions (Jennings, 1987; Torgerson, 1986), this model assumes that maximal outcomes can be achieved through the ordered gathering of relevant information allowing the 'best' alternative to be identified and selected (Weiss, 1977b). Decision-makers are assumed to operate as technicians or business managers, who collect and analyze information that allows them to adopt the most effective or efficient way of solving any problem they confront. It is for its 'neutral', technical application to problem-solving that this mode is also known as the 'scientific', 'engineering', or 'managerialist' approach (Elster, 1991: 115).

Early attempts to address organizational behaviour through a scientific mode of investigation identified the rational model of decision-making as a promising technique that would yield managerial advances in business and public administration. Elements of the model can be found in the work of early students of public administration such as Henri Fayol in France and Luther Gulick and Lyndal Urwick in Britain and the United States. Drawing on the insights gleaned by Fayol (1949) from his studies of the turn-of-the-century French coal industry, in the 1930s Gulick and Urwick, for example, promoted what they termed the 'POSDCORB' model of management in which they urged organizations to maximize their performance by systematically planning, organizing, staffing, directing, co-ordinating, reporting, and budgeting their activities (Gulick, 1937).

'Directing' a particular course of action, for Gulick and Urwick and the management theorists who followed in their footsteps, amounted to weighing the benefits of any decision against its expected costs and arriving at a 'steady stream' of maximizing decisions required for the organization to function (see, e.g., Kepner and Tregoe, 1965).

It was recognized from very early on, however, that it would not always be possible to achieve 'full' rationality in practice. This was because even if a decision-maker wished to adopt maximizing decisions, these might not be possible due to limitations of information and time. However, many analysts did not consider these to be insurmountable problems. Rather, they simply recognized the difficulties that could be found in translating decision-making theory into decision-making practice, which meant that the resulting decisions might not be perfectly rational or error-proof, but would normally be close enough to approximate 'perfect' rationality.

Some analysts, however, claimed that these limitations on rationality had much more serious implications for decision-making theory and practice. Perhaps the most noted critic of the rational model was Herbert Simon, until recently the only student of public administration ever to win a Nobel Prize. Simon and others argued that the limitations on rationality previously noted were not simply 'deviations' that might be overcome by more careful analysis, or that would crop up only in exceptional circumstances. Rather, these shortcomings represented the norm and were impossible to avoid and serious enough to undermine completely any notions of 'pure' rationality or outcome maximization embodied in the classical rational model.

Simon, in particular, argued in a series of books and articles in the 1950s that several hurdles prevented decision-makers from ever attaining 'pure' rationality in their decisions and put forward an alternate notion of '*bounded rationality*' to replace the maximizing one found in rational choice theory (Simon, 1955, 1957b; Jones 2002). First, he noted that this form of decision-making would generate maximal results only if *all* possible alternatives and the costs of each alternative were assessed before a decision was made. However, he noted that decision-makers faced cognitive limits in considering an almost infinite number of possible options, leading them to focus on only a limited number of alternatives that they deemed were likely, or probable, or feasible. Simon noted that such pre-decisional choices were typically made on ideological, professional, cultural, or similar grounds, if not randomly. When efficiency implications are ignored in such initial choices, the opportunity to select a rational course of action from among the remaining options is lost (see Fernandes and Simon, 1999).

Second, Simon noted that the rational model required that decision-makers know the consequences of each decision in advance, which is rarely, if ever, true. But without accurately predicting the future, Simon noted, it is impossible to assess the costs and benefits of different options as required by the rational model. Third, Simon noted that most policy options entail a 'bundle' of favourable and adverse consequences and the 'costing' of each 'bundle' is not straightforward, as it requires a preliminary ranking of relative potential gains that, again, cannot be validated on 'rational' grounds. Fourth, Simon also noted that very often the same option can be efficient or inefficient depending on other, and changing, circumstances. Hence, it is rarely possible for decision-makers to draw robust conclusions about which alternative is superior, as required by the rational model (see Einhorn and Hogarth, 1986).

Numerous efforts to modify the rational model followed criticisms such as these, all in the effort to preserve the idea of 'maximization' in decision-making (Kruse et al., 1991: ch. 1; Conlisk, 1996). Theories of *'fuzzy' decision-making*, for example, argued that even if costs and benefits associated with specific policy options could not be clearly stated or specified with great precision, probabilistic techniques could be used to illuminate the *range* of 'maximized' outcomes, allowing at least an approximately rational choice to be made (Bellman and Zadeh, 1970; Whalen, 1987; Mendoza and Sprouse, 1989).

Other studies, mainly in the field of psychology, attempted to specify, on the basis of field experiments, exactly what sorts of common biases decision-makers exhibited in dealing with the uncertainties described by Simon (see Slovic et al., 1977, 1985). This is the case, for example, with models linked to *prospect theory* (see Kahneman and Tversky, 1979; Tversky and Kahneman, 1981, 1982, 1986; Haas, 2001), which postulated that humans 'overweight losses relative to comparable gains, engage in risk-averse behaviour in choices but risk-acceptant behaviour in choices among losses, and respond to probabilities in a nonlinear manner' (Levy, 1997: 33). This was done in the hope of allowing some specification of the cognitive limits in decision-making raised by Simon, thus allowing the development of 'second-best' maximizing rational models that would take into account actual human behaviourial limitations in the face of uncertainty (see Yates and Zukowski, 1976; Suedfeld and Tetlock, 1992; Einhorn, 1982; Kanner, 2005).

Simon, however, concluded that public decisions ostensibly taken in accordance with the precepts and methods outlined by the rational model would never *maximize* benefits over costs, but would instead tend only to *satisfy* whatever criteria decision-makers had set for themselves at the time of a decision. This *'satisfycing'* criterion, as he put it, was a realistic one given the bounded rationality with which human beings are endowed and within which they must work when taking decisions (see March, 1978, 1994). Although he did not himself develop an alternative model of decision-making built on the notion of satisfycing (see Jones, 2001: ch. 3), his insights would later be taken up by Charles Lindblom, who would incorporate them into the best-known alternative to the rational model: the *incremental* model of decision-making based on limited analysis and political exchange or bargaining, rather than knowledge-based analysis (Thomson et al., 2003).

The Incremental Model

Doubts about the usefulness of the rational model led to development of a second major school of public policy decision-making theory that sought a closer approximation of theory to the actual behaviour of decision-makers in real-life decision-making situations. These efforts yielded the incremental model, which portrayed public policy decision-making as a political process characterized by bargaining and compromise among self-interested decision-makers (Braybrooke and Lindblom, 1963; Dahl and Lindblom, 1953; Lindblom, 1959). In this model, the decisions eventually made represent what is politically feasible rather than technically desirable, and what is possible or 'optimal' rather than 'maximal' in the rational model's meaning of getting the most output for the least cost.

The credit for developing the incremental model of public decision-making is attributed to Yale University political scientist Charles Lindblom and his colleagues at other North American universities in the late 1950s and early 1960s (Dahl and Lindblom, 1953; Lindblom, 1955, 1958, 1959). Lindblom took to heart the ideas of bounded rationality and satisfycing behaviour among decision-makers developed by Simon and, on the basis of his own observations of actual decision-making processes in governments, outlined what he suggested were the common elements of the 'strategies of decision' actually followed by public policy decision-makers (Jones, 2002). The model he put forward arranged these strategies into a 'mutually supporting set of simplifying and focusing stratagems' and included the following elements:

a. Limitation of analysis to a few somewhat familiar policy alternatives . . . differing only marginally from the status quo;
b. Mixing policy goals and other values along with the empirical aspects of a problem in policy analysis (that is, no obligation to specify values first before identifying the means to promote them);
c. A greater analytical preoccupation with ills to be remedied than positive goals to be sought;
d. A sequence of trials, errors, and revised trials;
e. Analysis that explores only those possible consequences of an alternative considered to be important;
f. Fragmentation of analytical work to many (partisan) participants in policy making (each attending to their piece of the overall problem domain). (Lindblom, 1979: 517)

In Lindblom's view, decision-makers both did and should develop policies through a process of making 'successive limited comparisons' with earlier decisions, those with which they are most familiar. As he put it in his oft-cited article on 'The Science of Muddling Through', decision-makers typically, and should, work through a process of 'continually building out from the current situation, step-by-step and by small degrees' (Lindblom, 1959: 81). Decisions thus arrived at are usually only marginally different from those that exist. In other words, the changes from the status quo in decision-making are *incremental*.

According to Lindblom, there are two reasons why decisions typically do not stray far from the status quo. First, since bargaining requires distributing limited resources among various participants, it is easier to continue the existing pattern of distribution rather than try to negotiate the redistribution that would be required under any radically new proposal. Since the benefits and costs of present arrangements are known to the policy actors, unlike the uncertainties surrounding new arrangements, securing agreement on major changes is more difficult. The result is typically either continuation of the status quo or agreement to make only small changes to it. Second, the standard operating procedures of bureaucracies also tend to promote the continuation of existing practices. The methods by which bureaucrats identify options and the procedures and criteria for choice are often laid out in advance, inhibiting innovation and perpetuating existing arrangements (Gortner et al., 1987: 257).

Lindblom also argued that the rational model's requirement of separation between ends and means in the calculus of decision-making was unworkable in practice not only due to the time, information, and cognitive constraints identified by Simon and others, but also because it assumed policy-makers could both clearly separate means from ends in assessing policies and then agree upon each. Lindblom argued that in most policy areas, discussion of ends are inseparable from the means to achieve them, since which goals are pursued often depends on whether or not viable means are available to accomplish them. The beneficial essence of incrementalism, Lindblom argued, was to try to systematize decision-making processes by stressing the need for political agreement and learning by trial and error, rather than simply stumbling into random decisions without any strategy at all, or failing to develop pseudo-maximal ones through the application of the rational method (Lindblom and Cohen, 1979).

Some critics of incrementalism have debated the extent to which the incremental model accurately describes how many public policy decisions are actually made in practice (see Berry, 1990; Jones et al., 1997), since decisions to significantly alter the status quo do occur with relative frequency. Others, however, found several faults with its theoretical implications (see Weiss and Woodhouse, 1992). First, the model was criticized for lacking any kind of goal orientation. As John Forester (1984: 23) put it, incrementalism 'would have us cross and recross intersections without knowing where we are going'. Second, the model was challenged for being inherently conservative, given its apparent suspicion of large-scale change and innovation. Third, it was censured for representing decision-making as inherently undemocratic, to the extent it confined decision-making to bargaining within a select group of senior policy-makers (Gawthrop, 1971). Fourth, by discouraging systematic analysis and planning and undermining the need to search for promising new alternatives, it was said to promote short-sighted decisions that can have adverse consequences for society in the long run (Lustick, 1980). In addition to these criticisms of the desirability of decisions made incrementally, the model was also criticized for its narrow analytic usefulness. Yehezkel Dror (1964), for example, noted that incrementalism can only work when there is a great deal of continuity in the nature of problems that policies are intended to address and in the means available to address them, a continuity that does not always exist. Incrementalism is more characteristic of decision-making in a relatively stable environment, rather than in situations that are unusual, such as a crisis or a novel policy issue (Nice, 1987; Lustick, 1980). Fifth, it was pointed out that in practice it is very difficult to know exactly what is an 'increment' and what is not in terms of the size of the difference moved from the previous status quo (Bailey and O'Connor, 1975).

Lindblom countered many of these criticisms in his own writings, stating that incrementalism was neither inherently conservative nor short-sighted, since the relative size and direction of increments were not predetermined but would emerge from the deliberative bargaining process that characterized incremental policy-making (Lindblom, 1979: 517). He also suggested that the incremental method was neither inherently democratic nor undemocratic, but would simply follow the structure of representation present in different political systems and situations (Lindblom, 1968).

However, in responding to one major criticism—that incrementalism was better suited for or more likely to occur in some policy-making contexts than others—adherents of the incremental model had to accept that the nature of the decision-making process would vary according to factors such as whether a policy was new, the number of decision-makers involved, and whether or not they shared a consensus on the goals and objectives of policy-making (Bendor, 1995; Jones, 2001). This meant that the model was neither the ideal method of decision-making, as had been suggested by some adherents, nor, as Lindblom had alleged in some of his writings, the *only* possible method of policy-making. Rather, it was only one of several possible types or styles of public policy decision-making (Hayes, 2007).

Efforts to Move beyond Rationalism and Incrementalism

By the early 1980s, it had become apparent to many observers that the continuing debate between the advocates of rationalism and those of incrementalism over the merits and demerits of their favoured models was interfering with empirical work and the theoretical development of the subject. As Smith and May (1980: 156) argued:

> A debate about the relative merits of rationalistic as opposed to incrementalist models of decision-making has featured for some years now and although the terms of this debate are relatively well known it has had comparatively little impact upon empirical research in the areas of either policy or administrative studies.

Rather than continue with this debate, the authors suggested that:

> we require more than one account to describe the several facets of organizational life. The problem is not to reconcile the differences between contrasting rational and incremental models, nor to construct some third alternative which combines the strongest features of each. The problem is to relate the two in the sense of spelling out the relationship between the social realities with which each is concerned.

This awareness of the limitations of both the rational and incremental models of decision-making led policy scholars to look for alternatives. These came in many forms. Despite Smith and May's admonition, some analysts attempted to synthesize the two models, an initially unlikely objective but one that is not impossible to achieve. Others embraced the elements of unpredictability and capriciousness opened by the fall of incrementalism as the main alternative to the rational model. While neither of these theoretical directions proved particularly fruitful, a third effort to clarify the exact nature of alternative decision-making modes or styles, and the likely conditions under which they would be employed, generated more lasting value and continues to inform present-day work on the subject.

Mixed-Scanning Model

The initial response of many scholars to criticisms of incrementalism as an alternative to the rational model was to attempt to 'rescue' both models by combining them in a kind of constructive synthesis. As early as 1967, for example, Amitai Etzioni developed his *mixed-scanning* model to bridge the shortcomings of both rational and incremental models by combining elements from both.

Accepting the criticisms of the rational model as largely unworkable in practice and of the incremental model as only appropriate to certain types of policy environments, Etzioni suggested that combining the two models allowed both criticisms to be overcome, while providing decision-makers with a practical guide to 'optimal' decision-making. Adopting a similar position to that of Simon, Etzioni, and later many others, suggested that the decision-making process in fact consisted of two stages, a 'pre-decisional' or 'representative' stage of assessing a problem and 'framing' it—which would utilize incremental analysis—and a second analytical phase in which specific solutions could be more carefully assessed—which would be more rational in nature (see Voss, 1998; Svenson, 1979; Alexander, 1979, 1982).

In Etzioni's 'mixed-scanning' model, optimal decisions would result from a cursory search ('scanning') for alternatives, followed by a detailed probe of the most promising alternatives. This would allow for more innovation than permitted by the incremental model, without imposing the unrealistic demands prescribed by the rational model. Etzioni argued that this was, indeed, how many decisions were made in reality, where it is not uncommon to find a series of incremental decisions followed by a substantially different decision when decision-makers are faced with a problem significantly different from those dealt with before. Thus, he presented his model as both a prescriptive and descriptive approach to decision-making that would overcome the conceptual limitations of earlier models while conforming to the actual practice of decision-makers on the ground.

In more recent work, students of US foreign policy decision-making developed a similar two-stage model of decision-making processes, sometimes referred to as the *'poliheuristic'* model (see Mintz and Geva, 1997; Mintz et al., 1997). In this view, decision-makers use a variety of cognitive shortcuts ('heuristics' or 'operational codes' or 'standard operating procedures') to compensate for limitations in knowledge and to achieve some initial winnowing of alternatives to a set of 'feasible' or 'acceptable' ones (Fernandes and Simon, 1999; Voss and Post,

1988; George, 1969, 1979; Drezner, 2000; Allison and Halperin, 1972; Brule, 2008). These heuristics include the use of historical analogies, a preference for incremental policies, the desire for consensus among competing policy actors, and the desire to claim credit or avoid blame for potential policy outcomes (see George, 1980; Weaver, 1986; Hood, 2002; Vertzberger, 1998; Sulitzeanu-Kenan and Hood, 2005; Hood and Rothstein, 2001). In the second stage, a limited number of alternatives are subjected to a more rational, 'maximizing' analysis (Mintz, 2004, 2005; Ye, 2007). As Mintzberg et al. found in their 1976 study of 'strategic' or non-routine decision-making with uncertain outcomes:

> When faced with a complex, unprogrammed situation, the decision makers seek to reduce the decision into subdecisions to which he [sic] applies general purpose, interchangeable sets of procedures or routines. In other words, the decision makers deal with unstructured situations by factoring them into familiar, structural elements. Furthermore, the individual decision maker uses a number of problem-solving shortcuts—satisficing instead of maximizing, not looking too far ahead, reducing a complex environment to a series of simplified conceptual 'models'. (Mintzberg et al., 1976: 247; see also Weiss, 1982)

It is not clear, however, exactly how these models differ from the incremental and rational ones they were ostensibly designed to replace. That is, the techniques of marginal analysis put forward by Lindblom and others already envisioned a limited search for, and selection of, alternatives, which would then be singled out for more detailed analysis. And it is also not clear how mixed scanning would overcome the problems associated with the rational model, since without the systematic comparison of all possible alternatives it is impossible to assure that a final decision is a maximizing one. Nevertheless, Etzioni's call for a less overtly political type of incrementalism than that based on Lindblom's 'partisan mutual adjustment' was well received by many public policy practitioners. Among policy scholars, however, it was quickly bypassed in favour of other models—such as the so-called 'garbage-can' theory discussed below—that purported to come more directly to terms with the reality of uncertainty and ambiguity facing policy-makers in day-to-day decision-making situations (Walker and Marchau, 2004; Driedger and Eyles, 2003; Gupta et al., 2003; Morgan and Henrion, 1990; Potoski, 1999).

The Garbage-Can Model: Embracing Irrationalism

In the late 1970s, a very different model asserted and, in fact, embraced the inherent lack of rationality in the decision-making process identified by Simon and others. Developed in part by one of Simon's co-authors, James March, and March's Norwegian colleague, Johan Olsen, the so-called *garbage-can model* of decision-making denied to the decision-making process even the limited rationality attributed to it by incrementalism (March and Olsen, 1979b; Cohen et al., 1972).

March and Olsen, working with Michael Cohen, began with the assumption that both the rational and incremental models presumed a level of intentionality, comprehension of problems, and predictability of relations among actors that simply did not obtain in reality. In their view, decision-making was a highly ambiguous and unpredictable process only distantly related to searching for means to achieve goals. Rejecting the instrumentalism that characterized most other models, Cohen, March, and Olsen (1979: 26) argued that most decision opportunities were:

> a garbage can into which various problems and solutions are dumped by participants. The mix of garbage in a single can depends partly on the labels attached to the alternative cans; but it also depends on what garbage is being produced at the moment, on the mix of cans available, and on the speed with which garbage is collected and removed from the scene.

Cohen, March, and Olsen deliberately used the garbage-can metaphor to strip away the aura of scientific authority attributed to decision-making by earlier theorists. They sought to drive home the point that goals are often unknown to policy-makers, as are causal relationships. In their view, actors simply define goals and choose means as they go along in a policy process that is necessarily contingent and unpredictable. As Gary Mucciaroni (1992: 461) phrased it, in this model:

> There is plenty of room for chance, human creativity, and choice to influence outcomes. What gets on the agenda at given points in time is the result of a fortuitous conjunction—whatever the combination of salient problems, available solutions, and political circumstances that exist. Events, such as the opening of a window of opportunity, are often unpredictable, and participants often are unable to control events once they are set in motion. Yet, individual actors are not completely without an ability to affect outcomes. Entrepreneurs decide which problems to dramatize, choose which solutions to push, and formulate political strategies to bring their issues onto the agenda. Actors in the process develop problem definitions and solutions that are plausible and compelling, link them together, and make them congruent with existing political conditions.

March and Olsen (1979a) provided evidence from several case studies of decision-making processes in European universities to substantiate their proposition that public decisions are often made in too ad-hoc and haphazard a fashion to be called incremental, much less rational. Others, such as Paul Anderson (1983), for example, also provided evidence that even decisions with respect to the important international events such as those surrounding the 1962 Cuban Missile Crisis, one of the most critical issues of the Cold War period, were made in terms of simplistic yes/no binary choices on proposals that would emerge in the course of discussion.

Be that as it may, while its key tenets may well be a fairly accurate description of how organizations make decisions some of the time, in other instances it would be reasonable to expect more order. As critics such as Mucciaroni argued, albeit in a national context, rather than present a general model of decision-making, the garbage-can idea represents only a type of decision-making characteristic of a particular political or organizational environment or context:

> Perhaps the mode of policy-making depicted by the garbage can model is itself embedded in a particular institutional structure. Put another way, the model may be better at depicting decision-making in the United States, where the institutional structure is fragmented and permeable, participation is pluralistic and fluid, and coalitions are often temporary and ad hoc. By contrast, policy-making in other countries takes place among institutions that are more centralized and integrated, where the number of participants is limited and their participation is highly structured and predictable. (Mucciaroni, 1992: 466)

This type of decision-making is also more likely to occur at points when policy paradigms are in transition, when the coherence commonly held core beliefs typically impose upon policy-making is lacking (Hood, 1999).

The 'Decision Accretion' Model of Decision-Making

Challenging and controversial, the main contribution of the garbage-can model was in helping to break the logjam of what had become a rather sterile debate between rationalists and incrementalists over the merits of their models, thereby allowing for more nuanced studies of decision-making within specific institutional and ideational contexts to be undertaken.

By the 1980s most studies pointed to the significance of understanding decision-making structures and contexts for the analysis of how decisions are actually taken in complex organizations. In her work on the use of knowledge in the policy process, for example, Carol Weiss noted that in many instances policy decisions are not decided in a 'brisk and clear-cut style' in a single institution or setting at a single point in time. Rather, many decisions, from the momentous to the inane, are actually taken piecemeal, without any overall plan of attack or conscious deliberation, but rather appear more like a pearl in an oyster, having been accreted in multiple layers over a relatively lengthy period of time through the actions of multiple decision-makers (Weiss, 1980).

Unlike incrementalism, which paints a similar portrait of policy-making as the buildup of previous decisions, or the garbage-can model, which also describes policy emergence as largely fortuitous, notions of decision accretion do not rely on intra-organizational bargaining processes or fluid sets of participants to explain this pattern. Instead, it is said to emerge due to the nature of the decision to be made and the structure of the organizations that make them. As Weiss argued:

> In large organizations, decisions on complex issues are almost never the province of one individual or one office. Many people in many offices

have a say, and when the outcomes of a course of action are uncertain, many participants have opportunities to propose, plan, confer, deliberate, advise, argue, forward policy statements, reject, revise, veto, and re-write. (Ibid., 399)

In such situations, Weiss suggested, individuals often do not even realize when a decision has been made. Each person takes only some small step in a large process with seemingly small consequences. But over the course of time, 'these many small steps foreclose alternative courses of action and limit the range of the possible. Almost imperceptibly, a decision has been made, (sometimes) without anyone's awareness that he or she was deciding' (ibid., 401).

This analysis highlights the significance of *multiple arenas* and *multiple rounds* of decision-making for many modern-day public policy decisions (Howlett, 2007). That is, as Weiss and others have suggested, decision-making often tends to occur in multiple locations or venues, each with a distinct set of actors, rules of procedure, and ability to influence the outcome of a decision process in a pre-ferred direction (see Klijn, 2001; Mintzberg et al., 1976; Timmermans, 2001). In each arena, different actors can 'score points' in terms of having their definition of a problem or solution adopted. These decisions are collected in a 'round' in which the results of each round are fed back into other arenas for continued dis-cussion and debate, a process in which new actors can be activated, new arenas become involved, and new or modified decisions emerge (see Teisman, 2000; Hammond, 1986).

In addition, each venue or arena can be involved in one or more simultaneous decision-making processes, increasing the likelihood that couplings and uncou-plings of issues can occur in a highly contingent fashion (see Roe, 1990; Perrow, 1984; van Bueren et al., 2001; Klijn and Teisman, 1991). Similar effects result from actor positions changing over time in lengthy multi-round decision-making processes (Klijn and Koppenjan, 2000b; Howlett, 2007).

Conclusion: Revisiting Public Policy Decision-Making Modes

Focusing on the interactions between actors both within and between organiza-tional arenas and on the strategies used to influence outcomes allows some pre-dictions to be made about the likely kinds of decisions that can emerge from these lengthy and complex policy processes (see Allison and Halperin, 1972; Sager, 2001; Stokman and Berveling, 1998). Moreover, it also allows for the conscious design of decision-making processes in order to clarify the roles of different actors and stages in the process and to ensure that outcomes are less 'irrational' and con-tingent than might otherwise be the case with instances of pure '*decision creep*' (de Bruijn and ten Heuvelhof, 2000; Klijn and Koppenjan, 2005).[2]

As we have seen, the early rational and incremental models suggested that disparate decision-making styles can be found animating the public policy process. Later models, such as the mixed-scanning, garbage-can, and decision round models, provide some indication of which variables are responsible for the predominance of a particular decision style in a specific circumstance: the nature of a policy problem; the number and type of actors involved; the nature of the informational, temporal, and institutional constraints within which they operate; and the pre-existing sets of ideas or 'frames' and decision-making routines with and through which decision-makers approach their tasks (Ley-Borras, 2005).

The idea that there is a range of possible decision-making styles is not a new one (see Wildavsky, 1962; Scharpf, 1991). In some of his earlier writings, for example, Charles Lindblom and several of his co-authors held out the possibility that incremental decision-making could coexist with efforts to achieve more 'rational' decisions. Thus, Braybrooke and Lindblom (1963), for example, argued that four different types of decision-making could be discerned, depending on the amount of knowledge at the disposal of decision-makers and the amount of change the selection involved from earlier decisions. In Braybrooke and Lindblom's view the overwhelming majority of decisions were likely to be taken in an incremental fashion, involving minimal change in situations of low available knowledge. However, three other possibilities also existed, the rational model emerging as one possibility and two other poorly defined styles—'revolutionary' and 'analytic'—also existing as infrequently utilized alternatives given specific change and knowledge configurations. Later in his career, Lindblom revisited this idea, arguing that a spectrum of decision-making styles existed according to how systematic the analysis supporting the decision was. These ranged from 'synoptic' decision-making, which is similar to the rational ideal, to 'blundering', that is, simply following hunches or guesses without any real effort at systematic analysis of alternative strategies, which is akin to the garbage-can model.

Neither of these early taxonomies took into account the principal variables identified as significant in the selection process by more recent decision-making models. A more promising start in this direction was made by John Forester in his work on decision-making styles. Forester (1984, 1989) argued that there were at least five distinct decision-making styles associated with six key sets of conditions. According to him, 'what is rational for administrators to do depends on the situations in which they work.' That is, the decision-making style and the type of decision made by decision-makers would be expected to vary according to issue and institutional contexts. As he put it:

Depending upon the conditions at hand, a strategy may be practical or ridiculous. With time, expertise, data, and a well-defined problem, technical calculations may be in order; without time, data, definition, and expertise, attempting those calculations could well be a waste of time. In a complex organizational environment, intelligence networks will be as, or more, important than documents when information is needed. In an environment of inter-organizational conflict, bargaining and compromise may be called for. Administrative strategies are sensible only in a political and organizational context. (Forester, 1984: 25)

Forester suggested that for decision-making to take place along the lines proposed by the rational model, the following conditions had to be met. First, the number of *agents* (decision-makers) had to be limited, possibly to as few as one person. Second, the organizational *setting* for the decision had to be simple, and insulated from the influences of other policy actors. Third, the *problem* had to be well defined; in other words, its scope, time horizon, value dimensions, and chains of consequences had to be well understood. Fourth, *information* must be as close to perfect as possible; in other words, it must be complete, accessible, and comprehensible. Finally, there must be no urgency for the decision, that is, *time* had to be infinitely available to the decision-makers to consider all possible contingencies and their present and anticipated consequences.

When these conditions are met completely, rational decision-making can be expected to prevail. However, since these five conditions are rarely met in practice, Forester argued that other styles of decision-making would be more likely to emerge. Thus, the number of agents (decision-makers) can expand and multiply almost to infinity; the setting can include many different organizations and can be more or less open to external influences (Heikkila and Isett, 2004; Hammond, 2003); the problem can be ambiguous or susceptible to multiple competing interpretations (Bozeman and Pandey, 2004); information can be incomplete, misleading, or purposefully withheld or manipulated; and time can be limited or artificially constrained and manipulated (Wright, 1974).

From this perspective, Forester suggested the existence of five possible styles of decision-making: what he termed 'optimization', 'satisfycing', 'search', 'bargaining', and 'organizational'. *Optimization* is the strategy that obtains when the conditions (mentioned above) of the rational-comprehensive model are met. The prevalence of other styles depends on the degree to which those conditions are not met. When the limitations are cognitive, for reasons mentioned earlier, we are likely to find the *satisfycing* style of decision-making. The other styles mentioned by Forester, however, are overlapping and therefore difficult to distinguish clearly. A *search* strategy is one he argued was likely to occur when the problem is vague. A *bargaining* strategy is likely to be employed when multiple actors deal with a problem facing a shortage of information and time. The *organizational* strategy involves multiple settings and actors with both time and informational resources but also multiple problems. Suffice it to say that these types involve greater numbers of actors, more complex settings, more intractable problems, incomplete or distorted information, and limited time for making decisions.

While a major improvement over earlier classifications and taxonomies, and certainly an improvement over the rational and incremental models and their 'garbage-can' challengers, Forester's was only a first step in surpassing earlier models of decision-making styles. A major problem with his particular taxonomy is that it does not actually flow very logically from his arguments. A close examination of his discussion of the factors shaping decision-making (Forester, 1984: 26) reveals that one would expect to find many more than five possible styles flowing from the cited combinations and permutations of the variables. Although many of these categories are indistinguishable in practice and would thus serve little analytical purpose, it remains unclear why one should expect only the five cited styles to emerge.

An improvement on Forester's model of decision-making styles can be made by recasting his variables to more clearly and consistently relate decision-making styles to the types of variables found to be significant in earlier investigations of public decision-making. Combining Forester's concepts of 'agent' and 'setting', for example, highlights the role of different kinds of policy subsystems—that is, different numbers and types of actors situated in different numbers and types of institutional settings—in the decision-making process (March, 1994; Beach and Mitchell, 1978). The complexity of the policy subsystem affects the number of venues, the nature of dominant policy ideas and interests, and the level of agreement or opposition to an option within the subsystem and among decision-makers (see Bendor and Hammond, 1992). Some options accord with the core values of the subsystem members while other do not, thereby structuring decisions into hard (e.g., contested and cognitively challenging) and easy (e.g., broadly understood and familiar) choices (Pollock et al., 1993).

Similarly, it is possible to combine Forester's notions of 'problem', 'information', and 'time' resources, which can all be seen to reflect the types of decision-making constraints identified by Simon and Lindblom and others (see Payne, 1982; Simon, 1973; Maule and Svenson, 1993; Payne et al., 1988). That is, the making of decisions is constrained to varying degrees by information and time limitations (Rochefort and Cobb, 1993; Webber, 1992; Pappi and Henning, 1998), as well as by the intractability or 'wickedness' of the problem (Weick, 1976; Rittel and Webber, 1973; Sharkansky, 1997: ch. 2; Hisschemoller and Hoppe, 1995). But it is often the case that these constraints run together because part of the issue of problem tractability is related to lack of information about potential solutions and a lack of time required to gather or develop it (Radford, 1977).

Thus, two pertinent variables can be used to construct an effective taxonomy of decision-making styles: (1) the cohesion of the policy subsystem involved in the decision and, specifically, whether or not decision-makers enjoy legitimacy within the subsystem, and (2) the severity of the constraints that decision-makers face in making their choices (see Lindquist, 1988; Martin, 1998: ch. 2). The constraints may be institutional or cognitive: political or social institutions may hinder dealing with a problem or decision-makers may simply not know how to deal with it. Figure 6.1 outlines the four basic decision-making styles that emerge on the basis of these two dimensions.

In this model, decisions made within cohesive policy subsystems are less likely to resort to adjustment strategies and, depending on the nature of the constraints they face, tend to promote either rational or negative decision-making. On the other hand, as incrementalists suggest, highly constrained policy contexts are likely to result in an incremental adjustment approach to decision-making in policy subsystems that lack cohesion (Holzmann and Rutkowski, 2003; Weyland, 2005). In situations of low constraint and low cohesion, decisions are likely to be

Figure 6.1   Decision-Making Styles

		Cohesion of Policy Subsystem	
		Low	High
	Low	**Ad hoc** (non-linear change)	**Rational** (linear and non-linear change)
Severity of Policy Constraints	High	**Incremental** (linear change)	**Negative** (status quo)

Note: Cells provide examples of instruments in each category.

non-linear and ad hoc, often shuttling between different alternatives over fairly short periods of time, as suggested by the garbage-can model (t'Hart and Kleiboer, 1995; de Bruijn and ten Heuvelhof, 2000).

This discussion demonstrates that the essential character of the public decision-making process is very much the same as that of the other policy stages we have examined. That is, like the earlier stages of agenda-setting and policy formulation, the decision-making stage is affected by the nature of the policy subsystem involved (the number and type of actors, their institutional setting, and the kinds of ideas they hold),[3] and by the constraints under which decision-makers operate (Agranoff and Yildiz, 2007; Woll, 2007). A focus on these variables can help predict the type of outcome likely to arise from the particular style of decision-making adopted in the policy process in question (Stokman and Berveling, 1998).

Ultimately, then, as John Forester (1984: 23) put it, what is rational for administrators and politicians to do:

> depends on the situations in which they work. Pressed for quick recommendations, they cannot begin long studies. Faced with organizational rivalries, competition and turf struggles, they may justifiably be less than candid about their plans. What is reasonable to do depends on the context one is in, in ordinary life no less than in public administration.

Study Questions

1. How do agenda-setting and formulation shape the decision-making process?
2. To what extent is it possible to make rational decisions?
3. Is incrementalism the default decision-making option? Why or why not?
4. Why is paradigmatic change a rare outcome of decision-making?
5. What subsystem features are likely to generate non-decisions?

Further Readings

Allison, Graham T., and Morton H. Halperin. 1972. 'Bureaucratic Politics: A Paradigm and Some Policy Implications', *World Politics* 24 (Suppl.): 40–79.

Cohen, M., J. March, and J. Olsen. 1972. 'A Garbage Can Model of Organizational Choice', *Administrative Science Quarterly* 17, 1: 1–25.

Forester, John. 1984. 'Bounded Rationality and the Politics of Muddling Through', *Public Administration Review* 44: 23–30.

Haas, M.L. 2001. 'Prospect Theory and the Cuban Missile Crisis', *International Studies Quarterly* 45: 241–70.

Jones, B.D. 2002. 'Bounded Rationality and Public Policy: Herbert A. Simon and the Decisional Foundation of Collective Choice', *Policy Sciences* 35: 269–84.

Lindblom, Charles. 1959. 'The Science of Muddling Through', *Public Administration Review* 19: 79–88.

Mintz, A. 2005. 'Applied Decision Analysis: Utilizing Poliheuristic Theory to Explain and Predict Foreign Policy and National Security Decisions', *International Studies Perspectives* 6, 1: 94–8.

Simon, Herbert. 1955. 'A Behavioral Model of Rational Choice', *Quarterly Journal of Economics* 69, 1: 99–118.

Smith, Gilbert, and David May. 1980. 'The Artificial Debate between Rationalist and Incrementalist Models of Decision-Making', *Policy and Politics* 8: 147–61.

Teisman, G.R. 2000. 'Models for Research into Decision-Making Processes: On Phases, Streams and Decision-Making Rounds', *Public Administration* 78, 4: 937–56.

Weiss, Carol H. 1980. 'Knowledge Creep and Decision Accretion', *Knowledge: Creation, Diffusion, Utilization* 1, 3: 381–404.

Chapter 7

Policy Implementation

After a public problem has reached the policy agenda, various options have been proposed to address it, and the government has set policy goals and decided on a course of action to attain them, it must put the decision into practice. The effort, knowledge, and resources devoted to translating policy decisions into action comprise the policy cycle's implementation stage. While most policy decisions identify the means to pursue their goals, subsequent choices are inevitably required to attain results. Funding must be allocated, personnel assigned, and rules of procedure developed to make a policy work.

Policy implementation often relies on civil servants and administrative officials to establish and manage the necessary actions. However, non-governmental actors who are part of the policy subsystem can also be involved in implementation activities. In some countries, like Sweden, there may be a tradition of non-governmental actors directly implementing some important social programs (Ginsburg, 1992; Johansson and Borell, 1999). In other countries, like the US, which have only recently attempted to implement some programs through community and religious ('faith-based') groups (Kuo, 2006), non-governmental actors are typically involved in the design and evaluation of policies but not their actual administration and management.

Actors and Activities in Policy Implementation

Once the direction and goals of a policy are officially decided, the number and type of actors involved begin to expand beyond the small subset of actors making policy decisions to encompass the policy universe of interested actors. Policy subsystems then become important contributors to implementation as their participants apply knowledge and values to shaping the launch and evolution of programs implementing policy decisions. Usually, however, only a narrow range of subsystem actors become involved in the implementation process. Bureaucrats are the most significant actors in most policy implementation, bringing the endemic intra- and inter-organizational conflicts of public agencies to the fore of this stage in the policy cycle (Dye, 2001).

Different bureaucratic agencies at various levels of government (national, state or provincial, and local) are usually involved in implementing policy, each carrying particular interests, ambitions, and traditions that affect the implementation process and shape its outcomes, in a process of 'multi-level' government or governance (see Bardach, 1977; Elmore, 1978; Bache and Flinders, 2004). Implementation by public agencies is often an expensive, multi-year effort, meaning that continued funding for programs and projects is usually neither permanent nor guaranteed but rather requires continual negotiation and discussions within and between the political and administrative arms of the state. If their preferred solution to a problem was not selected, this creates opportunities for politicians, agencies, and other members of policy subsystems to use the implementation process as simply another opportunity for continuing the conflicts they may have lost at earlier stages of the policy process. Such processes, of course, greatly complicate implementation and move it further away from being simply a 'technical' issue of decision-processing (Nicholson-Crotty, 2005).

While politicians are significant actors in the decisions that lead into the implementation process and can play an active role in subsequent oversight and evaluation efforts, most of the day-to-day activities of policy administration typically fall within the purview of salaried public servants. This is because of the key role played by laws codifying the results of decision-making and empowering specific state agencies to put those decisions into practice (Keyes, 1996; Ziller, 2005).

In most countries, traditional or *civil or common laws* form a 'default' or basic set of principles governing how individuals interact with each other and with the state in their day-to-day lives. These laws are often codified in writing—as is the case in many continental European countries—but they may also be found in less systematic form in the overall record of precedents set by judicial bodies, as is the case in Britain and its former colonies. Even in these so-called 'common-law' countries, *statutory laws* are passed by parliaments to replace or supplement the civil or common law (Gall, 1983; Bogart, 2002). These statutes take the form of Acts, which, among other things, usually also create a series of rules to be followed in implementing particular policies, as well as a range of offences and penalties for non-compliance with the law.

Statute law usually also designates a specific administrative agency or ministry as empowered to make whatever '*regulations*' or administrative rules are required to ensure the successful implementation of the principles and aims of the enabling legislation. Regulations giving effect in specific circumstances to the general principles codified in laws are then prepared by civil servants employed by administrative agencies, often in conjunction with target or 'clientele' groups (Kagan, 1994). Regulations cover such items as the standards of behaviour or performance that must be met by target groups and the criteria to be used to administer policy. These serve as the basis for licensing or approval and, although unlegislated, provide the de facto source of direction for most implementation processes. As was discussed in Chapter 5, this general form of implementation is sometimes referred to as '*command-and-control*' regulation whereby a command is given by an authorized body and the administration is charged with controlling the target group to ensure compliance (Sinclair, 1997; Kerwin, 1994, 1999; Baldwin and Cave, 1999).

Although many efforts have been made in recent years to supplement or replace this mode of governance with others in which implementation is based more on collaboration or incentives (Freeman, 1997; Armstrong and Lenihan, 1999; Kernaghan, 1993), in the modern era, such legal processes continue to form the basis for implementation in all but the worst instances of dictatorship or personal rule. Instructions may be issued through compliant legislatures but also directly from the executive to the administration. These types of legal processes are a necessary part of adapting general statements of intent, which usually result from the decision-making stage, to the specific circumstances and situations that administrators face on the ground in attempting to alter societal behaviour in the direction desired by decision-makers. Even in the case of efforts to develop more collaborative relationships with target groups, administrative actions must still be based on legal authority provided by legislatures and executives (Grimshaw, 2001; Klijn, 2002; Phillips, 2004).

The usual form of such administrative venues is the *ministry* or *department*, and the actual practice of administering policy and delivering services is performed overwhelmingly by civil servants in such agencies. However, other forms of quasi-governmental organizations (quangos) (Hood, 1986; Koppell, 2003) ranging from state-owned enterprises (Stanton, 2002; Chandler, 1983; Laux and Molot, 1988) to non-profit corporations and bodies (McMullen and Schellenberg, 2002; Advani and Borins, 2001) and public–private partnerships (English and Skelern, 1995; Hodge and Greve, 2007), as discussed in Chapter 5, can also be vehicles for service delivery.

This does not, however, exhaust the types of state agencies involved in implementation, which also include organizations designed to perform specific tasks related to service delivery without being directly or indirectly involved in its management. Among these are various kinds of tribunals, such as *independent regulatory commissions*, that exist at arm's-length from the government and develop the rules and regulations required for administration (Cushman, 1941; Braithwaite et al., 1987; Christensen and Laegreid, 2007). Another form of implementing agency is the administrative appeal *board* and other forms of *commissions and tribunals* created by statute or regulation to perform many quasi-judicial functions, including appeals concerning licensing, certification of personnel or programs, and the issuance of permits. Appointed by government, administrative tribunals and boards usually represent, or purport to represent, some diversity of interests and expertise and are expected to moderate the public–private interface in goods and service delivery without displacing non-state actors in the production and distribution of various kinds of goods and services. *Public hearings* may be statutorily defined as a component of such administrative process and operate to secure regulatory compliance. In most cases, however, such hearings are held at the discretion of a decision-making authority and are often after-the-fact public information sessions rather than true consultative devices (Talbert et al., 1995; Grima, 1985). *Specialized advisory boards and commissions* (Brown, 1955, 1972; Smith, 1977) often supplant public consultations, yielding more expert views on specific regulatory activities than open public hearings would typically provide, but also allowing some subsystem members to exercise inordinate influence on policy implementation (Dion, 1973).

Thus, while state officials remain an important force in the implementation stage of the policy process, advisory and quasi-governmental agencies allow them to be joined by members of the relevant policy subsystems, as the number and type of policy actors return to resembling those found at the formulation stage (Bennett and McPhail, 1992). Just as at that stage, *target groups*, that is, groups whose behaviour is intended or expected to be altered by government action, play a major role in the implementation process (Donovan, 2001; Kiviniemi, 1986; Schneider and Ingram, 1993). The political and economic resources of target groups certainly have an impact on the implementation of policies (Montgomery, 2000). Powerful groups affected by a policy can influence the character of implementation by supporting or opposing it. Thus, regulators will commonly strike compromises with groups, or attempt to use the groups' own resources in some cases, to make the task of implementation simpler or less expensive (Giuliani, 1999). Although this is typically done informally in some jurisdictions, such as the United States, more formal efforts have been made in many sectors to incorporate regulator–regulated negotiations in the development of administrative standards and other aspects of the regulatory process (Coglianese, 1997). Changing levels of public support for a policy can also affect implementation. Many policies witness a decline in support after a policy decision has been made, enabling administrators to vary the original intent of a decision (see Hood, 1983, 1986a). Despite the rule of law, bureaucrats thus possess considerable influence, whether they seek it or not, in realizing the policy initiatives they are called upon to implement.

Implementation Theory

Until the early 1970s, implementation was often regarded as unproblematic, despite the availability of large, century-old, literatures in public administration, organizational behaviour, and management concerned with effective execution of government decisions (Wilson, 1887; Goodnow, 1900; Gaus, 1931). Many policy researchers ignored or downplayed the political pitfalls arising at this stage in the policy cycle, assuming that once a policy decision was made, the administrative arm of government would simply carry it out (Hargrove, 1975). Within the policy sciences, this view began to change with the publication of Pressman and Wildavsky's 1973 work on program implementation. Their study of US federal programs for unemployed inner-city residents of Oakland, California, showed that job-creation programs were not actually being carried out in the manner anticipated by policy-makers. Other studies confirmed that the Great Society programs instituted by the Johnson administration (1963–8) in the US were not achieving their intended objectives and argued that the problem was rooted in the manner in which they were being implemented (see van Meter and van Horn, 1975; Bardach, 1977). Research in other countries arrived at similar conclusions (Hjern, 1982; Mayntz, 1979). The upshot of all these studies was a more systematic effort in the 1980s to understand the factors that influenced public policy implementation (Sabatier and Mazmanian, 1981).

This 'second generation' of implementation research in the policy sciences quickly became embroiled in a dispute over the most appropriate focus for describing and analyzing its subject matter: the so-called *'top-down'* versus *'bottom-up'* debate (Barrett, 2004). Some studies generated analyses and prescriptions that presented policy implementation to be most successful as a 'top-down' process whose mechanisms ensured that implementing officials could do their job more effectively. Effectiveness was defined as keeping to the original intent of the public officials who had ratified the policy. This top-down perspective was opposed by those who subscribed to a 'bottom-up' approach, which carefully examined the actions of those affected by and engaged in the implementation of a policy (Sabatier, 1986). Here, effectiveness was seen to arise from the adaptive behaviour of 'street-level bureaucrats' seeking to attain and sustain the means to achieve policy goals on the ground (Lipsky, 1980). While both of these approaches generated valuable insights, like many similar dichotomous debates in the field, they tended to ossify into hardened positions that stifled conceptual development and research, leading to calls in the late 1980s and 1990s for new approaches that would yield more 'scientific' implementation research methods and results (see Lester et al., 1987; Goggin et al., 1990; DeLeon, 1999a).

Many scholars moved beyond the top-down versus bottom-up debate during the 1990s, yielding a fertile decade that produced what Malcolm Goggin and his colleagues labelled the 'third generation' of implementation research (Lester and Goggin, 1998; O'Toole, 2000b). In addition to studies using the insights of recent models of administrative behaviour such as game theory and principal–agent models of behaviour (e.g., Scholz, 1984, 1991; Hawkins and Thomas, 1989a)— which focused on the nature of enforcement involved in traditional administrative techniques—an approach emerged that concentrated on policy tools or instruments. Rather than studying the purely administrative concerns of putting a program into practice, this approach considered implementation as an attempt to apply the various tools of government described in Chapter 5 to concrete cases through a process of more or less conscious policy design (see Salamon, 1981; Mayntz, 1983; Bobrow, 2006).

First- and Second-Generation Models of Public Policy Implementation

First- and second-generation theories were quite useful in setting out a variety of managerial and organizational design principles, or maxims of administration, which were expected to generate an optimal or maximizing match between political intent and administrative action. These included various statements about the best or most desirable size of administrative units and those surrounding optimal 'spans of control' within and between agencies, as well as other similar organizational principles. The most serious shortcoming of the first-generation approach, as noted above, was its virtually exclusive focus on senior politicians and officials, who often play, as second-generation 'bottom-up' analysts noted, only a marginal role in day-to-day implementation compared to lower-level officials and members of the public (see Hjern and Porter, 1993; Hjern, 1982; Barrett and Fudge, 1981).

Studies conducted in bottom-up fashion showed that the success or failure of many programs often depended on the commitment and skills of the actors directly involved in implementing programs (Lipsky, 1980), and these studies focused attention on the formal and informal relationships constituting the policy subsystems involved in both designing and implementing policies. The most serious shortcoming of both top-down and bottom-up analyses, though, was their common assumption that decision-makers provide implementers with clear goals and direction when, as we have seen in Chapter 6, in reality government intentions can emerge from bargaining, accretion, and other processes and thus result in often vague, unclear, or even contradictory goals and direction.

Seen in this light, these two approaches are not contradictory but complementary (Sabatier, 1993a; Matland, 1995) and, together, help to get at the reality of policy implementation. As we have seen, policy subsystems consisting of key private and public actors in a policy sector play a crucial role at all stages of the policy process. The top-down approach starts with the decisions of the government, examines the extent to which administrators carry out or fail to carry out these decisions, and seeks to find the reasons underlying the extent of the implementation conducted. The bottom-up approach merely begins at the other end of the implementation chain of command and urges that the activities of so-called street-level implementers be fully taken into account. Both, however, require a theory of why specific tools and policy mechanisms are used in specific circumstances, and not others, to carry out governmental tasks, and why implementers behave the way they do in carrying out their tasks. These questions about implementation design and behaviour are the focus of 'third-generation' implementation studies.

Third-Generation Implementation Theory

Implementing some programs can be relatively unproblematic, as in the case of closing down an illegal casino or opening a new school, because attaining these goals requires discrete decisions whose translation into practice is usually routine. The same is not true for programs designed to address long-term, chronic, or ill-defined problems such as eliminating compulsive gambling or improving pupils' educational achievements. Public problems such as domestic violence or dysfunctional schools are rooted in so many causes that programs designed to address single or even multiple causes can normally be expected to fall short of their objectives. The problem of speeding on city streets has more simple origins and, therefore, can be less challenging, even though it is unlikely to be eradicated. Similarly, programs designed to eliminate pollution or tax and welfare frauds must face the reality that no available technology will allow complete achievement of these objectives. Even if the technology is available, it may be more expensive than the society is willing to pay. As was discussed in earlier chapters, 'wicked' problems are particularly difficult to tackle because of their complex, novel, or interdependent nature and because they involve not a single decision but a series of determinations on how to carry out the government's policy (Churchman, 1967; Rittel and Webber, 1973).

Game Theory

Dealing with such problems enhances administrative discretion inasmuch as the more complex and difficult the problem, the greater the range of potential solutions that administrators will have to choose among in dealing with it. However, wicked problems also allow considerable leeway for policy subsystem members to evade or otherwise fail to fully comply with administrative edicts and plans. The nature of the target group identified by a policy can also influence the administrative discretion arising in its implementation because the larger and more diverse a group is, the more difficult it will be to affect behaviour in a desired fashion. For example, improving the safety features of automobiles is easier to implement and entails less bureaucratic discretion than making thousands of careless drivers observe traffic regulations (Hood, 1986a). The small number of manufacturers involved can be directed towards policy goals such as installing airbags and anti-lock brakes through regulations, while police enforcement of careless driving will entail many judgements about individual circumstances. In other words, the extent of the behavioural change sought in the target group and the relative size and homogeneity of the target group are key determinants of the level of difficulty faced in policy implementation. A policy of eradicating sexism, racism, or religious intolerance is more difficult to implement because of the deep roots of these attitudes in societies' cultural belief systems. By contrast, increasing the electricity supply requires almost no change in behaviour on the part of consumers (Schneider and Ingram, 1990, 1993a).

Game theory is one method used by third-generation analysts to assess how behavioural discretion influences implementation. Regulatory theorists such as Keith Hawkins (1984) and John Thomas (1989) noted how different levels of discretion could lead to very different regulatory styles in specific sectors and issue areas, not to mention jurisdictions (Kagan, 1994, 1996), as regulators could opt for or construct oversight systems based on either coercion or persuasion. This insight was used by analysts such as John Scholz (1984, 1991) to apply game-theoretic principles to the regulatory situation. Scholz demonstrated that the incentives and payoff for compliance and non-compliance on the part of the regulated could be matched to payoffs and incentives for regulators to use education or enforcement as implementation strategies.

A typical implementation game, therefore, would be one in which regulators would initiate implementation with efforts at persuasion, efforts that typically would be met by a failure of the regulated to comply. This would lead regulators to move towards more coercive rules in the next iteration, yielding a worse-off situation for both regulators and the regulated, who would face, respectively, high enforcement and high compliance costs. The game would then progress to an intermediate position in which coercion would be scaled back in exchange for compliance by the regulated, although this would be an unstable equilibrium requiring monitoring and temporary increases in coercion on the part of regulators to maintain ongoing compliance and avoid cheating.

This application of game theory to regulatory implementation generated interesting insights. However, it did not take into account a second key dimension of the implementation situation underscored in the top-down versus bottom-up debates: the divisions within the state itself that affect the ability of implementation on the ground to match the aims and expectations of enacting politicians.

This resulted in the application of a second type of game-theoretic model to the implementation stage; that of *principal–agent theory* (as discussed in Chapter 2).

Principal–Agent Theory

Administrative discretion is affected by the changing social, economic, technological, and political contexts of implementation (Hutter and Manning, 1990). Changes in social conditions may affect the interpretation of a policy problem that prompts adjustment of existing programs. For example, many of the challenges faced by social security programs in industrialized countries arise from the fact that they were not designed to cope with the ever-increasing proportion of the aged or continuous high rates of unemployment. Changes in economic conditions can have a similar impact. A program targeting the poor and unemployed, for instance, is more likely to change after an economic upturn or downturn. New technology also can be expected to change policy implementation options, such as when a more effective or cheaper pollution control technology yields adjustments in environmental policies. A new government may also trigger changes in the way policies are implemented. Conservative governments, for example, have been known to tighten the availability of social security programs established by labour or socialist governments without necessarily changing the policy itself (Mazmanian and Sabatier, 1983: 31).

Because of such variations in implementation contexts, civil servants can acquire a great deal of discretion in pursuing policy goals under changing environments. Civil servants also tend to become more expert in an administrative area than the generalists who staff political offices. Civil servants can then decide how and to whom the laws will be applied (Calvert et al., 1989; McCubbins et al., 1987, 1989), placing politicians and administrators in a particular kind of *principal–agent relationship*, such as those commonly found in associations between lawyer and client, physician and patient, or buyer–broker–seller, in which the principal is dependent on the goodwill of the agent to further his or her interests when it may not be in the interests of the agent to do so (Ellig and Lavoie, 1995; Francis, 1993; Banks, 1995). The particular dynamics of this relationship affects the tenor and quality of their interactions and limits the ability of political 'principals' to circumscribe effectively the behaviour of their erstwhile 'agents' (Bozeman, 1993; Milward and Provan, 1998).

One principal–agent problem that has long been recognized by policy researchers, for example, is the tendency for regulators (the agents in this case), over time, to identify more with the needs of the regulated than with their erstwhile political principals. At the extreme, this tendency is thought to undermine the regulatory structure and trigger its demise and replacement (Bernstein, 1955). This theory of *regulatory capture* is based on flaws in the principal–agent relationship that encourage such behaviour. Career patterns where individuals move back and forth between the government bureaucracy and industry employment over time, for example, allow the possibility that the individuals involved will consciously or unconsciously blur their interests and ambitions (Sabatier, 1975).

Principal–agent theorists argue that many noble efforts on the part of governments and citizens to create better and safer worlds have foundered on the 'realities' of implementation, where the actions of agents diverge from the intentions of their principals and thus distort policy outcomes. This insight has led not only to a greater appreciation of the difficulties encountered in policy implementation, but also has spurred attempts to design better policies in a manner offering a reasonable chance of success in implementation. While many government decisions continue to be taken without adequate attention to the difficulties of implementation, there is a growing recognition of the need to take these concerns into account at earlier stages of the policy process, such as policy formulation, through a process of complex *policy design* (Spence, 1999). It is usually easier and more effective for policy-makers to take implementation challenges into account and devise an appropriate response *ex ante* rather than *ex post* (Linder and Peters, 1984, 1988, 1990).

Implementation as Policy Design: Instrument Choices and Policy Mixes

Principal–agent theory pointed to the implications of the design of administrative structures for effective implementation and underlined the importance of mechanisms that ensure effective oversight of administrative actors by their political 'masters'. This focus extended the insight of 'bottom-up' implementation studies of the need for structures allowing senior officials to control street-level ones while granting those on the ground enough autonomy to perform their work effectively (McCubbins and McCubbins, 1994; McCubbins and Schwartz, 1984). This renewed emphasis on the significance of institutional design for effective policy implementation dovetailed in the 1990s with other efforts to study the characteristics of policy instruments and the reasons for their selection by governments, undertaken with the aim of improving the implementation process through improving the selection of tools for the job to be done.

The 'instrument choice' or 'policy design' approach to understanding policy implementation began from the observation that, to a great extent, policy implementation involves applying one or more of the basic techniques of government discussed in Chapter 5—variously known as *policy tools*, *policy instruments*, or *governing instruments*—to the resolution of policy problems in the form of a *policy mix* or blend of different instruments (see Bressers and Klok, 1988; Schneider and Ingram, 1990a: 513–14; McDonnell and Elmore, 1987; Elmore, 1978, 1987). This approach towards implementation begins from the premise that regardless of whether we study the implementation process in a top-down or bottom-up fashion, the process of giving substance to a government decision always involves choosing among several tools available that could each make a contribution to advancing policy (Hood, 1986a; Linder and Peters, 1991).

Systematic analyses of instrument choices usually begin with the attempt to identify a single or limited number of dimensions along which categories of policy instruments are said to vary. For this purpose, a useful distinction can be drawn among the instruments listed in Chapter 5 between their 'substantive' or 'procedural' nature, that is, between those affecting the substance of policy outputs and those directed instead towards the manipulation of policy processes associated with the delivery of those outputs. This distinction can be applied to taxonomies of policy instruments such as the 'NATO' scheme for classifying governing tools depending on the nature of the 'statecraft' resources, as identified by Christopher Hood (1986), that they primarily rely upon—nodality, authority, treasure, and organization (see also Anderson, 1977).

The four basic types of instruments in each category generated by this classification scheme are set out in Figure 7.1 below. These are the basic building blocks from which any policy mix is constructed (Howlett et al., 2006).

These kinds of instruments can be ranged on two scales depending on how particular instruments relate to the degree of manipulation of market and network actors they entail (see Figures 7.2 and 7.3).

After having developed these basic inventories and spectra of policy tools, as described in Chapter 5, the instrument choice perspective on policy implementation and design then addressed the question of why implementers do, or should, choose a particular instrument from among the many available: the question of the *rationale for instrument choice* (Doern and Phidd, 1983; Howlett, 1991).

Two different groups of scholars have worked on this question and the answers they have put forward have varied dramatically. Economists have for the most part tended to interpret the choice of policy instrument as, at least in theory, a technical exercise of matching the specific attributes of different types of tools to the characteristics of the job at hand. Political scientists, on the other hand, have

Figure 7.1   A Taxonomy of Basic Policy Instrument Components of a Policy Mix

		Resource Used			
		Nodality	Authority	Treasure	Organization
General Principle Governing Use	Substantive	Advice Training Reporting Registration	Regulation Self-regulation Licences Census-taking	Grants User charges Loans Tax credits Polling	Administration Public enterprises Policing Consultants Record-keeping
	Procedural	Information provision/ withdrawal	Treaties Advisory committees/ commissions	Interest group funding/ creation	Conferences Commissions of inquiry Government reorganizations

Note: Cells provide examples of instruments in each category.
Sources: Adapted from Christopher Hood, *The Tools of Government* (Chatham, NJ: Chatham House, 1986), 124–5; Michael Howlett, 'Managing the "Hollow State": Procedural Policy Instruments and Modern Governance', *Canadian Public Administration* 43, 4 (2000): 412–31.

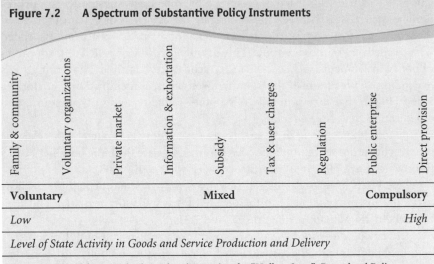

Figure 7.2   A Spectrum of Substantive Policy Instruments

Family & community | Voluntary organizations | Private market | Information & exhortation | Subsidy | Tax & user charges | Regulation | Public enterprise | Direct provision

Voluntary	Mixed	Compulsory
Low		High

Level of State Activity in Goods and Service Production and Delivery

Source: Adapted from Michael Howlett, 'Managing the "Hollow State": Procedural Policy Instruments and Modern Governance', *Canadian Public Administration* 43, 4 (2000): 412–31.

tended to argue that instruments are more or less substitutable on a purely technical basis, and have instead focused on the political forces they believe govern
instrument selection (see Peters and Van Nispen, 1998; Eliadis et al., 2005).

Studies by economists on the subject have been shaped by the theoretical
debates, discussed in Chapter 2, between neo-classical or public choice adherents
and welfare economists on the proper role of the state in the economy. While all
prefer voluntary instruments that allow markets to operate in the most unfettered

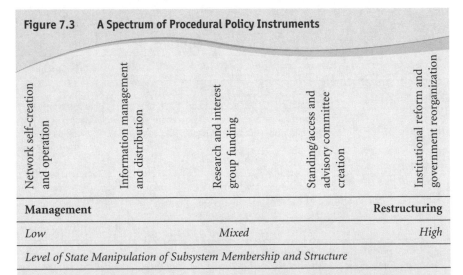

Figure 7.3   A Spectrum of Procedural Policy Instruments

Network self-creation and operation | Information management and distribution | Research and interest group funding | Standing/access and advisory committee creation | Institutional reform and government reorganization

Management		Restructuring
Low	Mixed	High

Level of State Manipulation of Subsystem Membership and Structure

Source: Adapted from Michael Howlett, 'Managing the "Hollow State": Procedural Policy Instruments and Modern Governance', *Canadian Public Administration* 43, 4 (2000): 412–31.

fashion, some welfare economists permit greater scope for the use of other kinds of instruments by governments in order to correct market failures (Bator, 1958; Economic Council of Canada, 1979; Utton, 1986; Howse et al., 1990). In contrast, neo-classical analysts approve the use of such instruments only for providing pure public goods; their use for any other reason is viewed as distorting the market process and leading to suboptimal aggregate social outcomes (Breyer, 1979, 1982; Posner, 1974; Stigler, 1975; Wolf, 1987). Welfare economists' greater theoretical acceptance of state intervention leads them to more systematic analyses of instrument choice. However, like their more ascetic colleagues, they still tend to treat the choice of instrument as a strictly technical exercise that consists of evaluating the features of various instruments, matching them to different types of market failures, estimating their relative costs, and choosing the instrument that most efficiently overcomes the market failure in question (Mitnick, 1980; Stokey and Zeckhauser, 1978; Weimer and Vining, 1992).

Other economists use public choice theory to explain patterns of instrument use. As we saw in Chapter 2, public choice theory argues that in a democracy the dynamic of self-serving behaviour by voters, politicians, and bureaucrats promotes an increasing tendency to tax and spend, and to regulate and nationalize private activity. It is argued that democratic politics leads states to choose instruments that provide concentrated benefits to marginal voters while spreading the costs to the entire population (see Buchanan, 1980; Trebilcock and Hartle, 1982; Wilson, 1974). For electoral reasons, it is claimed, governments make efforts to choose instruments that do not reveal their true costs to the voters who ultimately pay for them.

While the incorporation of political factors into the analysis of instrument choices is an improvement on some aspects of earlier economic approaches, public choice analyses ultimately do little to further the explanation of systematic patterns of instrument choices. It is very difficult, for example, to match types of instruments with patterns of the distribution of costs and benefits (Wilson, 1974) since one must first know whether governments want to claim credit or avoid blame for the action to be undertaken (Weaver, 1986; Hood, 2002). Most instruments can be used for both purposes, and which purpose motivates a government depends on highly idiosyncratic and contextual factors relatively far removed from the implementation process.

Economic theories of instrument choice tend to be overly deductive and lack a solid empirical base in studies of actual instrument choice by governments. The rationales for policy instrument choice they provide are for the most part based on theoretical assumptions concerning what governments ought to do, rather than on empirical investigations into what they actually do (Howard, 1995; Bohm and Russell, 1985; Peters, 2002). Studies by political scientists, the second group that has devoted much effort to implementation, instruments, and policy design studies, as the following discussion will show, tend to display a wider variety of factors influencing instrument choices and are generally more empirical in nature. To those looking for theoretical parsimony, however, they may not appear as elegant as the studies generated by economists, but they help to grapple with the complexity of actual policy instrument use and inductively develop a plausible theory of instrument choice in policy implementation (see Howlett, 1991).

One oft-cited political science approach to theorizing the question of policy instrument choice was developed in the 1970s by Bruce Doern and several of his Canadian associates (Doern, 1981; Phidd and Doern, 1983; Tupper and Doern, 1981). Assuming that all instruments are *technically substitutable*—that is, that at least in theory any instrument could be bent, shaped, and twisted to perform any task—they argued that in liberal-democratic societies governments would simply *prefer* to use the least coercive instruments available. These, generally, would involve the least cost and effort on their part while complying with the fundamental ideological faith in markets held by liberal-democratic governments and, often, while also complying with constitutional and other kinds of institutional constraints placed on government action. For Doern, a government would 'move up the scale' towards the use of more 'interventionist' or coercive instruments as necessary to overcome any societal resistance it encountered to the achievement of its aims. In other words, while any instrument can theoretically accomplish any chosen aim, governments choose the least coercive instruments possible for the task at hand, given the level of societal resistance they encounter to their actions. Overall, this conception led Doern and his colleagues to suggest that a typical pattern of instrument use in many states was for governments to begin with minimal activities such as exhortation and move slowly, if at all, towards direct provision.

Later, these studies turned to the question of whether these choices resulted in any distinctive implementation patterns that could be discerned among the policy efforts of different jurisdictions or sectors (Rothmayr et al., 1997). Answering this latter question moved implementation analysis further away from its roots in the study of public administration and helped to integrate implementation research with the policy sciences. Specifically, these studies highlighted the close links among policy formulation, decision-making, and implementation.

As we have seen in Chapter 5, instrument selection is a complex activity influenced by factors such as the nature of the subsystem involved and especially its propensity to allow new actors and new ideas to penetrate into policy deliberations. Whether or not the selected instrument will actually be able to address an issue depends both on the particular options chosen by governments and on the implementation context, including compliance games and principal–agent problems, as well as the manner in which current implementation choices relate to their articulated goals and to those goals and means already implemented in complex policy and program mixes.

This latter point is a significant one that will be discussed in further detail in Chapter 9. Suffice it to say at this point, however, that instrument choices, to be effective, must be closely and carefully related to policy goals, and that any new goals and tools must also be carefully integrated with existing policies if implementation is to succeed. New and old goals must be *coherent*, in the sense of being logically related, while new and old instrument choices must be *consistent*, in the sense of not operating at cross-purposes (see Figure 7.4).

Figure 7.4   Relationship of Policy Goals and Means in Policy Implementation

		Policy Tools	
		Consistent	Inconsistent
Policy Goals	Coherent	Optimal	Ineffective
	Incoherent	Misdirected	Failed or suboptimal

Note: Cells indicate likely outcome of implementation contexts.
Source: Michael Howlett and Jeremy Rayner. 'Design Principles for Policy Mixes: Cohesion and Coherence in "New Governance Arrangements"', *Policy and Society* 26, 4 (2007): 1–18.

Thus, in this perspective, policy design is a task that involves more than just policy formulation, but also decision-making and implementation if policies are to be successfully carried out. Policy-makers must strive to attain an optimal matching of goals and means in the implementation process in order to successfully attain those goals, but this process is fraught with challenges and the risk of failure.

Implementation Styles and Long-Term Instrument Preferences

Implementation research over the past 30 years has generated many insights into this stage of the policy cycle, which shed a great deal of light on the possibilities and constraints affecting instrument use and the ability of practitioners to design and improve these efforts (O'Toole, 2004). While some studies undertaken in this vein have been, and continue to be, influenced by the idea that implementation is purely technical in nature, and hence open to rapid change and reconfiguration, most studies have linked implementation activities to larger-scale and more permanent arrangements of policy actors and instruments, or 'modes of operation' and 'implementation styles' (Spicker, 2005, 2006).

Despite somewhat different methodologies and frameworks, these approaches share the view that implementation involves much more than simply executing previously arrived at decisions. They endorse the notion that policy implementation can only be meaningfully understood and evaluated in terms of the existing range of policy actors present in the policy subsystem, the kind of resources that policy actors have at their disposal, and the nature of the problem they are trying to address and the ideas they have about how to go about addressing it, all in the context of the policy regime in which they are working (Bressers and O'Toole, 1998, 2005; Bressers, 1998). This complexity and the ever-present possibility of failure lead implementers to develop distinct preferences for substantive and procedural instruments that they know work well together and that have succeeded previously in the sector involved or, in the event of a new issue area, in other similar sectors.

Instrument preferences or *implementation styles* develop as a function of these factors, which ultimately can be related to the kind of problems implementers face, especially their 'tractability', or ease of solution, and the severity of the constraints policy-makers face in implementing solutions to those problems. That is, as we have seen in other chapters, some problems are more 'resolvable' than others or, to put it another way, are more susceptible to resolution through simple solutions over relatively short periods of time, within the range of ideas found in the existing policy community about what constitutes an appropriate action (Schon, 1994; Hisschemoller and Hoppe, 1995). 'Tractability' is thus very much a function of the level of complexity of the policy subsystem involved, while the kinds of constraints policy actors face in terms of their endowments of specific types of governing resources also serve as a longer-term restriction on their ability to use specific types of policy tools.

These factors affect the choice of both procedural and substantive governing instruments (Saward, 1992; Rhodes, 1997; Howse et al., 1990; Bennett, 1992). Effective use of both types of instrument requires that a government has the capacity to effect changes, while the actual extent of resource use required will vary with the size and complexity of the policy actors it is attempting to influence (see Saward, 1990; Bryson and Crosby, 1993; Maloney, 2001). Governments with a high capacity for facing complex policy environments are often able to use 'directive' procedural instruments such as government reorganization to create new, or restructure existing, policy subsystems or markets (see Suchman, 1995; Heritier, 1997, 1999). Lower-capacity governments facing policy environments of lower complexity often can rely on instruments such as information manipulation to affect the behaviour of policy actors. Where low-capacity governments face complex implementation environments they are not able to rely on information provision to alter actor behaviour, but they can use selective funding to support specific actors or to create new ones to meet their needs (see King and Walker, 1991; Browne, 1991; Pal, 1993). In low-complexity situations, high-capacity governments can more directly alter subsystem and market structures by recognizing new actors or privileging old ones through authoritative means, for example, by establishing specialized independent regulatory commissions or quasi-independent advisory committees and/or quangos, which favour certain actors and ideas over others (see Hood, 1986b, 1988; Brown, 1972; Smith, 1977; Dion, 1973).

Although numerous permutations and combinations are possible, putting these two types of instruments and key variables together leads to the model of basic instrument preferences found in Figure 7.5.

This discussion does not delve into the detail of fine gradations of instrument use within each general category of instrument, of course, nor does it deal with the specific contexts of individual decisions, which can result in errors being made in instrument choices (see Varone and Landry, 1997), nor does it fully address the question about optimal and suboptimal instrument mixes in particular policy areas or sectors, a subject discussed in more detail in Chapter 9. However, it suggests that although instrument choices are complex, general patterns of such choices can nevertheless be discerned and explained by focusing on the actors, institutions, and ideas with which policy implementers work; and that on this basis, advice can be rendered to public managers about which types of instruments

Figure 7.5   A Model of Basic Instrument Preferences

		Nature of the Policy Subsystem	
		Complex	Simple
Severity of Constraints on State	High	Focus on directive instruments (e.g., direct provision and government reorganizations)	Focus on authoritative instruments (e.g., regulation and advisory committees)
	Low	Focus on subsidy instruments (e.g., grants and interest group funding)	Focus on information instruments (e.g., advertising campaigns and information disclosure)

are likely to succeed in specific implementation contexts (see Bressers, 1998; Bressers and O'Toole, 1998; Mandell, 2000).

Conclusion: Subsystem Complexity and Issue Tractability as Key Determinants of Implementation Success and Failure

The central assumption of most contemporary approaches to policy implementation is that this stage of the policy process is shaped by political factors related to state capacity to deal with specific issues and the complexity of the subsystem with which it must deal (Atkinson, 1989: 114). This explains why patterns of government instrument choices, as Doern suggested, exhibit a surprising amount of similarity and continuity within and across policy sectors over time, constituting relatively long-lasting implementation styles.

These styles vary by jurisdiction and issue so that what British policy-makers might typically accomplish through public enterprises, for example, might be implemented in the US through regulations. At the sectoral level, this is something economists repeatedly find, to their displeasure, when their proposals for using new types of complex economic instruments to control social ills such as pollution are rejected in favour of the continuing use of regulation, as has become almost habitual in many countries for dealing with this type of problem (Doern, 1998; Doern and Wilks, 1998; Stavins, 2001). A focus on relatively long-standing political factors related to state capacity and subsystem complexity helps to explain why these long-lasting styles of instrument choice exist at both the sectoral and national levels and also helps to assess their propensity for implementation success and failure.

Thus, tractable problems in low-constraint situations can result in 'full' implementation, where problems can be addressed in their entirety and fully resolved. Constructing a new highway route to a city, for example, can often result in the complete elimination of the transportation concerns that prompted its construction. At the other extreme, highly intractable problems are rarely completely

Figure 7.6	Implementation Modes and Their Potential to Resolve Problems

		Nature of the Problem	
		Tractable	*Non-tractable*
Severity Constraints	*Low*	Full implementation (highway construction)	Experimental implementation (children's reading ability)
	High	Contested implementation (health care)	Symbolic implementation (elimination of poverty)

Source: Adapted from R.E. Matland, 'Synthesizing the Implementation Literature: The Ambiguity-Conflict Model of Policy Implementation', *Journal of Public Administration Research and Theory* 5, 2 (1995): 145–74.

addressed and resolved. With low constraints, such issues might be dealt with by experimentation with new policy instruments and tools or, if constraints are higher, through only symbolic efforts at a resolution. The many experiments undertaken with child literacy programs are a good example of the former case, while the often token gestures made in the direction of the elimination of poverty are an unfortunate example of the latter. Finally, where problems are theoretically tractable or treatable but where practical constraints are high, it is often the case that implementation becomes a contested field in which implementers struggle to enhance their resources in order to fully resolve the issue concerned. These ideal types are set out in Figure 7.6.

Policy actors can try to enhance their capacity to deal with implementation problems and overcome resource constraints in numerous ways, including, in the case of administrators, through enhancement of their analytical capacity for environmental monitoring and forecasting and, hence, better policy design (Painter and Pierre, 2005; Anderson, 1996; Bakvis, 2000), and, in the case of politicians, through creation of specialized central agencies and implementation units designed to concentrate resources on difficult problems (Lindquist, 2006). However, many of these resource constraints and problems are very difficult to overcome and can result in long-standing modes of implementation developing in varied issue areas that are highly resistant to change.

Study Questions

1. Is it harder to implement solutions to wicked problems than it is to formulate solutions? Why?
2. Why is it common for a gap to emerge between the intentions of decision-makers and the outcomes of implementation?
3. How does the role of bureaucracy differ in implementation from other stages of the process?
4. What can governments do to solve intractable problems (e.g., ending poverty)?

Further Readings

Bardach, Eugene. 1977. *The Implementation Game: What Happens after a Bill Becomes a Law*. Cambridge, Mass.: MIT Press.

Ellig, Jerry, and Don Lavoie. 1995. 'The Principal–Agent Relationship in Organizations', in P. Foss, ed., *Economic Approaches to Organizations and Institutions: An Introduction*. Aldershot: Dartmouth.

Goggin, Malcolm L., et al. 1990. *Implementation Theory and Practice: Toward a Third Generation*. Glenview, Ill.: Scott, Foresman/Little, Brown.

Howlett, Michael. 2005. 'What Is a Policy Instrument? Policy Tools, Policy Mixes and Policy Implementation Styles', in P. Eliadis, M. Hill, and M. Howlett, eds, *Designing Government: From Instruments to Governance*. Montreal and Kingston: McGill-Queen's University Press, 31–50.

———— and Jeremy Rayner. 2007. 'Design Principles for Policy Mixes: Cohesion and Coherence in "New Governance Arrangements"', *Policy and Society* 26, 4: 1–18.

Howse, R., J.R.S. Prichard, and M.J. Trebilcock. 1990. 'Smaller or Smarter Government?', *University of Toronto Law Journal* 40: 498–541.

Kagan, Robert A. 1991. 'Adversarial Legalism and American Government', *Journal of Policy Analysis and Management* 10, 3: 369–406.

Lipsky, Michael. 1980. *Street-Level Bureaucracy: Dilemmas of the Individual in Public Services*. New York: Russell Sage Foundation.

O'Toole, Laurence J. 2000. 'Research on Policy Implementation: Assessment and Prospects', *Journal of Public Administration Research and Theory* 10, 2: 263–88.

Pressman, Jeffrey L., and Aaron B. Wildavsky. 1984. *Implementation: How Great Expectations in Washington Are Dashed in Oakland*, 3rd edn. Berkeley: University of California Press.

Schneider, Anne, and Helen Ingram. 1993. 'Social Construction of Target Populations: Implications for Politics and Policy', *American Political Science Review* 87, 2: 334–47.

Simon, H.A. 1946. 'The Proverbs of Administration', *Public Administration Review* 6: 53–67.

Chapter 8

Policy Evaluation:
Policy-Making as Learning

Once the need to address a public problem has been acknowledged, various possible solutions have been considered, and some among them have been selected and put into practice, a government often assesses how the policy is working. At the same time, various other interested members of policy subsystems and of the general public are engaged in their own assessment of the workings and effects of the policy in order to express support for or opposition to the policy, or to demand changes to it. The concept of *policy evaluation* thus refers broadly to the stage of the policy process at which it is determined how a public policy has actually fared in action. It involves the evaluation of the means being employed and the objectives being served. As Larry Gerston (1997: 120) has defined it, 'policy evaluation assesses the effectiveness of a public policy in terms of its perceived intentions and results.' How deep or thorough the evaluation is depends on those initiating and/or undertaking it, and what they intend to do with the findings.

After a policy has been evaluated, the problem and solutions it involves may be completely reconceptualized, in which case the cycle may swing back to agenda-setting or some other stage of the cycle, or the status quo may be maintained. Reconceptualization may consist of minor changes or fundamental reformulation of the problem, including terminating the policy altogether (DeLeon, 1983). How evaluation is conducted, the problems the exercise entails, and the range of results to which it typically leads are the concerns of this chapter. It then outlines the patterns of policy change that typically result from different types of policy evaluation.

Positivist and Post-Positivist Policy Evaluation

For the most part, policy evaluation has been the analytical domain of those who view such assessment as a neutral, technical exercise in determining the success (or failure) of government efforts to deal with policy problems. David Nachmias (1979: 4), an influential figure in the field's early development, captured this positivist spirit in defining policy evaluation as 'the objective systematic, empirical examination of the effects ongoing policies and public programs have on their targets in terms of the goals they are meant to achieve'. Discerning readers will have no difficulty detecting the rationalist premise underlying this definition. It specifies explicitly that examining a policy's effects on the achievement of its goals should be objective, systematic, and empirical, the hallmarks of the positivist approach to policy analysis. However, as we have mentioned before, public policy goals are often neither clear nor explicit, necessitating subjective interpretation to determine what exactly was achieved. Objective analysis is further limited by the difficulties encountered in developing neutral standards by which to evaluate government success in dealing with societal demands and socially constructed problems in a highly politicized environment.

After much work in the 1960s and 1970s to develop quantitative systems of policy evaluation, it became clear (Anderson, 1979a; Kerr, 1976; Manzer, 1984) that developing adequate and acceptable measures for evaluating policy was more contentious and problematic than was previously believed. Astute observers also noted that it was naive to believe that policy evaluation was always intended to reveal the effects of a policy. In fact, it is at times employed to disguise or conceal certain facts that a government fears will show it in a poor light. It is also possible for governments to design the terms of evaluation in such a way as to lead to conclusions that would show it in a better light. Or, if it wants to change or scrap a policy, it can adjust the terms of the evaluation accordingly. Similarly, evaluation by those outside the government is not always designed to improve a policy, but often to criticize it in order to gain partisan political advantage or to reinforce ideological postulates (Chelimsky, 1995; Bovens and t'Hart, 1995).

As a result, more recent thinking tends to view policy evaluation, like other stages of the policy process, as an inherently political activity, albeit, like the other stages, with a technical component. In its extreme, post-positivist form, it has been argued that since the same condition can be interpreted quite differently by different evaluators, there is no definitive way of determining the correct evaluation mode. Which interpretation prevails, in this view, is ultimately determined by political conflicts and compromises among the various actors (Ingram and Mann, 1980b: 852).

This is not to suggest that policy evaluation is an irrational or a purely political process, devoid of genuine intentions to assess the functioning of a policy and its effects. Rather, it serves as a warning that we must be aware that relying solely on formal evaluation for drawing conclusions about a policy's relative success or failure will yield unduly limited insights about policy outcomes and their assessment. To get the most out of policy evaluation, the limits of rationality and the political forces that shape it must also be taken into account, without going so far as to believe that the subjective nature of policy assessments allows no meaningful evaluation to take place.

Policy Evaluation as Policy Learning

One way of looking at policy evaluation, which combines elements of both the positivist and post-positivist perspectives, is to regard it as a very significant stage in an overall process of *policy learning* (Grin and Loeber, 2007; Lehtonen, 2005). That is, perhaps the greatest benefits of policy evaluation are not the direct results it generates in terms of definitive assessments of the success and failure of particular policies per se, but rather the educational dynamic that it can stimulate among policy-makers as well as others less directly involved in policy issues

(Pressman and Wildavsky, 1984). Whether they realize it or not, actors engaged in policy evaluation are often participating in a larger process of policy learning, in which improvements or enhancements to policy-making and policy outcomes can be brought about through careful and deliberate assessment of how past stages of the policy cycle affected both the original goals adopted by governments and the means implemented to address them (see Etheredge and Short, 1983; Sabatier, 1988; Lehtonen, 2006).

The concept of 'learning' is generally associated with intentional, progressive, cognitive consequences of the education that results from policy evaluation. However, policy learning also has a broader meaning that includes understanding both the intended and unintended (see Merton, 1936) consequences of policy-making activities, as well as both the 'positive' and 'negative' implications of existing policies and their alternatives on the status quo and efforts to alter it. From a learning perspective, public policy evaluation is conceived as an iterative process of active learning about the nature of policy problems and the potential of various solutions to address them (Rist, 1994; Levitt and March, 1988). This view shares some similarities with the idea of policy-making as a 'trial-and-error' process of policy experimentation, but with the added idea that successive 'rounds' of policy-making, if carefully evaluated after each 'round', can avoid repeating mistakes and move policy implementation ever closer towards the achievement of desired goals.

Like other concepts in policy science, there are differing interpretations of what is meant by 'policy learning' and whether its source and motivation are within or outside existing policy processes. Peter Hall makes the case for '*endogenous*' learning, defining the activity as a 'deliberate attempt to adjust the goals or techniques of policy in the light of the consequences of past policy and new information so as to better attain the ultimate objects of governance' (Hall, 1993: 278). Hugh Heclo, on the other hand, suggests that learning is a less conscious, '*exogenous*' activity, often occurring as a government's response to some kind of external or exogenous change in a policy environment. According to Heclo, this often takes the form of an almost automatic process, as 'learning can be taken to mean a relatively enduring alteration in behaviour that results from experience; usually this alteration is conceptualized as a change in response made in reaction to some perceived stimulus' (Heclo, 1974: 306). The two definitions describe the same relationship between policy learning and policy change, but differ substantially in their approach to the issue. For Hall, learning is a part of the normal public policy process in which policy-makers attempt to understand why certain initiatives may have succeeded while others failed. If policies change as a result of learning, the impetus for change originates within the normal policy process of the government. For Heclo, on the other hand, policy learning is seen as an activity undertaken by policy-makers largely in reaction to changes in external policy 'environments'. As the environment changes, policy-makers must adapt if their policies are to succeed.

Regardless of its external or internal causes, however, most scholars agree that several types of learning can result from different kinds of evaluations.

Assessments can be carried out by both governmental and non-governmental actors at this stage of the policy cycle, since the number of actors involved in evaluation expands towards the size of the policy universe existing during agenda-setting (Bennett and Howlett, 1991; May, 1992; Sabatier, 1988; Hall, 1993; Etheredge, 1981; see also Argyris, 1992; Argyris and Schon, 1978). Some lessons are likely to concern practical suggestions about specific aspects of the policy cycle, based on the actual experience with the policy on the part of policy implementers and target groups. These include, for example, their perceptions of the lessons they have learned about which policy instruments have 'succeeded' in which circumstances and which have 'failed' to accomplish expected tasks or goals, or which issues have enjoyed public support in the agenda-setting process and which have not, and therefore which are likely to do so in future. Richard Rose (1988, 1991) defined one such relatively specific and limited type of learning as *lesson-drawing*. This type of learning originates within the formal policy process and is aimed primarily at the choice of means or techniques employed by policy-makers in their efforts to achieve their goals; in Rose's formulation this often involves the analysis of, and derivation of lessons from, experiences in other sectors, issue areas, or jurisdictions.

Other lessons probe broader policy goals and their underlying ideas or paradigms, or the 'frames' in which lesson-drawing takes place. This is a more fundamental type of learning, which is accompanied by changes in the thinking underlying a policy that might result in a policy being terminated or drastically revised in light of new conceptions and ideas developed through the evaluation process. Following Hall (1993), this type of learning is often referred to as *social learning*. It tends to originate outside the formal policy process and affects the policy-makers' capacity to change society.

Evidence-based Policy-Making as Policy Learning

'Evidence-based policy-making' is a term that has come into use in recent years as policy practitioners have struggled to enhance the rationality of policy deliberations and promote improved policy learning on the part of governments. It represents an effort to reform or restructure policy processes by prioritizing data-based evidentiary decision-making criteria over less formal or more 'intuitive' or experiential policy assessments in order to avoid or minimize policy failures caused by a mismatch between government expectations and actual, on-the-ground conditions. The evidence-based policy movement (Pawson, 2006) is thus the latest in a series of efforts undertaken by reformers in governments over the past half-century to enhance the efficiency and effectiveness of public policy-making through the application of a systematic evaluative rationality to policy problems (Sanderson, 2006; Mintrom, 2007).

Exactly what constitutes 'evidence-based policy-making' and whether analytical efforts in this regard actually result in better or improved policies are contentious (Packwood, 2002; Pawson, 2002; Tenbensel, 2004; Jackson, 2007). Through a process of theoretically informed empirical analysis consciously directed towards promoting policy learning, however, proponents of this approach believe that governments can better learn from experience, avoid repeating the errors of the past, and better apply new techniques to the resolution of old and new problems (Sanderson, 2002a, 2002b).

Assessing Policy Success or Failure

Policy evaluation is made challenging by the difficulties that arise in assessing the success or failure of policy initiatives. As Bovens and t'Hart (1996: 4) have argued, 'the absence of fixed criteria for success and failure, which apply regardless of time and place, is a serious problem' for anyone who wants to understand policy evaluation. Policies can succeed or fail in numerous ways. Sometimes an entire policy regime can fail, while more often specific programs within a policy field may be designated as successful or unsuccessful (Mucciaroni, 1990; Moran, 2001; Gundel, 2005). And both policies and programs can succeed or fail either in substantive terms—that is, delivering or failing to deliver the goods—or in procedural terms—as being legitimate or illegitimate, fair or unfair, just or unjust (Bovens and t'Hart, 1995; Weaver, 1986; McGraw, 1990; Hood, 2002).

'Success' is always hard to define. In some instances of an unequivocal disaster, like an airplane crash or nuclear reactor meltdown, analyses can pinpoint obvious causes such as technical failures, managerial incompetence, or corruption (Bovens and t'Hart, 1996; Gray and t'Hart, 1998). Evaluation can also uncover lesser-known causes of breakdown such as 'practical drift', in which increasingly large deviations from expected norms are allowed to occur until, finally, significant system failure occurs (Vaughan, 1996). Although some of the lessons drawn from these spectacular accidents—such as the significant potential for failure of complex organizational systems when elements are either too loosely or too tightly coupled (Perrow, 1984)—can be translated into policy studies, the causes behind more typical policy failures, such as overspending on project development or the unintended consequences of a policy initiative, are harder to pin down.

Failures can occur at any stage of the policy cycle and do not necessarily have their source in the same stage (Michael, 2006). Thus, an overly ambitious government may agree to address intractable ('wicked') problems (Pressman and Wildavsky, 1973; Churchman, 1967) at the agenda-setting stage, a decision that can lead to failure at any succeeding stage of the policy cycle. Failure can also arise from a mismatch between goals and means at the formulation stage (Busenberg, 2000, 2001, 2004a, 2004b), or it can result from the consequences of lapses or mis-judgements at the decision-making stage (Bovens and t'Hart, 1995, 1996; Perrow, 1984; Roots, 2004; Merton, 1936). Another set of pitfalls arises through various 'implementation failures' in which the aims of decision-makers fail to be properly or accurately translated into practice (Kerr, 1976; Ingram and Mann, 1980). Policy failure can also arise from a lack of effective oversight by decision-makers over those who implement policy (McCubbins and Schwartz, 1984; McCubbins and Lupia, 1994; Ellig and Lavoie, 1995). Finally, failure can stem from governments and policy-makers not effectively evaluating policy processes and learning useful lessons from past experiences (May, 1992; Scharpf, 1986; Busenberg, 2000, 2001, 2004a, 2004b).

In many circumstances, the operation of a policy system is too idiosyncratic, the actors too numerous, and the number of outcomes too small to permit clear and unambiguous post-mortems of *policy outcomes*. Nevertheless, such efforts are made by many actors with varying degrees of formality and the results of these investigations, whether accurate or not, are fed back into the policy process, influencing the direction and content of further policy cycle iterations.

The role of actors at this stage is crucial. Different types of evaluations can be undertaken by different sets of actors and can have very different impacts on subsequent policy deliberations and activities (Fischer and Forester, 1987). As Bovens and t'Hart (ibid., 21) note, ultimately 'judgements about the failure or success of public policies or programs are highly malleable. Failure is not inherent in policy events themselves. "Failure" is a judgement about events.' These judgements about policy success and failure often depend partly on imputing notions of intentionality to government actors, assuming that there was a 'method to the madness' and that policy actors meant to achieve what their actions produced. Intentionality makes it possible to assess policy-making results against expectations. However, even with this rational assumption, assessment is not a simple task (see Sieber, 1981: ch. 2). First, as we have seen, government intentions may be vague and ambiguous, or even potentially contradictory or mutually exclusive. Second, labels such as 'success' and 'failure' are inherently relative and will be interpreted differently by different policy actors and observers. Moreover, such designations are also semantic tools used in public debates to seek political advantage. That is, policy evaluations affect considerations and consequences related to assessing blame and taking credit for government activities at all stages of the policy process, all of which can have electoral, administrative, and other consequences for policy actors (Bovens and t'Hart, 1996: 9; Brandstrom and Kuipers, 2003; Twight, 1991; Hood, 2002; Hood and Rothstein, 2001).

Such judgements, by nature, are at least partially linked to factors such as the nature of the causal theories used to frame policy problems at the agenda-setting and policy formulation stages and the conceptual solutions developed at the formulation stage. The expectations of decision-makers about likely program or policy results and the extent of time allowed for those results to materialize before evaluators make their assessments are other important factors (Bovens and t'Hart, 1996: 37). Policy evaluation processes, recognizing these built-in biases, often simply aim to provide enough information to make reasonably intelligent and defensible claims about policy outcomes, rather than offering definitive explanations that build airtight cases concerning their absolute level of success or failure.

Actors in the Policy Evaluation Process

A good part of the complexity of policy evaluation is due to the fact that different sets of actors in the policy universe and subsystem are simultaneously or sequentially involved in different kinds of formal and informal evaluation activities. Whatever the dynamic of these efforts—overlapping, competing, or co-ordinated—the need to understand who is involved and what they bring to policy evaluation points to the need to have a clear understanding of the different kinds of policy evaluators that exist.

Evaluation almost always involves bureaucrats and politicians within government dealing with the policy in question in a formalized and often institutionalized and regularized way, as is the case, for example, with ongoing budgetary and program reviews. But it typically also involves organized non-governmental members of policy subsystems—such as think-tanks and interest groups—that conduct their own, less formal, reviews of government behaviour and effectiveness. In addition, evaluations may also involve members of the public, who often will have the ultimate say on a government's policy record when they vote at elections (Brewer and DeLeon, 1983: 319–26) or comment to the media or pollsters about it.[1] Thus, the sites, range, and types of policy evaluation are much broader than often presented in the mainstream evaluation literature, which tends to concentrate overwhelmingly on evaluation by bureaucrats and 'outside' private consultants and think-tanks. Consultants are playing an increasingly important role in evaluation (Speers, 2007; Dent, 2002; Perl and White, 2002; Lapsley and Oldfield, 2001; Martin, 1998; Saint-Martin, 1998; Bakvis, 1997). Think-tanks, on the other hand, once played an important role in many countries in assessing and critiquing policies, but their proliferation and the trend towards their identification with specific partisan interests have greatly undermined their ability to affect policy discourses and directions through their evaluative activities (McGann and Johnson, 2005; Rich, 2004; Abelson, 2002, 2007; Ladi, 2005; Stone, 2007; Lindquist, 2004).

At one extreme, policy analysts working in departments or specialized units in the administration routinely apply formal techniques such as cost-benefit analysis (Boardman et al., 2001; Sinden and Thampapillai, 1995) or various kinds of performance measures to try to quantify program outputs and accurately assess program results (see Meltsner, 1976; Friedman, 2002). These analysts can have a substantial impact on subsequent rounds of policy-making because of several different roles they can play in the evaluation process. They can affect the 'framing' and assessment of policy success and failure by how they develop and apply various measures, indicators, and benchmarks to program outputs, or sometimes serve as critics or 'advocates' of particular approaches to problems (see Davies, 1999; de la Porte et al., 2001; Levy, 2001). They can also serve as 'brokers' linking policy-makers to implementers, or to those outside the formal institutions of government who are generating new knowledge on social problems and the techniques for resolving or attempting to resolve these problems (see Meltsner, 1976; Guess and Farnham, 2000).

At the other extreme, public protests by affected individuals and interest groups also represent an evaluation of the merits of existing policies, although this kind of evaluation is post hoc, informal, and external to the intra-governmental policy 'loop'. Such evaluations may involve critiques of both the substance and process of policy, and can lead to changes in administrative organizations and procedures, such as an increase or decrease in access to information by the public (see Snow and Benford, 1992). In between these two poles lie a variety of other venues and means of policy evaluation that involve institutionalized links between formal and informal policy evaluators in government and civil society. These include the judiciary, which is able to review legislative and administrative actions to determine the extent to which policies match up to larger, often constitutionally established principles of social justice and conduct (see de Smith, 1973; Edley, 1990; Humphries and Songer, 1999; Jaffe, 1965). They also include more recent efforts on the part of administrators to bring public views into the evaluative process through the use of such procedural instruments as focus groups, surveys, inquiries, citizens' juries, consensus conferences, and advisory committees (see Hastak et al., 2001; Peters and Parker, 1993; Schwartz, 1997; Wraith and Lamb, 1971).

Types of Policy Evaluation

Fundamental to policy evaluation is its impact on effecting policy changes. After all, the implicit purpose of policy evaluation is to change a policy if it is deemed necessary as a result of undertaking a review (Feick, 1992). This makes activity at this 'final' stage of the policy cycle critical, since in most cases new activities and new rounds of policy-making will result from, or follow, the output of evaluative processes. The activity of several distinct types of evaluators result in several distinct types of policy analysis and evaluation. At a general level, policy evaluations can be classified into three broad categories—*administrative evaluation*, *judicial evaluation*, and *political evaluation*—which differ in the way they are conducted, the actors they involve, and their effects.

Administrative Evaluation

Administrative evaluation is well represented in the academic literature on policy evaluation. It is usually undertaken within a government, occasionally by specialist agencies whose only task is to evaluate policies, but more often by financial, legal, and political overseers attached to existing government departments, specialized executive agencies, legislatures, and judiciaries. Private consultants may also be hired by the various branches and agencies of the government to conduct evaluation for a fee.

Administrative evaluation is usually, though not always, restricted to examining the efficient delivery of government services and attempting to determine whether 'value for money' is being achieved while still respecting principles of justice and democracy. It is intended to ensure that policies are accomplishing their expected goals at the least possible cost and with the least possible burden on individual citizens. This passion for efficiency has inspired numerous formal evaluative systems, such as managerial performance and personnel reviews, as well as the conduct of annual audits and the creation of budgeting systems that attempt to better match goals and expenditures than has been the case with traditional

administrative techniques. Administrative evaluation requires collection of precise information ('evidence') on program delivery and its compilation in a stan-
dardized fashion in order to allow comparisons of costs and outcomes over time
and across policy sectors. As such, these efforts are quite technical and increasingly sophisticated, although the increase in complexity is not necessarily
matched by a similar increase in usefulness (Friedman, 2002).

Administrative policy evaluations come in a variety of forms and differ widely
in levels of sophistication and formality. Those undertaken by government agencies and arm's-length 'non-partisan agencies' (Hird, 2005) are generally of five
different types: (1) process evaluation; (2) effort evaluation; (3) performance
evaluation; (4) efficiency evaluation; and (5) effectiveness evaluation (Suchman,
1967; Davidson, 2005).

Process evaluations examine the organizational methods, including rules and
operating procedures, used to deliver programs. The objective is usually to see if a
process can be streamlined and made more efficient. Towards this objective, implementation of a policy is usually broken down into discrete tasks, such as strategic
planning, financial management, and client relations, and then one or more of
these tasks are evaluated for efficiency, effectiveness, and/or accountability.

Effort evaluation attempts to measure the quantity of program inputs, that is,
the amount of effort governments put into accomplishing their goals. The input
may be personnel, office space, communication, transportation, and so on—all of
which are calculated in terms of the monetary costs involved. The purpose of this
evaluation is to establish baseline data that can be used for subsequent assessment
of efficiency or quality of service delivery.

Performance evaluation examines program outputs rather than inputs.
Examples of the outputs may be hospital beds or school enrolments, numbers of
patients seen or children taught. The main aim of performance evaluation is simply
to determine what the policy is producing, often regardless of the stated objectives.
This type of evaluation produces data ('performance measures') that are used as
inputs into the more comprehensive and intensive evaluations mentioned below.

Efficiency evaluation attempts to assess a program's costs and judge if the same
amount and quality of outputs could be achieved more efficiently, that is, at a lower
cost, through various kinds of production streamlining. Input and output evaluations are the building blocks of this evaluation method, whose significance
increases in times of budgetary restraint. The difficulties involved in the more comprehensive effectiveness evaluations mean that policy-makers must often content
themselves with efficiency evaluations as a 'second-best' alternative. This form of
evaluation is commonly conducted by outside consultants hired by governments.

Finally, *effectiveness evaluation* (also known as *adequacy of performance evaluation* or *'value-for-money' auditing*) involves an additional level of complexity to
simply adding up program inputs or outputs; it is intended to find out if the program is doing what it is supposed to be doing. In this type of evaluation, the performance of a given program is compared to its intended goals to determine
whether the program is meeting those goals and/or whether the goals need to be
adjusted in the light of the program's accomplishments. Findings can lead to

recommendations for altering or changing programs or policies. While this type of evaluation is most useful to policy-makers, it is also the most difficult to undertake. The information needs are immense and the level of sophistication required to carry it out is higher than is generally available in government, leading to the creation of specialized units in many jurisdictions, such as auditors general, to carry it out.

These different types of administrative evaluation of public policies have generated various formal evaluative systems or techniques whose implementation in many jurisdictions fostered the growth of the formal policy analysis profession (Nachmias, 1979; Suchman, 1967, 1979). In the 1970s and 1980s these included such systems as the Program Planning and Budgeting System (PPBS) first developed at the Ford Motor Company and then adopted by the US Department of Defense and ultimately the entire US federal government; Zero-Based Budgeting (ZBB), a variant of PPBS developed at the Xerox Corporation and adopted by the Carter administration in the US and, later, in many other countries; and Management by Objectives (MBO), a self-reporting managerial performance system implemented in the US (Reid, 1979; Rogers, 1978; Wildavsky, 1969).

These techniques have been employed to varying degrees by different governments around the world. In addition, different countries and governments developed their own evaluative systems. Thus, in Canada, for example, in the 1980s a Policy and Expenditure Management System (PEMS) was introduced at the federal level, along with a new Office of the Controller General (OCG) mandated specifically to carry out evaluation research, while the federal Treasury Board tried to introduce a new government-wide Operational Performance Measurement System (OPMS) (Canada, Treasury Board, 1976, 1981; Rogers et al., 1981). More recently, such techniques include efforts to establish performance indicators or *benchmarks* that can allow public-sector efforts and outcomes to be compared across agencies or with private-sector counterparts (Swiss, 1991; Kernaghan et al., 2000; Triantafillou, 2007). Such efforts have been popularized in North America in moves to 'reinvent' government, and have become a predominant tool of the so-called 'New Public Management', which has inspired administrative reform towards smaller, leaner government in Europe, Australasia, and Latin America as well as North America (Aucoin, 1990; Pollitt, 2001; Osborne and Gaebler, 1992; Abma and Noordegraaf, 2003).

While much effort has been put into developing these formal and systematic or system-wide policy evaluation techniques, they have largely failed to overcome the inherent limitations of rationalist policy analysis (Dobell and Zussman, 1981; Jordan and Sutherland, 1979): the prerequisites for their success are too steep to be met in the rough-and-tumble world of public policy-making. Any emphasis on examining the extent to which policy objectives are accomplished by a program must contend with the reality that policies often do not state their objectives precisely enough to permit rigorous analysis of whether they are being achieved; in addition, governments often do not desire to have their failures, unlike what they consider to be their successes, publicized and dissected. Moreover, the same policy may be directed at achieving a variety of objectives, without indicating their relative priority, thus making it difficult to find out if a particular objective is being achieved (Cahill and Overman, 1990; Formaini, 1990; McLaughlin, 1985; Palumbo, 1987; Weiss, 1977a). Social and economic problems tend to be tightly interrelated, as is the case, for example, with housing and employment, and it is virtually impossible to independently isolate and evaluate the effects of policies directed at either of them. In addition, each policy has effects on problems other than those intended, which a comprehensive evaluation must consider but which may make the task of evaluation unwieldy and unmanageable. The difficulties involved in gathering reliable and usable information and aggregating it into generally acceptable benchmarks further aggravate these problems.

The limitations faced by administrative evaluation—and we have noted only a few—increase with the level of sophistication and comprehensiveness expected of such analyses. Thus, effectiveness evaluations, which would clearly be of most use to policy-makers, are the most difficult to undertake. Because of these difficulties, the enthusiasm for rational administrative evaluation has been on the wane since the 1980s. Although the recent attention paid in some areas such as health care to the notion of evidence-based policy-making has revitalized the field somewhat, significant limits on the ability to collect and apply relevant program-level data continue to dampen enthusiasm for, or implementation of, this form of policy evaluation (Head, 2008; Hammersley, 2005; Laforest and Orsini, 2005; Moseley and Tierney, 2004).

To broaden administrative evaluation and attempt, somehow, to assess the question of program effectiveness, many governments have experimented with creating specialized internal audit agencies (Adair and Simmons, 1988; Good, 2003) and with promoting public participation in the evaluation process. The intention is both to better evaluate policies and to head off challenges to these policies on the grounds of a 'lack of consultation' with interested or affected members of the public. But the usefulness and legitimacy of these kinds of public forums have been challenged on many grounds. There are concerns with the extent to which participants are actually representative of a range of views and ideas and with the effects of issues such as funding on the quality and quantity of representation (see Pateman, 1970; Wagle, 2000; Englehart and Trebilcock, 1981; Mitchell et al., 1997).

Frustration with the difficulties involved in administrative evaluation, for example, led the Auditor General of Canada to conclude in his 1983 *Annual Report* that 'a significant proportion of evaluation assessments did not form an adequate basis for sound advice.' Ten years later, the Auditor General's review of program evaluation in the Canadian federal government found numerous changes in form but little in substance. According to the *Report*, evaluations were still:

> less likely to be an important source of information in support of program and policy decisions addressing questions of continued relevance and cost-effectiveness. Evaluations are more likely to provide information for accountability purposes but are often partial. The most complete information available is related to operational effectiveness, the way a program is working. (Canada, Auditor General, 1993)

Judicial Evaluation

A second major type of policy evaluation is not concerned with budgets, priorities, efficiencies, and expenditures, per se, but with the legal issues relating to the manner in which government programs are implemented. Such evaluations are carried out by the judiciary and are concerned with possible conflicts between government actions and constitutional provisions or established standards of administrative conduct and individual rights (Jacobson et al., 2001).

The judiciary is entitled to review government actions either on its own initiative or when asked to do so by an individual or organization filing a case against a government agency in a court of law. The grounds for judicial review differ considerably across countries but usually extend to the examination of the constitutionality of the policy being implemented, or whether its implementation or development violated principles of natural rights and/or justice in democratic societies, or religious or ideological doctrines in others. In the former case, judges typically assess such factors as whether the policy was developed and implemented in a non-capricious and non-arbitrary fashion according to principles of due process and accepted administrative law (Jaffe, 1965).

In countries governed through parliamentary systems, such as Australia, New Zealand, Sweden, Japan, Ireland, and Britain, judicial courts usually concentrate on whether or not an inferior court, tribunal, or government agency has acted within its powers or jurisdiction. If it has, and if it also has abided with principles of natural justice and has not acted in a capricious or arbitrary fashion, then its decision will usually be allowed to stand, subject to any existing statutory appeal provisions. Stated simply, judicial reviews in these countries focus on issues or errors in law (Jaffe, 1969; Wade, 1965, 1966). That is, courts in these systems do not review the facts specific to the case, but tend to restrict their evaluation to procedural issues. Thus, as long as administrative agencies operate within their jurisdiction and according to principles of fundamental justice and due process, their decisions are unlikely to be overturned. Courts in republican systems with constitutionally entrenched divisions of powers, on the other hand, have a very different constitutional role, providing them with more authority and the legitimacy required to question legislative and executive actions. As a result, they are much more active and willing to consider errors of fact as well as errors of law in their evaluations of administrative behaviour (Jaffe, 1965).

Political Evaluation

Political evaluation of government policy is undertaken by just about everyone with any interest in political life. Unlike administrative and judicial evaluations, political evaluations are usually neither systematic nor technically sophisticated. Indeed, many are inherently partisan, one-sided, and biased. Partisan political evaluations often simply attempt to label a policy a success or failure, followed by demands for continuation or change. The same is true of the work of many think-tanks, which, like political parties, bring a specific ideological or other more or less fixed perspective or 'frame' to the evaluation process (see Bovens and t'Hart, 1995; Abelson, 1996; Lindquist, 1998; Ricci, 1993; Weaver, 1989). This does not undermine their significance, however, because their initial objective in undertaking an evaluation is rarely to improve a government's policy, but rather to support or challenge it. Praise or criticism at this stage can lead to new iterations of the cycle as governments attempt to respond to criticisms, similar to what occurs with much of the more reasoned, technical evaluations.

While political evaluation is ongoing, it enters the policy process only on specialized occasions. One of the most important of these occasions in democracies is at election time, when citizens get their opportunity to render judgement on the government's performance. Votes at elections or in referendums express the voters' informal evaluations of the efficiency and effectiveness of governments and their programs and policies. However, in most democratic countries, referendums or plebiscites on particular policies are relatively rare. As was discussed in Chapter 3, while elections are held regularly, by their very nature they usually involve a range of issues, so when citizens express their preferences and sentiments through the ballot box at election time, their evaluation is usually made as an aggregate judgement on a government's overall record of activities in office rather than about the effectiveness or usefulness of specific policies. Nevertheless, public perceptions of the ineffectiveness or harmful effects of specific high-profile government activities can and do affect voting behaviour, a reality governments ignore at their peril come election day (King, 1981).

A more common type of political policy evaluation involves consulting with members of relevant policy subsystems. There are many mechanisms for such consultations, which involve the use of some of the procedural policy instruments discussed in Chapters 5 and 7. These include setting up administrative forums for public hearings and establishing special consultative committees, task forces, and inquiries for evaluative purposes (see Cairns, 1990a; Bulmer, 1993; Clokie and Robinson, 1969), and can range from small meetings of less than a dozen participants lasting several minutes to multi-million dollar inquiries that hear thousands of individual briefs and can take years to complete (Doern, 1967; Salter, 1981; Wilson, 1971). In many countries, political evaluation of government action is built into the system, in the form, for example, of congressional or parliamentary oversight committees (see McCubbins and McCubbins, 1994; McCubbins and Schwartz, 1984). While in some countries, such as the US, these tend to meet on a regular basis, in others, such as Canada and Australia, the process may be less routine and undertaken in a much more ad hoc fashion (see de la Mothe, 1996; Banting, 1995).

These political mechanisms for policy evaluation are usually capable of ascertaining the views of many members of the policy subsystem and affected public on specific policy issues. However, it is not certain that the simple fact of a government hearing the public's views makes a difference to its policy, much less that this leads to change in policy. Effectiveness often depends on whether the views heard are congruent with those of the current government (Dye, 1972:

353–75), which in turn depends on the criteria government members and political officials use to assess success or failure of particular policies or programs.

The Outcomes of Policy Evaluation: Policy Feedback and Policy Termination

There are three possible outcomes that may result from the policy evaluation stage of the policy cycle. First, a policy can be judged successful and continued in its present form. Second, and much more typically, a policy can be judged wanting in some respect and efforts are suggested for its reform (see Patton and Sawicki, 1993). Finally, a policy can be judged a complete failure (or success), leading to the recommendation that it be terminated (see DeLeon, 1978; Geva-May, 2001; Bovens and t'Hart, 1996; Bovens et al., 2001). In the first two outcomes, the policy evaluation stage serves to feed the policy back to some other stage of the policy process. While it is not clear to which stage the process will proceed, in many cases it returns to the agenda-setting stage, hence providing the policy cycle with its cyclical, iterative shape (see Pierson, 1993; Anglund, 1999; Coleman et al., 1997; Billings and Hermann, 1998).

The third alternative option for policy reform is, of course, simply to terminate or end a policy or program. Like more limited proposals for reform, this option involves feeding the results of the evaluation back into the policy process, usually directly to the decision-making stage. Unlike proposals for more limited reform or simply accepting the status quo, the option of policy termination envisions a complete cessation of the policy cycle, at least in its then-current form, at a very near point in the future (DeLeon, 1978, 1983).

Although it is fairly common for evaluations, especially political ones, to suggest the adoption of the termination option, observers have noted the reluctance of decision-makers to adopt this course of action and the general tendency for policies to persist even when they are considered by many to have failed to achieve their goals (Weaver, 1988). This is partially due to the inherent difficulties, mentioned above, of arriving at agreement on policy success or failure. Although, occasionally, a problem may be seen as so pernicious that no possible option can reasonably be expected to resolve it—in other words, that all options will fail—or as having been so successful that government action is no longer required, all observers note that the attainment of unified opinion on these matters among relevant policy actors is an exceedingly rare circumstance (see Daniels, 1997; Kaufman, 1976; Lewis, 2002; Franz, 2002). Much more typically, existing programs and policies will have developed established beneficiaries who will define their continuation and, often, have become so institutionalized that their cessation would trigger a costly battle involving considerable legal, bureaucratic, and political expense (Weaver, 1988; Bardach, 1976; Geva-May, 2001). Handbooks and guidelines for would-be terminators all stress the need to develop political coalitions and circumstances allowing these costs to be overcome if termination is to proceed (see Behn, 1977; Geva-May and Wildavsky, 1997: ch. 5).

These observations all underscore the extent to which termination represents, in effect, an effort to overcome *path dependencies* or *policy legacies* in the policy process; that is, the manner in which earlier decisions affect the course of future ones by altering the context in which future decisions are made (Mulvale et al., 2007; Kay, 2005; Greener, 2005; Pierson, 2000a). Such legacies from the past make the achievement of termination very difficult, often requiring an ideological shift in government and society to allow the more or less uniform judgements of success or failure to emerge, and such broad consensus is most frequently required for uncontested terminations to be made (Kirkpatrick et al., 1999; DeLeon, 1997). It also bears mentioning that a successful termination in the short term does not guarantee a similar long-term result. Thus, if the perception of a problem persists, a termination will usually feed back directly into a reconceptualization of problems and policy alternatives and a new round of policy-making. If no other suitable alternative emerges in this deliberation, this can result in the reversal of a termination and the reinstatement of a terminated program or policy.

Linking Policy Evaluation and Learning: Evaluation Styles in Government

Understanding the links between the evaluation process and its outcomes requires an understanding of the reasons why learning, 'non-learning', and other forms of 'limited learning' occur in complex organizations. Non-learning involves failing to undertake any evaluations, while limited learning occurs when lessons of only a very restricted scope are drawn from the evaluation process (Abrahamson and Fairchild, 1999; Tamuz, 2001; May, 1999; Simon, 1991; March and Olsen, 1975). Research in the administrative and organizational sciences suggests that which type of learning will occur depends on the capacity and willingness of policy-makers to absorb new information (see Huber, 1991; Peters, 1998; Zarkin, 2008).

As Cohen and Levinthal have observed with reference to private firms:

the ability to evaluate and utilize outside knowledge is largely a function of the level of prior related knowledge. At the most elemental level, this prior knowledge includes basic skills or even a shared language but may also include knowledge of the most recent scientific or technological developments in a given field. Thus, prior related knowledge confers an ability to recognize the value of new information, assimilate it, and apply it to commercial ends. These abilities collectively constitute what we call a firm's 'absorptive capacity'. (Cohen and Levinthal, 1990: 132; also see Lane and Lubatkin, 1998)

In a complex organization such as a large firm or government, this implies that learning is a cumulative process and that the existing store of knowledge largely determines what will be done with any new information that flows into the organization. That store of knowledge resides, of course, in the personnel who staff such organizations, and their training and experience on the job thus constitute a key determinant of the propensity for learning within the organizations, whether private firms or governments.

Also critical in this regard, as Aldrich and Herker (1977) note, are 'boundary-spanning' links between the organization and its environment, links receptive to new information and capable of disseminating it within the organization. That is, learning requires policy elites and administrators to be open to these new inputs and not threatened by their dissemination across the organization. Hall (1993) and Sabatier (1987) have suggested that this engagement and transmission of new ideas must be found in larger sets of the policy universe. The impact of this latter form of *social learning*, as discussed above, both authors have argued, is likely to be more profound than the more limited effects generated by closed elite or insider evaluation and reflection.

Hence, in the case of policy evaluation, this implies that, similar to what we have found at the other stages of the policy cycle, two relevant variables affecting the potential for evaluations to lead to learning are (1) the capacity of government in terms of the level of training, skill, and professionalism of its employees; and (2) the nature of the policy subsystem and especially its open or closed nature.

Thus, a state must have a high-capacity civil service operating within a large and complex subsystem in order for 'social learning' to take place. When personnel are poorly trained or inexperienced and subsystems are closed, only perfunctory or limited forms of learning can be expected to result. Low-capacity civil services dealing with large and complex subsystems are likely to generate only limited forms of learning, most likely contested learning—whereby different actors draw dissimilar conclusions from any results obtained; while high-capacity evaluators dealing with closed subsystems are likely to fixate on technical issues. These outcomes are set out in Figure 8.1, along with examples of each outcome drawn from the case of transportation policy-making.

Policies meant to address the problems posed by growing motor vehicle traffic, for instance, illustrate the divergent evaluations that are possible. Debates over 'what is to be done about traffic' are commonplace in affluent urban areas, particularly where economic activity and population are growing. Where civil engineers, who are trained to produce road infrastructure, are primarily responsible for transportation policy, road use is evaluated through traffic counts, a simple metric that captures the volume of driving but ignores both the causes behind it and the consequences beyond transportation impacts. The typical response to such evaluations documenting growing traffic volume, and identifying the primary impact of road congestion, is to propose building new roads or removing bottlenecks. The extra road, of course, is soon choked up again as the number of cars increases, a lesson that evaluators are unlikely to learn under this mode of evaluation.

If the same transportation policy subsystem adopts a broader assessment framework, such as measuring energy efficiency and air pollution in addition to traffic volume, policy evaluation moves to the upper right quadrant of Figure 8.1 and raises the opportunity for technical learning. Here, enabling automobile use to provide growing levels of urban mobility remains the policy goal, but by using

Figure 8.1   Types of Learning Outcomes Expected from Different Evaluative Modes

		Evaluative Capacity	
		Low	High
	Low	**Non- or perfunctory learning** Perfunctory evaluation that validates existing policy. e.g.: Highway expansion planning	**Technical learning** Consideration of alternative means, within same goal structures. e.g.: Traffic management planning
Subsystem Complexity	High	**Contested learning** Competing/partial evaluations by different organizations and actors. e.g.: Separate evaluation by agricultural, environmental, industry, and other road user interests of traffic patterns and use.	**Social learning** Consideration of paradigmatic alternatives. e.g.: Car-free days; reducing roads by reserving lanes for buses; taxing cars and earmarking the revenues thus generated to public transportation.

additional assessment tools, civil engineers and other transport policy actors gain feedback on the energy and environmental challenges that also arise from auto use, in addition to the traffic congestion. This can show the value of transportation demand management options, such as road pricing or incentives to carpool, bike, or telecommute. Such feedback represents an opportunity for technical learning, and has been used to initiate road pricing in cities as diverse as Singapore, Trondheim, and London, while other cities (including New York City) are considering its imposition (Cardwell, 2008).

When a broader set of assessment techniques is applied by policy actors with a wide range of viewpoints, the result is likely to be contested learning, depicted in the lower left quadrant of Figure 8.1. Here one set of evaluators, such as environmental groups, will evaluate the automobile's impacts in relation to goals that extend well beyond transportation performance while another set sticks with the established mobility goals. Environmental sustainability, conservation of agricultural lands, and public health improvements will then be pitted against mobility goals. To those who assess environmental, energy, and public health impacts, the car's costs will clearly outweigh its benefits, while those who assess automobile travel in terms of mobility will not recognize these costs and dispute the conclusions for policy change that flow from them. Such contested learning is characterized by the phenomenon of 'duelling experts', who often contribute to a policy stalemate where rival organizations assert their findings, which are used mainly to block changes based on each others' evaluative conclusions.

Finally, when the policy subsystem is open to comprehensive evaluation of an urban transportation policy, such as when a change in government introduces new officials to policy deliberations, and the evaluation techniques cover a broad range of assessment tools, the opportunity for a paradigmatic shift in policy exists. Here, in the lower right quadrant of Figure 8.1, we would find transportation breakthroughs like the decision to close large sections of Bogota, Colombia, to automobiles on weekends, to restrict daily driving into the city on weekdays, and to reallocate road space away from automobiles to rapid bus services. Such policy decisions, of course, require a recognition that automobiles can never meet the demand for urban mobility in a truly sustainable manner (Cohen, 2008).

Conclusion: The Key Role of Evaluation and Feedback in the Policy Cycle

Different forms of evaluation take place in the public policy process under the direction, and with the involvement, of different types of policy actors in the policy subsystem, and result in different learning outcomes. These feed back into succeeding phases or rounds of the policy cycle. Despite inherent difficulties with assessing the success or failure of policy efforts, past writings on the subject of policy evaluation have tended overwhelmingly to concentrate on developing, criticizing, and refining the techniques of formal administrative evaluations. In the process, the limits of rationality in the policy process were often forgotten, along with the lesson that policy evaluation is an inherently political exercise (Hellstern, 1986; Chelimsky, 1995).

Analysts who do account for the politics underlying policy evaluation see it as a continuation of the struggle over scarce resources or contested ideologies, but also as a key part of a policy cycle because of its function as a learning process in which policies develop and change on the basis of assessments of past successes and failures and conscious efforts to emulate successes and avoid failures (see Sanderson, 2002a, 2002b). This conception not only helps to make sense of policy evaluation and removes it from the narrow technocratic concerns characteristic of administrative evaluation, but also helps to identify the different learning styles that can emerge in the evaluative process and their propensities to contribute to different types of policy outcomes and dynamics. It highlights the significant role played by all forms of evaluation in the animation of the policy cycle as decisions play out over time, the subject of the final chapter of the book.

Study Questions

1. What are the potential and limitations of different evaluation techniques?
2. What capacity is required to carry out effective evaluation? How can this be developed?
3. To what extent is it possible to engage the public in policy evaluation?
4. What is policy learning and how would you recognize it?
5. How do the types of evaluation undertaken by different policy actors differ from each other?

Further Readings

Adair, John J., and Rex Simmons. 1988. 'From Voucher Auditing to Junkyard Dogs: The Evolution of Federal Inspectors General', *Public Budgeting and Finance* 8, 2: 91–100.

Bennett, Colin, and Michael Howlett. 1991. 'The Lessons of Learning: Reconciling Theories of Policy Learning and Policy Change', *Policy Sciences* 25, 3: 275–94.

Cardwell, Dianne. 2008. 'City Council Approves Fee to Drive Below 60th', *New York Times*, 1 Apr., 1.

Cohen, Jon. 2008. 'Calming Traffic on Bogota's Killing Streets', *Science* 319, 5864: 742–3.

Cohen, Wesley M., and Daniel A. Levinthal. 1990. 'Absorptive Capacity: A New Perspective on Learning and Innovation', *Administrative Science Quarterly* 35: 128–52.

Davies, I. 1999. 'Evaluation and Performance Management in Government', *Evaluation* 8, 2: 150–9.

DeLeon, Peter. 1983. 'Policy Evaluation and Program Termination', *Policy Studies Review* 2, 4: 631–47.

Huber, George P. 1991. 'Organization Learning: The Contributing Processes and the Literatures', *Organization Science* 2, 1: 88–115.

Jaffe, Louis L. 1965. *Judicial Control of Administrative Action*. Boston: Little, Brown.

May, Peter J. 1999. 'Fostering Policy Learning: A Challenge for Public Administration', *International Review of Public Administration* 4, 1: 21–31.

Nachmias, David. 1979. *Public Policy Evaluation: Approaches and Methods*. New York: St Martin's Press.

Pierson, Paul. 1993. 'When Effect Becomes Cause: Policy Feedback and Political Change', *World Politics* 45: 595–628.

Rose, Richard. 1993. *Lesson-Drawing in Public Policy: A Guide to Learning across Time and Space*. Chatham, NJ: Chatham House.

Part III

Long-Term Policy Dynamics

Chapter 9

Patterns of Policy Change

The ideas and information presented in this book have shown that public policy-making is rarely as simple a matter as either analysts or policy-makers might wish for, but neither is it so complex that it calls into questions any analysis and informed judgement and commentary. It consists of a series of decisions, involving a large number of actors operating within the confines of an amorphous, yet inescapable, context of ideas and institutions, and employing a variety of diverse and multi-faceted policy instruments to try to achieve the goals of government (Braun, 1999). This intricacy poses real difficulties for those seeking a comprehensive understanding of the subject, requiring the development of a distinct vocabulary of policy-related terms and concepts that can be tied together into testable hypotheses and theories.

As the chapters in this volume have shown, one of the most straightforward and effective ways to deal with such complexity is to break down the public policy-making process into a series of discrete but related sub-processes that, together, form an entire policy cycle. The stages in that cycle correspond to the five stages found in other instances of applied problem-solving, whereby problems are recognized, possible solutions are proposed, a solution is chosen, the selected choice is put into effect, and finally the outcomes are monitored and evaluated. In the policy process, these stages are manifested as agenda-setting, policy formulation, decision-making, policy implementation, and policy evaluation.

Of course, the public policy process is not necessarily as tightly sequential or goal-driven as the model makes it appear. Policy actors, it is justifiably argued, do not go about making and implementing policies in quite the systematic manner suggested by the policy cycle model. While this is no doubt a legitimate complaint against conceiving of public policy as being carried out in a series of stages, it is also true that the limitation can be mitigated to a large extent with diligent examination and cautious inference from what is found. The advantage of employing the cycle model lies in its role as a methodological heuristic: facilitating the understanding of the public policy process by breaking it into parts, each of which can be investigated alone or in terms of its relationship to the other stages of the cycle. This allows the integration of empirical materials derived from individual cases, comparative studies of several cases, and the study of one or many stages of one or several cases into policy theories and analyses. The policy literature is replete with these distinct perspectives on policy and models such as the one presented in this book, derived from the accumulated knowledge gained from earlier studies.

The model's greatest virtue is this empirical orientation, which enables the systematic evaluation of the diverse factors driving public policy-making at the various procedural stages. While abstract conceptualization is necessary to develop a broad picture of the policy process, an analytical framework that takes into account the details of the sub-processes in developing a picture of the entire process is essential.

The factors considered at each stage of the policy cycle have been the actors, institutions, and ideas involved in developing the content and processes that create the policy in question, and the instruments available to carry it out. These aspects of the policy-making process are intricate phenomena in their own right, and the general nature of these elements has been sketched out in the book. Ultimately, it has been argued, policy-making can be thought of as both a process in which interests and ideas collide as actors contest and deliberate over what to do, and also one in which all actors learn from past successes and mistakes as the cycle repeats itself through successive rounds or iterations.

Studying policy-making using the policy cycle model thus highlights the dynamic nature of policy-making and helps to organize the otherwise difficult-to-grasp relations among actors, ideas, institutions, and instruments that explain these dynamics. However, while disaggregation has permitted the detailed examination of each stage of the policy process found in Chapters 4–8, these beg the question of what the whole process looks like over time. Are there typical overall patterns of policy development and change? And, if so, how do such patterns come into being and how do they influence policy actions and outcomes? These issues will be examined in this concluding chapter.

Outcomes of Policy Succession: Policy Feedback and Policy Termination

Policy Feedback

As E.E. Schattschneider (1935: 38) noted, 'new policies create new politics'. That is, the outcomes of the policy process tend to 'feed back' into the policy environment, thus altering important aspects of the context in which policy was created, including institutional rules and operations, the distribution of wealth and power in society, the nature of the ideas and interests relevant to policies, and even the selection of personnel assigned to deal with policy problems. As we have discussed in Chapter 8, the feedback process from formal and informal evaluations can easily affect the identification and interpretation of policy problems, assessments of the feasibility of potential solutions, and target groups' response to them, thereby altering the conditions under which policies are further developed and implemented. Policies can create new 'spoils' for policy actors to argue over, new ideas about 'what works' and why in terms of policy actions, or can result in the mobilization or 'countermobilization' of actors who feel they have been disadvantaged by an existing policy or program (Pierson, 1993). Hence, it is not at all unusual— in fact, it is typical—for policy-making to reiterate the policy process following the outcome of the evaluation stage, as captured in the policy cycle's logic of recurring deliberation and cyclical processing.

Exactly where or to which stage a policy process may go following the evaluation stage depends on the nature of the feedback provided and the types of actors involved. Formal evaluations by governmental actors, for example, tend to result in limited critiques that typically might involve alterations to the policy implementation process, such as the creation of new agencies or regulations to deal with an issue raised in the evaluative process. However, these and other types of evaluations can also result in new ways of thinking about a problem and solutions to it, feeding back into 'earlier' stages such as agenda-setting and policy formulation where problems and options are initially framed and assessed.

New iterations of the policy cycle are a typical output of evaluation processes and often involve larger or smaller reforms of existing policies and processes. It is important to note, however, that subsequent iterations of the cycle take on a distinctive form from the development of entirely new policies, since they build on an already existing policy framework or 'regime'. As incrementalists such as Charles Lindblom have suggested, future rounds of policy-making typically build on the basis of earlier rounds and, as a result, successive rounds and their outcomes tend to incorporate many aspects of existing policies rather than develop completely new forms of policy action. Although dramatic shifts in policies can occur, typically only more minor changes occur because the general configuration of existing policy processes—subsystem membership, political and other relevant policy institutions, policy ideas, discourses and frames, and state and societal capacities and constraints—do not change substantially between iterations of the cycle. Thus, typical feedback processes emerging from the policy evaluation stage of the cycle, as Paul Pierson has noted, underscore and help to explain the historical or '*path-dependent*' nature of policy-making in modern states (Pierson, 2000a, 2004).

'Path dependency' is a general term used by economists, sociologists, and others to capture the manner in which previous conditions affect future conditions (see Mahoney, 2000; Pierson, 2000a; Haydu, 1998); in short, the term is a kind of shorthand for the idea that, in policy-making, 'history matters'. That is, the continuity of policies over time due to the existence of '*policy legacies*' limits the nature and extent of choice policy-makers have in making subsequent decisions (see Weir, 1992; Rose, 1990; Kay, 2006). It describes the situation whereby once a system is in place, it tends to perpetuate itself by limiting the range of choices or the ability of forces both outside ('exogenous') and inside ('endogenous') the system to alter that trajectory. In other words, once a trajectory is in place it tends to 'lock in' the previous state of the system and the direction of its dynamics (Arthur, 1989; Duit, 2007). Examples of this phenomenon range from how decisions on the initial location of hospitals and schools affect their operation to that of decisions to ban nuclear power, which are much harder and more expensive to take once plants have been built than if they had never been constructed in the first place (Wilsford, 1994; Pollock et al., 1989; Rona-Tas, 1998; Davidson, 2004).[1]

While the concept of path dependency may over-exaggerate the extent to which policy lock-in occurs (Kay, 2005; Greener, 2002; Dobrowolsky and Saint-Martin, 2005; Howlett and Rayner, 2006; Ross, 2007; Peters et al., 2005), it is quite clear that policy legacies affect policy-making by creating institutional routines and procedures that can force decision-making in particular directions—by either eliminating or distorting the range of options available to governments (see Wilsford, 1985, 1994; Pierson, 2000a; Rona-Tas, 1998).[2] Policies continue to develop through iterations of the policy cycle, and a common theme in the literature on policy dynamics is the manner in which aspects of policy subsystems and dominant ideas become institutional obstacles to making a new start.

Policy Styles and Policy Regimes

Numerous case studies over the last three decades have highlighted the manner in which these pre-established ideological and institutional factors insulate policies from pressures for change. By the mid-1970s it was apparent to many observers that actors in the policy processes, as Simmons, Davis, Chapman, and Sager (1974: 461) put it, tended to 'take on, over a period of time, a distinctive style which affects . . . policy decisions, i.e. they develop tradition and history which constrains and refines their actions and concerns.' The concept of a *policy style* is useful not only for describing such typical policy processes but also for capturing an important aspect of policy dynamics, that is, the relatively enduring nature of these arrangements (Larsen et al., 2006).

A policy style can be thought of as existing as part of a larger 'policy regime' that emerges over time as policy succession takes place. Such a regime includes not only how policy deliberations take place but also, as we have seen in earlier chapters, the kinds of actors and ideas present. In his comparative work on social policy, for example, Gosta Esping-Andersen found different countries to have 'specific institutional arrangements adopted by societies in the pursuit of work and welfare. A given organization of state–economy relations is associated with a particular social policy logic' (Rein et al., 1987). Eisner, similarly, defined a regime as a 'historically specific configuration of policies and institutions which establishes certain broad goals that transcend the problems' specific to particular sectors (Eisner, 1993: xv; see also Eisner, 1994a). In their work on US policy-making, Harris and Milkis (1989: 25) found regimes in many sectors that they argued had developed as a 'constellation' of (1) ideas justifying governmental activity, (2) institutions that structure policy-making, and (3) a set of policies themselves.

A policy regime, hence, can be seen to combine several of the concepts discussed in earlier chapters. It can be thought of as integrating a common set of policy ideas (a policy paradigm), a long-lasting governance arrangement (or policy mix), a common or typical policy process (a policy style), and a more or less fixed set of policy actors (a policy subsystem or policy monopoly). As such, it is a useful term for describing long-term patterns found in both the substance and process of public policy-making in a particular jurisdiction or sector. The general idea is that such policy-making tends to develop in such a way that the same actors, institutions, instruments, and governing ideas tend to dominate for extended periods of time, infusing a policy sector with both a consistent content and a set of typical policy processes or procedures. Understanding how styles, paradigms, and regimes form, how they are maintained, and how they change is thus an important aspect of the study of public policy (Kuks, 2004; de Vries, 2005b).

Policy Termination

Before we discuss common patterns of policy change, however, we should recall that another possibility always exists: policy termination. That is, while many per-mutations of policy feedback processes exist, one major option for policy reform is simply to terminate or end a policy or program. Like more limited proposals for reform, this option involves feeding the results of an evaluative process back into the policy process, usually directly to the decision-making stage. Unlike pro-posals for more limited reform or simply accepting the status quo, the option of *policy termination* envisions a complete cessation of the policy cycle at a very near point in the future (DeLeon, 1978, 1983).

As we saw in Chapter 8, although it is fairly common for evaluations, especially political ones, to suggest the termination option, decision-makers find it difficult to adopt this course of action and, as a result, most policies tend to persist over long periods once they have been established (Weaver, 1988). This is partially due to the inherent difficulties, mentioned in Chapter 8, of reaching agreement about a policy's success or failure. Only rarely may a problem be seen to be so pernicious that no possible option can be expected to improve it—in other words, that all options will fail—or as having been so successful that further government action is no longer required (see Daniels, 1997; Kaufman, 1976; Lewis, 2002; Frantz, 2002; Geva-May, 2001; Behn, 1977; Geva-May and Wildavsky, 1997: ch. 5).

Types of Policy Change: Normal and Atypical

Most observers of policy dynamics recognize that two common types or patterns of change are typical of public policy-making. The more 'normal' pattern involves relatively minor tinkering with policies and programs already in place through successive rounds of policy-making, which results in new policies being 'layered' on top of existing ones. Such changes are 'incremental' and do not individually affect the essential substance of existing policy styles or paradigms, although col-lectively, as is discussed below, they can affect the coherence and consistency of the elements of a policy regime. The second, more substantial pattern relates to the fundamental transformation of policy-making and involves changes in basic sets of policy ideas, institutions, interests, and processes. Termination is one such transformation, but other similarly major changes also are possible. Like termina-tion, though, all major changes run up against the impediments of previous policy legacies, making such changes difficult, and rare.

Normal Policy Change

There is a surprising degree of continuity in public policy, for most policies made by governments are, for the most part and most of the time, in some way a con-tinuation of past policies and practices. Even what are often portrayed as 'new' policy initiatives are often simply variations on existing practices (Polsby, 1984; Lindblom, 1959; Hayes, 1992). This is because, as we have seen, the principal elements of policy-making—the actors, ideas, and institutions involved, and the constraints and capacities with which they operate—change very slowly, if at all, between iterations of a policy process, while the iterations, by comparison, occur more frequently. The structure of policy subsystems in particular affects the over-arching sets of policy ideas that determine the recognition of policy problems, the construction of options to resolve them, and the implementation and evaluation of means to achieve solutions in practice. As we have seen, subsystem structure shapes the policy discourse by conditioning the members' perception of what is desirable and possible, and affects the choice of policy instruments and the eval-uation of policy outcomes. The sources of these ideas are varied, not to mention contentious; they range from purely ideological constructs, to manifestations of material conditions, to developments in science and the knowledge base of soci-ety and policy-makers and analysts.

Rhodes (1997a) and Schaap and van Twist (1997), as well as many others, have argued that policy stability is greatly enhanced by the fact that all subsystems tend to construct 'policy monopolies' in which the interpretation and general approach to a subject are more or less fixed (see Baumgartner and Jones, 1991, 1993). Only when a monopoly is broken by the emergence of new members or the departure of old ones can we expect to find substantial policy change in any significant sense (see Kubler, 2001; Dudley and Richardson, 1998; de Vries, 2000, 2005a, 2005b). These 'closed networks' are a key source of policy stability, which is based simply on the ability of existing policy actors to keep new members from entering into policy debates and discourses or to marginalize their participation (see Daugbjerg, 1997; Hammond and Knott, 2000). This can occur, for example, when govern-ments refuse to appoint prominent critics to advisory boards or regulatory tri-bunals, when funding is not provided for interveners at hearings, when the creation of such boards and procedures is resisted, or when the behaviour of inter-est groups in pursuing specialized issue niches restricts competition in a policy network (Browne, 1990, 1991; Greenaway, 2007; Raphael, 2008).

Atypical Policy Change

Within a policy regime considerable fluctuations and marginal changes can occur without altering the overall nature of the long-term pattern of policy procedures or contents (Hayes, 2001). Forces promoting policy stability and limited change are powerful, yet sometimes we do find a deep change in the normal substance and process of policy-making. This type of atypical policy change involves a sub-stantial transformation in the components of policy regimes, including policy paradigms and styles.

Policy 'monopolies' are able to retain control over policy deliberations and outcomes through a variety of means, including denying room on policy agendas for new ideas and actors, closing membership in policy networks at the formula-tion stage and thus restricting the range and type of policy alternatives enunciated or articulated, promoting status quo decision-making, limiting the resources and ability of implementers to alter policies, and promoting only limited forms of learning emerging from the evaluation stage of the policy cycle (Greenaway, 2007). All of these activities inhibit change at various stages of the policy cycle and thus promote policy stability. They help to maintain stable policy 'frames', or relatively stable sets of overarching policy ideas, and filter out alternative visions of public policy that could inspire efforts towards more fundamental change (Schon and Rein, 1994). These activities and others like them explain why a 'normal' pattern of policy change typically involves tinkering with or altering various aspects of existing policies without changing the basic configuration of a policy regime.

While there may be a great deal of continuity in policy succession, however, over time it is possible for the addition of new layers of complexity to result in duplication of initiatives, confusion in policy goals, and the inconsistent use of policy instruments. These factors can lead to policy failures or can make existing regimes vulnerable to the criticisms raised by actors within a policy subsystem as well as by excluded members of the policy universe. This can lead to the development of increasingly suboptimal policy mixes (Pierson, 2000c; Greener, 2002; Stead and Meijers, 2004; Meijers and Stead, 2004).

In their studies of institutional and policy change in Europe and elsewhere, Kathleen Thelen (2003, 2004) and Joseph Hacker (2004a, 2004b), among others, have identified several common processes of policy development that can result in, or correct, these suboptimal policy outcomes: layering, drift, conversion, and replacement or redesign. *Layering* is a process in which new ends and means are simply added to existing ones without abandoning the previous ones. This is likely to promote incoherence among the policy ends as well as inconsistency with respect to policy means (Howlett and Rayner, 1995; Rayner et al., 2001). *Drift* is said to occur when policy ends change while policy means remain constant, thus making the means inconsistent with respect to the changed ends and hence often ineffective in achieving them (Torenvlied and Akkerman, 2004). *Conversion* is a process in which there is an attempt to change the mix of policy means in order to meet goals (Falkenmark, 2004; Hacker, 2004a, 2004b). In policy *redesign or replacement* there is a conscious effort to fundamentally restructure both the means and ends of

Figure 9.1   Relationship of Policy Elements and Outcomes to Policy Development Processes

		New Policy Means Relationship to Existing Means	
		Consistent	*Inconsistent*
New Policy Goals Relationship to Existing Goals	*Coherent*	Redesign (optimal policies)	Drift (ineffective policies)
	Incoherent	Conversion (misdirected policies)	Layering (misdirected and ineffective policies)

Note: Brackets represent likely outcomes.

policy so that they are consistent and coherent in terms of their goals and means orientations (Eliadis et al., 2004; Gunningham and Sinclair, 1998) (see Figure 9.1).

Many existing policy regimes have been developed haphazardly through layering processes in which new tools and objectives have simply been piled on top of older ones, creating a palimpsest-like mixture of overwritten policy elements (Scrase and Sheate, 2002; May et al., 2007; Thomas, 2003; May et al., 2005; Lafferty and Hovden, 2003; Evers and Wintersberger, 1990; Evers, 2005). As these layers build up, however, they can result in failed policies that can undermine the ability of an existing policy monopoly to continue to control policy processes and outcomes, leading to a second pattern of atypical policy change.

Atypical policy changes often occur as a result of the activities of specialized policy actors reacting to discordances or 'anomalies'—discrepancies between events on the ground and their theorization within the dominant paradigm—which occur more frequently as the layers of policy build up over multiple rounds of policy-making. As Sabatier (1987), Kingdon (1984), and others have argued, anomalous events and activities are those which are not expected or understandable in terms of prevalent policy discourses. These deviations from the expected policy norm upset calculations of actor self-interest and subsystem legitimacy and allow innovative actors—'policy entrepreneurs'—to leverage changing circumstances in order to introduce new ideas into the policy milieu (Bundgaard and Vrangbaek, 2007). These new actors are often seen as engaged in a struggle with established ones, who usually resist the introduction of new ideas and defend the status quo or, at least, attempt to limit changes to those compatible with existing arrangements (see Nunan, 1999; Howlett and Rayner, 1995; Jenkins-Smith et al., 1991).

Two situations with exogenous origins, which often promote discontent with the status quo and can lead to atypical policy change, have received detailed examination in the literature: *systemic perturbations* and *policy spillovers*. Paul Sabatier, for example, has argued that 'changes in the core aspects of a policy are usually the results of perturbations in non-cognitive factors external to the subsystem such as macro-economic conditions or the rise of a new systemic governing coalition' (Sabatier, 1988: 140; see also Sabatier, 1987; Sabatier and Jenkins-Smith. 1993a). 'Systemic perturbations' is a thus a term used to describe one of the oldest known forces that can trigger atypical policy changes—external crises that upset established policy routines (Meyer, 1982; Brandstrom and Kuipers, 2003). These can include idiosyncratic phenomena such as wars or disasters, or repeating events such as critical elections and leadership rotations (Meijerink, 2005; Birkland, 2004). The principal mechanism by which change occurs is through the introduction of new actors into policy processes, very often in the form of enhanced public attention being paid to a policy issue as a result of a perceived crisis situation (Cobb and Primo, 2003; Kindleberger, 1996).

'*Subsystem spillovers*' refers to exogenous change processes that occur when activities in otherwise distinct subsystems transcend old boundaries and affect the structure or behaviour of other subsystems (Dery, 1999; Lynggaard, 2001; Djelic and Quack, 2007; Kay, 2006). Instances such as those that have occurred when Internet-based computing collided with existing telecommunications regimes and when long-established natural resource policy actors find it necessary to deal with Aboriginal land claims exemplify this phenomenon (Hoberg and Morawaski, 1997; Grant and MacNamara, 1995; Rosendal, 2000; Gehring and Oberthur, 2000; Marion, 1999; Rayner et al., 2001). Although this particular process of regime change has just begun to be examined, it would appear that spillovers can occur in specific issues without any permanent change in subsystem membership (*subsystem intersection*) or they can be more long-term in nature (*subsystem convergence*). This general process, like systemic perturbations, affects policy processes largely through the introduction of new actors into otherwise stable regimes. Unlike systemic perturbations, however, the new actors tend to be policy specialists and interested parties, rather than simply members of the aroused public (Deeg, 2007; May et al., 2007).

Two endogenous processes have also been linked to important atypical policy regime changes: *venue change* and *policy learning*. 'Venue change' refers to changes in the strategies policy actors follow in pursuing their interests. In their work on policy formation in the United States, for example, Baumgartner and Jones (1993: 26, 239–41) noted several strategies employed by actors excluded from policy subsystems to gain access to policy deliberations and affect policy outcomes. They noted that venue-shifting strategies usually involved the redefinition of a policy issue or 'frame' in order to facilitate alteration of the location where policy deliberations, especially formulation and decision-making, occur. The internationalization of public policy-making and its impact on policy change—often addressed in short-hand as 'globalization'—results in policy regime change largely through the proliferation of new venues for actors to exploit (Epstein, 1997; Cerny, 2001; Doern et al., 1996a; Melo, 2004; Bleich, 2002, 2006). Not all policy issues are susceptible to reframing or image manipulation, and not all political systems contain any, or as many, alternate policy venues (Perl and Dunn, 2007; Meijerink, 2005; Wood, 2006). Notable instances of policy change through venue-shifting include those in many jurisdictions when environmental groups have attempted to redefine the image of an issue like waste disposal from a technical regulatory issue to a public health or property rights one susceptible to lawsuits and recourse to the courts (see Jordan, 1998; Hoberg, 1998; Richardson, 1999).

'Policy learning' is a second endogenous change-enhancing process. As discussed in Chapter 8, it refers to the manner in which, as Hugh Heclo (1974) has noted, a relatively enduring alteration in policy results from policy-makers and participants learning from their own and others' experience with similar policies. While some types of learning are limited to reflections on existing practices, others are much more far-reaching and can affect a wide range of policy elements (see Bennett and Howlett, 1991; May, 1992). All involve the development and diffusion of new ideas into existing policy processes. As was discussed in Chapter 8, these different conceptions all describe a common tendency for policies to change as the result of alterations in policy ideas circulating in policy subsystems, as knowledge of past experiences influences member judgements as to the feasibility or desirability of certain present courses of action (Knoepfel and Kissling-Naf, 1998; Benz and Furst, 2002; Nilsson, 2005; de Jong and Edelenbos, 2007).

Punctuated Equilibrium: Linking Normal and Atypical Policy Change

Much anecdotal and other evidence suggests that normal and atypical policy dynamics are connected in an overarching pattern of policy change that can be described as a 'punctuated equilibrium'. In punctuated equilibrium models, first developed in the areas of natural history and paleobiology, change occurs as an irregular, non-linear, or stepped function in which relatively long periods of policy stability are interspersed with infrequent periods of substantial change (see Eldredge and Gould, 1972; Gould and Eldredge, 1977; Gersick, 1991).

In the policy realm this refers to normal policy-making, which involves fairly common, routine, non-innovative changes at the margin of existing policies, followed by bouts of atypical, or non-incremental, change involving new policies that represent a sharp break from how policies were developed and implemented in the past (Baumgartner and Jones, 1993; Berry, 1990; Rose, 1976; True et al., 1999; Hayes, 2001). Frequently cited examples of such patterns include shifts in fiscal and monetary policy in most Western countries from a balanced-budget orthodoxy to Keynesian demand management in the late 1940s and the subsequent shift to forms of monetarism in the late 1970s (Hall, 1989, 1992). Similar shifts occurred in many resource policy sectors, as policies shifted from pure exploitation to conservation in the nineteenth century, and then from conservation to sustainable management in the twentieth (see Hays, 1959, 1987; Cashore and Howlett, 2007; Gould, 2007; Robinson, 2007; Robinson et al., 2007; Robinson and Caver, 2006; John, 2003).

While many cases of punctuated equilibrium have been well explored (Schrad, 2007; Heron and Richardson, 2008; Greer, 2008), a fully elaborated theory of when this particular policy dynamic emerges and how it establishes a new paradigm remains a work in progress. The extent to which examples from economic policy transformation can be generalized to support the assessment of change in other sectors such as security policy or environmental policy is far from settled. Among the questions remaining to be answered is the degree to which the dynamics of profound policy change transcend political systems and sectors, and the extent to which they depend on the substantive character of the policy that is changing (Mortensen, 2005; Howlett and Cashore, 2007; Kuhner, 2007; Bannink and Hoogenboom, 2007; John, 2003).

The general argument that has been proposed to explain punctuated equilibrium patterns of policy dynamics, however, is that atypical change ultimately occurs because anomalies build up between the policy regime and the reality it 'regulates', causing a crisis within the existing regime and making it susceptible to both endogenous and exogenous forces and processes of change (Linz, 1978). The process of regime change is initially quite unstable as conflicting ideas emerge and compete for dominance when an existing paradigm or subsystem breaks down. The process becomes complete, until the next upheaval, when a new set of ideas wins out over others and is accepted by most, or at least the most powerful, members of the policy subsystem then in place. The new regime's hegemony is eventually established when it is institutionalized and its legitimacy yields recognition

Figure 9.2   A General Model of the Punctuated Equilibrium Model of Policy Regime Change: Stage Characteristics

1. *Regime stability.* The reigning orthodoxy is institutionalized and policy adjustments are made largely by a closed group of experts and officials and other members of a closed subsystem.

2. *Accumulation of real-world anomalies.* Developments are neither anticipated nor fully explicable in terms of the reigning orthodoxy, thereby undermining its effectiveness and legitimacy.

3. *Experimentation.* Efforts are made by subsystem members to stretch the existing regime to account for the anomalies.

4. *Fragmentation of authority.* Experts and officials become discredited and new participants challenge the existing subsystem, paradigm, and regime.

5. *Contestation.* Debate spills into the public arena and involves the larger political process, including electoral and partisan considerations.

6. *Institutionalization of a new regime.* After a period of time, the advocates of a new regime secure positions of authority and alter existing organizational and decision-making arrangements in order to institutionalize the new subsystem, paradigm, and regime.

Sources: Adapted from Peter A. Hall, 'Policy Paradigms, Social Learning and the State: The Case of Economic Policy Making in Britain', *Comparative Politics* 25, 3 (1993): 275–96; M.S. de Vries, 'Generations of Interactive Policy-Making in the Netherlands', *International Review of Administrative Sciences* 71, 4 (2005): 577–91.

of policy ideas and options as normal (see Wilson, 2000; Skogstad, 1998; Jenson, 1989; Legro, 2000). Alternatives that do not fit within the new normalcy then appear unusual, lack support, and are less likely to be considered by policymakers. A general model of this punctuated equilibrium model of policy regime change is set out in Figure 9.2.

The more stable the subsystem and the more established and embedded the ideas within it are about how policy should operate, the greater the propensity to resist change. When this is combined with a stable political regime where state agents are most comfortable reacting to change (e.g., adopting a 'wait-and-see' approach to dealing with anomalies), the level of policy dysfunction will have to rise quite high before delegitimation yields a 'big bang' political realignment that breaks away from an established policy monopoly (Menahem, 2008). The resulting change will, by its nature, seem quite innovative.

Conversely, chaotic policy subsystems can become fertile ground for debating policy change, without necessarily yielding substantial innovation (McBeth et al., 2007). In their contest over different paradigms, an unstable mix of participants will introduce diverse ideas in pursuit of disparate interests (Loughlin, 2004; Van Kersbergen and Van Waarden, 2004; Jones and Baumgartner, 2005).

Conclusion

Discussion of the key roles played by policy actors, ideas, and institutions at all stages of the policy process helped us throughout this book to provide an alternative way to view the operation of a policy cycle than that typically found in the literature (see DeLeon and Kaufmanis, 2001; Schmidt, 2008).

Chapters 1–3 set out the basic intentions of the policy sciences and discussed the manner in which existing general theories of political life fail to provide a satisfactory understanding of public policy-making and the roles played by actors, institutions, and instruments found in the policy process of modern liberal-democratic states. Chapters 4–8 discussed the various stages of the policy cycle and identified the different styles in which policy deliberations proceed, but said little about how these stages fit together, or whether characteristic patterns of policy change existed in public policy processes or contents.

This chapter addressed the issue of policy change and the existence of long-term patterns of relative stability in policy-making, highlighting the manner in which actors, institutions, and ideas combine to produce reasonably stable policy styles, subsystems, paradigms, and regimes. This analysis showed how public policy-making is a process characterized by two patterns of policy change—normal and atypical—linked together in an overall punctuated equilibrium pattern. Policy dynamics typically involve the establishment of an equilibrium characterized by normal change—wherein policies change only incrementally through layering, conversion, and drift—until periodically interrupted by more fundamental change affecting the nature of policy regimes and resulting in policy replacement or redesign. These policy dynamics are complex and characterized by different forces and processes enhancing policy stability and turbulence in specific cases. Processes such as policy learning and path-dependence often overlap and their interactive effects can lead to minor or major change, depending on the presence or absence of other conditions that enhance the opportunities for new actors and ideas to penetrate established policy regimes (see Thomas, 1999; Alink et al., 2001; Nisbet, 1972; Campbell, 1997; Studlar, 2007).

Analyzing the policy process in terms of policy cycles and policy subsystems both aids in the conceptualization of these fundamental dynamics and facilitates their analysis. Identifying the characteristic policy styles, subsystems, paradigms, and policy regimes through analysis of the stages of the policy cycle allows the establishment of a baseline against which change can be measured. Only careful observation of subsystem behaviour will clarify tendencies towards atypical policy change involving a significant, though not necessarily complete, break from the past in terms of the overall policy goals, the understanding of public problems and their solutions, and the policy instruments used to put decisions into effect (Mortensen, 2007; Liefferink, 2006; Kenis, 1991; Menahem, 1998, 2001). Such deep changes occur in circumstances when normal policy changes come to be regarded as insufficient for the task at hand. By their very nature such changes are infrequent, but when they do take place, the effects are felt throughout the entire policy regime (Baumgartner and Jones, 2002).

The notion of fundamental policy change as synonymous with changes in policy regimes brings to the fore the insight that public policy-making is not simply a process of conflict resolution, as most past economic and political science-based theories allege, nor is it a process solely comprised of policy-makers responding to external shocks or jolts. Policy-making is influenced largely by the activities of policy subsystem members attempting to shape the structure and operation of policy-making through activities such as venue-shifting, image reframing, and policy learning.

This move away from a traditional linear interpretation of the policy cycle and towards a more nuanced position on the investigation and conceptualization of the public policy process is reflected in some 'post-positivist' modes of analysis in policy science as a whole, but is not synonymous with it (see Dudley et al., 2000; Howlett and Ramesh, 1998; Lynn, 1999). Policy scholars now recognize that policy phenomena are shaped by highly contingent and complex processes, but that they also require an appropriate research methodology to move beyond statements of their uncertainty and complexity (see Hilgartner and Bosk, 1981; Holzner and Marx, 1979).

Policy analysis itself is just as much a subject of analysis and reflection as the object of the analysis. In contemporary policy studies, grand theories are eschewed and have been replaced by the recognition that social problems and the government's response to them are affected by a range of factors whose general form, but not specific content, can be assumed in advance (see Cook, 1985; Jennings, 1987). The emphasis is now very much upon considering as many factors as possible in assessing the causes, consequences, and dynamics of public policy-making. Studying public policy is demanding and difficult because government decision-making is complex and nuanced. But careful conceptualization and systematic analysis along the lines set out in this volume go a long way towards bringing some light into what has been, for many years, the 'black box' of government activity (see Roe, 1990, 2000; Bernstein et al., 2000).

Study Questions

1. Is policy feedback an inherently conservative force that entrenches established ideas and interests? Can it unlock established organizational and administrative patterns and promote new policy dynamics?
2. To what degree is policy knowledge unique to a specific context? How much insight into policy can be acquired from studying the experience of other sectors and events?
3. How are patterns of normal and atypical change linked together?
4. What are some of the processes that typically engender policy punctuations?
5. How do new policy regimes become institutionalized?

Further Readings

Abbott, A. 1983. 'Sequences of Social Events: Concepts and Methods for the Analysis of Order in Social Processes', *Historical Methods* 16, 4: 129–47.

———. 1997. 'On the Concept of Turning Point', *Comparative Social Research* 16: 85–105.

———. 2001. *Time Matters: On Theory and Method*. Chicago: University of Chicago Press.

Baumgartner, Frank R., and Bryan D. Jones. 1991. 'Agenda Dynamics and Policy Subsystems', *Journal of Politics* 53, 4: 1044–74.

Campbell, John L. 1998. 'Institutional Analysis and the Role of Ideas in Political Economy', *Theory and Society* 27, 5: 377–409.

Coleman, William D., Grace D. Skogstad, and Michael Atkinson. 1996. 'Paradigm Shifts and Policy Networks: Cumulative Change in Agriculture', *Journal of Public Policy* 16, 3: 273–302.

Eisner, Marc Allen. 1994. 'Discovering Patterns in Regulatory History: Continuity, Change and Regulatory Regimes', *Journal of Policy History* 6, 2: 157–87.

Esping-Andersen, Gosta. 1985. 'Power and Distributional Regimes', *Politics and Society* 14, 2: 223–56.

Gersick, Connie J.G. 1991. 'Revolutionary Change Theories: A Multilevel Exploration of the Punctuated Equilibrium Paradigm', *Academy of Management Review* 16, 1: 10–36.

Hall, Peter A. 1993. 'Policy Paradigms, Social Learning and the State: The Case of Economic Policy-making in Britain', *Comparative Politics* 25, 3: 275–96.

Jones, Bryan D., and Frank R. Baumgartner. 2005. *The Politics of Attention: How Government Prioritizes Problems*. Chicago: University of Chicago Press.

Perl, Anthony, 1991. 'Financing Transport Infrastructure: The Effects of Institutional Durability in French and American Policymaking," *Governance* 4, 4: 365–402.

Richardson, Jeremy, Gunnel Gustafsson, and Grant Jordan. 1982. 'The Concept of Policy Style', in Richardson, ed., *Policy Styles in Western Europe*. London: George Allen and Unwin, 1–16.

True, James L., Bryan D. Jones, and Frank R. Baumgartner. 1999. 'Punctuated-Equilibrium Theory: Explaining Stability and Change in American Policymaking', in P.A. Sabatier, ed., *Theories of the Policy Process*. Boulder, Colo.: Westview Press, 97–115.

Wilson, Carter A. 2000. 'Policy Regimes and Policy Change', *Journal of Public Policy* 20, 3: 247–71.

Notes

Chapter 2

1. Keohane (1989: 163) described them as 'persistent and connected sets of rules (formal or informal) that prescribe behavioural roles, constrain activity, and shape expectations'.
2. Identifying the institutional logic of appropriate behaviour regarding economic transactions can be applied to many other areas of social and political life. Policy-relevant activities such as the negotiation of international treaties, the operation of multi-level systems of government, and issues of regulatory enforcement are subject to similar analyses in which the actions and decisions of policy actors are modelled as the outcomes of multiple, nested games occurring within the confines, costs, and payoffs established by institutional orders (Scharpf, 1997; Putnam, 1988; Scholz, 1984; Sproule-Jones, 1989).
3. See the efforts to accomplish this in the synthesis of deductive and inductive neo-institutionalisms in Aspinwall and Schneider (2000) and Hollingsworth (2000). On the limits of these efforts, see Hay and Wincott (1998).

Chapter 3

1. Even more significantly, some institutional arrangements are believed to be more conducive to effective policy-making and implementation than others (Stoker, 1989; May, 1993; Siedschlag, 2000).
2. The normative and ideological nature of much discussion on this subject is apparent in the titles and terms used to describe many findings. This can be seen in the otherwise excellent comparative and historical studies of Joel Brooks, who, finding very little relationship between public opinion and policy-making, terms this phenomenon 'democratic frustration', suggesting it results from a problem with the policy system failing to react properly to the democratic one. See Brooks (1985, 1987, 1990). More recently, see Petry (1999).
3. That is to say, not discriminating against imports once they have crossed the border after meeting all legal requirements, including payment of applicable tariffs.

Chapter 4

1. This is a type of threshold model of social behaviour. On these, see Wood and Doan (2003); Granovetter (1978); Schelling (1971).

Chapter 5

1. Bardach (1980), for instance, argued that government had three 'technologies' at its disposal—enforcement, inducement, and benefaction—and that these required different combinations of four critical governmental resources: money, political support, administrative competency, and creative leadership. Rondinelli suggested that all policy instruments depended on a limited set of 'methods of influence' that governments had at their disposal: in his case, persuasion, exchange, and authority (Rondinelli, 1983: 125).

2. Much of this criticism relied heavily on works by authors of the Chicago and Virginia schools of political economy, who showed how regulations were inefficient as well inequitable (for examples of the former, see Becker, 1983; Peltzman, 1974; Stigler, 1971; for the latter, see Buchanan and Tollison, 1984; Landes and Posner, 1975; Posner, 1974; Tollison, 1991). Neo-conservative politicians, led by Britain's Margaret Thatcher and US President Ronald Reagan, further fanned popular sentiments against regulations, which put deregulation at the centre of the economic policy reform agenda right around the world (Eisner, 1994b; Ramesh and Howlett, 2006; Crew and Rowley, 1986; Derthick and Quirk, 1985).

3. Other policy instruments not technically considered as subsidies may involve some component of subsidy. Thus, regulations that restrict the quantity of a particular good or service produced or sold also involve subsidy to the producers because they can often artificially increase prices. Restrictive licensing, such as that received by the taxi-cab industry in most places, is another example of this kind of subsidy through regulation. Government procurement from local producers at a price higher than the market price is also a subsidy to these producers to the extent of the difference between the purchase price and the market price (Howard, 1997). Where government is purchasing leading-edge products and services, as can occur in defence and aerospace contracts, the way in which the uncertain costs of deploying new technology are dealt with can be critical to policy success or failure (Bajari and Tadelis, 2001). Public procurement can also be targeted to advance policy priorities such as the promotion of minority-owned enterprises and transnational human rights (McCrudden, 2004).

4. Payroll taxes of various sorts are used in most countries to fund social security programs. Under such schemes, the employer typically withholds a specified portion of the employee's salary, matches the amount by a proportion determined by the government, and then transmits both the employee's and employer's contributions to the government. Payroll taxes often build an insurance pool for designated risks such as unemployment, sickness, industrial injury, and old age pensions. When the specified contingency occurs, the insured collects from the fund. In a sense this is no different from private insurance one can buy, except that some risks are regarded as crucial to the society and hence government makes insurance against them compulsory. Compulsory participation in an insurance fund expands the number of insured and thus reduces the cost of premiums by spreading the risk for specific individual activities among the general populace (Katzman, 1988; Feldman, 2002).

5. Another innovative example of user charges is provided by the efforts of Singapore and, more recently, London to control downtown traffic congestion. During peak hours, commuters in Singapore are required to pay a set fee to enter the downtown area, which forces them to compare the costs of entering the area in their own vehicles with the cost of taking a bus or underground train, which are exempt from the charge (Lam and Toan, 2006). The charge has had a marked impact, reducing traffic inflow into the downtown area (Phang and Toh, 2004). London, England, has followed Singapore's lead in charging drivers for centre city roads, yielding a 30 per cent decrease in driving delays and an 18 per cent reduction in traffic volume (Leape, 2006). Other cities, such as New York, are now considering similar schemes.

6. All societies regard looking after the needs of family members and others close to them as an essential individual responsibility. Children, the aged, and the sick are ordinarily looked after in this manner, mainly in terms of care, but financial assistance is also common. It has been calculated that in 1978 the total cost of the transfer of cash, food, and housing within families in the United States amounted to US$86 billion (Gilbert and Gilbert, 1989: 281). Non-monetary transfers are almost impossible to estimate, however, because families provide a range of services whose value cannot be priced. It

is estimated, for example, that about 80 per cent of home health-care services for the elderly in the US are provided by family members (ibid., 19).

7. Initial findings suggest that as non-profit organizations funded primarily from donations shift their focus to activities that generate fees and sales revenue, they become more focused on program delivery to client group(s) and less engaged with the broader community of related organizations (Galaskiewicz et al., 2006). Despite the possibility that focusing voluntary and faith-based organizations on service delivery can have indirect costs in their ability to contribute to the broader community, budgetary pressures have prompted governments in many countries to rely more on the voluntary sector as a way to lower program costs (Brock and Banting, 2001).

8. Toll goods include semi-public goods, such as bridges or highways, which do not diminish in quantity after use but for the use of which it is possible to charge. Common-pool goods are those, like fish in the ocean, whose usage cannot be directly charged to individuals but whose quantity is reduced after use.

9. Examples of first-order changes in a health sector, for example, would include altering staffing levels in hospitals or altering physician fee schedules. Second-order changes would involve changing the type of instrument used to deliver health care, such as moving from user fees to mandatory insurance arrangements. Third-order change would involve a shift in policy goals, such as moving away from a biomedical focus on the individual to a more holistic goal of collective, social, or community well-being.

10. For similar models based on a similar critique of Hall, see Daugbjerg (1997); Smith (2000).

11. Although this insight is similar to that used to generate a simple spectrum or continuum of subsystem types—ranging from integrated to unintegrated and usually related to a single variable such as subsystem size—this does not fully capture the complexity of subsystem structure. See Marsh and Rhodes (1992b). While it is common to associate small subsystems with integration and large ones with a lack of cohesion, many studies have shown that small subsystems can exhibit unintegrated communities and networks, while being large, similarly, does not prevent subsystems from being unified and cohesive. See, for example, Giuliani (1999); Kriesi and Jegen (2001).

12. Hence, one of the most significant aspects of subsystem structure involves the nature of the relationship, or the configuration, that exists between the two component parts of the subsystem: the discourse community and the interest network (see Bulkley, 2000; Schaap and van Twist, 1997). This is because subsystems featuring closely integrated communities and networks will be more cohesive and better able to resist the entrance of new ideas and actors into policy processes than will those with sizable intellectual and psychological distances between the two subsets of actors (Howlett, 2002).

Chapter 6

1. For a very good and comprehensive survey, see Abelson and Levi (1985).

2. Much work on decision tools and strategies, such as environmental impact statements, risk analysis, and intergovernmental diplomacy, has involved the study of these multi-round decision processes so that governments seeking particular policy outcomes might better design their form and structure (see Kennett, 2000; Bregha et al., 1990; Koppenjan, 2001; Gregory et al., 2001).

3. On the significance of the organizational context and the ideational frames constructed by decision-makers within these contexts for decision-making, see Black (1997); Hammond and Knott (1999); Metcalfe (1978); Mintz (1993).

Chapter 8

1. The literature on the poor quality of media analysis and its distorting influence (e.g., fixation on scandals and symbolic politics, and efforts of government to control media content) is of interest here. See, especially, Murray (2007); Tumber and Waisbord (2004); Cobb and Primo (2003); Lodge and Hood (2002); Nisbet and Lewenstein (2002); Callaghan and Schnell (2001); Lee (2001).

Chapter 9

1. 'Path dependency' is often used simply as a synonym for the idea that 'history matters' in policy studies (Pierson, 2000a). This is useful insofar as it points to the idea that 'sequence matters' in terms of when and how policies develop (Abbott, 1983, 2001). However, a more specific view of path dependency includes the idea that policy development is essentially chance-like, at least insofar as initial events establishing policy trajectories are concerned. Mahoney, for example, outlines the three principal elements of a path-dependent model of historical evolution as: (1) only early events in sequence matter; (2) these early events are contingent; and (3) later events are inertial (Mahoney, 2000). These elements separate this model from narrative analyses and from other historical models, such as process sequencing (see Howlett and Rayner, 2006). Identifying these 'turning points' or 'conjunctures' is thus critical to path-dependency analyses of historical processes, although there is significant debate in the literature over exactly what is meant by characterizing an event as 'contingent' (Wilsford, 1985, 1994; Abbott, 1997). At its simplest, contingency implies that, although the particular sequence of events is not a strictly necessary one, predictable from the conditions of the starting point according to general laws, an explicable pattern nonetheless relates one point to another, especially in the early part of the sequence. While a random sequence implies that any event has an equal probability of following from any other, in a contingent sequence each turning point renders the occurrence of the next point more likely until, finally, 'lock-in' occurs and a general explanatory principle, such as increasing returns, takes over the work of explanation (Mahoney and Schensul, 2006; Liebowitz and Margolis, 1995).

2. As Pierson (2000b), Weir (1992), and March and Olsen (1989: 52), among others, have argued, policy stability emerges when a problem definition or policy solution is routinized, increasing the constituency for its preservation and raising the costs and difficulty of its alteration or termination (see Haydu, 1998; Torfing, 2001; David, 2005; Goodin and Rein, 2001).

Bibliography

Aaron, H.J. 1967. 'Social Security: International Comparison', in O. Eckstein, ed., *Studies in the Economics of Income Maintenance*. Washington: Brookings Institution, 13–49.

Abbott, A. 1990. 'Conceptions of Time and Events in Social Science Methods', *Historical Methods* 23, 4: 140–51.

———. 1997. 'On the Concept of Turning Point', *Comparative Social Research* 16: 85–105.

Abelson, Donald E. 1996. *American Think Tanks and Their Role in U.S. Foreign Policy*. London: Macmillan.

———. 1999. 'Public Visibility and Policy Relevance: Assessing the Impact and Influence of Canadian Policy Institutes', *Canadian Public Administration* 42, 2: 240–70.

———. 2002. *Do Think Tanks Matter? Assessing the Impact of Public Policy Institutes*. Montreal and Kingston: McGill-Queen's University Press.

———. 2007. 'Any Ideas? Think Tanks and Policy Analysis in Canada', in Dobuzinskis et al. (2007: 298–310).

Abelson, R.P., and A. Levi. 1985. 'Decision Making and Decision Theory', in G. Lindzey and E. Aronson, eds, *Handbook of Social Psychology: Vol. 1: Theory and Method*. New York: Random House, 231–309.

Aberbach, Joel D., Robert D. Putnam, and Bert A. Rockman. 1981. *Bureaucrats and Politicians in Western Democracies*. Cambridge, Mass.: Harvard University Press.

Abma, Tineke A., and Mirko Noordegraaf. 2003. 'Public Managers amidst Ambiguity: Towards a Typology of Evaluative Practices in Public Management', *Evaluation* 9, 3: 285–306.

Abrahamson, Eric, and Gregory Fairchild. 1999. 'Management Fashion, Lifecycles, Triggers, and Collective Learning Processes', *Administrative Science Quarterly* 44: 708–40.

Adair, John J., and Rex Simmons. 1988. 'From Voucher Auditing to Junkyard Dogs: The Evolution of Federal Inspectors General', *Public Budgeting and Finance* 8, 2: 91–100.

Adams, Greg D. 1997. 'Abortion: Evidence of an Issue Evolution', *American Journal of Political Science* 41, 3: 718–37.

Adcroft, A., and R. Willis. 2005. 'The (Un)Intended Outcome of Public Sector Performance Measurement', *International Journal of Public Sector Management* 18, 5: 386–400.

Adie, R.F., and P.G. Thomas. 1987. *Canadian Public Administration: Problematical Perspectives*, 2nd edn. Scarborough, Ont.: Prentice-Hall.

Adler, Robert S., and R. David Pittle. 1984. 'Cajolery or Command: Are Education Campaigns an Adequate Substitute for Regulation', *Yale Journal on Regulation* 1: 159–93.

Advani, Asheesh, and Sandford Borins. 2001. 'Managing Airports: A Test of the New Public Management', *International Public Management Journal* 4: 91–107.

Afonso, Alexandre. 2007. 'Policy Change and the Politics of Expertise: Economic Ideas and Immigration Control Reforms in Switzerland', *Swiss Political Science Review* 13, 1: 1–38.

Aglietta, Michel. 1979. *A Theory of Capitalist Regulation*. London: New Left Books.

Agranoff, R., and M. McGuire. 1999. 'Managing in Network Settings', *Policy Studies Review* 16, 1: 18–41.

——— and Mete Yildiz. 2007. 'Decision Making in Public Management Networks', in Morcöl (2007: 319–45).

Ahroni, Yair. 1986. *Evolution and Management of State-Owned Enterprises*. Cambridge, Mass.: Ballinger.

Aldrich, Howard, and Diane Herker. 1977. 'Boundary Spanning Roles and Organizational Structure', *Academy of Management Review* 2 (Apr.): 217–30.

——— and David A. Whetten. 1980. 'Organization-sets, Action-sets, and Networks: Making the Most of Simplicity', in P. Nystrom and W.H. Starbuck, eds, *Handbook of Organizational Design*. Oxford: Oxford University Press.

Alexander, Ernest R. 1979. 'The Design of Alternatives in Organizational Contexts: A Pilot Study', *Administrative Sciences Quarterly* 24: 382–404.

———. 1982. 'Design in the Decision-Making Process', *Policy Sciences* 14: 279–92.

Alford, Robert R. 1972. 'The Political Economy of Health Care: Dynamics without Change', *Politics and Society* 2, 2: 127–64.

———. 1975. *Health Care Politics: Ideological and Interest Group Barriers to Reform*. Chicago: University of Chicago Press.

Alink, Fleur, Arjen Boin, and Paul t'Hart. 2001. 'Institutional Crises and Reforms in Policy Sectors: The Case of Asylum Policy in Europe', *Journal of European Public Policy* 8, 2: 286–306.

Allison, Graham. 1969. 'Conceptual Models and the Cuban Missile Crisis', *American Political Science Review* 63: 689–718.

———. 1971. *Essence of Decision: Explaining the Cuban Missile Crisis*. Boston: Little, Brown.

——— and Morton H. Halperin. 1972. 'Bureaucratic Politics: A Paradigm and Some Policy Implications', *World Politics* 24 (supp.): 40–79.

Almond, Gabriel A. 1988. 'The Return to the State', *American Political Science Review* 82, 3: 853–901.

——— and Stephen J. Genco. 1977. 'Clouds, Clocks and the Study of Politics', *World Politics* 29: 489–522.

Althusser, L., and E. Balibar. 1977. *Reading 'Capital'*. London: New Left Books.

Amariglio, Jack L., Stephen A. Resnick, and Richard D. Wolff. 1988. 'Class, Power, and Culture', in C. Nelson and L. Grossberg, eds, *Marxism and the Interpretation of Culture*. Urbana: University of Illinois Press.

Aminzade, Ronald. 1992. 'Historical Sociology and Time', *Sociological Methods and Research* 20, 4: 456–80.

Anderson, Charles W. 1971. 'Comparative Policy Analysis: The Design of Measures', *Comparative Politics* 4, 1: 117–31.

———. 1977. *Statecraft: An Introduction to Political Choice and Judgement*. New York: John Wiley and Sons.

———. 1979a. 'The Place of Principles in Policy Analysis', *American Political Science Review* 73, 3: 711–23.

———. 1979b. 'Political Design and the Representation of Interests', in P.C. Schmitter and G. Lehmbruch, eds, *Trends towards Corporatist Intermediation*. London: Sage, 271–97.

Anderson, G. 1996. 'The New Focus on the Policy Capacity of the Federal Government', *Canadian Public Administration* 39, 4: 469–88.

Anderson, James E. 1975. *Public Policy-Making*. New York: Praeger.

———, ed. 1976. *Economic Regulatory Policies*. Lexington, Mass.: Lexington Books.

———. 1984. *Public Policy-Making: An Introduction*, 3rd edn. Boston: Houghton Mifflin.

Anderson, Paul A. 1983. 'Decision Making by Objection and the Cuban Missile Crisis', *Administrative Science Quarterly* 28: 201–22.

Andrews, Richard. 1998. 'Environmental Regulation and Business "Self-Regulation"', *Policy Sciences* 31: 177–97.

Anglund, Sandra M. 1999. 'Policy Feedback: The Comparison Effect and Small Business Procurement Policy', *Policy Studies Journal* 27, 1: 11–27.

Angus, William H. 1974. 'Judicial Review: Do We Need It?', in D.J. Baum, ed., *The Individual and the Bureaucracy*. Toronto: Carswell.

Argyris, Chris. 1992. *On Organizational Learning*. London: Blackwell.

———— and Donald A. Schon. 1978. *Organizational Learning: A Theory of Action Perspective*. Reading, Mass.: Addison-Wesley.

Armstrong, Jim, and Donald G. Lenihan. 1999. *From Controlling to Collaborating; When Governments Want to be Partners: A Report on the Collaborative Partnership Project*. Toronto: Institute of Public Administration of Canada New Directions, Number 3.

Arthur, W. Brian. 1989. 'Competing Technologies, Increasing Returns, and Lock-In by Historical Events', *Economic Journal* 99: 116–31.

Ascher, Kate. 1987. *The Politics of Privatisation: Contracting Out Public Services*. Basingstoke: Macmillan.

Ascher, William. 1986. 'The Evolution of the Policy Sciences: Understanding the Rise and Avoiding the Fall', *Journal of Policy Analysis and Management* 5: 365–89.

Aspinwall, Mark D., and Gerald Schneider. 2000. 'Same Menu, Separate Tables: The Institutionalist Turn in Political Science and the Study of European Integration', *European Journal of Political Research* 38: 1–36.

Atkinson, Michael M., and William D. Coleman. 1989a. 'Strong States and Weak States: Sectoral Policy Networks in Advanced Capitalist Economies', *British Journal of Political Science* 19, 1: 47–67.

———— and ————. 1989b. *The State, Business, and Industrial Change in Canada*. Toronto: University of Toronto Press.

———— and ————. 1992. 'Policy Networks, Policy Communities and the Problems of Governance', *Governance* 5, 2: 154–80.

———— and Robert A. Nigol. 1989. 'Selecting Policy Instruments: Neo-Institutional and Rational Choice Interpretations of Automobile Insurance in Ontario', *Canadian Journal of Political Science* 22, 1: 107–35.

Aucoin, Peter. 1990. 'Administrative Reform in Public Management: Paradigms, Principles, Paradoxes and Pendulums', *Governance* 3, 2: 115–37.

————. 1997. 'The Design of Public Organizations for the 21st Century: Why Bureaucracy Will Survive in Public Management', *Canadian Public Administration* 40, 2: 290–306.

————. 2006. 'Accountability and Coordination with Independent Foundations: A Canadian Case of Autonomization', in Tom Christensen and Per Laegreid, eds, *Autonomy and Regulation: Coping with Agencies in the Modern State*. Cheltenham: Edward Elgar, 110–33.

Averch, Harvey. 1990. *Private Markets and Public Interventions: A Primer for Policy Designers*. Pittsburgh: University of Pittsburgh Press.

Axworthy, Thomas S. 1988. 'Of Secretaries to Princes', *Canadian Public Administration* 31, 2: 247–64.

Bache, I., and M. Flinders. 2004. *Multi-Level Governance*. New York: Oxford University Press.

Bachrach, Peter, and Morton S. Baratz. 1962. 'Decisions and Non-decisions: An Analytical Framework', *American Political Science Review* 56, 2: 632–42.

———— and ————. 1970. *Power and Poverty: Theory and Practice*. New York: Oxford University Press.

———— and ————. 1975. 'Power and Its Two Faces Revisited: A Reply to Geoffrey Debnam', *American Political Science Review* 69, 3: 900–7.

Bailey, J.J., and R.J. O'Connor. 1975. 'Operationalizing Incrementalism: Measuring the Muddles', *Public Administration Review* 35: 60–6.

Bajari, P., and S. Tadelis. 2001. 'Incentives versus Transaction Costs: A Theory of Procurement Contracts', *Rand Journal of Economics* 32, 3: 387–407.

Baksi, Soham, and Pinaki Bose. 2007. 'Credence Goods, Efficient Labelling Policies, and Regulatory Enforcement', *Environmental and Resource Economics* 37: 411–30.

Bakvis, Herman. 1997. 'Advising the Executive: Think Tanks, Consultants, Political Staff and Kitchen Cabinets', in P. Weller, H. Bakvis, and R.A.W. Rhodes, eds, *The Hollow Crown: Countervailing Trends in Core Executives.* New York: St Martin's Press, 84–125.

———. 2000. 'Rebuilding Policy Capacity in the Era of the Fiscal Dividend: A Report from Canada', *Governance* 13, 1: 71–103.

——— and David MacDonald. 1993. 'The Canadian Cabinet: Organization, Decision-Rules, and Policy Impact', in M. Michael Atkinson, ed., *Governing Canada: Institutions and Public Policy.* Toronto: Harcourt Brace Jovanovich.

Balch, George I. 1980. 'The Stick, the Carrot, and Other Strategies: A Theoretical Analysis of Governmental Intervention', *Law and Policy Quarterly* 2, 1: 35–60.

Baldwin, David A. 1985. *Economic Statecraft.* Princeton, NJ: Princeton University Press.

Baldwin, Robert, and Martin Cave. 1999. *Understanding Regulation: Theory, Strategy and Practice.* Oxford: Oxford University Press.

Balla, Steven J., and John R. Wright. 2001. 'Interest Groups, Advisory Committees, and Congressional Control of the Bureaucracy', *American Journal of Political Science* 45, 4: 799–812.

Banks, Jeffrey S. 1995. 'The Design of Institutions', in D.L. Weimer, ed., *Institutional Design.* Boston: Kluwer, 17–36.

Bannink, Duco, and Marcel Hoogenboom. 2007. 'Hidden Change: Disaggregation of Welfare Regimes for Greater Insight into Welfare State Change', *Journal of European Social Policy* 17, 1: 19–32.

Banting, Keith G. 1982. *The Welfare State and Canadian Federalism.* Kingston, Ont.: Queen's University Institute of Intergovernmental Relations.

———. 1995. 'The Social Policy Review: Policy-Making in a Semi-Sovereign Society', *Canadian Public Administration* 38, 2: 283–90.

Bardach, Eugene. 1976. 'Policy Termination as a Political Process', *Policy Sciences* 7, 2: 123–31.

———. 1977. *The Implementation Game: What Happens after a Bill Becomes a Law.* Cambridge, Mass.: MIT Press.

———. 1980. 'Implementation Studies and the Study of Implements', paper presented at the annual meeting of the American Political Science Association.

———. 1989. 'Social Regulation as a Generic Policy Instrument', in Salamon (1989a).

———. 2006. 'Policy Dynamics', in Michael Moran, Martin Rein, and Robert E. Goodin, eds, *The Oxford Handbook of Public Policy.* Oxford: Oxford University Press, 336–66.

——— and Robert A. Kagan. 1982. *Going by the Book: The Problem of Regulatory Unreasonableness.* Philadelphia: Temple University Press.

Barker, Anthony, and B. Guy Peters, eds. 1993. *The Politics of Expert Advice: Creating, Using and Manipulating Scientific Knowledge for Public Policy.* Pittsburgh: University of Pittsburgh Press.

Barnett, Michael N., and Martha Finnemore. 1999. 'The Politics, Power, and Pathologies of International Organizations', *International Organization* 53, 4: 699–732.

Barrett, S.M. 2004. 'Implementation Studies: Time for a Revival? Personal Reflections on 20 Years of Implementation Studies', *Public Administration* 82, 2: 249–62.

Barrett, Susan, and Colin Fudge. 1981. *Policy and Action: Essays on the Implementation of Public Policy.* London: Methuen.

Bator, Francis M. 1958. 'The Anatomy of Market Failure', *Quarterly Journal of Economics* 72, 3: 351–79.

Baumgartner, Frank R., and Bryan D. Jones. 1991. 'Agenda Dynamics and Policy Subsystems', *Journal of Politics* 53, 4: 1044–74.

——— and ———. 1993. *Agendas and Instability in American Politics*. Chicago: University of Chicago Press.

——— and ———. 1994. 'Attention, Boundary Effects, and Large-Scale Policy Change in Air Transportation Policy', in D.A. Rochefort and R.W. Cobb, eds, *The Politics of Problem Definition: Shaping the Policy Agenda*. Lawrence: University Press of Kansas.

——— and Beth L. Leech. 1998. *Basic Interests: The Importance of Groups in Politics and in Political Science*. Princeton, NJ: Princeton University Press.

——— and ———. 2001. 'Interest Niches and Policy Bandwagons: Patterns of Interest Group Involvement in National Politics', *Journal of Politics* 63, 4: 1191–1213.

Baxter-Moore, Nicolas. 1987. 'Policy Implementation and the Role of the State: A Revised Approach to the Study of Policy Instruments', in Robert J. Jackson, Doreen Jackson, and N. Baxter-Moore, eds, *Contemporary Canadian Politics: Readings and Notes*. Scarborough, Ont.: Prentice-Hall, 336–55.

Beach, L.R., and T.R. Mitchell. 1978. 'A Contingency Model for the Selection of Decision Strategies', *Academy of Management Review* 3, 3: 439–49.

Beam, David A., and Timothy J. Conlan. 2002. 'Grants', in Salamon (2002a: 340–80).

Becker, Gary S. 1958. 'Competition and Democracy', *Journal of Law and Economics* 1: 105–9.

Beesley, M.E. 1992. *Privatization, Regulation and Deregulation*. New York: Routledge.

Behn, Robert D. 1977. 'How to Terminate a Public Policy: A Dozen Hints for the Would-be Terminator', *Policy Analysis* 4, 3: 393–414.

Bekke, H.A.G.M., J.L. Perry, T.A.J. Toonen,. 1996. *Civil Service Systems in Comparative Perspective*. Bloomington: Indiana University Press.

——— and F.M. van der Meer. 2000. *Civil Service Systems in Western Europe*. Cheltenham: Edward Elgar.

Beland, Daniel. 2007. 'Ideas and Institutional Change in Social Security: Conversion, Layering and Policy Drift', *Social Science Quarterly* 88, 1: 20–38.

Bellehumeur, Robert. 1997. 'Review: An Instrument of Change', *Optimum* 27, 1: 37–42.

Bellman, R.E., and L.A. Zadeh. 1970. 'Decision-Making in a Fuzzy Environment', *Management Science* 17, 4: B141–64

Bemelmans-Videc, Marie-Louise, Ray C. Rist, and Evert Vedung, eds. 1998. *Carrots, Sticks and Sermons: Policy Instruments and Their Evaluation*. New Brunswick, NJ: Transaction.

Bendor, Jonathan. 1995. 'A Model of Muddling Through', *American Political Science Review* 89, 4: 819–40.

——— and Thomas H. Hammond. 1992. 'Re-Thinking Allison's Models', *American Political Science Review* 86, 2: 301–22.

Bennett, Colin J. 1990. 'The Formation of a Canadian Privacy Policy: The Art and Craft of Lesson-Drawing', *Canadian Public Administration* 33, 4: 551–70

———. 1991. 'What Is Policy Convergence and What Causes It?', *British Journal of Political Science* 21, 2: 215–33.

———. 1992a. *Regulating Privacy: Data Protection and Public Policy in Europe and the United States*. Ithaca, NY: Cornell University Press.

———. 1992b. 'The International Regulation of Personal Data: From Epistemic Community to Policy Sector', paper presented at the annual meeting of the Canadian Political Science Association, Charlottetown, PEI.

———. 1997. 'Understanding Ripple Effects: The Cross-National Adoption of Policy Instruments for Bureaucratic Accountability', *Governance* 10, 3: 213–33.

——— and Michael Howlett. 1991. 'The Lessons of Learning: Reconciling Theories of Policy Learning and Policy Change', *Policy Sciences* 25, 3: 275–94.

Bennett, Scott, and Margaret McPhail. 1992. 'Policy Process Perceptions of Senior Canadian Federal Civil Servants: A View of the State and Its Environment', *Canadian Public Administration* 35, 3: 299–316.

Bennett, W. Lance. 1980. *Public Opinion in American Politics*. New York: Harcourt Brace Jovanovich.

Benson, J. Kenneth. 1982. 'A Framework for Policy Analysis', in Rogers and Whetton (1982: 137–76).

Bentley, Arthur F. 1908. *The Process of Government*. Chicago: University of Chicago Press.

Benz, A., and D. Furst. 2002. 'Policy Learning in Regional Networks', *European Urban and Regional Studies* 9, 1: 21–35.

Berelson, Bernard. 1952. 'Democratic Theory and Public Opinion', *Public Opinion Quarterly* 16 (Fall): 313–30.

Berger, Peter L., and Thomas Luckmann. 1966. *The Social Construction of Reality: A Treatise in the Sociology of Knowledge*. New York: Doubleday.

Berle, Adolf. 1959. *Power without Property*. New York: Harcourt Brace.

Bernier, Luc, Keith Brownsey, and Michael Howlett. 2005. *Executive Styles in Canada: Cabinet Structures and Leadership Practices in Canadian Government*. Institute of Public Administration of Canada Series in Public Management and Governance. Toronto: University of Toronto Press.

Bernstein, Marver H. 1955. *Regulating Business by Independent Commission*. Princeton, NJ: Princeton University Press.

Bernstein, Steven, and Benjamin Cashore. 2000. 'Globalization, Four Paths of Internationalization and Domestic Policy Change: The Case of EcoForestry in British Columbia, Canada', *Canadian Journal of Political Science* 33, 1: 67–100.

Bernstein, S., R.N. Lebow, J.G. Stein, and S. Weber. 2000. 'God Gave Physics the Easy Problems: Adapting Social Science to an Unpredictable World', *European Journal of International Relations* 6, 1: 43–76.

Berridge, V. 2005. 'Issue Network versus Producer Network? ASH, the Tobacco Products Research Trust and UK Smoking Policy', *Clio Medica* 75, 1: 101–24.

Berry, Jeffrey M. 1989. 'Subgovernments, Issue Networks, and Political Conflicts', in R.A. Harris and S.M. Milkis, eds, *Remaking American Politics*. Boulder, Colo.: Westview Press, 239–60.

Berry, William T. 1990. 'The Confusing Case of Budgetary Incrementalism: Too Many Meanings for a Single Concept', *Journal of Politics* 52: 167–96.

Bertelli, Anthony, and Sven E. Feldmann. 2007. 'Strategic Appointments', *Journal of Public Administration Research and Theory* 17, 1: 19–38.

Besley, T., and A. Case. 2003. 'Political Institutions and Policy Choices: Evidence from the United States', *Journal of Economic Literature* 41 (Mar.): 7–73.

Best, Samuel J. 1999. 'The Sampling Problem in Measuring Policy Mood: An Alternative Solution', *Journal of Politics* 61, 3: 721–40.

Bickers, Kenneth N., and John T. Williams. 2001. *Public Policy Analysis: A Political Economy Approach*. Boston: Houghton Mifflin.

Billings, Robert S., and Charles F. Hermann. 1998. 'Problem Identification in Sequential Policy Decision-Making: The Re-representation of Problems', in D.A. Sylvan and J.F. Voss, eds, *Problem Representation in Foreign Policy Decision-Making*. Cambridge: Cambridge University Press, 53–79.

Bilodeau, Nancy, Claude Laurin, and Aidan Vining. 2007. '"Choice of Organizational Forms Makes a Real Difference": The Impact of Corporatization on Government Agencies in Canada', *Journal of Public Administration Research and Theory* 17: 119–47.

Birch, Anthony H. 1972. *Representation*. New York: Praeger.

Birkland, Thomas A. 1997. *After Disaster: Agenda Setting, Public Policy and Focusing Events*. Washington: Georgetown University Press.

———. 1998. 'Focusing Events, Mobilization, and Agenda Setting', *Journal of Public Policy* 18, 1: 53–74.

———. 2001. *An Introduction to the Policy Process: Theories, Concepts, and Models of Public Policy-Making*. Armonk, NY: M.E. Sharpe.

———. 2004. '"The World Changed Today": Agenda-Setting and Policy Change in the Wake of the September 11 Terrorist Attacks', *Review of Policy Research* 21, 2: 179–200.

Black, Julia. 1997. 'New Institutionalism and Naturalism in Socio-Legal Analysis: Institutionalist Approaches to Regulatory Decision-Making', *Law and Policy* 19, 1: 51–93.

Blais, André, Donald Blake, and Stéphane Dion. 1996. 'Do Parties Make a Difference? A Re-Appraisal', *American Journal of Political Science* 40, 2: 514–20.

Bleich, Erik. 2002. 'Integrating Ideas into Policy-Making Analysis: Frames and Race Policies in Britain and France', *Comparative Political Studies* 35, 9: 1054–76.

———. 2006. 'Institutional Continuity and Change: Norms, Lesson-Drawing, and the Introduction of Race-Conscious Measures in the 1976 British Race Relations Act', *Policy Studies* 27, 3: 219–34.

Block, Fred. 1980. 'Beyond Relative Autonomy: State Managers as Historical Subjects', *Socialist Register*: 227–42.

Blom-Hansen, Jens. 1997. 'A "New Institutional" Perspective on Policy Networks', *Public Administration* 75, 4: 669–93.

———. 2001. 'Organized Interests and the State: A Disintegrating Relationship? Evidence from Denmark', *European Journal of Political Research* 39: 391–416.

Blyth, Mark M. 1997. ' "Any More Bright Ideas?" The Ideational Turn of Comparative Political Economy', *Comparative Politics* 29: 229–50.

———. 2007. 'Powering, Puzzling or Persuading? The Mechanisms of Building Institutional Orders', *International Studies Quarterly* 51: 761–77.

Boardman, A.E., D.H. Greenberg, A.R. Vining, and D.L. Weimer. 2001. *Cost-Benefit Analysis: Concepts and Practice*. Upper Saddle River, NJ: Prentice-Hall.

Bobrow, Davis B. 2006. 'Policy Design: Ubiquitous, Necessary and Difficult', in B. Guy Peters and Jon Pierre, eds, *Handbook of Public Policy*. London: Sage, 75–96.

——— and John S. Dryzek. 1987. *Policy Analysis by Design*. Pittsburgh: University of Pittsburgh Press.

Boddy, Raford, and James Crotty. 1975. 'Class Conflict and Macro-Policy: The Political Business Cycle', *Review of Radical Political Economics* 7, 1: 1–19.

Bogart, W.A. 2002. *Consequences: The Impact of Law and Its Complexity*. Toronto: University of Toronto Press.

Bogason, Peter. 2000. *Public Policy and Local Governance: Institutions in Postmodern Society*. Cheltenham: Edward Elgar.

Bohm, Peter, and Clifford S. Russell. 1985. 'Comparative Analysis of Alternative Policy Instruments', in A.V. Kneese and J.L. Sweeney, eds, *Handbook of Natural Resource and Energy Economics*, vol. 1. Dordrecht: Elsevier.

Boin, R. Arjen, and Marc H.P. Otten. 1996. 'Beyond the Crisis Window for Reform: Some Ramifications for Implementation', *Journal of Contingencies and Crisis Management* 4, 3: 149–61.

Bolom, Jan-Tjeerd. 2000. 'International Emissions Trading Under the Kyoto Protocol: Credit Trading', *Energy Policy* 29: 605–13.

Boockmann, Bernhard. 1998. 'Agenda Control by Interest Groups in EU Social Policy', *Journal of Theoretical Politics* 10, 2: 215–36.

Borzel, Tanja A. 1998. 'Organizing Babylon—On the Different Conceptions of Policy Networks', *Public Administration* 76 (Summer): 253–73.

Bos, Dieter. 1991. *Privatization: A Theoretical Treatment*. Oxford: Clarendon Press.

Bosso, Christopher J. 1989. 'Setting the Agenda: Mass Media and the Discovery of Famine in Ethiopia', in M. Margolis and G.A. Mauser, eds, *Manipulating Public Opinion: Essays on Public Opinion as a Dependent Variable*. Pacific Grove, Calif.: Brooks/Cole, 153–74.

Bourgault, Jacques, and Stéphane Dion. 1989. 'Governments Come and Go, But What of Senior Civil Servants? Canadian Deputy Ministers and Transitions in Power (1867–1987)', *Governance* 2, 2: 124–51.

Bovens, Mark, and Paul t'Hart. 1995. 'Frame Multiplicity and Policy Fiascoes: Limits to Explanation', *Knowledge and Policy* 8, 4: 61–83.

———— and ————. 1996. *Understanding Policy Fiascoes*. New Brunswick, NJ: Transaction.

————, ————, and B. Guy Peters. 2001. 'Analysing Governance Success and Failure in Six European States', in Bovens, t'Hart, and Peters, eds, *Success and Failure in Public Governance: A Comparative Analysis*. Cheltenham: Edward Elgar, 12–32.

Boychuk, Gerard. 1997. 'Are Canadian and U.S. Social Assistance Policies Converging?', *Canadian-American Public Policy* 30: 1–55.

Boyer, B., and L. Cremieux. 1999. 'The Anatomy of Association: NGOs and the Evolution of Swiss Climate and Biodiversity Policies', *International Negotiation* 4: 255–82.

Bozeman, Barry, ed. 1993. *Public Management: The State of the Art*. San Francisco: Jossey-Bass.

————. 2002. 'Public-Value Failure: When Efficient Markets May Not Do', *Public Administration Review* 62, 2: 145–61.

———— and S.K. Pandey. 2004. 'Public Management Decision Making: Effect of Decision Content', *Public Administration Review* 64, 5: 553–65.

Bradford, Neil. 1999. 'The Policy Influence of Economic Ideas: Interests, Institutions and Innovation in Canada', *Studies in Political Economy* 59: 17–60.

Braithwaite, J., J. Walker, et al. 1987. 'An Enforcement Taxonomy of Regulatory Agencies', *Law and Policy* 9, 3: 323–51.

Brandsen, T., M. Boogers, and P. Tops. 2006. 'Soft Governance, Hard Consequences: The Ambiguous Status of Unofficial Guidelines', *Public Administration Review* 66, 4: 546–53.

Brandstrom, A., and S. Kuipers. 2003. 'From "Normal Incidents" to Political Crises: Understanding the Selective Politicization of Policy Failures', *Government and Opposition* 38, 3: 279–305.

Braun, Dietmar. 1999. 'Interests or Ideas? An Overview of Ideational Concepts in Public Policy Research', in D. Braun and A. Busch, eds, *Public Policy and Political Ideas*. Cheltenham: Edward Elgar, 11–29.

Braybrooke, David, and Charles Lindblom. 1963. *A Strategy of Decision: Policy Evaluation as a Social Process*. New York: Free Press of Glencoe.

Bregha, Francois, et al. 1990. *The Integration of Environmental Considerations into Government Policy*. Ottawa: Canadian Environmental Assessment Research Council.

Brenner, Neil. 1999. 'Beyond State-Centrism? Space, Territoriality, and Geographical Scale in Globalization Studies', *Theory and Society* 28: 39–78.

Bressers, Hans Th.A. 1998. 'The Choice of Policy Instruments in Policy Networks', in Peters and Van Nispen (1998: 85–105).

———— and Pieter-Jan Klok. 1988. 'Fundamentals for a Theory of Policy Instruments', *International Journal of Social Economics* 15, 3 and 4: 22–41.

———— and Laurence J. O'Toole. 1998. 'The Selection of Policy Instruments: A Network-based Perspective', *Journal of Public Policy* 18, 3: 213–39.

———— and ————. 2005. 'Instrument Selection and Implementation in a Networked Context', in P. Eliadis, M. Hill, and M. Howlett, eds, *Designing Government: From*

Instruments to Governance. Montreal and Kingston: McGill-Queen's University Press, 132–53.

Brewer, Garry D. 1974. 'The Policy Sciences Emerge: To Nurture and Structure a Discipline', *Policy Sciences* 5, 3: 239–44.

———— and Peter DeLeon. 1983. *The Foundations of Policy Analysis*. Homewood, NJ: Dorsey.

Breyer, Stephen. 1979. 'Analyzing Regulatory Failure: Mismatches, Less Restrictive Alternatives, and Reform', *Harvard Law Review* 92, 3: 549–609.

————. 1982. *Regulation and Its Reform*. Cambridge, Mass.: Harvard University Press.

Briassoulis, H. 2005. *Policy Integration for Complex Environmental Problems: The Example of Mediterranean Desertification*. Aldershot: Ashgate.

Brock, K.L., and K.G. Banting. 2001. *The Nonprofit Sector and Government in a New Century*. Montreal and Kingston: McGill-Queen's University Press.

Bromley, Daniel W. 1989. *Economic Interests and Institutions: The Conceptual Foundations of Public Policy*. New York: Blackwell.

Brooks, Joel E. 1985. 'Democratic Frustration in the Anglo-American Polities: A Quantification of Inconsistency between Mass Public Opinion and Public Policy', *Western Political Quarterly* 38, 2: 250–61.

————. 1987. 'The Opinion-Policy Nexus in France: Do Institutions and Ideology Make a Difference?', *Journal of Politics* 49, 2: 465–80.

————. 1990. 'The Opinion-Policy Nexus in Germany', *Public Opinion Quarterly* 54, 3: 508–29.

Brooks, Sarah M. 2005. 'Interdependent and Domestic Foundations of Policy Change: The Diffusion of Pension Privatization around the World', *International Studies Quarterly* 49: 273–94.

————. 2007. 'When Does Diffusion Matter? Explaining the Spread of Structural Pension Reforms across Nations', *Journal of Politics* 69, 3: 701–15.

Brooks, Stephen. 1998. *Public Policy in Canada: An Introduction*, 3rd edn. Toronto: Oxford University Press.

———— and Alain-G. Gagnon, eds. 1990. *Social Scientists, Policy, and the State*. New York: Praeger.

Brown, David S. 1955. 'The Public Advisory Board as an Instrument of Government', *Public Administration Review* 15: 196–201.

————. 1972. 'The Management of Advisory Committees: An Assignment for the '70's', *Public Administration Review* 32: 334–42.

Brown, M. Paul. 1992. 'Organizational Design as a Policy Instrument', in R. Boardman, ed., *Canadian Environmental Policy: Ecosystems, Politics, and Processes*. Toronto: Oxford University Press, 24–42.

Browne, William P. 1990. 'Organized Interests and Their Issue Niches: A Search for Pluralism in a Policy Domain', *Journal of Politics* 52, 2: 477–509.

————. 1991. 'Issue Niches and the Limits of Interest Group Influence', in Allan J. Cigler and Burdett A. Loomis, eds, *Interest Group Politics*. Washington: CQ Press, 345–70.

Brule, David J. 2008. 'The Poliheuristic Research Program: An Assessment and Suggestions for Further Progress', *International Studies Review* 10, 2: 266–93.

Brunori, David. 1997. 'Principle of Tax Policy and Targeted Tax Incentives', *State and Local Government Review* 29, 1: 50–61.

Bruton, Jim, and Michael Howlett. 1992. 'Differences of Opinion: Round Tables, Policy Networks and the Failure of Canadian Environmental Strategy', *Alternatives* 19, 1: 25.

Bryman, Alan. 1988. *Quantity and Quality in Social Research*. London: Unwin Hyman.

Bryson, John M., and Barbara C. Crosby. 1993. 'Policy Planning and the Design and Use of Forums, Arenas, and Courts', in Bozeman (1993).

Buchanan, James. 1975. *The Limits of Liberty*. Chicago: University of Chicago Press.

———. 1980. 'Rent Seeking and Profit Seeking', in Buchanan et al. (1980).

——— et al. 1978. *The Economics of Politics*. London: Institute of Economic Affairs.

———, R.O. Tollison, and G. Tullock, eds. 1980. *Toward a Theory of the Rent-Seeking Society*. College Station: Texas A&M Press.

Buckley, Walter. 1968. 'Society as a Complex Adaptive System', in Buckley, ed., *Modern System Research for the Behavioural Scientist*. Chicago: Aldine, 490–513.

Bulkley, Harriet. 2000. 'Discourse Coalition and the Australian Climate Change Policy Network', *Environment and Planning C: Government and Policy* 18: 727–48.

Bulmer, Martin. 1993. 'The Royal Commission and Departmental Committee in the British Policy-Making Process', in Peters and Parker (1993: 37–49).

Bundgaard, Ulrik, and Karsten Vrangbaek. 2007. 'Reform by Coincidence? Explaining the Policy Process of Structural Reform in Denmark', *Scandinavian Political Studies* 30, 4: 491–520.

Burgess, Michael, and Alain-G. Gagnon, eds. 1993. *Comparative Federalism and Federation: Competing Traditions and Future Directions*. New York: Harvester Wheatsheaf.

Burns, J.P., and B. Bowornwathana, 2001. *Civil Service Systems in Asia*. Cheltenham: Edward Elgar.

Burstein, Paul. 1991. 'Policy Domains: Organization, Culture and Policy Outcomes', *Annual Review of Sociology* 17: 327–50.

Burt, Sandra. 1990. 'Canadian Women's Groups in the 1980s: Organizational Development and Policy Influence', *Canadian Public Policy* 16, 1: 17–28.

Burton, P. 2006. 'Modernising the Policy Process: Making Policy Research More Significant?', *Policy Studies Journal* 27, 3: 173–95.

Busenberg, George J. 2000. 'Innovation, Learning and Policy Evolution in Hazardous Systems', *American Behavioral Scientist* 44, 4: 679–91.

———. 2001. 'Learning in Organizations and Public Policy', *Journal of Public Policy* 21, 2: 173–89.

———. 2004a. 'Wildfire Management in the United States: The Evolution of a Policy Failure', *Review of Policy Research* 21, 2: 145–56.

———. 2004b. 'Adaptive Policy Design for the Management of Wildfire Hazards', *American Behavioral Scientist* 48, 3: 314–26.

Butkiewicz, J.L., and H Yanikkaya. 2005. 'The Impact of Sociopolitical Instability on Economic Growth: Analysis and Implications', *Journal of Policy Modeling* 27, 5: 629–45.

Butler, David, H.R. Penniman, and Austin Ranney, eds. 1981. *Democracy at the Polls: A Comparative Study of Competitive National Elections*. Washington: American Enterprise Institute for Public Policy Research.

——— and Austin Ranney, eds. 1994. *Referendums Around the World: A Comparative Study of Practice and Theory*. Washington: American Enterprise Institute.

Cahill, Anthony G., and E. Sam Overman. 1990. 'The Evolution of Rationality in Policy Analysis', in S.S. Nagel, ed., *Policy Theory and Policy Evaluation: Concepts, Knowledge, Causes, and Norms*. New York: Greenwood Press.

Cairns, Alan C. 1974. 'Alternative Styles in the Study of Canadian Politics', *Canadian Journal of Political Science* 7: 102–28.

———. 1990a. 'Reflections on Commission Research', in A.P. Pross, I. Christie, and J.A. Yogis, eds, *Commissions of Inquiry*. Toronto: Carswell, 87–110.

———. 1990b. 'The Past and Future of the Canadian Administrative State', *University of Toronto Law Journal* 40: 310–61.

Callaghan, Karen, and Frauke Schnell. 2001. 'Assessing the Democratic Debate: How the News Media Frame Elite Policy Discourse', *Political Communication* 18: 183–212.

Calvert, Randall L., Mathew D. McCubbins, and Barry R. Weingast. 1989. 'A Theory of Political Control and Agency Discretion', *American Journal of Political Science* 33, 3: 588–611.

Cameron, David R. 1984. 'Social Democracy, Corporatism, Labour Quiescence and the Representation of Economic Interest in Advanced Capitalist Society', in J.H. Goldthorpe, ed., *Order and Conflict in Contemporary Capitalism*. Oxford: Clarendon Press.

Cammack, Paul. 1992. 'The New Institutionalism: Predatory Rule, Institutional Persistence, and Macro-Social Change', *Economy and Society* 21, 4: 397–429.

Campbell, Colin, and George J. Szablowski. 1979. *The Superbureaucrats: Structure and Behaviour in Central Agencies*. Toronto: Macmillan.

Campbell, John L. 1997. 'Mechanisms of Evolutionary Change in Economic Governance: Interaction, Interpretation and Bricolage', in Lars Magnusson and Jan Ottosson, eds, *Evolutionary Economics and Path Dependence*. Cheltenham: Edward Elgar.

———. 1998. 'Institutional Analysis and the Role of Ideas in Political Economy', *Theory and Society* 27, 5: 377–409.

Canada, Auditor General. 1983. *Annual Report of the Auditor General*. Ottawa: Parliament of Canada.

———. 1993. *Report of the Auditor General to the House of Commons*. Ottawa: Supply and Services Canada.

Canada, Treasury Board. 1976. *A Manager's Guide to Performance Measurement*. Ottawa: Treasury Board of Canada.

———. 1981. *The Policy and Expenditure Management System*. Ottawa: Treasury Board of Canada.

Canes-Wrone, Brandice, Michael C. Herron, and Kenneth W. Shotts. 2001. 'Leadership and Pandering: A Theory of Executive Policymaking', *American Journal of Political Science* 45, 3: 532–50.

Cantor, Robin, Stuart Henry, and Steve Rayner. 1992. *Making Markets: An Interdisciplinary Perspective on Economic Exchange*. Westport, Conn.: Greenwood Press.

Cardozo, Andrew. 1996. 'Lion Taming: Downsizing the Opponents of Downsizing', in G. Swimmer, ed., *How Ottawa Spends 1996–97: Life Under the Knife*. Ottawa: Carleton University Press, 303–36.

Carley, Michael. 1980. *Rational Techniques in Policy Analysis*. London: Heinemann Educational Books.

Carlsson, Lars. 2000. 'Policy Networks as Collective Action', *Policy Studies Journal* 28, 3: 502–22.

Carpenter, R. Charli. 2007. 'Studying Issue (Non)-Adoption in Transnational Advocacy Networks', *International Organization* 61: 643–67.

Carver, John. 2001. 'A Theory of Governing the Public's Business: Redesigning the Jobs of Boards, Councils and Commissions', *Public Management Review* 3, 1: 53–72.

Cashore, Benjamin, and Michael Howlett. 2007. 'Punctuating Which Equilibrium? Understanding Thermostatic Policy Dynamics in Pacific Northwest Forestry', *American Journal of Political Science* 51, 3.

Castles, Francis G. 1982. 'The Impact of Parties on Public Expenditure', in Castles, ed., *The Impact of Parties: Politics and Policies in Democratic Capitalist States*. London: Sage.

———. 1998. *Comparative Public Policy: Patterns of Post-War Transformation*. Cheltenham: Edward Elgar.

——— and R.D. McKinlay. 1979. 'Does Politics Matter? An Analysis of the Public Welfare Commitment in Advanced Democratic States', *European Journal of Public Research* 7, 2: 169–86.

—— and ——. 1997. 'Does Politics Matter? Increasing Complexity and Renewed Challenges', *European Journal of Political Research* 31: 102–7.

—— and Vance Merrill. 1989. 'Towards a General Model of Public Policy Outcomes', *Journal of Theoretical Politics* 1, 2: 177–212.

Cater, Douglas. 1964. *Power in Washington: A Critical Look at Today's Struggle in the Nation's Capital*. New York: Random House.

Cavaillès, Henri. 1946. *La route française: son histoire, sa fonction*. Paris: Librarie Armand Colin.

Cavanagh, Michael, David Marsh, and Martin Smith. 1995. 'The Relationship between Policy Networks at the Sectoral and Sub-Sectoral Levels: A Response to Jordan, Maloney and McLaughlin', *Public Administration* 73 (Winter): 627–9.

Cawson, Alan. 1978. 'Pluralism, Corporatism and the Role of the State', *Government and Opposition* 13, 2: 178–98.

——. 1986. *Corporatism and Political Theory*. Oxford: Blackwell.

Cerny, Philip G. 1996. 'International Finance and the Erosion of State Policy Capacity', in Gummett (1996: 83–104).

——. 2001. 'From "Iron Triangles" to "Golden Pentangles"? Globalizing the Policy Process', *Global Governance* 7: 397–410.

Chadwick, Andrew. 2000. 'Studying Political Ideas: A Public Political Discourse Approach', *Political Studies* 48: 283–301.

Chandler, M.A. 1982. 'State Enterprise and Partisanship in Provincial Politics', *Canadian Journal of Political Science* 15: 711–40.

——. 1983. 'The Politics of Public Enterprise', in Prichard (1983: 185–218).

—— and W.M. Chandler. 1979. *Public Policy and Provincial Politics*. Toronto: McGraw-Hill Ryerson.

Chapman, Richard A. 1973. 'Commissions in Policy-Making', in Chapman, ed., *The Role of Commissions in Policy-Making*. London: George Allen and Unwin, 174–88.

Chari, R.S., and H. McMahon. 2003. 'Reconsidering the Patterns of Organised Interests in Irish Policy Making', *Irish Political Studies* 18, 1: 27–50.

Chelimsky, Eleanor. 1995. 'Where We Stand Today in the Practice of Evaluation: Some Reflections', *Knowledge and Policy* 8, 3: 8–20.

Chenier, John A. 1985. 'Ministers of State to Assist: Weighing the Costs and the Benefits', *Canadian Public Administration* 28, 3: 397–412.

Christensen, Tom, and Per Laegreid, eds. 2001. *New Public Management: The Transformation of Ideas and Practice*. Aldershot: Ashgate.

—— and ——. 2003. 'Coping with Complex Leadership Roles: The Problematic Redefinition of Government-Owned Enterprises', *Public Administration* 81, 4: 803–31.

—— and ——. 2007. 'Regulatory Agencies—The Challenges of Balancing Agency Autonomy and Political Control', *Governance* 20, 3: 499–520.

Churchman, C. West. 1967. 'Wicked Problems', *Management Science* 14, 4: B141–2.

Clark, B.T. 2004. 'Agenda Setting and Issue Dynamics: Dam Breaching on the Lower Snake River', *Society and Natural Resources* 17: 599–609.

Clark, William Roberts. 1998. 'Agents and Structures: Two Views of Preferences, Two Views of Institutions', *International Studies Quarterly* 42: 245–70.

Clarke, Michael. 1992. 'Implementation', in Martin Harrop, ed., *Power and Policy in Liberal Democracies*. Cambridge: Cambridge University Press.

Clarke-Jones, M. 1987. *A Staple State: Canadian Industrial Resources in Cold War*. Toronto: University of Toronto Press.

Clemens, E.S., and J.M. Cook. 1999. 'Politics and Institutionalism: Explaining Durability and Change', *Annual Review of Sociology* 25: 441–66.

Clemons, Randall S., and Mark K. McBeth. 2001. *Public Policy Praxis: Theory and Pragmatism, a Case Approach*. Upper Saddle River, NJ: Prentice-Hall.

Clokie, Hugh McDowall, and J. William Robinson. 1969. *Royal Commissions of Inquiry: The Significance of Investigations in British Politics*. New York: Octagon Books.

Cnossen, S. 2005. *Theory and Practice of Excise Taxation: Smoking, Drinking, Gambling, Polluting and Driving*. Oxford: Oxford University Press.

Coase, R.H. 1937. 'The Nature of the Firm', *Economica* 4, 13–16 (Nov.): 386–405.

———. 1960. 'The Problem of Social Cost', *Journal of Law and Economics* 3: 1–44.

Coates, David, ed. 2005. *Varieties of Capitalism, Varieties of Approaches*. New York: Palgrave Macmillan.

Cobb, Roger W., and Charles D. Elder. 1972. *Participation in American Politics: The Dynamics of Agenda-Building*. Boston: Allyn and Bacon.

——— and D.M. Primo. 2003. *The Plane Truth: Airline Crashes, the Media, and Transportation Policy*. Washington: Brookings Institution.

———, J.K. Ross, and M.H. Ross. 1976. 'Agenda Building as a Comparative Political Process', *American Political Science Review* 70, 1: 126–38.

——— and Marc Howard Ross, eds. 1997a. *Cultural Strategies of Agenda Denial: Avoidance, Attack and Redefinition*. Lawrence: University Press of Kansas.

——— and ———. 1997b. 'Denying Agenda Access: Strategic Considerations', in Cobb and Ross (1997a).

Coglianese, Cary. 1997. 'Assessing Consensus: The Promise and Performance of Negotiated Rulemaking', *Duke Law Journal* 46, 6: 1255–1349.

Cohen, G.A. 1978. *Karl Marx's Theory of History: A Defense*. Oxford: Clarendon Press.

Cohen, Mark A., and V. Santhakumar. 2007. 'Information Disclosure as Environmental Regulation: A Theoretical Analysis', *Environmental and Resource Economics* 37: 599–620.

Cohen, Michael D., James G. March, and Johan P. Olsen. 1972. 'A Garbage Can Model of Organizational Choice', *Administrative Science Quarterly* 17, 1: 1–25.

———, ———, and ———. 1979. 'People, Problems, Solutions and the Ambiguity of Relevance', in March and Olsen (1979a).

Cohen, M.G., and S. McBride. 2003. *Global Turbulence: Social Activists' and State Responses to Globalization*. Aldershot: Ashgate.

Cohen, Wesley M., and Daniel A. Levinthal. 1990. 'Absorptive Capacity: A New Perspective on Learning and Innovation', *Administrative Science Quarterly* 35: 128–52.

Cohn, D. 2004. 'The Best of Intentions, Potentially Harmful Policies: A Comparative Study of Scholarly Complexity and Failure', *Journal of Comparative Policy Analysis* 6, 1: 39–56.

———. 2006. 'Jumping into the Political Fray: Academics and Policy-Making', *IRPP Policy Matters* 7, 3.

Coleman, William D. 1988. *Business and Politics: A Study of Collective Action*. Montreal and Kingston: McGill-Queen's University Press.

———. 1994. 'Policy Convergence in Banking: A Comparative Study', *Political Studies* 42: 274–92.

———, Michael M. Atkinson, and Eric Montpetit. 1997. 'Against the Odds: Retrenchment in Agriculture in France and the United States', *World Politics* 49: 435–81.

——— and Wyn P. Grant. 1998. 'Policy Convergence and Policy Feedback: Agricultural Finance Policies in a Globalizing Era', *European Journal of Political Research* 34: 225–47.

——— and Anthony Perl. 1999. 'Internationalized Policy Environments and Policy Network Analysis', *Political Studies* 47: 691–709.

——— and Grace Skogstad, eds. 1990. *Policy Communities and Public Policy in Canada: A Structural Approach*. Mississauga, Ont.: Copp Clark Pitman.

——, ——, and Michael Atkinson. 1996. 'Paradigm Shifts and Policy Networks: Cumulative Change in Agriculture', *Journal of Public Policy* 16, 3: 273–302.

Conlisk, J. 1996. 'Why Bounded Rationality?', *Journal of Economic Literature* 34: 669–700.

Connolly, William E. 1969. 'The Challenge to Pluralist Theory', in Connolly, ed., *The Bias of Pluralism*. New York: Atherton Press.

Cook, Brian, and B. Dan Wood. 1989. 'Principal-Agent Models of Political Control of Bureaucracy', *American Political Science Review* 83: 965–78.

Cook, D. 2002. 'Consultation, for a Change? Engaging Users and Communities in the Policy Process', *Social Policy and Administration* 36, 5: 516–31.

Cook, F.L., et al. 1983. 'Media and Agenda Setting: Effects on the Public, Interest Group Leaders, Policy Makers, and Policy', *Public Opinion Quarterly* 47, 1: 16–35.

Cook, Thomas D. 1985. 'Postpositivist Critical Multiplism', in Shotland and Mark (1985).

Cooney, Kate. 2007. 'Field, Organizations, and Agency: Toward a Multilevel Theory of Institutionalization in Action', *Administration and Society* 39, 6: 687–18.

Cordes, Joseph J. 2002. 'Corrective Taxes, Charges and Tradable Permits', in Salamon (2002a: 255–81).

Cortell, Andrew P., and James W. Davis. 1996. 'How Do International Institutions Matter? The Domestic Impact of International Rules and Norms', *International Studies Quarterly* 40: 451–78.

—— and Susan Peterson. 1999. 'Altered States: Explaining Domestic Institutional Change', *British Journal of Political Science* 29: 177–203.

—— and ——. 2001. 'Limiting the Unintended Consequences of Institutional Change', *Comparative Political Studies* 34, 7: 768–99.

Cox, Robert W. 1987. *Production, Power and World Order: Social Forces in the Making of History*. New York: Columbia University Press.

Crenson, Matthew A. 1971. *The Un-Politics of Air Pollution: A Study of Non-Decision-making in the Cities*. Baltimore: Johns Hopkins University Press.

Crew, M.A., and C.K. Rowley. 1986. 'Deregulation as an Instrument in Industrial Policy', *Journal of Institutional and Theoretical Economics* 142: 52–70.

Cushman, Robert E. 1941. *The Independent Regulatory Commissions*. London: Oxford University Press.

Cutler, A.C., V. Haufler, and T. Porter. 1999. 'The Contours and Significance of Private Authority in International Affairs', in Cutler, Haufler, and Porter, eds, *Private Authority and International Affairs*. Albany: State University of New York, 333–76.

Cutright, P. 1965. 'Political Structure, Economic Development, and National Security Programs', *American Journal of Sociology* 70, 5: 537–50.

Dahl, Robert A. 1956. *A Preface to Democratic Theory*. Chicago: University of Chicago Press.

——. 1961. *Who Governs? Democracy and Power in an American City*. New Haven: Yale University Press.

——. 1967. *Pluralist Democracy in the United States: Conflict and Consent*. Chicago: Rand McNally.

—— and Charles E. Lindblom. 1953. *Politics, Economics and Welfare: Planning and Politico-economic Systems Resolved into Basic Social Processes*. New York: Harper and Row.

Daneke, Gregory A. 1992. 'Back to the Future: Misplaced Elements of Political Inquiry and the Advanced Systems Agenda', in William N. Dunn and Rita Mae Kelly, eds, *Advances in Policy Studies Since 1950*. New Brunswick, NJ: Transaction, 267–90.

Daniels, Mark R. 1997. *Terminating Public Programs: An American Political Paradox*. Armonk, NJ: M.E. Sharpe.

Danziger, Marie. 1995. 'Policy Analysis Postmodernized: Some Political and Pedagogical Ramifications', *Policy Studies Journal* 23, 3: 435–50.

Daugbjerg, Carsten. 1997. 'Policy Networks and Agricultural Policy Reforms: Explaining Deregulation in Sweden and Re-regulation in the European Community', *Governance* 10, 2: 123–42.

———— and David Marsh. 1998. 'Explaining Policy Outcomes: Integrating the Policy Network Approach with Macro-Level and Micro-Level Analysis', in Marsh, ed., *Comparing Policy Networks*. Buckingham: Open University Press, 52–71.

———— and A.B. Perdersen. 2004. 'New Policy Ideas and Old Policy Networks: Implementing Green Taxation in Scandinavia', *Journal of Public Policy* 24, 2: 219–49.

———— and J. Studsgaard. 2005. 'Issue Redefinition, Venue Change and Radical Agricultural Policy Reforms in Sweden and New Zealand', *Scandinavian Political Studies* 28, 2: 103–24.

David, Paul A. 1985. 'Clio and the Economics of QWERTY', *American Economic Review* 75, 2: 332–7.

————. 2005. 'Path Dependence in Economic Processes: Implications for Policy Analysis in Dynamical System Contexts', in Kurt Dopfer, ed, *The Evolutionary Foundations of Economics*. Cambridge: Cambridge University Press, 151–94

David, Wilfred L. 1985. *The IMF Policy Paradigm: The Macroeconomics of Stabilization, Structural Adjustment, and Economic Development*. New York: Praeger.

Davidson, A. 2004. 'Dynamics without Change: Continuity of Canadian Health Policy', *Canadian Public Administration* 47, 3: 251–79.

Davidson, E. Jane. 2005. *Evaluation Methodology Basics*. Thousand Oaks, Calif.: Sage.

Davies, I. 1999. 'Evaluation and Performance Management in Government', *Evaluation* 8, 2: 150–9.

Davis, G., P. Weller, E. Craswell, and S. Eggins. 1999. 'What Drives Machinery of Government Change? Australia, Canada and the United Kingdom 1950–1997', *Public Administration* 77, 1: 7–50.

Dearing, James W., and Everett M. Rogers. 1996. *Agenda-Setting*. Thousand Oaks, Calif.: Sage.

Debnam, Geoffrey. 1975. 'Non-decisions and Power: The Two Faces of Bachrach and Baratz', *American Political Science Review* 69, 3: 889–900.

de Bruijn, Johan A., and Ernst F. ten Heuvelhof. 1991. 'Policy Instruments for Steering Autopoietic Actors', in Roeland In't Veld et al., eds, *Autopoiesis and Configuration Theory: New Approaches to Societal Steering*. Dordrecht: Kluwer, 161–70.

———— and ————. 1995. 'Policy Networks and Governance', in David L. Weimer, ed., *Institutional Design*. Boston: Kluwer, 161–79.

———— and ————. 1997. 'Instruments for Network Management', in W.J.M. Kickert, E.-H. Klijn, and J.F.M. Koppenjan, eds, *Managing Complex Networks: Strategies for the Public Sector*. London: Sage, 119–36.

———— and ————. 2000. *Networks and Decision-Making*. Utrecht: Lemma Publishers.

Deeg, Richard. 2007. 'Complementarity and Institutional Change in Capitalist Systems', *Journal of European Public Policy* 14, 4: 611–30.

deHaven-Smith, Lance, and Carl E. Van Horn. 1984. 'Subgovernment Conflict in Public Policy', *Policy Studies Journal* 12, 4: 627–42.

DeHoog, Ruth Hoogland, and Lester M. Salamon. 2002. 'Purchase-of-Service Contracting', in Salamon (2002a: 319–39).

de Jong, Martin, and Jurian Edelenbos. 2007. 'An Insider's Look into Policy Transfer in Transnational Expert Networks', *European Planning Studies* 15, 5: 687–706.

de la Mothe, John. 1996. 'One Small Step in an Uncertain Direction: The Science and Technology Review and Public Administration in Canada', *Canadian Public Administration* 39, 3: 403–17.

de la Porte, Caroline, Phillipe Pochet, and Graham Room. 2001. 'Social Benchmarking, Policy Making and New Governance in the EU', *Journal of European Social Policy* 11, 1: 291–307.

DeLeon, Peter. 1978. 'A Theory of Policy Termination', in J.V. May and A.B. Wildavsky, eds, *The Policy Cycle*. Beverly Hills, Calif.: Sage, 279–300.

———. 1983. 'Policy Evaluation and Program Termination', *Policy Studies Review* 2, 4: 631–47.

———. 1986. 'Trends in Policy Sciences Research: Determinants and Developments', *European Journal of Political Research* 14, 1 and 2: 3–22.

———. 1988. *Advice and Consent: The Development of the Policy Sciences*. New York: Russell Sage Foundation.

———. 1992. 'Policy Formulation: Where Ignorant Armies Clash By Night', *Policy Studies Review* 11, 3 and 4: 389–405.

———. 1994. 'Reinventing the Policy Sciences: Three Steps Back to the Future', *Policy Sciences* 27, 1: 77–95.

———. 1997. *Democracy and the Policy Sciences*. Albany: State University of New York Press.

———. 1997. 'Afterward: The Once and Future State of Policy Termination', *International Journal of Public Administration* 20: 33–46.

———. 1999a. 'The Missing Link Revisited: Contemporary Implementation Research', *Policy Studies Review* 16, 3 and 4: 311–38.

———. 1999b. 'The Stages Approach to the Policy Process: What Has It Done? Where Is It Going?', in Sabatier (1999a: 19–34).

———. 2006. 'The Historical Roots of the Field', in Michael Moran, Martin Rein, and Robert E. Goodin, eds, *The Oxford Handbook of Public Policy*. Oxford: Oxford University Press, 39–57.

——— and Katie Kaufmanis. 2001. 'Public Policy Theory: Will It Play in Peoria?', *Policy Currents* 10, 4: 9–13.

——— and Christine R. Martell. 2006. 'The Policy Sciences: Past, Present and Future', in B. Guy Peters and Jon Pierre, eds, *Handbook of Public Policy*. London: Sage, 31–48.

Demaret, Paul. 1997. 'The Reciprocal Influence of Multilateral and Regional Trade Rules: A Framework of Analysis', in Demaret, J.-F. Bellis, and G.G. Jimenez, eds, *Regional and Multilateralism after the Uruguay Round: Convergence, Divergence and Interaction*. Liège: Institute d'Études Juridiques Européennes de Université Liège, 805–38.

Dent, Helen. 2002. 'Consultants and the Public Service', *Australian Journal of Public Administration* 61, 1: 108–13

Derthick, M., and P.J. Quirk. 1985. *The Politics of Deregulation*. Washington: Brookings Institution.

Dery, David. 1984. *Agenda-Setting and Problem Definition*. Lawrence: University Press of Kansas.

———. 1999. 'Policy by the Way: When Policy is Incidental to Making Other Policies', *Journal of Public Policy* 18, 2: 163–76.

de Smith, S.A. 1973. *Judicial Review of Administrative Action*. London: Stevens and Son.

Dessler, David. 1999. 'Constructivism within a Positivist Social Science', *Review of International Studies* 25: 123–37.

Desveaux, James A., Evert Lindquist, and Glen Toner. 1994. 'Organizing for Innovation in Public Bureaucracy: AIDS, Energy and Environment Policy in Canada', *Canadian Journal of Political Science* 27, 3: 493–528.

Devas, N., S. Delay, and M. Hubbard. 2001. 'Revenue Authorities: Are They the Right Vehicle for Improved Tax Administration?', *Public Administration and Development* 21, 3: 211–22.

De Vita, C.J., and E.C. Twombly. 2005. 'Who Gains from Charitable Tax Credit Programs? The Arizona Model', *Public Administration Review* 65, 1: 57–63.

de Vries, M.S. 2000. 'The Secret and Cost of Success: Institutional Change and Policy Change', in O. Van Heffen, W.J.M. Kickert, and J.J.A. Thomassen, eds, *Governance in Modern Society: Effects, Change and Formation of Government Institutions*. Dordrecht: Kluwer, 61–86.

————. 2005. 'Generations of Interactive Policy-Making in the Netherlands', *International Review of Administrative Sciences* 71, 4: 577–91.

————. 2005b. 'Changing Policy Views at the Local Level: The Effect of Age, Generations and Policy Periods in Five European Countries', *European Journal of Political Research* 44: 1–15.

Dimitrakopoulos, Dionyssis G. 2005. 'Norms, Interests and Institutional Change', *Political Studies* 53: 676–93.

Dion, Leon. 1973. 'The Politics of Consultation', *Government and Opposition* 8, 3: 332–53.

Djelic, Marie-Laure, and Sigrid Quack. 2007. 'Overcoming Path Dependency: Path Generation in Open Systems', *Theory and Society* 36: 161–86.

Dobbin, Frank, Beth Simmons, and Geoffrey Garrett. 2007. 'The Global Diffusion of Public Policies: Social Construction, Coercion, Competition, or Learning?', *Annual Review of Sociology* 33: 449–72.

Dobell, Rodney, and David Zussman. 1981. 'An Evaluation System for Government: If Politics Is Theatre, Then Evaluation Is (Mostly) Art', *Canadian Public Administration* 24, 3: 404–27.

Dobrowolsky, Alexandra, and Denis Saint-Martin. 2005. 'Agency, Actors and Change in a Child-Focused Future: "Path Dependency" Problematised', *Commonwealth and Comparative Politics* 43, 1: 1–33.

Dobuzinskis, Laurent. 1992. 'Modernist and Postmodernist Metaphors of the Policy Process: Control and Stability vs Chaos and Reflexive Understanding', *Policy Sciences* 25: 355–80.

————. 1996. 'Trends and Fashions in the Marketplace of Ideas', in Dobuzinskis, M. Howlett, and D. Laycock, eds, *Policy Studies in Canada: The State of the Art*. Toronto: University of Toronto Press, 91–124.

————. 2000. 'Global Discord: The Confusing Discourse of Think Tanks', in T. Cohn, S. McBride, and J. Wiseman, eds, *Power in the Global Era*. London: Macmillan.

————, M. Howlett, and D. Laycock. 2007. *Policy Analysis in Canada: The State of the Art*. Toronto: University of Toronto Press

Dodge, Martin, and Christopher Hood. 2002. 'Pavlovian Policy Responses to Media Feeding Frenzies? Dangerous Drugs Regulation in Comparative Perspective', *Journal of Contingencies and Crisis Management* 10, 1: 1–13.

Doern, G. Bruce. 1967. 'The Role of Royal Commissions in the General Policy Process and in Federal–Provincial Relations', *Canadian Public Administration* 10, 4: 417–33.

————. 1971. 'The Role of Central Advisory Councils: The Science Council of Canada', in Doern and Aucoin (1971: 246–66).

————. 1981. *The Nature of Scientific and Technological Controversy in Federal Policy Formation*. Ottawa: Science Council of Canada.

————. 1998. 'The Interplay among Regimes: Mapping Regulatory Institutions in the United Kingdom, the United States, and Canada', in Doern and Wilks (1998: 29–50).

———— and Peter Aucoin, eds. 1971. *The Structures of Policy-Making in Canada*. Toronto: Macmillan.

—————— et al. 1999. 'Canadian Regulatory Institutions: Converging and Colliding Regimes', in Doern, M.M. Hill, M.J. Prince, and R.J. Schultz, eds, *Changing the Rules: Canadian Regulatory Regimes and Institutions*. Toronto: University of Toronto Press, 3–26.

——————, L. Pal, and B.W. Tomlin, eds. 1996a. *Border Crossings: The Internationalization of Canadian Public Policy*. Toronto: Oxford University Press.

——————, ——————, and ——————. 1996b. 'The Internationalization of Canadian Public Policy', in Doern, Pal, and Tomlin (1996a: 1–26).

—————— and Richard W. Phidd. 1992. *Canadian Public Policy: Ideas, Structure, Process*, 2nd edn. Toronto: Nelson Canada.

—————— and Ted Reed. 2001. 'Science and Scientists in Regulatory Governance: A Mezzo-Level Framework for Analysis', *Science and Public Policy* 28, 3: 195–204.

—————— and S. Wilks, eds. 1998. *Changing Regulatory Institutions in Britain and North America*. Toronto: University of Toronto Press.

—————— and V.S. Wilson, eds. 1974a. *Issues in Canadian Public Policy*. Toronto: Macmillan.

—————— and ——————. 1974b. 'Conclusions and Observations', in Doern and Wilson (1974).

Dollery, Brian E., and Joe L. Wallis. 2003. *The Political Economy of the Voluntary Sector: A Reappraisal of the Comparative Institutional Advantage of Voluntary Organisations*. Cheltenham: Edward Elgar.

—————— and Andrew Worthington. 1996. 'The Evaluation of Public Policy: Normative Economic Theories of Government Failure', *Journal of Interdisciplinary Economics* 7, 1: 27–39.

d'Ombrain, N. 1997. 'Public Inquiries in Canada', *Canadian Public Administration* 40, 1: 86–107.

Donahue, John D. 1989. *The Privatization Decision: Public Ends, Private Means*. New York: Basic Books.

—————— and Joseph S. Nye Jr, eds. 2001. *Governance and Bigger, Better Markets*. Washington: Brookings Institution.

—————— and Richard J. Zeckhauser. 2006. 'Public–Private Collaboration', in Michael Moran, Martin Rein, and Robert E. Goodin, eds, *The Oxford Handbook of Public Policy*. Oxford: Oxford University Press, 496–525.

Donovan, M.C. 2001. *Taking Aim: Target Populations and the Wars on AIDS and Drugs*. Washington: Georgetown University Press.

Doorenspleet, Renske. 2000. 'Reassessing the Three Waves of Democratization', *World Politics* 52, 3: 384–406.

Dosi, G., et al., eds. 1988. *Technical Change and Economic Theory*. London: Pinter.

Dostal, J.M. 2004. 'Campaigning on Expertise: How the OECD Framed Welfare and Labour Market Policies—and Why Success Could Trigger Failure', *Journal of European Public Policy* 11, 3: 440–60.

Dowding, Keith. 1994. 'The Compatibility of Behaviouralism, Rational Choice and "New Institutionalism"', *Journal of Theoretical Politics* 6, 1: 105–17.

Downs, Anthony. 1957. *An Economic Theory of Democracy*. New York: Harper.

——————. 1967. *Inside Bureaucracy*. New York: Harper and Row.

——————. 1972. 'Up and Down with Ecology—the "Issue-Attention Cycle"', *The Public Interest* 28: 38–50.

Drezner, Daniel W. 2000. 'Ideas, Bureaucratic Politics, and the Crafting of Foreign Policy', *American Journal of Political Science* 44, 4: 733–49.

Driedger, S.M., and J. Eyles. 2003. 'Charting Uncertainty in Science-Policy Discourses: The Construction of the Chlorinated Drinking-Water Issue and Cancer', *Environment and Planning C: Government and Policy* 21: 429–44.

Dror, Yehezkel. 1964. 'Muddling Through—"Science" or Inertia', *Public Administration Review* 24, 3: 154–7.

————. 1968. *Public Policymaking Re-examined*. San Francisco: Chandler.

————. 1969. 'The Prediction of Political Feasibility', *Futures* (June): 282–8.

Druckman, James N. 2001. 'On the Limits of Framing Effects: Who Can Frame?', *Journal of Politics* 63, 4: 1041–66.

Dryzek, John S. 1990. *Discursive Democracy: Politics, Policy and Political Science*. Cambridge: Cambridge University Press.

————. 1992. 'How Far Is It From Virginia and Rochester to Frankfurt? Public Choice as Global Theory', *British Journal of Political Science* 22, 4: 397–418.

————. 2002. 'A Post-Positivist Policy-Analytic Travelogue', *The Good Society* 11, 1: 32–6.

————. 2005. 'Handle with Care: The Deadly Hermeneutics of Deliberative Instrumentalism', *Acta Politica* 40: 197–211.

———— and Brian Ripley. 1988. 'The Ambitions of Policy Design', *Policy Studies Review* 7, 4: 705–19.

Duchacek, Ivo D. 1970. *Comparative Federalism: The Territorial Dimension of Politics*. New York: Holt, Rinehart and Winston.

Dudley, Geoffrey, Wayne Parsons, and Claudio M. Radaelli. 2000. 'Symposium: Theories of the Policy Process', *Journal of European Public Policy* 7, 1: 122–40.

———— and Jeremy Richardson. 1998. 'Arenas without Rules and the Policy Change Process: Outsider Groups and British Roads Policy', *Political Studies* 46: 727–47.

———— and ————. 1999. 'Competing Advocacy Coalitions and the Process of "Frame Reflection": A Longitudinal Analysis of EU Steel Policy', *Journal of European Public Policy* 6, 2: 225–48.

Duit, Andreas. 2007. 'Path Dependency and Institutional Change: The Case of Industrial Emission Control in Sweden', *Public Administration* 85, 4: 1097–1118.

Dunleavy, Patrick. 1986. 'Explaining the Privatization Boom: Public Choice versus Radical Approaches', *Public Administration* 64, 1: 13–34.

———— and Christopher Hood. 1994. 'From Old Public Administration to New Public Management', *Public Money and Management* 14, 3: 9–16.

———— and B. O'Leary. 1987. *Theories of the State: The Politics of Liberal Democracy*. Basingstoke: Macmillan Education.

Dunn, James, Jr, and Anthony Perl. 1994. 'Policy Networks and Industrial Revitalization: High Speed Rail Initiatives in France and Germany', *Journal of Public Policy* 14, 3: 311–43.

Dunn, William N. 1988. 'Methods of the Second Type: Coping with the Wilderness of Conventional Policy Analysis', *Policy Studies Review* 7, 4: 720–37.

Dunsire, Andrew. 1986. 'A Cybernetic View of Guidance, Control and Evaluation in the Public Sector', in Franz-Xavier Kaufman, Giandomenico Majone, and Vincent Ostrom, eds, *Guidance, Control, and Evaluation in the Public Sector*. Berlin: Walter de Gruyter, 327–46.

————. 1993a. *Manipulating Social Tensions: Collaboration as an Alternative Mode of Government Intervention*. Koln: Max Plank Institute, 1993a.

————. 1993b. 'Modes of Governance', in J. Kooiman, ed., *Modern Governance*. London: Sage, 21–34.

Duquette, Michel. 1999. *Building New Democracies: Economic and Social Reform in Brazil, Chile and Mexico*. Toronto: University of Toronto Press.

Durning, Dan. 1999. 'The Transition from Traditional to Postpositivist Policy Analysis: A Role for Q-Methodology', *Journal of Policy Analysis and Management* 18, 3: 389–410.

Durr, Robert H. 1993. 'What Moves Policy Sentiment?', *American Political Science Review* 87, 1: 158–72.

Durant, Robert F., and Paul F. Diehl. 1989. 'Agendas, Alternatives and Public Policy: Lessons from the U.S. Foreign Policy Agenda', *Journal of Public Policy* 9, 2: 179–205.

Dwivedi, O.P., ed. 1982. *Administrative State in Canada: Essays in Honour of J.E. Hodgetts.* Toronto: University of Toronto Press.

Dye, Thomas R. 1972. *Understanding Public Policy.* Englewood Cliffs, NJ: Prentice-Hall.

———. 2001. *Top-Down Policymaking.* New York: Chatham House.

Dyerson, Romano, and Frank Mueller. 1993. 'Intervention by Outsiders: A Strategic Perspective on Government Industrial Policy', *Journal of Public Policy* 13, 1: 69–88.

Dyson, Kenneth H.F. 1980. *The State Tradition in Western Europe: A Study of an Idea and Institution.* Oxford: Martin Robertson.

Economic Council of Canada. 1979. *Responsible Regulation: An Interim Report.* Ottawa: Supply and Services Canada.

Edelenbos, J., and E.-H. Klijn. 2006. 'Managing Stakeholder Involvement in Decision-Making: A Comparative Analysis of Six Interactive Processes in the Netherlands', *Journal of Public Administration Research and Theory* 16, 3: 417–46.

Edelman, Murray. 1964. *The Symbolic Uses of Politics.* Chicago: University of Chicago Press.

———. 1988. *Constructing the Political Spectacle.* Chicago: University of Chicago Press.

Edley, Christopher F., Jr. 1990. *Administrative Law: Rethinking Judicial Control of Bureaucracy.* New Haven: Yale University Press.

Edwards, George C., and Ira Sharkansky. 1978. *The Policy Predicament: Making and Implementing Public Policy.* San Francisco: Freeman.

Edwards, Ward. 1954. 'The Theory of Decision Making', *Psychological Bulletin* 51, 4: 380–417.

Einhorn, Hillel J. 1982. 'Learning from Experience and Suboptimal Rules in Decision Making', in D. Kahneman, P. Slovic, and A. Tversky, eds, *Judgement Under Uncertainty: Heuristics and Biases.* Cambridge: Cambridge University Press, 268–83.

——— and Robin M. Hogarth. 1986. 'Decision Making under Ambiguity', *Journal of Business* 59, 4, part 2: S225–S251.

Eisner, Marc Allen. 1993. *Regulatory Politics in Transition.* Baltimore: Johns Hopkins University Press.

———. 1994a. 'Discovering Patterns in Regulatory History: Continuity, Change and Regulatory Regimes', *Journal of Policy History* 6, 2: 157–87.

———. 1994b. 'Economic Regulatory Policies: Regulation and Deregulation in Historical Context', in Rosenbloom and Schwartz (1994: 91–116).

Eldredge, Niles, and Stephen Jay Gould. 1972. 'Punctuated Equilibria: An Alternative to Phyletic Gradualism', in T.J.M. Schopf, ed., *Paleobiology.* San Francisco: Freeman, Cooper, 82–115.

Eliadis, P., M. Hill, and M. Howlett. 2005. *Designing Government: From Instruments to Governance.* Montreal and Kingston: McGill-Queen's University Press.

Elkin, Stephen L. 1986. 'Regulation and Regime: A Comparative Analysis', *Journal of Public Policy* 6, 1: 49–72.

Ellig, Jerry, and Don Lavoie. 1995. 'The Principle–Agent Relationship in Organizations', in P. Foss, ed., *Economic Approaches to Organizations and Institutions: An Introduction.* Aldershot: Dartmouth.

Elliott, Chris, and Rodolphe Schlaepfer. 2001. 'The Advocacy Coalition Framework: Application to the Policy Process for the Development of Forest Certification in Sweden', *Journal of European Public Policy* 8, 4: 642–61.

Elliott, Dominic, and Martina McGuinness. 2001. 'Public Inquiry: Panacea or Placebo?', *Journal of Contingencies and Crisis Management* 10, 1: 14–25.

Elliott, Euel, and Andrew I.E. Ewoh. 2000. 'The Evolution of an Issue: The Rise and Decline of Affirmative Action', *Policy Studies Review* 17, 2 and 3: 212–37.

Elmore, Richard F. 1978. 'Organizational Models of Social Program Implementation', *Public Policy* 26, 2: 185–228.

————. 1987. 'Instruments and Strategy in Public Policy', *Policy Studies Review* 7, 1: 74–186.

Elster, Jon, ed. 1986. *Rational Choice*. Cambridge: Cambridge University Press.

————. 1991. 'The Possibility of Rational Politics', in D, Held, ed., *Political Theory Today*. Oxford: Polity.

Englehart, Kenneth G., and Michael J. Trebilcock. 1981. *Public Participation in the Regulatory Process: The Issue of Funding*. Ottawa: Economic Council of Canada.

English, L.M., and M. Skellern. 2005. 'Public–Private Partnerships and Public Sector Management Reform: A Comparative Analysis', *International Journal of Public Policy* 1, 1 and 2: 1–21.

Epstein, Paul J. 1997. 'Beyond Policy Community: French Agriculture and the GATT', *Journal of European Public Policy* 4, 3: 355–72.

Erbring, Lutz, Edie N. Goldenberg, and Arthur H. Miller. 1980. 'Front Page News and Real World Cues: A New Look at Agenda-Setting by the Media', *American Journal of Political Science* 24, 1: 16–49.

Erikson, Robert S., Norman R. Luttbeg, and Kent L. Tedin, eds. 1980. *American Public Opinion*. New York: John Wiley and Sons.

————, Gerald C. Wright Jr, and John P. McIver. 1989. 'Political Parties, Public Opinion and State Policy in the United States', *American Political Science Review* 83, 3: 729–39.

Esping-Andersen, Gosta. 1981. 'From Welfare State to Democratic Socialism: The Politics of Economic Democracy in Denmark and Sweden', in M. Zeitlin, ed., *Political Power and Social Theory*, 111–40.

————. 1985. *Politics Against Markets: The Social Democratic Road to Power*. Princeton, NJ: Princeton University Press.

————. 1990. *The Three Worlds of Welfare Capitalism*. Cambridge: Polity.

———— and Walter Korpi. 1984. 'Social Policy as Class Politics in Post-War Capitalism: Scandinavia, Austria, and Germany', in J.H. Goldthorpe, ed., *Order and Conflict in Contemporary Capitalism*. Oxford: Clarendon Press.

Etheredge, Lloyd S. 1981. 'Government Learning: An Overview', in S.L. Long, ed., *The Handbook of Political Behavior*. New York: Plenum.

———— and James Short. 1983. 'Thinking about Government Learning', *Journal of Management Studies* 20, 1: 41–58.

Etzioni, Amitai. 1967. 'Mixed-Scanning: A "Third" Approach to Decision-Making', *Public Administration Review* 27, 5: 385–92.

Evans, Mark, and Jonathan Davies. 1999. 'Understanding Policy Transfer: A Multi-Level, Multi-Disciplinary Perspective', *Public Administration* 77, 2: 361–85.

Evans, Peter. 1992. 'State as Problem and Solution: Predation, Embedded Autonomy, and Structural Change', in Stephen Haggard and Robert R. Kaufman, eds, *The Politics of Economic Adjustment: International Constraints, Distributive Conflicts, and the State*. Princeton, NJ: Princeton University Press, 139–81.

————. 1995. *Embedded Autonomy: States and Industrial Transformation*. Princeton, NJ: Princeton University Press.

————, D. Rueschemeyer, and T. Skocpol, eds. 1985. *Bringing the State Back In*. Cambridge: Cambridge University Press.

Everett, S. 2003. 'The Policy Cycle: Democratic Process of Rational Paradigm Revisited', *Australian Journal of Public Administration* 62, 2: 65–70.

Evers, A. 2005. 'Mixed Welfare Systems and Hybrid Organizations: Changes in the Governance and Provision of Social Services', *International Journal of Public Administration* 28: 737–48.

———— and H. Wintersberger. 1990. *Shifts in the Welfare Mix: Their Impact on Work, Social Services and Welfare Policies*. Boulder, Colo.: Westview Press.

Fabbrini, Sergio, and Daniela Sicurelli. 2008. 'Bringing Policy-Making Structure Back In: Why Are the US and the EU Pursuing Different Foreign Policies?', *International Politics* 45: 292–309.

Falk, Richard. 1997. 'State of Siege: Will Globalization Win Out?', *International Affairs* 73, 1: 123–36.

Falkenmark, M. 2004. 'Towards Integrated Catchment Management: Opening the Paradigm Locks between Hydrology, Ecology and Policy-Making', *Water Resources Development* 20, 3: 275–82.

Falkner, G. 2000. 'Policy Networks in a Multi-Level System: Convergence towards Moderate Diversity?', *West European Politics* 23, 4: 94–120.

Farr, J., J.S. Hacker, and N. Kazee. 2006. 'The Policy Scientist of Democracy', *American Political Science Review* 100, 4: 579–87.

Fayol, Henri. 1949. *General and Industrial Management*. London: Pitman.

Feick, Jurgen. 1992. 'Comparing Comparative Policy Studies—A Path towards Integration?', *Journal of Public Policy* 12, 3: 257–86.

Feldman, Martha S., and Anne M. Khademian. 2007. 'The Role of the Public Manager in Inclusion: Creating Communities of Participation', *Governance* 20, 2: 305–24.

Feldman, Ron J. 2002. 'Government Insurance', in Salamon (2002a: 186–216).

Felstiner, W.L., Richard L. Abel, and Austin Sarat. 1980–1. 'The Emergence and Trans-formation of Disputes: Naming, Blaming, Claiming', *Law and Society Review* 15, 3 and 4: 631–54.

Fernandes, Ronald, and Herbert A. Simon. 1999. 'A Study of How Individuals Solve Complex and Ill-Structured Problems', *Policy Sciences* 32: 225–45.

Finkle, Peter, et al. 1994. *Federal Government Relations with Interest Groups: A Reconsidera-tion*. Ottawa: Privy Council Office.

Finnemore, Martha, and Kathryn Sikkink. 1998. 'International Norm Dynamics and Political Change', *International Organization* 52, 4: 887–917.

Firestone, O.J. 1970. *The Public Persuader: Government Advertising*. Toronto: Methuen.

Fischer, Frank. 1993. 'Policy Discourses and the Politics of Washington Think Tanks', in Fischer and Forester (1993: 21–42).

———. 1998. 'Beyond Empiricism: Policy Inquiry in Postpostivist Perspective', *Policy Studies Journal* 26, 1: 129–46.

———. 2007a. 'Policy Analysis in Critical Perspective: The Epistemics of Discursive Practices', *Critical Policy Analysis* 1, 1: 97–109.

———. 2007b. 'Deliberative Policy Analysis as Practical Reason: Integrating Empirical and Normative Arguments', in Fischer, Gerald Miller, and Mara Sidney, eds, *Handbook of Public Policy Analysis: Theory, Politics, and Methods*, Boca Raton, Fla: CRC Press, 223–36.

——— and John Forester, eds. 1987. *Confronting Values in Policy Analysis: The Politics of Criteria*. Beverly Hills, Calif.: Sage.

——— and ———, eds. 1993. *The Argumentative Turn in Policy Analysis and Planning*. Durham, NC: Duke University Press.

Fischoff, Baruch. 1977. 'Cost-Benefit Analysis and the Art of Motorcycle Maintenance', *Policy Sciences* 8, 2: 177–202.

Fishman, Ethan. 1991. 'Political Philosophy and the Policy Studies Organization', *PS: Political Science and Politics* 24: 720–3.

Flathman, Richard E. 1966. *The Public Interest: An Essay Concerning the Normative Discourse of Politics*. New York: Wiley.

Flemming, Roy B., B. Dan Wood, and John Bohte. 1999. 'Attention to Issues in a System of Separated Powers: The Macrodynamics of American Policy Agendas', *Journal of Politics* 61, 1: 76–108.

Flinders, Matthew V., and Hugh McConnel. 1999. 'Diversity and Complexity: The Quango-Continuum', in Flinders and Martin J. Smith, eds, *Quangos, Accountability and Reform: The Politics of Quasi-Government*. Sheffield: Political Economy Research Centre, 17–39.

Flitner, D. 1986. *The Politics of Presidential Commissions*. New York: Transnational Publishers.

Foley, Duncan K. 1978. 'State Expenditure from a Marxist Perspective', *Journal of Public Economics* 9, 2: 221–38.

Foot, David K. 1979. 'Political Cycles, Economic Cycles and the Trend in Public Employment in Canada', in Meyer W. Bucovetsky, ed., *Studies in Public Employment and Compensation in Canada*. Toronto: Butterworths for Institute for Research on Public Policy, 65–80.

Forester, John. 1984. 'Bounded Rationality and the Politics of Muddling Through', *Public Administration Review* 44, 1: 23–31.

———. 1989. *Planning in the Face of Power*. Berkeley: University of California Press.

———. 1993. *Critical Theory, Public Policy, and Planning: Toward a Critical Pragmatism*. New York: SUNY Press.

Formaini, Robert. 1990. *The Myth of Scientific Public Policy*. New Brunswick, NJ: Transaction.

Foucault, Michel. 1972. 'The Discourse on Language', in Foucault, ed., *The Archaeology of Knowledge*. New York: Pantheon.

Fowler, Edmund P., and David Siegel, eds. 2002. *Urban Policy Issues*. Toronto: Oxford University Press.

Fox, Charles J. 1990. 'Implementation Research: Why and How to Transcend Positivist Methodology', in Palumbo and Calista (1990).

Francis, John G. 1993. *The Politics of Regulation: A Comparative Perspective*. Oxford: Blackwell.

Franke, George R. 2001. 'Applications of Meta-Analysis for Marketing and Public Policy: A Review', *Journal of Public Policy and Marketing* 20, 2: 186–200.

Frantz, J.E. 2002. 'Political Resources for Policy Terminators', *Policy Studies Journal* 30, 1: 11–28.

Freeman, Gary P. 1985. 'National Styles and Policy Sectors: Explaining Structured Variation', *Journal of Public Policy* 5, 4: 467–96.

Freeman, Jody. 1997. 'Collaborative Governance in the Administrative State', *UCLA Law Review* 45, 1: 1–98.

Freeman, John Leiper. 1955. *The Political Process: Executive Bureau–Legislative Committee Relations*. New York: Random House.

——— and Judith Parris Stevens. 1987. 'A Theoretical and Conceptual Reexamination of Subsystem Politics', *Public Policy and Administration* 2, 1: 9–24.

French, John R.P., and Bertram Raven. 1959. 'The Bases of Social Power', in D. Cartwright, ed., *Studies in Social Power*. Ann Arbor: University of Michigan Press, 150–67.

French, M., and J. Phillips. 2004. 'Windows and Barriers in Policy-Making: Food Poisoning in Britain, 1945–56', *Social History of Medicine* 17, 2: 269–84.

Frey, Bruno S. 1978. 'Politico-Economic Models and Cycles', *Journal of Public Economics* 9: 203–20.

Frey, Frederick W. 1971. 'Comment: On Issues and Non-issues in the Study of Power', *American Political Science Review* 65: 1081–1101.

Friedman, Lee S. 2002. *The Microeconomics of Public Policy Analysis*. Princeton, NJ: Princeton University Press.

Galaskiewicz, Joseph, Wolfgang Bielefeld, and Myron Dowell. 2006. 'Networks and Organizational Growth: A Study of Community Based Nonprofits', *Administrative Science Quarterly* 51: 337–80.

Gall, Gerald L. 1983. *The Canadian Legal System*, 2nd edn. Toronto: Carswell.

Garson, G. David. 1986. 'From Policy Science to Policy Analysis: A Quarter Century of Progress', in W.N. Dunn, ed., *Policy Analysis: Perspectives, Concepts, and Methods*. Greenwich, Conn.: JAI Press, 3–22.

Gaus, John M. 1931. 'Notes on Administration', *American Political Science Review* 25, 1: 123–34.

Gawthrop, Louis C. 1971. *Administrative Politics and Social Change*. New York: St Martin's Press.

Gehring, Thomas, and Sebastian Oberthur. 2000. 'Exploring Regime Interaction: A Framework of Analysis', paper presented to the Final Conference of the EU-financed Concerted Action Programme on the Effectiveness of International Environmental Agreements and EU Legislation—Fridtjof Nansen Institute, Barcelona, 9–11 Nov. 2000.

Genschel, P. 1997. 'The Dynamics of Inertia: Institutional Persistence and Change in Telecommunications and Health Care', *Governance* 10, 1: 43–66.

Gent, Chariti E. 2000. 'Needle Exchange Policy Adoption in American Cities: *Why Not?*', *Policy Sciences* 33: 125–53.

George, Alexander L. 1969. 'The "Operational Code": A Neglected Approach to the Study of Political Leaders and Decision-Making', *International Studies Quarterly* 13: 190–222.

———. 1979. 'The Causal Nexus between Cognitive Beliefs and Decision-Making Behaviour: The "Operational Code" Belief System', in L.S. Falkowski, ed., *Psychological Models in International Politics*. Boulder, Colo.: Westview Press, 95–124.

———. 1980. *Presidential Decision-making in Foreign Policy: The Effective Use of Information and Advice*. Boulder, Colo.: Westview Press.

Gersick, Connie J.G. 1991. 'Revolutionary Change Theories: A Multilevel Exploration of the Punctuated Equilibrium Paradigm', *Academy of Management Review* 16, 1: 10–36.

Gerston, Larry N. 1997. *Public Policy Making: Process and Principles*. Armonk, NY: M.E. Sharpe.

Gerth, Hans, and C. Wright Mills, eds. 1958. *From Max Weber: Essays in Sociology*. New York: Oxford University Press.

Geva-May, Iris. 2001. 'When the Motto is "Till Death Do Us Part": The Conceptualization and the Craft of Termination in the Public Policy Cycle', *International Journal of Public Administration* 24, 3: 263–88.

——— and Aaron Wildavsky. 1997. *An Operational Approach to Policy Analysis: The Craft-Prescriptions for Better Analysis*. Boston: Kluwer.

Gibson, Robert B., ed. 1999. *Voluntary Initiatives: The New Politics of Corporate Greening*. Peterborough, Ont.: Broadview Press.

Gierke, Otto von. 1958a. *Natural Law and the Theory of Society, 1500–1800*. Cambridge: Cambridge University Press.

———. 1958b. *Political Theories of the Middle Age*. Cambridge: Cambridge University Press.

Gilbert, Neil, and Barbara Gilbert. 1989. *The Enabling State: Modern Welfare Capitalism in America*. New York: Oxford University Press.

Gill, Norman N. 1940. 'Permanent Advisory Committees in the Federal Government', *Journal of Politics* 2: 411–25.

Gillroy, John Martin, and Maurice Wade, eds. 1992. *The Moral Dimensions of Public Policy Choice: Beyond the Market Paradigm*. Pittsburgh: University of Pittsburgh Press.

Gilmore, Thomas N., and James Krantz. 1991. 'Innovation in the Public Sector: Dilemmas in the Use of Ad Hoc Processes', *Journal of Policy Analysis and Management* 10, 3: 455–68.

Ginsburg, N. 1992. *Divisions of Welfare: A Critical Introduction to Comparative Social Policy*. London: Sage.

Girginov, V., and I. Sandanski. 2004. 'The Politics of Sport Sponsorship: A Policy Network Perspective', *European Sport Management Quarterly* 4: 123–49.

Giuliani, Mark. 1999. '"Soft" Institutions for Hard Problems: Instituting Air Pollution Policies in Three Italian Regions', in W. Grant, A. Perl, and P. Knoepfel, eds, *The Politics of Improving Urban Air Quality*. Cheltenham: Edward Elgar, 31–51.

Glicken, Jessica. 2000. 'Getting Stakeholder Participation "Right": A Discussion of Participatory Processes and Possible Pitfalls', *Environmental Science and Policy* 3: 305–10.

Goffman, Erving. 1974. *Frame Analysis: An Essay on the Organization of Experience*. Cambridge, Mass.: Harvard University Press.

Goggin, Malcolm L., et al. 1990. *Implementation Theory and Practice: Toward a Third Generation*. Glenview, Ill.: Scott, Foresman/Little, Brown.

Goldfinch, Shaun. 2000. *Remaking New Zealand and Australia Economic Policy: Ideas, Institutions and Policy Communities*. Washington: Georgetown University Press.

Goldmann, K. 2005. 'Appropriateness and Consequences: The Logic of Neo-Institutionalism', *Governance* 18, 1: 35–52.

Goldsmith, S., and W.D. Eggers. 2004. *Governing by Network: The New Shape of the Public Sector*. Washington: Brookings Institution.

Goldstein, Judith, and Robert O. Keohane, eds. 1993a. *Ideas and Foreign Policy: Beliefs, Institutions and Political Change*. Ithaca, NY: Cornell University Press.

——— and ———. 1993b. 'Ideas and Foreign Policy: An Analytical Framework', in Goldstein and Keohane (1993a: 3–30).

Good, D. 2003. *The Politics of Public Management: The HRDC Audit of Grants and Contributions*. Toronto: University of Toronto Press.

Goodin, R.E., and M. Rein. 2001. 'Regimes on Pillars: Alternative Welfare State Logics and Dynamics', *Public Administration* 79, 4: 769–801.

Goodnow, Frank J. 1900. *Politics and Administration: A Study in Government*. New York: Russell and Russell.

Gordon, I., J. Lewis, and K. Young. 1977. 'Perspectives on Policy Analysis', *Public Administration Bulletin* 25: 26–30.

Gorges, Michael J. 2001. 'The New Institutionalism and the Study of the European Union: The Case of the Social Dialogue', *West European Politics* 24, 4: 152–68.

Gormley, William T. 1989. *Taming the Bureaucracy: Muscles, Prayers and Other Strategies*. Princeton, NJ: Princeton University Press.

———. 2007. 'Public Policy Analysis: Ideas and Impact', *Annual Review of Political Science* 10: 297–313.

——— and B. Guy Peters. 1992. 'National Styles of Regulation: Child Care in Three Countries', *Policy Sciences* 25: 381–99.

Gortner, Harold, Julianne Mahler, and Jeanne Bell Nicholson. 1987. *Organization Theory: A Public Perspective*. Chicago: Dorsey Press.

Gough, Ian. 1975. 'State Expenditure in Advanced Capitalism', *New Left Review* 92: 53–92.

Gould, Stephen Jay. 2002. *The Structure of Evolutionary Theory*. Cambridge, Mass.: Harvard University Press.

———. 2007. *Punctuated Equilibrium*. Cambridge, Mass.: Belknap Press.

——— and Niles Eldredge. 1977. 'Punctuated Equilibria: The Tempo and Mode of Evolution Reconsidered', *Paleobiology* 3: 115–51.

Gourevitch, P. 1993. 'Democracy and Economic Policy: Elective Affinities and Circumstantial Conjunctures', *World Development* 21, 8: 1271–80.

Graber, Doris Appel. 1989. *Mass Media and American Politics*. Washington: Congressional Quarterly Press.

Grabosky, Peter N. 1995. 'Using Non-Governmental Resources to Foster Regulatory Compliance', *Governance* 8, 4: 527–50.

Grande, E. 1996. 'The State and Interest Groups in a Framework of Multi-Level Decision-Making: The Case of the European Union', *Journal of European Public Policy* 3: 313–38.

Granovetter, M. 1978. 'Threshold Models of Collective Behaviour', *American Journal of Sociology* 83, 6: 1420–43.

Grant, Wyn, and Anne MacNamara. 1995. 'When Policy Communities Intersect: The Cases of Agriculture and Banking', *Political Studies* 43: 509–15.

Grantham, Andrew. 2001. 'How Networks Explain Unintended Policy Implementation Outcomes: The Case of UK Rail Privatization', *Public Administration* 79, 4: 851–70.

Gray, Pat, and Paul t'Hart. 1998. *Public Policy Disasters in Western Europe*. London: Routledge.

Green, Donald, and Ian Shapiro. 1994. *Pathologies of Rational Choice Theory*. New Haven: Yale University Press.

Greenaway, John, Brian Salter, and Stella Hart. 2007. 'How Policy Networks Can Damage Democratic Health: A Case Study in the Government of Governance', *Public Administration* 85, 3: 717–38.

Greenberg, George D., et al. 1977. 'Developing Public Policy Theory: Perspectives from Empirical Research', *American Political Science Review* 71: 1532–43.

Greener, I. 2002. 'Understanding NHS Reform: The Policy-Transfer, Social Learning and Path Dependency Perspectives', *Governance* 15, 2: 161–83.

———. 2005. 'The Potential of Path Dependence in Political Studies', *Politics* 25, 1: 62–72.

Green-Pedersen, Christoffer. 2004. 'The Dependent Variable Problem within the Study of Welfare State Retrenchment: Defining the Problem and Looking for Solutions', *Journal of Comparative Policy Analysis* 6, 1: 3–14.

Greer, Scott. 2008. 'Choosing Paths in European Health Services Policy: A Political Analysis of a Critical Juncture', *Journal of European Social Policy* 18, 3: 219–31.

Gregory, Robin, Tim McDaniels, and Daryl Fields. 2001. 'Decision Aiding, Not Dispute Resolution: Creating Insights through Structured Environmental Decisions', *Journal of Policy Analysis and Management* 20, 3: 415–32.

Greif, A., and D.D. Laitin. 2004. 'A Theory of Endogenous Institutional Change', *American Political Science Review* 98, 4: 633–52.

Griggs, Steven. 1999. 'Restructuring Health Policy Networks: A French Policy Style?', *West European Politics* 22, 4: 185–204.

Grima, A.P. 1985. 'Participatory Rites: Integrating Public Involvement in Environmental Impact Assessment', in J.B.R. Whitney and V.W. Maclaren, eds, *Environmental Impact Assessment: The Canadian Experience*. Toronto: University of Toronto Institute for Environmental Studies, 33–51.

Grimshaw, Damian, Steven Vincent, and Hugh Willmott. 2001. 'New Control Modes and Emergent Organizational Forms: Private–Public Contracting in Public Administration', *Administrative Theory and Practice* 23, 3: 407–30.

Grin, John, and Anne Loeber. 2007. 'Theories of Policy Learning: Agency, Structure and Change', in Frank Fischer, Gerald D. Miller, and Mara S. Sidney, eds, *Handbook of Public Policy Analysis*. London: Taylor and Francis, 201–19.

Guess, George M., and Paul G. Farnham. 2000. *Cases in Public Policy Analysis*. Washington: Georgetown University Press.

Gulick, Luther H. 1937. 'Notes on the Theory of Organization', in Gulick and Urwick (1937).

——— and Lyndal Urwick, eds. 1937. *Papers on the Science of Administration*. New York: Institute of Public Administration.

——— and ———, eds. 1947. *Papers on the Science of Administration*. New York: A.M. Kelley.

Gummett, P., ed. 1996. *Globalization and Public Policy*. Cheltenham: Edward Elgar.

Gundel, S. 2005. 'Towards a New Typology of Crises', *Journal of Contingencies and Crisis Management* 13, 3: 106–15.

Gunningham, Neil, Peter Grabosky, and Darren Sinclair. 1998. *Smart Regulation: Designing Environmental Policy*. Oxford: Clarendon Press.

——— and Joseph Rees. 1997. 'Industry Self-Regulation: An Institutional Perspective', *Law and Policy* 19, 4: 363–414.

——— and Darren Sinclair. 1999. 'Regulatory Pluralism: Designing Policy Mixes for Environmental Protection', *Law and Policy* 21, 1: 49–76.

——— and Mike D. Young. 1997. 'Toward Optimal Environmental Policy: The Case of Biodiversity Conservation', *Ecology Law Quarterly* 24: 243–98.

Guo, Chao. 2007. 'When Government Becomes the Principal Philanthropist: The Effects of Public Funding on Patterns of Nonprofit Governance', *Public Administration Review* (May–June): 458–73.

Gupta, J., X. Olsthoorn, and E. Rotenberg. 2003. 'The Role of Scientific Uncertainty in Compliance with the Kyoto Protocol to the Climate Change Convention', *Environmental Science and Policy* 6: 475–86.

Gustafsson, Gunnel, and J.J. Richardson. 1979. 'Concepts of Rationality and the Policy Process', *European Journal of Political Research* 7: 415–36.

Haas, Ernst B. 1958. *The Uniting of Europe: Political, Social and Economical Forces 1950–1957*. London: Stevens and Sons.

———. 1975. 'Is there a Hole in the Whole? Knowledge, Technology, Interdependence, and the Construction of International Regimes', *International Organization* 29, 3: 827–76.

Haas, Mark L. 2001. 'Prospect Theory and the Cuban Missile Crisis', *International Studies Quarterly* 45: 241–70.

Haas, Peter M. 1992. 'Introduction: Epistemic Communities and International Policy Coordination', *International Organization* 46, 1: 1–36.

Hacker, Joseph S. 2004a. 'Reform without Change, Change without Reform: The Politics of US Health Policy Reform in Comparative Perspective', in M.A. Levin and M. Shapiro, eds, *Transatlantic Policymaking in an Age of Austerity: Diversity and Drift*. Washington: Georgetown University Press, 13–63.

———. 2004b. 'Review Article: Dismantling the Health Care State? Political Institutions, Public Policies and the Comparative Politics of Health Reform', *British Journal of Political Science* 34: 693–724.

Haggard, Stephen, and Chung-In Moon. 1990. 'Institutions and Economic Policy: Theory and a Korean Case Study', *World Politics* 42, 2: 210–37.

——— and Beth A. Simmons. 1987. 'Theories of International Regimes', *International Organization* 41, 3: 491–517.

Hahn, Robert W., and John A. Hird. 1991. 'The Costs and Benefits of Regulation: Review and Synthesis', *Yale Journal of Regulation* 8, 1: 233–78.

Haider, Donald. 1989. 'Grants as a Tool of Public Policy', in Salamon (1989a: 93–124).

Haider-Markel, Donald P., and Mark R. Joslyn. 2001. 'Gun Policy, Opinion, Tragedy and Blame Attribution: The Conditional Influence of Issue Frames', *Journal of Politics* 63, 2: 520–43.

Hajer, Maarten A. 1993. 'Discourse Coalitions and the Institutionalization of Practice: The Case of Acid Rain in Britain', in Fischer and Forester (1993: 43–76).

———. 1997. *The Politics of Environmental Discourse: Ecological Modernization and the Policy Process*. Oxford: Oxford University Press.

———. 2005. 'Setting the Stage: A Dramaturgy of Policy Deliberation', *Administration and Society* 36, 6: 624–47.

——— and Hendrik Wagenaar, eds. 2003. *Deliberative Policy Analysis: Understanding Governance in the Network Society*. Cambridge: Cambridge University Press.

Hall, John A., and G. John Ikenberry. 1989. *The State*. Minneapolis: University of Minnesota Press.

Hall, Michael, and Keith Banting. 2000. 'The Nonprofit Sector in Canada: An Introduction', in Banting, ed., *The NonProfit Sector in Canada: Roles and Relationships*. Montreal and Kingston: McGill-Queen's University Press, 1–28.

Hall, Peter A. 1986. *Governing the Economy: The Politics of State Intervention in Britain and France*. Cambridge: Polity Press.

———, ed. 1989. *The Political Power of Economic Ideas: Keynesianism across Nations*. Princeton, NJ: Princeton University Press.

———. 1990. 'Policy Paradigms, Experts, and the State: The Case of Macroeconomic Policy-Making in Britain', in Brooks and Gagnon (1990).

———. 1992. 'The Change from Keynesianism to Monetarism: Institutional Analysis and British Economic Policy in the 1970s', in S. Steinmo et al., eds, *Structuring Politics: Historical Institutionalism in Comparative Analysis*. Cambridge: Cambridge University Press, 90–114.

———. 1993. 'Policy Paradigms, Social Learning and the State: The Case of Economic Policy Making in Britain', *Comparative Politics* 25, 3: 275–96.

———. 1997. 'The Role of Interests, Institutions and Ideas in the Comparative Political Economy of Industrialized Nations', in M.I. Lichbach and A.S. Zuckerman, eds, *Comparative Politics: Rationality, Culture and Structure*. Cambridge: Cambridge University Press, 174–207.

——— and David Soskice, eds. 2001a. *Varieties of Capitalism: The Institutional Foundations of Comparative Advantage*. Oxford: Oxford University Press.

——— and ———. 2001b. 'Varieties of Capitalism: The Institutional Foundations of Comparative Advantage', in Hall and Soskice (2001a: 1–70).

——— and Rosemary C.R. Taylor. 1996. 'Political Science and the Three New Institutionalisms', *Political Studies* 44: 936–57.

Hall, Thad E., and Laurence J. O'Toole. 2000. 'Structures for Policy Implementation: An Analysis of National Legislation 1965–1966 and 1993–1994', *Administration and Society* 31, 6: 667–86.

——— and ———. 2004. 'Shaping Formal Networks through the Regulatory Process', *Administration and Society* 36, 2: 186–207.

Halligan, J. 2003. *Civil Service Systems in Anglo-American Countries*. Cheltenham: Edward Elgar.

Hamm, Keith E. 1983. 'Patterns of Influence among Committees, Agencies, and Interest Groups', *Legislative Studies Quarterly* 8, 3: 379–426.

Hammersley, M. 2005. 'Is the Evidence-Based Practice Movement Doing More Good Than Harm? Reflections on Iain Chalmers' Case for Research-Based Policy Making and Practice', *Evidence and Policy* 1, 1: 85–100.

Hammond, Thomas H. 1986. 'Agenda Control, Organizational Structure, and Bureaucratic Politics', *American Journal of Political Science* 30, 2: 379–420.

———. 2003. 'Veto Points, Policy Preferences, and Bureaucratic Autonomy in Democratic Systems', in G.A. Krause and K.J. Meier, eds, *Politics, Policy and Organizations: Frontiers in the Scientific Study of Bureaucracy*. Ann Arbor: University of Michigan Press, 73–103.

——— and Jack H. Knott. 1999. 'Political Institutions, Public Management, and Policy Choice', *Journal of Public Administration Research and Theory* 9, 1: 33–85.

——— and ———. 2000. 'Public Management, Administrative Leadership and Policy Change', in J.L. Brudney, L.J. O'Toole, and H.G. Rainey, eds, *Advancing Public Management: New Developments in Theory, Methods and Practice*. Washington: Georgetown University Press, 49–74.

Hancock, M. Donald. 1983. 'Comparative Public Policy: An Assessment', in A.W. Finifter, ed., *Political Science: The State of the Discipline*. Washington: American Political Science Association, 283–308.

Hansen, Randal, and Desmond King. 2001. 'Eugenic Ideas, Political Interests, and Policy Variance: Immigration and Sterilization Policy in Britain and the U.S.', *World Politics* 53 (Jan.): 237–63.

Hansen, Susan B. 1983. 'Public Policy Analysis: Some Recent Developments and Current Problems', *Policy Studies Journal* 12: 14–42.

Hansford, T.G. 2004. 'Lobbying Strategies, Venue Selection, and Organized Interest Involvement at the U.S. Supreme Court', *American Politics Research* 32, 2: 170–97.

Hansmann, Henry B. 1980. 'The Role of Nonprofit Enterprise', *Yale Law Journal* 89, 5: 835–901.

Hargrove, E.L. 1975. *The Missing Link: The Study of the Implementation of Social Policy*. Washington: Urban Institute.

Harris, Richard, and Sidney Milkis. 1989. *The Politics of Regulatory Change*. New York: Oxford University Press.

Harrison, Kathryn. 2001. 'Too Close to Home: Dioxin Contamination of Breast Milk and the Political Agenda', *Policy Sciences* 34: 35–62.

Harrow, Jenny. 2001. '"Capacity Building" as a Public Management Goal: Myth, Magic of the Main Chance', *Public Management Review* 3, 2: 209–30.

Harsanyi, John C. 1977. *Rational Behaviour and Bargaining Equilibrium in Games and Social Situations*. Cambridge: Cambridge University Press.

Hastak, Manoj, Michael B. Mazis, and Louis A. Morris. 2001. 'The Role of Consumer Surveys in Public Policy Decision Making', *Journal of Public Policy and Marketing* 20, 2: 170–85.

Haufler, Virginia. 2000. 'Private Sector International Regimes', in R.A. Higgott and G.R.D. Underhill, eds, *Andreas Bieler*. London: Routledge, 121–37.

———. 2001. *A Public Role for the Private Sector: Industry Self-Regulation in a Global Economy*. Washington: Carnegie Endowment for International Peace.

Hawkesworth, Mary. 1992. 'Epistemology and Policy Analysis', in W. Dunn and R.M. Kelly, eds, *Advances in Policy Studies*. New Brunswick, NJ: Transaction, 291–329.

Hawkins, Keith. 1984. *Environment and Enforcement: Regulation and the Social Definition of Pollution*. Oxford: Clarendon Press.

——— and John M. Thomas, eds. 1989a. *Making Regulatory Policy*. Pittsburgh: University of Pittsburgh Press.

——— and ———. 1989b. 'Making Policy in Regulatory Bureaucracies', in Hawkins and Thomas (1989a: 3–30).

Hay, Colin. 2004. 'Common Trajectories, Variable Paces, Divergent Outcomes? Models of European Capitalism under Conditions of Complex Economic Interdependence', *Review of International Political Economy* 11, 2: 231–62.

——— and Daniel Wincott. 1998. 'Structure, Agency and Historical Institutionalism', *Political Studies* 46: 951–7.

Haydu, Jeffrey. 1998. 'Making Use of the Past: Time Periods as Cases to Compare and as Sequences of Problem Solving', *American Journal of Sociology* 104, 2: 339–71.

Hayes, Michael T. 1978. 'The Semi-Sovereign Pressure Groups: A Critique of Current Theory and an Alternative Typology', *Journal of Politics* 40, 1: 134–61.

———. 1992. *Incrementalism and Public Policy*. New York: Longmans.

———. 2001. *The Limits of Policy Change: Incrementalism, Worldview and the Rule of Law*. Washington: Georgetown University Press.

———. 2007. 'Policy Making through Disjointed Incrementalism', in Morcöl (2007: 39–59).

Hays, Samuel P. 1959. *Conservation and the Gospel of Efficiency: The Progressive Conservation Movement 1890–1920*. Cambridge, Mass.: Harvard University Press.

———. 1987. *Beauty, Health and Permanence: Environmental Politics in the United States, 1955–1985*. New York: Cambridge University Press.

Head, Brian W. 2008. 'Three Lenses of Evidence-Based Policy', *Australian Journal of Public Administration* 67, 1: 1–11.

Heclo, Hugh. 1974. *Modern Social Politics in Britain and Sweden: From Relief to Income Maintenance*. New Haven: Yale University Press.

———. 1976. 'Conclusion: Policy Dynamics', in Rose (1976: 237–66).

———. 1978. 'Issue Networks and the Executive Establishment', in A. King, ed., *The New American Political System*. Washington: American Enterprise Institute for Public Policy Research, 87–124.

———. 1994. 'Ideas, Interests and Institutions', in L.C. Dodd and C. Jillson, eds, *The Dynamics of American Politics: Approaches and Interpretations*. San Francisco: Westview, 366–92.

Heichel, Stephan, Jessica Pape, and Thomas Sommerer. 2005. 'Is There Convergence in Convergence Research? An Overview of Empirical Studies on Policy Convergence', *Journal of European Public Policy* 12, 5: 797–816.

Heidenheimer, Arnold J., Hugh Heclo, and Carolyn Teich Adams, eds. 1975. *Comparative Public Policy: The Politics of Social Choice in Europe and America*. New York: St Martin's Press.

Heikkila, Tanya. 1999. 'The Role of Science and Research in Policy Making: The Case of the San Pedro River Basin', paper presented at the annual meeting of the Western Political Science Association, Seattle.

——— and K.R. Isett. 2004. 'Modeling Operational Decision Making in Public Organizations: An Integration of Two Institutional Theories', *American Review of Public Administration* 34, 1: 3–19.

Heinz, John P., et al. 1990. 'Inner Circles or Hollow Cores', *Journal of Politics* 52, 2: 356–90.

——— et al. 1993. *The Hollow Core: Private Interests in National Policy Making*. Cambridge, Mass.: Harvard University Press.

Held, David, and Anthony McGrew. 1993. 'Globalization and the Liberal Democratic State', *Government and Opposition* 28, 2: 261–85.

Hellstern, Gerd-Michael. 1986. 'Assessing Evaluation Research', in Kaufman et al. (1986: 279–312).

Hendrick, Rebecca M., and David Nachmias. 1992. 'The Policy Sciences: The Challenge of Complexity', *Policy Studies Review* 11, 3 and 4: 310–28.

Heritier, Adrienne. 1997. 'Policy-Making by Subterfuge: Interest Accommodation, Innovation and Substitute Democratic Legitimation in Europe—Perspectives from Distinctive Policy Areas', *Journal of European Public Policy* 4, 2: 171–89.

———. 1999. 'Elements of Democratic Legitimation in Europe: An Alternative Perspective', *Journal of European Public Policy* 6, 2: 269–82.

Herman, Edward S., and Noam Chomsky. 1988. *Manufacturing Consent: The Political Economy of the Mass Media*. New York: Pantheon Books.

Hermann, Charles F. 1982. 'Instruments of Foreign Policy', in P. Callahan, L.P. Brady, and M.G. Hermann, eds, *Describing Foreign Policy Behaviour*. Beverly Hills, Calif.: Sage, 153–74.

Hernes, Gudmund. 1976. 'Structural Change in Social Processes', *American Journal of Sociology* 82, 3: 513–47.

Heron, Tony, and Ben Richardson. 2008. 'Path Dependency and the Politics of Liberalisation in the Textiles and Clothing Industry', *New Political Economy* 13, 1: 1–18.

Hesse, Joachim Jens. 1997. 'Rebuilding the State: Public Sector Reform in Central and Eastern Europe', in J.-E. Lane, ed., *Public Sector Reform: Rationale, Trends and Problems*. London: Sage, 114–45.

Hibbing, John R., and Elizabeth Theiss-Morse. 2002. *Stealth Democracy: Americans' Beliefs about How Government Should Work*. Cambridge: Cambridge University Press.

Hibbs, Douglas A., Jr. 1977. 'Political Parties and Macroeconomic Policy', *American Political Science Review* 71: 1467–87.

———. 1978. 'On the Political Economy of Long-run Trends in Strike Activity', *British Journal of Political Science* 8, 2: 153–75.

———. 1987. *The Political Economy of Industrial Democracies*. Cambridge, Mass.: Harvard University Press.

Hilgartner, Stephen, and Charles L. Bosk. 1981. 'The Rise and Fall of Social Problems: A Public Arenas Model', *American Journal of Sociology* 94, 1: 53–78.

Hill, Larry B., ed. 1992. *The State of Public Bureaucracy*. Armonk, NY: M.E. Sharpe.

Hill, Michael, ed. 1993. *The Policy Process: A Reader*. London: Harvester Wheatsheaf.

Hintze, Otto. 1975. *The Historical Essays of Otto Hintze*. New York: Oxford University Press.

Hird, J.A. 2005. 'Policy Analysis for What? The Effectiveness of Nonpartisan Policy Research Organizations', *Policy Studies Journal* 33, 1: 83–105.

Hirschman, Albert O. 1958. *The Strategy of Economic Development*. New Haven: Yale University Press.

Hirst, Paul, and Grahame Thompson. 1996. *Globalization in Question*. Oxford: Polity Press.

Hisschemoller, Matthijs, and Rob Hoppe. 1995. 'Coping with Intractable Controversies: The Case for Problem Structuring in Policy Design and Analysis', *Knowledge and Policy* 8, 4: 40–61.

Hjern, Benny. 1982. 'Implementation Research—The Link Gone Missing', *Journal of Public Policy* 2, 3: 301–8.

——— and David O. Porter. 1993. 'Implementation Structures: A New Unit of Administrative Analysis', in Hill (1993).

Hoberg, George. 1996. 'Putting Ideas in Their Place: A Response to "Learning and Change in the British Columbia Forest Policy Sector" ', *Canadian Journal of Political Science* 29, 1: 135–44.

———. 1998. 'Distinguishing Learning from Other Sources of Policy Change: The Case of Forestry in the Pacific Northwest', paper presented to the annual meeting of the American Political Science Association, Boston.

——— and E. Morawaski. 1997. 'Policy Change through Sector Intersection: Forest and Aboriginal Policy in Clayoquot Sound', *Canadian Public Administration* 40, 3: 387–414.

Hobson, John, and M. Ramesh. 2002. 'Globalisation Makes of States What States Make of It: Between Agency and Structure in the State/Globalisation Debate', *New Political Economy* 7, 1: 5–22.

Hockin, Thomas A. 1977. 'Mass Legitimate Parties and Their Implications for Party Leaders', in Hockin, ed., *Apex of Power: The Prime Minister and Political Leadership in Canada*. Scarborough, Ont.: Prentice-Hall, 70–85.

Hodge, Graeme A., and Carsten Greve. 2007. 'Public–Private Partnerships: An International Performance Review', *Public Administration Review* 67, 3: 545–58.

Hodgetts, J.E. 1973. *The Canadian Public Service: A Physiology of Government, 1867–1970*. Toronto: University of Toronto Press.

Hoekman, Bernard, and Michel Kostecki. 1995. *The Political Economy of the World Trading System: From GATT to WTO*. Oxford: Oxford University Press.

Hofferbert, Richard I. 1974. *The Study of Public Policy*. Indianapolis: Bobbs-Merrill.

Hoffman, Andrew J. 1999. 'Institutional Evolution and Change: Environmentalism and the U.S. Chemical Industry', *Academy of Management Journal* 42, 4: 351–71.

Hogwood, Brian W. 1992. *Ups and Downs: Is There an Issue-Attention Cycle in Britain?* Glasgow: Strathclyde Papers in Government and Politics no. 89.

———— and Lewis A. Gunn. 1984. *Policy Analysis for the Real World*. New York: Oxford University Press.

Hollingsworth, J. Rogers. 1998. 'New Perspectives on the Spatial Dimensions of Economic Coordination: Tensions between Globalization and Social Systems of Production', *Review of International Political Economy* 5, 3: 482–507.

————. 2000. 'Doing Institutional Analysis: Implications for the Study of Innovations', *Review of International Political Economy* 7, 4: 595–644.

Holzmann, Robert, M. Orenstein, and M. Rutkowski, eds. 2003. *Pension Reform in Europe: Process and Progress*. Washington: World Bank.

Holzner, Burkart, and John H. Marx. 1979. *Knowledge Application: The Knowledge System in Society*. Wellesley, Mass.: Allyn and Bacon.

Hood, Christopher. 1983. 'Using Bureaucracy Sparingly', *Public Administration* 61, 2: 197–208.

————. 1986a. *The Tools of Government*. Chatham, NJ: Chatham House.

————. 1986b. 'The Hidden Public Sector: The "Quangocratization" of the World?', in Kaufman et al. (1986: 183–207).

————. 1988. 'Keeping the Centre Small: Explanation of Agency Type', *Political Studies* 36, 1: 30–46.

————. 1991. 'A Public Management for All Seasons?', *Public Administration* 69 (Spring): 3–19.

————. 1995. 'Contemporary Public Management: A New Global Paradigm?', *Public Policy and Administration* 10, 2: 104–17.

————. 1998. *The Art of the State: Culture, Rhetoric and Public Management*. Oxford: Clarendon Press.

————. 1999. 'The Garbage Can Model of Organization: Describing a Condition of Prescriptive Design Principle', in M. Egeberg and P. Laegreid, eds, *Organizing Political Institutions: Essays for Johan P. Olsen*. Oslo: Scandinavian University Press, 59–78.

————. 2002. 'The Risk Game and the Blame Game', *Government and Opposition* 37, 1: 15–54.

———— and H. Rothstein. 2001. 'Risk Regulation under Pressure: Problem Solving or Blame Shifting?', *Administration and Society* 33, 1: 21–53.

Horn, Murray J. 1995. *The Political Economy of Public Administration: Institutional Choice in the Public Sector*. Cambridge: Cambridge University Press.

Hosseus, Daniel, and Leslie A. Pal. 1997. 'Anatomy of a Policy Area: The Case of Shipping', *Canadian Public Policy* 23, 4: 399–416.

Hough, Jerry F. 1972. 'The Soviet System: Petrification or Pluralism', *Problems of Communism* 21 (Mar.–Apr.): 25–45.

Howard, Christopher. 1993. 'The Hidden Side of the American Welfare States', *Political Science Quarterly* 108, 3: 403–36.

————. 1995. 'Testing the Tools Approach: Tax Expenditures versus Direct Expenditures', *Public Administration Review* 55, 5: 439–47.

————. 1997. *The Hidden Welfare State: Tax Expenditures and Social Policy in the United States*. Princeton, NJ: Princeton University Press.

————. 2002. 'Tax Expenditures', in Salamon (2002a: 410–44).

Howard, Cosmo. 2005. 'The Policy Cycle: A Model of Post-Machiavellian Policy Making?', *Australian Journal of Political Science* 64, 3: 3–13.

Howard, S. Kenneth. 1971. 'Analysis, Rationality, and Administrative Decision-Making', in F. Marini, ed., *Toward a New Public Administration: The Minnowbrook Perspective.* Scranton, Penn.: Chandler.

Howe, R. Brian, and David Johnson. 2000. *Restraining Equality: Human Rights Commissions in Canada.* Toronto: University of Toronto Press.

Howell, Chris. 2003. 'Varieties of Capitalism—and Then There Was One?', *Comparative Politics* 36, 1: 103–24.

Howells, G. 2005. 'The Potential and Limits of Consumer Empowerment by Information', *Journal of Law and Society* 32, 3: 349–70.

Howlett, Michael. 1986. 'Acts of Commission and Acts of Omission: Legal-Historical Research and the Intentions of Government in a Federal State', *Canadian Journal of Political Science* 19: 363–71.

———. 1990. 'The Round Table Experience: Representation and Legitimacy in Canadian Environmental Policy Making', *Queen's Quarterly* 97, 4: 580–601.

———. 1991. 'Policy Instruments, Policy Styles, and Policy Implementation: National Approaches to Theories of Instrument Choice', *Policy Studies Journal* 19, 2: 1–21.

———. 1994. 'Policy Paradigms and Policy Change: Lessons from the Old and New Canadian Policies towards Aboriginal Peoples', *Policy Studies Journal* 22, 4: 631–51.

———. 1997a. 'Issue-Attention and Punctuated Equilibria Models Reconsidered: An Empirical Examination of the Dynamics of Agenda-Setting in Canada', *Canadian Journal of Political Science* 30, 1: 3–29.

———. 1997b. 'Predictable and Unpredictable Policy Windows: Issue, Institutional and Exogenous Correlates of Canadian Federal Agenda-Setting', paper presented to the annual meeting of the Canadian Political Science Association, St John's.

———. 1999. 'Federalism and Public Policy', in J. Bickerton and A. Gagnon, eds, *Canadian Politics*, 3rd edn. Peterborough, Ont.: Broadview Press.

———. 2000. 'Managing the "Hollow State": Procedural Policy Instruments and Modern Governance', *Canadian Public Administration* 43, 4: 412–31.

———. 2002. 'Do Networks Matter? Linking Policy Network Structure to Policy Outcomes: Evidence from Four Canadian Policy Sectors, 1990–2000', *Canadian Journal of Political Science* 35, 2: 235–68.

———. 2007. 'Analyzing Multi-Actor, Multi-Round Public Policy Decision-Making Processes in Government: Findings from Five Canadian Cases', *Canadian Journal of Political Science* 40, 3: 659–84.

——— and Benjamin Cashore. 2007. 'Re-Visiting the New Orthodoxy of Policy Dynamics: The Dependent Variable and Re-Aggregation Problems in the Study of Policy Change', *Canadian Political Science Review* 1, 2: 50–62.

———, Alex Netherton, and M. Ramesh. 1999. *The Political Economy of Canada: An Introduction*, 2nd edn. Toronto: Oxford University Press.

——— and M. Ramesh. 1993. 'Patterns of Policy Instrument Choice: Policy Styles, Policy Learning and the Privatization Experience', *Policy Studies Review* 12, 1: 3–24.

——— and ———. 1995. *Studying Public Policy: Policy Cycles and Policy Subsystems.* Toronto: Oxford University Press.

——— and ———. 1998. 'Policy Subsystem Configurations and Policy Change: Operationalizing the Postpositivist Analysis of the Politics of the Policy Process', *Policy Studies Journal* 26, 3: 466–82.

——— and ———. 2002. 'The Policy Effects of Internationalization: A Subsystem Adjustment Analysis of Policy Change', *Journal of Comparative Policy Analysis* 4, 3: 31–50.

——— and Jeremy Rayner. 1995. 'Do Ideas Matter? Policy Subsystem Configurations and Policy Change in the Canadian Forest Sector', *Canadian Public Administration* 38, 3: 382–410.

———— and ————. 2006. 'Understanding the Historical Turn in the Policy Sciences: A Critique of Stochastic, Narrative, Path Dependency and Process-Sequencing Models of Policy-Making over Time', *Policy Sciences* 39, 1: 1–18.

———— and ————. 2007. 'Design Principles for Policy Mixes: Cohesion and Coherence in "New Governance Arrangements"', *Policy and Society* 26, 4: 1–18.

Howse, Robert, J. Robert S. Prichard, and Michael J. Trebilcock. 1990. 'Smaller or Smarter Government?', *University of Toronto Law Journal* 40: 498–541.

Huber, Evelyne, and John D. Stephens. 1998. 'Internationalization and the Social Democratic Model: Crisis and Future Prospects', *Comparative Political Studies* 31, 3: 353–97.

Huber, George P. 1991. 'Organization Learning: The Contributing Processes and the Literatures', *Organization Science* 2, 1: 88–115.

Huitt, Ralph K. 1968. 'Political Feasibility', in A. Ranney, ed., *Political Science and Public Policy*. Chicago: Markham Publishing, 263–76.

Hula, Richard C. 1988. 'Using Markets to Implement Public Policy', in Hula, ed., *Market-Based Public Policy*. London: Macmillan, 3–18.

————, Cynthia Jackson-Elmoore, and Laura Reese. 2007. 'Mixing God's Work and the Public Business: A Framework for the Analysis of Faith-Based Service Delivery', *Review of Policy Research* 24, 1: 67–89.

Humphries, Martha Anne, and Donald R. Songer. 1999. 'Law and Politics in Judicial Oversight of Federal Administrative Agencies', *Journal of Politics* 61, 1: 207–20.

Huntington, Samuel P. 1952. 'The Marasmus of the ICC: The Commissions, the Railroads and the Public Interest', *Yale Law Review* 61, 4: 467–509.

Hupe, Peter L., and Michael J. Hill. 2006. 'The Three Actions Levels of Governance: Re-Framing the Policy Process beyond the Stages Model', in B. Guy Peters and Jon Pierre, eds, *Handbook of Public Policy*. London: Sage, 13–30.

Hustinx, L., and F. Lammertyn. 2003. 'Collective and Reflexive Styles of Volunteering: A Sociological Modernization Perspective', *Voluntas: International Journal of Voluntary and Nonprofit Organizations* 14, 2: 167–87.

Hutter, Bridget M., and P.K. Manning. 1990. 'The Contexts of Regulation: The Impact upon Health and Safety Inspectorates in Britain', *Law and Policy* 12, 2: 103–36.

Iannuzzi, Alphonse. 2001. *Industry Self-Regulation and Voluntary Environmental Compliance*. Boca Raton, Fla: Lewis Publishers.

Ikenberry, G. John. 1988. 'Conclusion: An Institutional Approach to American Foreign Economic Policy', *International Organization* 42, 1: 219–43.

————. 1990. 'The International Spread of Privatization Policies: Inducements, Learning, and "Policy Bandwagoning"', in Suleiman and Waterbury (1990).

Imbeau, Louis M., and Guy Lachapelle. 1993. 'Les Déterminants des politiques provinciales au Canada: une synthèse des études comparatives', *Revue Québécoise de Science Politique* 23: 107–41.

Ingram, Helen M., and Dean E. Mann, eds. 1980a. *Why Policies Succeed or Fail*. Beverly Hills, Calif.: Sage.

———— and ————. 1980b. 'Policy Failure: An Issue Deserving Analysis', in Ingram and Mann (1980a).

Jacek, H.J. 1986. 'Pluralist and Corporatist Intermediation, Activities of Business Interest Associations, and Corporate Profits: Some Evidence from Canada', *Comparative Politics* 18, 4: 419–37.

Jackson, Peter M. 2007. 'Making Sense of Policy Advice', *Public Money and Management* 27, 4: 257–64.

Jacobsen, John Kurt. 1995. 'Much Ado about Ideas: The Cognitive Factor in Economic Policy', *World Politics* no. 47: 283–310.

Jacobson, Peter D., Elizabeth Selvin, and Scott D. Pomfret. 2001. 'The Role of the Courts in Shaping Health Policy: An Empirical Analysis', *Journal of Law, Medicine and Ethics* 29: 278–89.

Jacoby, William G. 2000. 'Issue Framing and Public Opinion on Government Spending', *American Journal of Political Science* 44, 4: 750–67.

Jaffe, Louis L. 1965. *Judicial Control of Administrative Action*. Boston: Little, Brown.

———. 1969. *English and American Judges as Lawmakers*. Oxford: Clarendon.

Jahn, G., M. Schramm, and A. Spiller. 2005. 'The Reliability of Certification: Quality Labels as a Consumer Policy Tool', *Journal of Consumer Policy* 28: 53–73.

James, Simon. 1993. 'The Idea Brokers: The Impact of Think Tanks on British Government', *Public Administration* 71: 491–506.

Jenkins, William I. 1978. *Policy Analysis: A Political and Organizational Perspective.* London: Martin Robertson.

Jenkins-Smith, Hank C., and Paul A. Sabatier. 1993. 'The Study of Public Policy Processes', in Sabatier and Jenkins-Smith (1993a).

———, Gilbert K. St Clair, and Brian Woods. 1991. 'Explaining Change in Policy Subsystems: Analysis of Coalition Stability and Defection over Time', *American Journal of Political Science* 35, 4: 851–80.

Jennings, Bruce. 1987. 'Interpretation and the Practice of Policy Analysis', in Fischer and Forester (1987).

Jenson, Jane. 1989. 'Paradigms and Political Discourse: Protective Legislation in France and the United States before 1914', *Canadian Journal of Political Science* 22, 2: 235–58.

———. 1991. 'All the World's a Stage: Ideas about Political Space and Time', *Studies in Political Economy* 36: 43–72.

———. 1994. 'Commissioning Ideas: Representation and Royal Commissions', in S.D. Phillips, ed., *How Ottawa Spends 1994–95: Making Change*. Ottawa: Carleton University Press, 39–69.

Jeon, Yongjoo, and Donald P. Haider-Markel. 2001. 'Tracing Issue Definition and Policy Change: An Analysis of Disability Issue Images and Policy Response', *Policy Studies Journal* 29, 2: 215–31.

Jervis, Robert. 1997. *System Effects: Complexity in Political and Social Life*. Princeton, NJ: Princeton University Press.

Johansson, R., and K. Borell. 1999. 'Central Steering and Local Networks: Old-Age Care in Sweden', *Public Administration* 77, 3: 585–98.

John, Peter. 2003. 'Is There Life after Policy Streams, Advocacy Coalitions and Punctuations: Using Evolutionary Theory to Explain Policy Change?', *Policy Studies Journal* 31, 4: 481–98.

——— and H. Margetts. 2003. 'Policy Punctuations in the UK: Fluctuations and Equilibria in Central Government Expenditure since 1951', *Public Administration* 81, 3: 411–32.

Johnsen, A. 2005. 'What Does 25 Years of Experience Tell Us about the State of Performance Measurement in Public Policy and Management?', *Public Money and Management* 25, 1: 9–17.

Johnson, A.F., and A. Stritch, eds. 1997. *Canadian Public Policy: Globalization and Political Parties*. Toronto: Copp Clark Pitman.

Johnson, Genevieve Fuji. 2007. 'The Discourse of Democracy in Canadian Nuclear Waste Management Policy', *Policy Science* 40: 79–99.

Johnson, Norman. 1987. *The Welfare State in Transition: The Theory and Practice of Welfare Pluralism*. Brighton, Sussex: Wheatsheaf Books.

Johnston, Richard. 1986. *Public Opinion and Public Policy in Canada: Questions of Confidence*. Toronto: University of Toronto Press.

Jones, Bryan D. 1994. *Reconceiving Decision-Making in Democratic Politics: Attention, Choice and Public Policy*. Chicago: University of Chicago Press.

———. 2001. *Politics and the Architecture of Choice: Bounded Rationality and Governance*. Chicago: University of Chicago Press.

———. 2002. 'Bounded Rationality and Public Policy: Herbert A. Simon and the Decisional Foundation of Collective Choice', *Policy Sciences* 35: 269–84.

——— and Frank R. Baumgartner. 2002. 'Punctuations, Ideas and Public Policy', in Baumgartner and Jones, eds, *Policy Dynamics*. Chicago: University of Chicago Press, 293–306.

——— and ———. 2005. *The Politics of Attention: How Government Prioritizes Problems*. Chicago: University of Chicago Press.

———, James L. True, and Frank R. Baumgartner. 1997. 'Does Incrementalism Stem from Political Consensus or from Institutional Gridlock?', *American Journal of Political Science* 41, 4: 1319–39.

Jones, Charles O. 1984. *An Introduction to the Study of Public Policy*, 3rd edn. Monterey, Calif.: Brooks/Cole.

Jonsson, G., and I. Zakrisson. 2005. 'Organizational Dilemmas in Voluntary Associations', *International Journal of Public Administration* 28: 849–56.

Jordan, A. Grant. 1981. 'Iron Triangles, Woolly Corporatism and Elastic Nets: Images of the Policy Process', *Journal of Public Policy* 1, 1: 95–123.

———. 1990a. 'Policy Community Realism versus "New" Institutionalist Ambiguity', *Political Studies* 38, 3: 470–84.

———. 1990b. 'Sub-governments, Policy Communities and Networks: Refilling the Old Bottles?', *Journal of Theoretical Politics* 2, 3: 319–38.

———. 1998. 'Indirect Causes and Effects in Policy Change: Shell, Greenpeace and the Brent Spar', paper presented to the annual meeting of the American Political Science Association, Boston.

———. 2000. 'The Process of Government and the Governmental Process', *Political Studies* 48: 788–801.

——— and William A. Maloney. 1997. 'Accounting for Subgovernments', *Administration and Society* 29, 5: 557–84.

——— and ———. 1998. 'Manipulating Membership: Supply-Side Influences on Group Size', *British Journal of Political Science* 28, 2: 389–409.

———, ———, and Andrew M. McLaughlin. 1994. 'Characterizing Agricultural Policy-Making', *Public Administration* 72 (Winter): 505–26.

——— and Klaus Schubert. 1992. 'A Preliminary Ordering of Policy Network Labels', *European Journal of Political Research* 21, 1 and 2: 7–27.

Jordan, J.M., and S.L. Sutherland. 1979. 'Assessing the Results of Public Expenditure: Program Evaluation in the Federal Government', *Canadian Public Administration* 22, 4: 581–609.

Jordana, J., and D. Sancho. 2005. 'Policy Networks and Market Opening: Telecommunications Liberalization in Spain', *European Journal of Political Research* 44: 519–46.

Kagan, Robert A. 1991. 'Adversarial Legalism and American Government', *Journal of Policy Analysis and Management* 10, 3: 369–406.

———. 1994. 'Regulatory Enforcement', in Rosenbloom and Schwartz (1994: 383–422).

———. 1996. 'The Political Construction of American Adversarial Legalism', in A. Ranney, ed., *Courts and the Political Process*. Berkeley, Calif.: Institute of Governmental Studies Press, 19–39.

——— and Lee Axelrad. 1997. 'Adversarial Legalism: An International Perspective', in P.S. Nivola, ed., *Comparative Disadvantages? Social Regulations and the Global Economy*. Washington: Brookings Institution, 146–202.

Kagel, John H., and Dan Levin. 2002. *Common Value Auctions and the Winner's Curse*. Princeton, NJ: Princeton University Press.

Kahneman, Daniel, and Amos Tversky. 1979. 'Prospect Theory: An Analysis of Decision under Risk', *Econometrica* 47: 263–89.

Kanner, Michael D. 2005. 'A Prospect Dynamic Model of Decision-Making', *Journal of Theoretical Politics* 17, 3: 311–38.

Karamanos, Panagiotis. 2001. 'Voluntary Environmental Agreements: Evolution and Definition of a New Environmental Policy Approach', *Journal of Environmental Planning and Management* 44, 1: 67–84.

Kasza, Gregory J. 2002. 'The Illusion of Welfare "Regimes"', *Journal of Social Policy* 31, 2: 271–87.

Kato, Junko. 1996. 'Review Article: Institutions and Rationality in Politics—Three Varieties of Neo-Institutionalists', *British Journal of Political Science* 26: 553–82.

Katzenstein, Peter J. 1977. 'Conclusion: Domestic Structures and Strategies of Foreign Economic Policy', *International Organization* 31, 4: 879–920.

————. 1985. *Small States in World Markets: Industrial Policy in Europe*. Ithaca, NY: Cornell University Press.

Katzman, Martin T. 1988. 'Societal Risk Management through the Insurance Market', in R.C. Hula, ed., *Market-Based Public Policy*. London: Macmillan, 21–42.

Kaufman, F.-X., G. Majone, and V. Ostrom, eds. 1986. *Guidance, Control, and Evaluation in the Public Sector*. Berlin: Walter de Gruyter.

Kaufman, Herbert. 1976. *Are Government Organizations Immortal?* Washington: Brookings Institution.

————. 2001. 'Major Players: Bureaucracies in American Government', *Public Administration Review* 61, 1: 18–42.

Kay, Adrian. 2005. 'A Critique of the Use of Path Dependency in Policy Studies', *Public Administration* 83, 3: 553–71.

————. 2006. *The Dynamics of Public Policy: Theory and Evidence*. Cheltenham: Edward Elgar.

Keck, Margaret E., and Kathryn Sikkink, eds. 1998. *Activists beyond Borders: Advocacy Networks in International Politics*. Ithaca, NY: Cornell University Press.

Keeler, John T.S. 1993. 'Opening the Window for Reform: Mandates, Crises and Extraordinary Policy-Making', *Comparative Political Studies* 25, 4: 433–86.

Keller, Ann C. 1999. 'Innovation and Influence: Scientists as Advocates in Environmental Policy Change', paper presented to the Western Political Science Association, Seattle.

Kelman, Steven. 1981. *Regulating America, Regulating Sweden: A Comparative Study of Occupational Safety and Health Policy*. Cambridge, Mass: MIT Press.

————. 2002. 'Contracting', in Salamon (2002a: 282–318).

Keman, H. 1997. 'Approaches to the Analysis of Institutions', in B. Steunenberg and F.V. Vught, eds, *Political Institutions and Public Policy: Perspectives on European Decision Making*. Dordrecht: Kluwer, 1–27.

———— and P. Pennings. 1995. 'Managing Political and Societal Conflict in Democracies: Do Consensus and Corporatism Matter?', *British Journal of Political Science* 25: 271–81.

Kenis, Patrick. 1991. 'The Pre-Conditions for Policy Networks: Some Findings from a Three Country Study on Industrial Re-Structuring', in Marin and Mayntz (1991: 297–330).

Kennamer, J. David, ed. 1992. *Public Opinion, the Press, and Public Policy*. Westport, Conn.: Praeger.

Kennett, Steven A. 2000. 'The Future for Cumulative Effects Management: Beyond the Environmental Assessment Paradigm', *Resources* 69: 1–7.

Keohane, Robert O. 1989. *International Institutions and State Powers: Essays in International Relations Theory*. Boulder, Colo.: Westview Press.

———. 1990. 'Multilateralism: An Agenda for Research', *International Journal* 45, 4: 731–64.

———and Stanley Hoffman. 1991. 'Institutional Change in Europe in the 1980s', in Keohane and Hoffman, eds, *The New European Community: Decision-Making and Institutional Change*. Boulder, Colo.: Westview Press, 1–40.

——— and Helen V. Milner, eds. 1996. *Internationalization and Domestic Politics*. New York: Cambridge University Press.

——— and Joseph S. Nye. 1989. *Power and Interdependence*. Glenview, Ill.: Scott, Foresman.

Kepner, Charles H., and Benjamin B. Tregoe. 1965. *The Rational Manager: A Systematic Approach to Problem Solving and Decision Making*. New York: McGraw-Hill.

Kernaghan, Kenneth. 1979. 'Power, Parliament and Public Servants in Canada: Ministerial Responsibility Reexamined', *Canadian Public Policy* 5, 3: 383–96.

———. 1985a. 'The Public and Public Servants in Canada', in Kernaghan, ed., *Public Administration in Canada. Selected Readings*. Toronto: Methuen, 323–33.

———. 1985b. 'Judicial Review of Administration Action', in Kernaghan ed., *Public Administration in Canada: Selected Readings*. Toronto: Methuen, 358–73.

———. 1993. 'Partnership and Public Administration: Conceptual and Practical Considerations', *Canadian Public Administration* 36, 1: 57–76.

———, Brian Marson, and Sandford Borins. 2000. *The New Public Organization*. Toronto: Institute of Public Administration of Canada.

Kerr, Clark. 1983. *The Future of Industrial Societies: Convergence or Continuing Diversity?* Cambridge, Mass.: Harvard University Press.

Kerr, Donna H. 1976. 'The Logic of "Policy" and Successful Policies', *Policy Sciences* 7, 3: 351–63.

Kerwin, Cornelius M. 1994. 'The Elements of Rule-Making', in Rosenbloom and Schwartz (1994: 345–81).

———. 1999. *Rulemaking: How Government Agencies Write Law and Make Policy*. Washington: Congressional Quarterly Press.

Key, V.O., Jr. 1967. *Public Opinion and American Democracy*. New York: Knopf.

Keyes, J.M. 1996. 'Power Tools: The Form and Function of Legal Instruments for Government Action', *Canadian Journal of Administrative Law and Practice* 10: 133–74.

Kickert, Walter J.M. 2001. 'Public Management of Hybrid Organizations: Governance of Quasi-Autonomous Executive Agencies', *International Public Management Journal* 4: 135–50.

Kim, Young-Jun, and Chui-Young Roh. 2008. 'Beyond the Advocacy Coalition Framework in Policy Process', *International Journal of Public Administration* 31: 668–89.

Kindleberger, C.P. 1996. *Manias, Panics and Crashes: A History of Financial Crises*. New York: John Wiley and Sons.

King, Anthony. 1973. 'Ideas, Institutions and the Policies of Governments: A Comparative Analysis: Part III', *British Journal of Political Science* 3, 4: 409–23.

———. 1981. 'What Do Elections Decide?', in Butler et al. (1981).

King, David C., and Jack L. Walker. 1991. 'An Ecology of Interest Groups in America', in Walker (1991: 57–73).

King, Gary, and Michael Laver. 1993. 'Party Platforms, Mandates and Government Spending', *American Political Science Review* 87, 3: 744–50.

King, M.R. 2005. 'Epistemic Communities and the Diffusion of Ideas: Central Bank Reform in the United Kingdom', *West European Politics* 28, 1: 94–123.

Kingdon, John W. 1984. *Agendas, Alternatives and Public Policies*. Boston: Little, Brown.

Kirkpatrick, Susan E., James P. Lester, and Mark R. Peterson. 1999. 'The Policy Termination Process: A Conceptual Framework and Application to Revenue Sharing', *Policy Studies Review* 16, 1: 209–36.

Kirschen, E.S., et al. 1964. *Economic Policy in Our Time*, vol. 1—*General Theory*. Chicago: Rand McNally.

Kisby, Ben. 2007. 'Analysing Policy Networks: Towards and Ideational Approach', *Policy Studies* 28, 1: 71–90.

Kiser, Larry L., and Elinor Ostrom. 1982. 'The Three Worlds of Action: A Metatheoretical Synthesis of Institutional Approaches', in Ostrom, ed., *Strategies of Political Inquiry*. Beverly Hills, Calif.: Sage, 179–222.

Kiviniemi, Markku. 1986. 'Public Policies and Their Targets: A Typology of the Concept of Implementation', *International Social Science Journal* 38, 108: 251–66.

Klijn, Erik-Hans. 1996. 'Analyzing and Managing Policy Processes in Complex Networks: A Theoretical Examination of the Concept Policy Network and Its Problems', *Administration and Society* 28, 1: 90–119.

———. 2001. 'Rules as Institutional Context for Decision Making in Networks: The Approach to Postwar Housing Districts in Two Cities', *Administration and Society* 33, 2: 133–64.

———. 2002. 'Governing Networks in the Hollow State: Contracting Out, Process Management, or a Combination of the Two?', *Public Management Review* 4, 2: 149–65.

——— and Joop F.M. Koppenjan. 2000a. 'Public Management and Policy Networks: Foundations of a Network Approach to Governance', *Public Management* 2, 2: 135–58.

——— and ———. 2000b. 'Politicians and Interactive Decision Making: Institutional Spoilsports or Playmakers', *Public Administration* 78, 2: 365–87.

——— and ———. 2005. 'Interactive Decision Making and Representative Democracy: Institutional Collisions and Solutions', *International Review of Administrative Sciences* 71, 4: 109–34.

———, ———, and Katrien Termeer. 1995. 'Managing Networks in the Public Sector: A Theoretical Study of Management Strategies in Policy Networks', *Public Administration* 73: 437–54.

——— and G.R. Teisman. 1991. 'Effective Policymaking in a Multi-Actor Setting: Networks and Steering', in Roeland In't Veld et al., eds, *Autopoiesis and Configuration Theory: New Approaches to Societal Steering*. Dordrecht: Kluwer, 99–111.

Knill, Christoph. 1998. 'European Policies: The Impact of National Administrative Traditions', *Journal of Public Policy* 18, 1: 1–28.

———. 1999. 'Explaining Cross-National Variance in Administrative Reform: Autonomous versus Instrumental Bureaucracies', *Journal of Public Policy* 19, 2: 113–39.

———. 2001. 'Private Governance across Multiple Arenas: European Interest Associations as Interface Actors', *Journal of European Public Policy* 8, 2: 227–46.

——— and Dirk Lehmkuhl. 2002. 'Private Actors and the State: Internationalization and Changing Patterns of Governance', *Governance* 15, 1: 41–63.

Knoepfel, Peter, Corinne Larrue, Frederic Varone, and Michael Hill. 2007. *Public Policy Analysis*. Bristol, UK: Policy Press.

——— and Ingrid Kissling-Naf. 1998. 'Social Learning in Policy Networks', *Policy and Politics* 26, 3: 343–67.

——— et al. 1987. 'Comparing Environmental Policies: Different Styles, Similar Content', in M. Dierkes, H.N. Weiler, and A.B. Antal, eds, *Comparative Policy Research: Learning from Experience*. Aldershot: Gower, 171–85.

Knoke, David. 1993. 'Networks as Political Glue: Explaining Public Policy-Making', in W.J. Wilson, ed., *Sociology and the Public Agenda*. London: Sage, 164–84.

——— and Edward O. Laumann. 1982. 'The Social Organization of National Policy Domains: An Exploration of Some Structural Hypotheses', in P. Marsden and N. Lin, eds, *Social Structure and Network Analysis*. Beverly Hills, Calif.: Sage, 255–70.

Knott, Jack H., and Diane McCarthy. 2007. 'Policy Venture Capital: Foundations, Government Partnerships, and Child Care Programs', *Administration and Society* 39, 3: 319–53.

Koh, Winston T.H., and David K.C. Lee. 1994. 'The Vehicle Quota System in Singapore: An Assessment', *Transportation Research Part A, Policy and Practice* 28A: 31–47.

Kolberg, Jon Eivind, and Gosta Esping-Andersen. 1992. 'Welfare States and Employment Regimes', in Kolberg, ed, *The Study of Welfare State Regimes*. New York: M.E. Sharpe.

Koppell, J.G.S. 2003. *The Politics of Quasi-Government: Hybrid Organizations and the Dynamics of Bureaucratic Control*. Cambridge: Cambridge University Press.

Koppenjan, Joop F.M. 2001. 'Project Development in Complex Environments: Assessing Safety in Design and Decision-Making', *Journal of Contingencies and Crisis Management* 9, 3: 121–30.

Korpi, Walter. 1983. *The Democratic Class Struggle*. London: Routledge & Kegan Paul.

Krasner, Stephen D. 1982. 'Structural Causes and Regime Consequences: Regimes as Intervening Variables', *International Organization* 36, 2: 185–205.

———, ed. 1983. *International Regimes*. Ithaca, NY: Cornell University Press.

———. 1984. 'Approaches to the State: Alternative Conceptions and Historical Dynamics', *Comparative Politics* 16, 2: 223–46.

———. 1988. 'Sovereignty: An Institutional Perspective', *Comparative Political Studies* 21, 1: 66–94.

Krause, George A. 1997. 'Policy Preference Formation and Subsystem Behaviour: The Case of Commercial Bank Regulation', *British Journal of Political Science* 27: 525–50.

Kreuger, Anne O. 1974. 'The Political Economy of the Rent-Seeking Society', *American Economic Review* 64, 3: 291–303.

Kriesi, Hanspeter, and Maya Jegen. 2000. 'Decision-Making in the Swiss Energy Policy Elite', *Journal of Public Policy* 20, 1: 21–53.

——— and ———. 2001. 'The Swiss Energy Policy Elite: The Actor Constellation of a Policy Domain in Transition', *European Journal of Political Research* 39: 251–87.

Kruse, R., E. Schwecke, and J. Heinsohn. 1991. *Uncertainty and Vagueness in Knowledge-Based Systems*. Berlin: Springer-Verlag.

Kubler, Daniel. 2001. 'Understanding Policy Change with the Advocacy Coalition Framework: An Application to Swiss Drug Policy', *Journal of European Public Policy* 8, 4: 623–41.

Kuhn, Thomas S. 1962. *The Structure of Scientific Revolutions*. Chicago: University of Chicago Press.

———. 1974. 'Second Thoughts on Paradigms', in F. Suppe, ed., *The Structure of Scientific Theories*. Urbana: University of Illinois Press, 459–82.

Kuhner, Stefan. 2007. 'Country-Level Comparisons of Welfare State Change Measures: Another Facet of the Dependent Variable Problem within the Comparative Analysis of the Welfare State', *Journal of European Social Policy* 17, 1: 5–18.

Kuks, S. 2004. 'Comparative Review and Analysis of Regime Changes in Europe', *Environmental Politics* 40, 2: 329–68.

Kuo, D. 2006. *Tempting Faith: An Inside Story of Political Seduction*. New York: Free Press.

Kurzer, Paulette, and Alice Cooper. 2007a. 'Consumer Activism, EU Institutions and Global Markets: The Struggle over Biotech Foods', *Journal of Public Policy* 27, 2: 103–28.

——— and ———. 2007b. 'What's for Dinner? European Farming and Food Traditions Confront American Biotechnology', *Comparative Political Studies* 40, 9: 1035–58.

Kuttner, Robert. 1997. *Everything For Sale: The Virtues and Limits of Markets*. New York: Alfred A. Knopf.

Lacroix, L. 1986. 'Strike Activity in Canada', in W.C. Riddell, ed., *Canadian Labour Relations*. Toronto: University of Toronto Press.

Ladi, Stella. 2005. *Globalisation, Policy Transfer and Policy Research Institutes*. Cheltenham: Edward Elgar.

Lafferty, W.M., and E. Hovden. 2003. 'Environmental Policy Integration: Towards an Analytical Framework', *Environmental Politics* 12, 3: 1–22.

Laforest, R., and M. Orsini. 2005. 'Evidence-Based Engagement in the Voluntary Sector: Lessons from Canada', *Social Policy and Administration* 39, 5: 481–97.

Lam, Soi Hoi, and Trinh Dinh Toan. 2006. 'Land Transport Policy and Public Transit in Singapore', *Transportation* 33: 171–88.

Lane, Jan-Erik. 2001. 'From Long-Term to Short-Term Contracting', *Public Administration* 79, 1: 29–48.

Lane, Peter J., and Michael Lubatkin. 1998. 'Relative Absorptive Capacity and Inter-organizational Learning', *Strategic Management Journal* 19: 461–77.

Lane, Wheaton. 1950. 'The Early Highway in America', in Jean Labatut and Wheaton Lane, *Highways in Our National Life*. Princeton, NJ: Princeton University Press, 68–75.

Langbein, L.I., and C.M. Kerwin. 2000. 'Regulatory Negotiation versus Conventional Rulemaking: Claims, Counterclaims, and Empirical Evidence', *Journal of Public Administration Research and Theory* 10, 3: 599–632.

Lapsley, Irvine, and Rosie Oldfield. 2001. 'Transforming the Public Sector: Management Consultants as Agents of Change', *European Accounting Review* 10, 3: 523–43.

Larsen, T.P., P. Taylor-Gooby, and J. Kananen. 2006. 'New Labour's Policy Style: A Mix of Policy Approaches', *International Social Policy* 35, 4: 629–49.

Lasswell, Harold D. 1951. 'The Policy Orientation', in Lerner and Lasswell (1951: 3–15).

———. 1956. *The Decision Process: Seven Categories of Functional Analysis*. College Park: University of Maryland Press.

———. 1958. *Politics: Who Gets What, When, How*. New York: Meridian.

———. 1971. *A Pre-View of Policy Sciences*. New York: American Elsevier.

Latham, Earl. 1952. 'The Group Basis of Politics: Notes for a Theory', *American Political Science Review* 46, 2: 376–97.

Laughlin, Richard C. 1991. 'Environmental Disturbances and Organizational Transitions and Transformations: Some Alternative Models', *Organization Studies* 12, 2: 209–32.

Laumann, Edward O., and David Knoke. 1987. *The Organizational State: Social Choice in National Policy Domains*. Madison: University of Wisconsin Press.

Laux, Jeanne Kirk, and Maureen Appel Molot. 1988. *State Capitalism: Public Enterprise in Canada*. Ithaca, NY: Cornell University Press.

Laver, Michael J., and Ian Budge. 1992. *Party Policy and Government Coalitions*. New York: St Martin's Press.

——— and W.B. Hunt. 1992. *Policy and Party Competition*. London: Routledge.

Leape, Jonathan. 2006. 'The London Congestion Charge', *Journal of Economic Perspectives* 20, 4: 157–76.

Lee, Mordecai. 2001. 'The Agency Spokesperson: Connecting Public Administration and the Media', *Public Administration Quarterly* 25, 1: 101–30.

Lee, Simon, and Stephen McBride, eds. 2007. *Neo-Liberalism, State Power and Global Governance*. New York: Springer.

Leech, B.L., F.R. Baumgartner, T.M. La Pira, and N.A. Semanko. 2005. 'Drawing Lobbyists to Washington: Government Activity and the Demand for Advocacy', *Political Research Quarterly* 58, 1: 19–30.

Leeuw, Frans L. 1998. 'The Carrot: Subsidies as a Tool of Government', in Bemelmans-Videc et al. (1998: 77–102).

Le Gales, P., and M. Thatcher, eds. 1995. *Les Reseaux de Politique Publique*. Paris: Editions L'Harmattan.

Le Grand, Julian. 1991. 'The Theory of Government Failure', *British Journal of Political Science* 21, 4: 423–42.

―――― and Ray Robinson, eds. 1984. *Privatization and the Welfare State*. London: George Allen and Unwin.

Legro, Jeffrey W. 2000. 'The Transformation of Policy Ideas', *American Journal of Political Science* 44, 3: 419–32.

Lehne, Richard. 2001. *Government and Business: American Political Economy in Comparative Perspective*. New York: Chatham House.

Lehtonen, Markku. 2005. 'OECD Environmental Performance Review Programme: Accountability (F)or Learning?', *Evaluation* 11, 2: 169–88.

――――. 2006. 'Deliberative Democracy, Participation, and OECD Peer Reviews of Environmental Policies', *American Journal of Evaluation* 27, 2: 185–200.

Leik, Robert K. 1992. 'New Directions for Network Exchange Theory: Strategic Manipulation of Network Linkages', *Social Networks* 14: 309–23.

Leman, Christopher. 1977. 'Patterns of Policy Development: Social Security in the United States and Canada', *Public Policy* 25, 2: 261–91.

――――. 1989. 'The Forgotten Fundamental: Successes and Excesses of Direct Government', in Salamon (1989a).

――――. 2002. 'Direct Government', in Salamon (2002a: 48–79).

Lerner, Daniel, and Harold D. Lasswell, eds. 1951. *The Policy Sciences: Recent Developments in Scope and Method*. Stanford, Calif.: Stanford University Press.

Lester, James P., and Malcolm L. Goggin. 1998. 'Back to the Future: The Rediscovery of Implementation Studies', *Policy Currents* 8, 3: 1–9.

―――― et al. 1987. 'Public Policy Implementation: Evolution of the Field and Agenda for Future Research', *Policy Studies Review* 7: 200–16.

Levi-Faur, D., and E. Vigoda-Gadot. 2006. 'New Public Policy, New Policy Transfers: Some Characteristics of a New Order in the Making', *International Journal of Public Administration* 29: 247–62.

Levin-Waldman, O.M. 2005. 'Welfare Reform and Models of Public Policy: Why Policy Sciences Are Required', *Review of Policy Research* 22, 4: 519–39.

Levitt, Barbara, and James G. March. 1988. 'Organizational Learning', *Annual Review of Sociology* 14: 319–40.

Levy, J.D. 2006. *The State after Statism: New State Activities in the Age of Liberalization*. Cambridge, Mass.: Harvard University Press.

Levy, Jack S. 1997. 'Prospect Theory and the Cognitive-Rational Debate', in N. Geva and A. Mintz, eds, *Decision-making on War and Peace: The Cognitive-Rational Debate*. Boulder, Colo.: Lynne Rienner, 33–50.

Levy, Roger. 2001. 'EU Performance Management 1977–96: A Performance Indicators Analysis', *Public Administration* 79, 2: 423–44.

Lewis, David E. 2002. 'The Politics of Agency Termination: Confronting the Myth of Agency Immortality', *Journal of Politics* 64, 1: 89–107.

Lewis-Beck, Michael S. 1988. *Economics and Elections: The Major Western Democracies*. Ann Arbor: University of Michigan Press.

Ley-Borras, R. 2005. 'A Decision Analysis Approach to Policy Issues: The NAFTA Case', *Review of Policy Research* 22, 5: 687–708.

Libecap, Gary D. 1986. 'Deregulation as an Instrument in Industrial Policy; Comment', *Journal of Institutional and Theoretical Economics* 142: 70–4.

Liebowitz, S.J., and Stephen E. Margolis. 1995. 'Path Dependence, Lock-In, and History', *Journal of Law, Economics and Organization* 11, 1: 205–25.

Liefferink, Duncan. 2006. 'The Dynamics of Policy Arrangements: Turning Round the Tetrahedron', in Bas Arts and Pieter Leroy, eds, *Institutional Dynamics in Environmental Governance*. Dordrecht: Springer, 45–68.

Lijphart, A. 1969. 'Consociational Democracy', *World Politics* 21, 2: 207–25.

Lindblom, Charles E. 1955. *Bargaining: The Hidden Hand in Government*. Los Angeles: Rand Corporation.

———. 1958. 'Policy Analysis', *American Economic Review* 48, 3: 298–312.

———. 1959. 'The Science of Muddling Through', *Public Administration Review* 19, 2: 79–88.

———. 1968. *The Policy-Making Process*. Englewood Cliffs, NJ: Prentice-Hall.

———. 1977. *Politics and Markets: The World's Political Economic Systems*. New York: Basic Books.

———. 1979. 'Still Muddling, Not Yet Through', *Public Administration Review* 39, 6: 517–26.

——— and D.K. Cohen. 1979. *Usable Knowledge: Social Science and Social Problem Solving*. New Haven: Yale University Press.

Linder, Stephen H. 1999. 'Coming to Terms with Public–Private Partnership', *American Behavioural Scientist* 43, 1: 35–51.

——— and B. Guy Peters. 1984. 'From Social Theory to Policy Design', *Journal of Public Policy* 4, 3: 237–59.

——— and ———. 1988. 'The Analysis of Design or the Design of Analysis?', *Policy Studies Review* 7, 4: 738–50.

——— and ———. 1989. 'Instruments of Government: Perceptions and Contexts', *Journal of Public Policy* 9, 1: 35–58.

——— and ———. 1990. 'Research Perspectives on the Design of Public Policy: Implementation, Formulation, and Design', in Palumbo and Calista (1990a).

——— and ———. 1991. 'The Logic of Public Policy Design: Linking Policy Actors and Plausible Instruments', *Knowledge in Society* 4: 125–51.

Lindquist, Evert A. 1988. 'What Do Decision Models Tell Us about Information Use?', *Knowledge in Society* 1, 2: 86–111.

———. 1992. 'Public Managers and Policy Communities: Learning to Meet New Challenges', *Canadian Public Administration* 35, 2: 127–59.

———. 1993. 'Think Tanks or Clubs? Assessing the Influence and Roles of Canadian Policy Institutes', *Canadian Public Administration* 36, 4: 547–79.

———. 2004. 'Three Decades of Canadian Think Tanks: Evolving Institutions, Conditions and Strategies', in D. Stone and A. Denham, eds, *Think Tank Traditions: Policy Research and the Politics of Ideas*. Manchester: Manchester University Press, 264–80.

———. 2006. 'Organizing for Policy Implementation: The Emergence and Role of Implementation Units in Policy Design and Oversight', *Journal of Comparative Policy Analysis: Research and Practice* 8, 4: 311–24.

Linz, Juan J. 1978. 'Crisis, Breakdown, and Reequilibration', in Linz and A. Stepan, eds, *The Breakdown of Democratic Regimes*. Baltimore: Johns Hopkins University Press, 3–124.

Lipietz, Alain. 1982. 'Towards Global Fordism', *New Left Review* 132: 33–48.

Lipsky, Michael. 1980. *Street-Level Bureaucracy: Dilemmas of the Individual in Public Services*. New York: Russell Sage Foundation.

Livingston, Steven G. 1992. 'Knowledge Hierarchies and the Politics of Ideas in American International Commodity Production', *Journal of Public Policy* 12, 3: 223–42.

Lober, Douglas J. 1997. 'Explaining the Formation of Business–Environmentalist Collaborations: Collaborative Windows and the Paper Task Force', *Policy Sciences* 30: 1–24.

Locksley, Gareth. 1980. 'The Political Business Cycle: Alternative Interpretations', in Paul Whiteley, ed., *Models of Political Economy*. London: Sage.

Lodge, M., and C. Hood. 2002. 'Pavlovian Policy Responses to Media Feeding Frenzies? Dangerous Dogs Regulation in Comparative Perspective', *Journal of Contingencies and Crisis Management* 10, 1: 1–13.

Loughlin, J. 2004. 'The "Transformation" of Governance: New Directions in Policy and Politics', *Australian Journal of Politics and History* 50, 1: 8–22.

Lovan, W.R., M. Murray, and R. Shaffer. 2004. 'Participatory Governance in a Changing World', in Lovan, Murray, and Shaffer, eds, *Participatory Governance: Planning, Conflict Mediation and Public Decision-Making in Civil Society*. Aldershot: Ashgate, 1–20.

Lowell, A. Lawrence. 1926. *Public Opinion and Popular Government*. New York: David McKay Company.

Lowi, Theodore J. 1966. 'Distribution, Regulation, Redistribution: The Functions of Government', in R.B. Ripley, ed., *Public Policies and Their Politics: Techniques of Government Control*. New York: Norton, 27–40.

———. 1969. *The End of Liberalism: Ideology, Policy and the Crisis of Public Authority*. New York: Norton.

———. 1972. 'Four Systems of Policy, Politics and Choice', *Public Administration Review* 32, 4: 298–310.

———. 1985. 'The State in Politics: The Relation between Policy and Administration', in R.G. Noll, ed., *Regulatory Policy and the Social Sciences*. Berkeley: University of California Press, 67–105.

———. 1998. 'Foreword: New Dimensions in Policy and Politics', in R. Tatalovich and B.W. Daynes, eds, *Moral Controversies in American Social Politics: Cases in Social Regulatory Policy*. Armonk, NY: M.E. Sharpe, xiii–xxvii.

Lowry, R.C. 1999. 'Foundation Patronage toward Citizen Groups and Think Tanks: Who Gets Grants?', *Journal of Politics* 81, 3: 758–76.

Lund, Michael S. 1989. 'Between Welfare and the Market: Loan Guarantees as a Policy Tool', in Salamon (1989a: 125–66).

Lundquist, Lennart J. 1987. *Implementation Steering: An Actor-Structure Approach*. Bickley, UK: Chartwell-Bratt.

Lustick, Ian. 1980. 'Explaining the Variable Utility of Disjointed Incrementalism: Four Propositions', *American Political Science Review* 74, 2: 342–53.

Luttbeg, Norman R. 1981. 'Where We Stand on Political Linkage', in Luttbeg, ed., *Public Opinion and Public Policy: Models of Political Linkage*. Itasca, Ill.: F.E. Peacock, 455–62.

Lutz, James M. 1989. 'Emulation and Policy Adoptions in the Canadian Provinces', *Canadian Journal of Political Science* 22, 1: 147–54.

Lyden, Fremont J., George A. Shipman, and Robert W. Wilkinson. 1968. 'Decision-Flow Analysis: A Methodology for Studying the Public Policy-Making Process', in P.P. Le Breton, ed., *Comparative Administrative Theory*. Seattle: University of Washington Press, 155–68.

Lynggaard, Kennet. 2001. 'The Study of Policy Change: Constructing an Analytical Strategy', paper presented at the ECPR 29th Joint Session Workshops, Grenoble, 6–11 Apr.

Lynn, Laurence E. 1987. *Managing Public Policy*. Boston: Little, Brown.

———. 1999. 'A Place at the Table: Policy Analysis, Its Postpositive Critics, and the Future of Practice', *Journal of Policy Analysis and Management* 18, 3: 411–24.

McAllister, James A. 1989. 'Do Parties Make a Difference?', in A.G. Gagnon and A.B. Tanguay, eds, *Canadian Parties in Transition: Discourse, Organization, Representation*. Toronto: Nelson, 485–511.

MacAvoy, Paul, et al., eds. 1989. *Privatization and State-Owned Enterprises: Lessons from the United States, Great Britain, and Canada*. Boston: Kluwer.

McBeth, Mark K., Elizabeth A. Shanahan, Ruth J. Arnell, and Paul L. Hathaway. 2007. 'The Intersection of Narrative Policy Analysis and Policy Change Theory', *Policy Studies Journal* 35, 1: 87–108.

———, ———, and Michael D. Jones. 2005. 'The Science of Storytelling: Measuring Policy Briefs in Greater Yellowstone', *Society and Natural Resources* 18: 413–29.

McCallum, B. 1978. 'The Political Business Cycle: An Empirical Test', *Southern Economic Journal* 44: 504–15.

McCombs, Maxwell E. 1981. 'The Agenda-Setting Approach', in D.D. Nimmo and K.R. Sanders, eds, *Handbook of Political Communication*. Beverly Hills, Calif.: Sage, 121–40.

McConnell, Grant. 1966. *Private Power and American Democracy*. New York: Knopf.

McCool, Daniel. 1989. 'Subgovernments and the Impact of Policy Fragmentation and Accommodation', *Policy Studies Review* 8, 2: 264–87.

———. 1998. 'The Subsystem Family of Concepts: A Critique and a Proposal', *Political Research Quarterly* 51, 2: 551–70.

McCrudden, C. 2004. 'Using Public Procurement to Achieve Social Outcomes', *Natural Resources Journal* 28: 257–67.

McCubbins, Arthur Lupia and Mathew D. 1994. 'Learning from Oversight: Fire Alarms and Policy Patrols Reconstructed', *Journal of Law, Economics and Organization* 10, 1: 96–125.

McCubbins, Mathew D., Roger G. Noll, and Barry R. Weingast. 1987. 'Administrative Procedures as Instruments of Political Control', *Journal of Law, Economics, and Organization* 3, 2: 243–77.

———, ———, and ———. 1989. 'Structure and Process, Politics and Policy: Administrative Arrangements and the Political Control of Agencies', *Virginia Law Review* 75, 2: 431–82.

——— and Thomas Schwartz. 1984. 'Congressional Oversight Overlooked: Policy Patrols versus Fire Alarms', *American Journal of Political Science* 28, 1: 165–79.

McDaniel, Paul R. 1989. 'Tax Expenditures as Tools of Government Action', in Salamon (1989a).

McDonnell, Lorraine M., and Richard F. Elmore. 1987. *Alternative Policy Instruments*. Santa Monica, Calif.: Center for Policy Research in Education.

McFarland, Andrew S. 1987. 'Interest Groups and Theories of Power in America', *British Journal of Political Science* 17, 2: 129–47.

———. 1991. 'Interest Groups and Political Time: Cycles in America', *British Journal of Political Science* 21, 3: 257–85.

———. 2004. *Neopluralism: The Evolution of Political Process Theory*. Lawrence: University Press of Kansas.

———. 2007. 'Neopluralism', *Annual Review of Political Science* 10: 45–66.

McGann, James G. 2008. *The Global 'Go-To Think Tanks': The Leading Public Policy Research Organizations in the World*. Philadelphia: Think Tanks and Civil Societies Program.

——— and E.C. Johnson. 2005. *Comparative Think Tanks, Politics and Public Policy*. Cheltenham: Edward Elgar.

——— and R. Kent Weaver, eds. 1999. *Think Tanks and Civil Societies: Catalysts for Ideas and Action*. New Brunswick, NJ: Transaction.

McGraw, Kathleen M. 1990. 'Avoiding Blame: An Experimental Investigation of Political Excuses and Justifications', *British Journal of Political Science* 20: 199–242.

McGuire, Michael. 2002. 'Managing Networks: Propositions on What Managers Do and Why They Do It', *Public Administration Review* 62, 5: 599–609.

McLaughlin, Milbrey W. 1985. 'Implementation Realities and Evaluation Design', in Shotland and Mark (1985).

McLean, Iain. 1987. *Public Choice: An Introduction*. Oxford: Blackwell.

———. 2000. 'Review Article: The Divided Legacy of Mancur Olson', *British Journal of Political Science* 30: 651–68.

McLennan, Gregor. 1989. *Marxism, Pluralism and Beyond: Classic Debates and New Departures*. Cambridge: Polity Press.

McMullen, K., and G. Schellenberg. 2002. *Mapping the Non-Profit Sector*. Ottawa: Canadian Policy Research Networks.

Macpherson, C.B. 1962. *The Political Theory of Possessive Individualism: Hobbes to Locke*. Oxford: Clarendon Press.

———. 1978. *The Life and Times of Liberal Democracy*. Oxford: Oxford University Press.

MacRae, Duncan, Jr. 1993. 'Guidelines for Policy Discourse: Consensual versus Adversarial', in Fischer and Forester (1993: 291–318).

McRobbie, A., and S.L. Thornton. 1995. 'Rethinking "Moral Panic" for Multi-Mediated Social Worlds', *British Journal of Sociology* 46, 4: 559–74.

McRoberts, Kenneth. 1993. 'Federal Structures and the Policy Process', in M. Michael Atkinson, ed., *Governing Canada: Institutions and Public Policy*. Toronto: Harcourt Brace Jovanovich.

Maddison, Sarah, and Richard Denniss. 2005. 'Democratic Constraint and Embrace: Implications for Progressive Non-Government Advocacy Organisations in Australia', *Australian Journal of Political Science* 40, 3: 373–89.

Madison, James, and Alexander Hamilton. 1961. *The Federalist Papers: A Collection of Essays Written in Support of the Constitution of the United States*. Garden City, NY: Anchor Books.

Mahoney, James. 2000. 'Path Dependence in Historical Sociology', *Theory and Society* 29, 4: 507–48.

——— and D. Schensul. 2006. 'Historical Contact and Path Dependence', in R. Goodin and C. Tilly, eds, *The Oxford Handbook of Contextual Political Analysis*. Oxford: Oxford University Press, 454–71.

Majone, Giandomenico. 1975. 'On the Notion of Political Feasibility', *European Journal of Political Research* 3: 259–74.

———. 1989. *Evidence, Argument, and Persuasion in the Policy Process*. New Haven: Yale University Press.

———. 1991. 'Cross-National Sources of Regulatory Policymaking in Europe and the United States', *Journal of Public Policy* 11, 1: 79–106.

Malloy, James M. 1993. 'Statecraft, Social Policy, and Governance in Latin America', *Governance* 6, 2: 220–74.

———. 1999. 'What Makes a State Advocacy Structure Effective? Conflicts between Bureaucratic and Social Movements Criteria', *Governance* 12, 3: 267–88.

———. 2003. *Between Colliding Worlds: The Ambiguous Existence of Government Agencies for Aboriginal and Women's Policy*. Toronto: University of Toronto Press.

Maloney, William A. 2001. 'Regulation in an Episodic Policy-Making Environment: The Water Industry in England and Wales', *Public Administration* 79, 3: 625–42.

———, Grant Jordan, and Andrew M. McLaughlin. 1994. 'Interest Groups and Public Policy: The Insider/Outsider Model Revisited', *Journal of Public Policy* 14, 1: 17–38.

Mandell, M.P. 2000. 'A Revised Look at Management in Network Structures', *International Journal of Organizational Theory and Behavior* 3, 1 and 2: 185–210.

Mann, Michael. 1984. 'The Autonomous Power of the State: Its Origins, Mechanisms and Results', *European Journal of Sociology* 25, 2: 185–213.

Manzer, Ronald. 1984. 'Policy Rationality and Policy Analysis: The Problem of the Choice of Criteria for Decision-making', in O.P. Dwivedi, ed., *Public Policy and Administrative Studies*. Guelph, Ont.: University of Guelph.

March, James G. 1978. 'Bounded Rationality, Ambiguity, and the Engineering of Choice', *Bell Journal of Economics* 9, 2: 587–608.

————. 1981. 'Decision Making Perspective: Decisions in Organizations and Theories of Choice', in A.H. van de Ven and W.F. Joyce, eds, *Perspectives on Organization Design and Behaviour*. New York: Wiley, 205–44.

————. 1994. *A Primer on Decision-Making: How Decisions Happen*. New York: Free Press.

———— and Johan P. Olsen. 1975. 'The Uncertainty of the Past: Organizational Learning under Ambiguity', *European Journal of Political Research* 3: 147–71.

———— and ————. 1979a. *Ambiguity and Choice in Organizations*. Bergen: Universitetsforlaget.

———— and ————. 1979b. 'Organizational Choice under Ambiguity', in March and Olsen (1979a).

———— and ————. 1983. 'Organizing Political Life: What Administrative Reorganization Tells Us about Government', *American Political Science Review* 77, 2: 281–96.

———— and ————. 1984. 'The New Institutionalism: Organizational Factors in Political Life', *American Political Science Review* 78, 3: 734–49.

———— and ————. 1989. *Rediscovering Institutions: The Organizational Basis of Politics*. New York: Free Press.

———— and ————. 1994. 'Institutional Perspectives on Political Institutions', paper presented to the International Political Science Association, Berlin.

———— and ————. 1995. *Democratic Governance*. New York: Free Press.

———— and ————. 1996. 'Institutional Perspectives on Political Institutions', *Governance* 9, 3: 247–64.

———— and ————. 1998a. 'The Institutional Dynamics of International Political Orders', in P.J. Katzenstein, R.O. Keohane, and S.D. Krasner, eds, *Exploration and Contestation in the Study of World Politics*. Cambridge, Mass.: MIT Press, 303–30.

———— and ————. 1998b. 'The Institutional Dynamics of International Political Orders', *International Organization* 52: 943–69.

————, Martin Schulz, and Xueguang Zhou. 2000. *The Dynamics of Rules: Change in Organizational Codes*. Stanford, Calif.: Stanford University Press.

Marier, Patrik. 2008. 'Empowering Epistemic Communities: Specialized Politicians, Policy Experts and Policy Reform', *West European Politics* 31, 3: 513–33.

Marin, Bernd, and Renate Mayntz, eds. 1991. *Policy Networks: Empirical Evidence and Theoretical Considerations*. Boulder, Colo.: Westview Press.

Marion, Justin, and Erich Muehlegger. 2007. *Measuring Illegal Activity and the Effects of Regulatory Innovation: A Study of Diesel Fuel Tax Evasion*. Cambridge, Mass.: John F. Kennedy School of Government Faculty Research Working Paper Series RWP07–026.

Marion, Russ. 1999. *The Edge of Organization: Chaos and Complexity Theories of Formal Social Systems*. London: Sage.

Markoff, John. 1975. 'Governmental Bureaucratization: General Processes and an Anomalous Case', *Comparative Studies in Society and History* 17, 4: 479–503.

———— and Veronica Montecinos. 1993. 'The Ubiquitous Rise of Economists', *Journal of Public Policy* 13, 1: 37–68.

Marsh, David, and R.A.W. Rhodes, eds. 1992a. *Policy Networks in British Government*. Oxford: Clarendon Press.

———— and ————. 1992b. 'Policy Communities and Issue Networks: Beyond Typology', in Marsh and Rhodes (1992a: 248–68).

Martin, John F. 1998. *Reorienting a Nation: Consultants and Australian Public Policy*. Aldershot: Ashgate.

Maslove, Allan, ed. 1994. *Taxing and Spending: Issues of Process*. Toronto: University of Toronto Press.

Masterman, Margaret. 1970. 'The Nature of a Paradigm', in I. Lakatos and A. Musgrave, eds, *Criticism and the Growth of Knowledge*. Cambridge: Cambridge University Press.

Mathiason, John. 2007. *Invisible Governance: International Secretariats in Global Politics.* Bloomfield, NJ: Kumarian Press.

Matland, R.E. 1995. 'Synthesizing the Implementation Literature: The Ambiguity-Conflict Model of Policy Implementation', *Journal of Public Administration Research and Theory* 5, 2: 145–74.

Maule, A. John, and Ola Svenson. 1993. 'Theoretical and Empirical Approaches to Behavioural Decision Making and Their Relations to Time Constraints', in Svenson and Maule, eds, *Time Pressure and Stress in Human Judgement and Decision Making.* New York: Plenum Press, 3–25.

Maurer, Andreas, and Roderick Parkes. 2007. 'The Prospects for Policy-Change in EU Asylum Policy: Venues and Image at the European Level', *European Journal of Migration and Law* 9: 173–205.

May, Peter J. 1991. 'Reconsidering Policy Design: Policies and Publics', *Journal of Public Policy* 11, 2: 187–206.

———. 1992. 'Policy Learning and Failure', *Journal of Public Policy* 12, 4: 331 54.

———. 1993. 'Mandate Design and Implementation: Enhancing Implementation Efforts and Shaping Regulatory Styles', *Journal of Policy Analysis and Management* 12, 4: 634–63.

———. 1999. 'Fostering Policy Learning: A Challenge for Public Administration', *International Review of Public Administration* 4, 1: 21–31.

———. 2002. 'Social Regulation', in Salamon (2002a: 156–85).

———. 2005. 'Policy Maps and Political Feasibility', in I. Geva-May, ed., *Thinking Like a Policy Analyst: Policy Analysis as a Clinical Profession.* London: Palgrave Macmillan, 127–51.

——— et al. 1997. *Environmental Management and Governance: Intergovernmental Approaches to Hazards and Sustainability.* London: Routledge.

———, B.D. Jones, B.E. Beem, E.A. Neff-Sharum, and M.K. Poague. 2005. 'Policy Coherence and Component-Driven Policymaking: Arctic Policy in Canada and the United States', *Policy Studies Journal* 33, 1: 37–63.

———, Joshua Sapotichne, and Samuel Workman. 2007. 'Policy Disruption across Subsystems: Terrorism, Public Risks, and Homeland Security', paper presented at the American Political Science Association annual meeting.

Mayer, I., P. Bots, and E. van Daalen. 2004. 'Perspectives on Policy Analysis: A Framework for Understanding and Design', *International Journal of Technology, Policy and Management* 4, 1: 169–91.

Mayntz, Renate. 1979. 'Public Bureaucracies and Policy Implementation', *International Social Science Journal* 31, 4: 633–45.

———. 1983. 'The Conditions of Effective Public Policy: A New Challenge for Policy Analysis', *Policy and Politics* 11, 2: 123–43.

———. 1993a. 'Governing Failure and the Problem of Governability: Some Comments on a Theoretical Paradigm', in J. Kooiman, ed., *Modern Governance: New Government–Society Interactions.* London: Sage.

———. 1993b. 'Modernization and the Logic of Interorganizational Networks', in J. Child et al., eds, *Societal Change between Market and Organization.* Aldershot: Avebury, 3–18.

Mazmanian, Daniel A., and Paul A. Sabatier. 1980. 'A Multivariate Model of Public Policy-Making', *American Journal of Political Science* 24, 3: 439–68.

——— and ———. 1983. *Implementation and Public Policy.* Glenview, Ill.: Scott, Foresman.

Mead, Lawrence M. 1985. 'Policy Studies and Political Science', *Policy Studies Review* 5, 2: 319–35.

Meijerink, S. 2005. 'Understanding Policy Stability and Change. The Interplay of Advocacy Coalitions and Epistemic Communities, Windows of Opportunity and Dutch Coastal Flooding Policy 1945–2003', *Journal of European Public Policy* 12, 6: 1060–77.

Meijers, E., and D. Stead. 2004. 'Policy Integration: What Does It Mean and How Can It Be Achieved? A Multi-Disciplinary Review', paper presented at the Berlin Conference on the Human Dimensions of Global Environmental Change: Greening of Policies— Interlinkages and Policy Integration.

Melo, M.A. 2004. 'Institutional Choice and the Diffusion of Policy Paradigms: Brazil and the Second Wave of Pension Reform', *International Political Science Review* 25, 3: 320–41.

Meltsner, Arnold J. 1972. 'Political Feasibility and Policy Analysis', *Public Administration Review* 32: 859–67.

———. 1976. *Policy Analysts in the Bureaucracy*. Berkeley: University of California Press.

Menahem, Gila. 1998. 'Policy Paradigms, Policy Networks and Water Policy in Israel', *Journal of Public Policy* 18, 3: 283–310.

———. 2001. 'Water Policy in Israel 1948–2000: Policy Paradigms, Policy Networks and Public Policy', *Israel Affairs* 7, 4: 21–44.

———. 2008. 'The Transformation of Higher Education in Israel since the 1990s: The Role of Ideas and Policy Paradigms', *Governnance* 21, 4: 499–526.

Mendoza, Guillermo A., and William Sprouse. 1989. 'Forest Planning and Decision Making under Fuzzy Environments: An Overview and Illustration', *Forest Science* 35, 2: 481–502.

Mertha, Andrew C., and William R. Lowry. 2006. 'Seminal Events and Policy Change in China, Australia and the United States', *Comparative Politics* 39, 1: 1–20.

Merton, Robert K. 1936. 'The Unanticipated Consequences of Purposive Social Action', *American Sociological Review* 6, 1: 894–904.

———. 1948. 'The Self-Fulfilling Prophecy', *Antioch Review* 8, 2: 193–210.

Metcalfe, Les. 1978. 'Policy Making in Turbulent Environments', in K. Hanf and F.W. Scharpf, eds, *Interorganizational Policy Making: Limits to Coordination and Central Control*. London: Sage, 37–55.

Meyer, Alan D. 1982. 'Adapting to Environmental Jolts', *Administrative Science Quarterly* 27: 515–37.

———, Geoffrey R. Brooks, and James B. Goes. 1990. 'Environmental Jolts and Industry Revolutions: Organizational Responses to Discontinuous Change', *Strategic Management Journal* 11: 93–110.

Michael, E.J. 2006. *Public Policy: The Competitive Framework*. Melbourne: Oxford University Press.

Migdal, Joel S. 1988. *Strong Societies and Weak States: State–Society Relations and State Capabilities in the Third World*. Princeton, NJ: Princeton University Press.

Mikalsen, K.H., and S. Jentoft. 2001. 'From User-Groups to Stakeholders? The Public Interest in Fisheries Management', *Marine Policy* 25: 281–92.

Miller, Leonard S. 1976. 'The Structural Determinants of the Welfare Effort: A Critique and a Contribution', *Social Service Review* 50, 1: 57–79.

Milner, Helen V., and Robert O. Keohane. 1996. 'Internationalization and Domestic Politics: A Conclusion', in Keohane and Milner (1996: 243–58).

Milward, H. Brinton, and Ronald A. Francisco. 1983. 'Subsystem Politics and Corporatism in the United States', *Policy and Politics* 11, 3.

——— and Keith G. Provan. 1998. 'Principles for Controlling Agents: The Political Economy of Network Structure', *Journal of Public Administration Research and Theory* 8, 2: 203–22.

——— and Gary L. Walmsley. 1984. 'Policy Subsystems, Networks and the Tools of Public Management', in R. Eyestone, ed., *Public Policy Formation*. Greenwich. Conn.: JAI Press, 3–25.

Minkenberg, Michael. 2001. 'The Radical Right in Public Office: Agenda-Setting and Policy Effects', *West European Politics* 24, 4: 1–21.

Minogue, Martin. 1983. 'Theory and Practice in Public Policy and Administration', *Policy and Politics* 1, 1.

Mintrom, Michael. 1997. 'Policy Entrepreneurs and the Diffusion of Innovation', *American Journal of Political Science* 41, 3: 738–70.

———. 2007. 'The Policy Analysis Movement', in Dobuzinskis et al. (2007: 71–84).

Mintz, Alex. 1993. 'The Decision to Attack Iraq', *Journal of Conflict Resolution* 37, 4: 595–618.

———. 2004. 'How Do Leaders Make Decisions?', *Journal of Conflict Resolution* 48, 1: 3–13.

———. 2005. 'Applied Decision Analysis: Utilizing Poliheuristic Theory to Explain and Predict Foreign Policy and National Security Decisions', *International Studies Perspectives* 6, 1: 94–8.

——— and Nehemia Geva. 1997. 'The Poliheuristic Theory of Foreign Policy Decision Making', in Geva and Mintz, eds, *Decision-Making in War and Peace: The Cognitive-Rational Debate*. Boulder, Colo.: Lynne Rienner.

——— et al. 1997. 'The Effect of Dynamic and Static Choice Sets on Political Decision Making: An Analysis Using the Decision Board Platform', *American Political Science Review* 91, 3: 553–66.

Mintzberg, Henry, Duru Raisinghani, and Andre Theoret. 1976. 'The Structure of "Unstructured" Decision Processes', *Administrative Science Quarterly* 21: 246–75.

Mitchell, K. 2001. 'Transnationalism, Neo-Liberalism and the Rise of the Shadow State', *Economy and Society* 30, 2: 165–89.

Mitchell, Ronald K., Bradley R. Age, and Donna J. Wood. 1997. 'Toward a Theory of Stakeholder Identification and Salience: Defining the Principle of Who and What Really Counts', *Academy of Management Review* 22, 4: 853–86.

Mitnick, Barry M. 1978. 'The Concept of Regulation', *Bulletin of Business Research* 53, 5: 1–20.

———. 1980. *The Political Economy of Regulation: Creating, Designing, and Removing Regulatory Forms*. New York: Columbia University Press.

Moe, Terry M. 1984. 'The New Economics of Organization', *American Journal of Political Science* 28: 739–77.

Monroe, Alan D. 1979. 'Consistency between Public Preferences and National Policy Decisions', *American Politics Quarterly* 7, 1: 3–19.

Monroe, Kristen Renwick. 1991. 'The Theory of Rational Action: Origins and Usefulness for Political Science', in Monroe, ed., *The Economic Approach to Politics: A Critical Reassessment of the Theory of Rational Action*. New York: HarperCollins, 1–31.

Montgomery, John D. 2000. 'Social Capital as a Policy Resource', *Policy Sciences* 33: 227–43.

Montpetit, Eric. 2002. 'Policy Networks, Federal Arrangements, and the Development of Environmental Regulations: A Comparison of the Canadian and American Agricultural Sectors', *Governance* 15, 1: 1–20.

———. 2003. 'Public Consultations in Policy Network Environments', *Canadian Public Policy* 29, 1: 95–110.

Moran, M. 2001. 'Not Steering but Drowning: Policy Catastrophes and the Regulatory State', *Political Quarterly* 72: 414–27.

Morcöl, Göktug. 2002. *A New Mind for Policy Analysis: Toward a Post-Newtonian and Postpositivist Epistemology and Methodology*. New York: Praeger.

———, ed. 2007. *Handbook of Decision Making*. New York: CRC Taylor and Francis.

Morgan, M.G., and M. Henrion. 1990. *Uncertainty: A Guide to Dealing with Uncertainty in Quantitative Risk and Policy Analysis*. Cambridge: Cambridge University Press.

Mortensen, Peter B. 2005. 'Policy Punctuations in Danish Local Budgeting', *Public Administration* 83, 4: 931–50.

———. 2007. 'Stability and Change in Public Policy: A Longitudinal Study of Comparative Subsystem Dynamics', *Policy Studies Journal* 35, 3: 373–94.

Moseley, A., and S. Tierney. 2004. 'Evidence-Based Practice in the Real World', *Evidence and Policy* 1, 1: 113–19.

Moss, David A. 2002. *When All Else Fails: Government as the Ultimate Risk Manager.* Cambridge, Mass.: Harvard University Press.

Mossberger, Karen. 2000. *The Politics of Ideas and the Spread of Enterprise Zones.* Washington: Georgetown University Press.

Moynihan, D.P. 2006. 'Ambiguity in Policy Lessons: The Agentification Experience', *Public Administration* 84, 4: 1029–50.

Mucciaroni, Gary. 1990. *The Political Failure of Employment Policy, 1945–1982.* Pittsburgh: University of Pittsburgh Press.

———. 1992. 'The Garbage Can Model and the Study of Policy Making: A Critique', *Polity* 24, 3: 460–82.

Mulford, Charles L. 1978. 'Why They Don't Even When They Ought To: Implications of Compliance Theory for Policymakers', in A. Etzioni, ed., *Policy Research.* Leiden: E.J. Brill, 47–62.

Mulvale, Gillian, Julia Abelson, and Paula Goering. 2007. 'Mental Health Service Delivery in Ontario, Canada: How Do Policy Legacies Shape Prospects for Reform?', *Health Economics, Policy and Law* 2: 363–89.

Munns, Joyce M. 1975. 'The Environment, Politics, and Policy Literature: A Critique and Reformulation', *Western Political Quarterly* 28, 4: 646–67.

Muntigl, Peter. 2002. 'Policy, Politics and Social Control: A Systemic Functional Linguistic Analysis of EU Employment Policy', *Text* 22, 3: 393–441.

Murray, Catherine. 2007. 'The Media', in Dobuzinskis et al. (2007: 286–97).

Musolf, Lloyd D. 1989. 'The Government Corporation Tool: Permutations and Possibilities', in Salamon (1989a: 231–52).

Mutersbaugh, T. 2005. 'Fighting Standards with Standards: Harmonization, Rents and Social Accountability in Certified Agrofood Networks', *Environment and Planning A* 37: 2033–51.

Nachmias, David. 1979. *Public Policy Evaluation: Approaches and Methods.* New York: St Martin's Press.

Nathanson, Constance A. 2000. 'Social Movements as Catalysts for Policy Change: The Case of Smoking and Guns', *Journal of Health Politics, Policy and Law* 24, 3: 421–88.

Nelson, Thomas E., and Zoe M. Oxley. 1999. 'Issue Framing Effects on Belief Importance and Opinion', *Journal of Politics* 61, 4: 1040–67.

Nettl, J.P. 1968. 'The State as a Conceptual Variable', *World Politics* 20, 4: 559–92.

Newig, Jens. 2004. 'Public Attention, Political Action: The Example of Environmental Regulation', *Rationality and Society* 16, 2: 149–90.

———. 2007. 'Symbolic Environmental Legislation and Societal Self-Deception', *Environmental Politics* 16, 2: 276–96.

Nice, D.C. 1987. 'Incremental and Non-incremental Policy Responses: The States and the Railroads', *Polity* 20: 145–56.

Nicholson-Crotty, S. 2005. 'Bureaucratic Competition in the Policy Process', *Policy Studies Journal* 33, 3: 341–61.

Nicolaus, Martin. 1967. 'Proletariat and Middle Class in Marx: Hegelian Choreography and the Capitalist Dialectic', *Studies on the Left* 7, 1: 22–49.

Nilsson, M. 2005. 'Learning, Frames and Environmental Policy Integration: The Case of Swedish Energy Policy', *Environment and Planning C* 23: 207–26.

Nisbet, M.C., and B.V. Lewenstein. 2002. 'Biotechnology and the American Media: The Policy Process and the Elite Press, 1970–1999', *Science Communication* 23, 4: 359–91.

Nisbet, Robert. 1972. 'Introduction: The Problem of Social Change', in Nisbet, ed., *Social Change.* New York: Harper and Row, 1–45.

Niskanen, William A. 1971. *Bureaucracy and Representative Government*. Chicago: University of Chicago Press.

Nohrstedt, D. 2005. 'External Shocks and Policy Change: Three Mile Island and Swedish Nuclear Energy Policy', *Journal of European Public Policy* 12, 6: 1041–59.

Norberg-Bohm, V. 1999. 'Stimulating "Green" Technological Innovation: An Analysis of Alternative Policy Mechanisms', *Policy Sciences* 32: 13–38.

Nordhaus, W. 1975. 'The Political Business Cycle', *Review of Economic Studies* 42: 169–90.

Nordlinger, Eric A. 1981. *On the Autonomy of the Democratic State*. Cambridge, Mass.: Harvard University Press.

———. 1987. 'Taking the State Seriously', in M. Weiner and S.P. Huntington, eds, *Understanding Political Development*. Boston: Little, Brown.

———. 1988. 'The Return to the State: Critiques', *American Political Science Review* 82, 3: 875–85.

North, Douglas C. 1990. *Institutions, Institutional Change and Economic Performance*. Cambridge: Cambridge University Press.

Nownes, Anthony J. 1995. 'The Other Exchange: Public Interest Groups, Patrons, and Benefits', *Social Science Quarterly* 76, 2: 381–401.

———. 2000. 'Policy Conflict and the Structure of Interest Communities', *American Politics Quarterly* 28, 3: 309–27.

———. 2004. 'The Population Ecology of Interest Group Formation: Mobilizing for Gay and Lesbian Rights in the United States, 1950–98', *British Journal of Political Science* 34, 1: 49–67.

——— and Allan J. Cigler. 1995. 'Public Interest Groups and the Road to Survival', *Polity* 27, 3: 380–404.

——— and Grant Neeley. 1996. 'Toward an Explanation for Public Interest Group Formation and Proliferation: "Seed Money", Disturbances, Entrepreneurship, and Patronage', *Policy Studies Journal* 24, 1: 74–92.

Nunan, Fiona. 1999. 'Policy Network Transformation: The Implementation of the EC Directive on Packaging and Packaging Waste', *Public Administration* 77, 3: 621–38.

Nyland, Julie. 1995. 'Issue Networks and Non-Profit Organizations', *Policy Studies Review* 14, 1 and 2: 195–204.

Obinger, Herbert, and Uwe Wagschal. 2001. 'Families of Nations and Public Policy', *West European Politics* 24, 1: 99–114.

Offe, C. 2006. 'Political Institutions and Social Power: Conceptual Explorations', in I. Shapiro, S. Skowronek, and D. Galvin, eds, *Rethinking Political Institutions: The Art of the State*. New York: New York University Press, 9–31.

O'Hagan, Emer. 2004. 'Too Soft to Handle? A Reflection on Soft Law in Europe and Accession States', *European Integration* 26, 4: 379–403.

Ohmae, K. 1995. *The End of the Nation State*. London: HarperCollins.

Oliveira, M.D., J.M. Magone, and J.A. Pereira. 2005. 'Nondecision Making and Inertia in Portuguese Health Policy', *Journal of Health Politics, Policy and Law* 30, 1 and 2: 211–30.

Oliver, Pamela E. 1993. 'Formal Models of Collective Action', *Annual Review of Sociology* 19: 271–300.

Olsen, J.P. 2005. 'Maybe It Is Time to Rediscover Bureaucracy', *Journal of Public Administration Research and Theory* 16, 1: 1–24.

Olson, David M., and Michael L. Mezey, eds. 1991. *Legislatures in the Policy Process: The Dilemmas of Economic Policy*. Cambridge: Cambridge University Press.

Olson, Mancur. 1965. *The Logic of Collective Action: Public Goods and the Theory of Groups*. Cambridge, Mass.: Harvard University Press.

———. 1982. *The Rise and Decline of Nations: Economic Growth, Stagflation, and Social Rigidities*. New Haven: Yale University Press.

————. 1986. 'A Theory of the Incentives Facing Political Organizations: Neo-Corporatism and the Hegemonic State', *International Political Science Review* 7, 2: 165–89.

Organization for Economic Co-operation and Development (OECD). 1993. *Managing with Market-Type Mechanisms*. Paris: OECD.

————. 2006. *The Political Economy of Environmentally Related Taxes*. Paris: OECD.

Orren, Karen, and Stephen Skowronek. 1993. 'Beyond the Iconography of Order: Notes for a "New Institutionalism"', in L.C. Dodd and C. Jillson, eds, *The Dynamics of American Politics: Approaches and Interpretations*. Boulder, Colo.: Westview Press.

———— and ————. 1998–9. 'Regimes and Regime Building in American Government: A Review of Literature on the 1940s', *Political Science Quarterly* 113, 4: 689–702.

Osborne, D., and E. Gaebler. 1992. *Reinventing Government*. Reading, Mass.: Addison-Wesley.

Ossowski, Stanislaw. 1963. *Class Structure in the Social Consciousness*, trans. Sheila Patterson. New York: Free Press of Glencoe.

Ostrander, Susan A., and Stuart Langton, eds. 1987. *Shifting the Debate: Public/Private Sector Relations in the Modern Welfare State*. New Brunswick, NJ: Transaction.

Ostrom, Elinor. 1986a. 'A Method of Institutional Analysis', in Kaufman et al. (1986).

————. 1986b. 'An Agenda for the Study of Institutions', *Public Choice* 48: 3–25.

————. 1999. 'Institutional Rational Choice: An Assessment of the Institutional Analysis and Development Framework', in Sabatier (1999a: 35–71).

————. 2003. 'How Types of Goods and Property Rights Jointly Affect Collective Action', *Journal of Theoretical Politics* 15, 3: 239–70.

Ostrom, Vincent, David Feeny, and Hartmut Picht, eds. 1993. *Rethinking Institutional Analysis and Development: Issues, Alternatives and Choices*. San Francisco: Institute for Contemporary Studies Press.

O'Sullivan, Deborah, and Barry Down. 2001. 'Policy Decision-making Models in Practice: A Case Study of the Western Australian "Sentencing Acts"', *Policy Studies Journal* 29, 1: 56–70.

O'Toole, Laurence J. 2000a. 'Different Public Managements? Implications of Structural Context in Hierarchies and Networks', in J.L. Brudney, L.J. O'Toole, and H.G. Rainey, eds, *Advancing Public Management: New Developments in Theory, Methods and Practice*. Washington: Georgetown University Press, 19–48.

————. 2000b. 'Research on Policy Implementation: Assessment and Prospects', *Journal of Public Administration Research and Theory* 10, 2: 263–88.

————. 2004. 'The Theory–Practice Issue in Policy Implementation Research', *Public Administration* 82, 2: 309–29.

Ouimet, Mathieu, and Vincent Lemieux. 2000. *Les Réseaux de Politique Publique: Un Bilan Critique et Une Voie de Formilization*. Québec: Université Laval Centre d'Analyse des Politiques Publiques.

Owens, Susan, and Tim Rayner. 1999. '"When Knowledge Matters": The Role and Influence of the Royal Commission on Environmental Pollution', *Journal of Environmental Policy and Planning* 1: 7–24.

Packwood, A. 2002. 'Evidence-Based Policy: Rhetoric and Reality', *Social Policy and Society* 1, 3: 267–72.

Padberg, D.I. 1992. 'Nutritional Labeling as a Policy Instrument', *American Journal of Agricultural Economics* 74, 5: 1208–13.

Page, Benjamin I., and Robert Y. Shapiro. 1992. *The Rational Public: Fifty Years of Trends in American Policy Preferences*. Chicago: University of Chicago Press.

Page, Christopher. 2006. *The Roles of Public Opinion Research in Canadian Government*. Toronto: University of Toronto Press.

Page, Edward C. 1985a. *Political Authority and Bureaucratic Power: A Comparative Analysis*. Brighton, Sussex: Wheatsheaf.

———. 1985b. 'Laws as an Instrument of Policy: A Study in Central–Local Government Relations', *Journal of Public Policy* 5, 2: 241–65.

Painter, M., and J. Pierre. 2005. *Challenges to State Policy Capacity: Global Trends and Comparative Perspectives*. London: Palgrave Macmillan.

Pal, Leslie A. 1987. *Public Policy Analysis: An Introduction*. Toronto: Methuen.

———. 1988. 'Hands at the Helm? Leadership and Public Policy', in Pal and David Taras, eds, *Prime Ministers and Premiers: Political Leadership and Public Policy in Canada*. Scarborough, Ont.: Prentice-Hall, 16–26.

———. 1992. *Public Policy Analysis: An Introduction*, 2nd edn. Scarborough, Ont.: Nelson.

———. 1993a. *Interests of State: The Politics of Language, Multiculturalism, and Feminism in Canada*. Montreal and Kingston: McGill-Queen's University Press.

———. 1993b. 'Advocacy Organizations and Legislative Politics: The Effects of the Charter of Rights and Freedoms on Interest Lobbying of Federal Legislation, 1989–1991', in F.L. Seidle, ed., *Equity and Community: The Charter, Interest Advocacy and Representation*. Montreal: Institute for Research on Public Policy, 119–57.

———. 1997. *Beyond Policy Analysis: Public Issue Management in Turbulent Times*. Toronto: ITP Nelson.

Palumbo, Dennis J. 1987. *The Politics of Program Evaluation*. Beverly Hills, Calif.: Sage.

——— and D.J. Calista. 1990a. *Implementation and the Policy Process: Opening Up the Black Box*. New York: Greenwood Press.

——— and ———. 1990b. 'Opening Up the Black Box: Implementation and the Policy Process', in Palumbo and Calista (1990a).

Panitch, Leo. 1977. 'The Development of Corporatism in Liberal Democracies', *Comparative Political Studies* 10, 1: 61–90.

———. 1979. 'Corporatism in Canada', *Studies in Political Economy* 1, 1: 43–92.

Papadopoulos, Yannis, and Philippe Warin. 2007. 'Are Innovative, Participatory and Deliberative Procedures in Policy Making Democratic and Effective?', *European Journal of Political Research* 46: 445–72.

Papaioannou, H. Rush, and J. Bassant. 2006. 'Performance Management: Benchmarking as a Policy-Making Tool: From the Private to the Public Sector', *Science and Public Policy* 33, 2: 91–102.

Pappi, Franz Urban, and Christian H.C.A. Henning. 1998. 'Policy Networks: More Than a Metaphor', *Journal of Theoretical Politics* 10, 4: 553–75.

——— and ———. 1999. 'The Organization of Influence on the EC's Common Agricultural Policy: A Network Approach', *European Journal of Political Research* 36: 257–81.

Parag, Yael. 2006. 'A System Perspective for Policy Analysis and Understanding: The Policy Process Networks', *The Systemist* 28, 2: 212–24.

———. 2008. 'Who Governs the Air We Breathe? Lessons from Israel's Industrialist Covenant', *Journal of Environmental Policy and Planning* 10, 2: 133–52.

Parenti, Michael. 1986. *Inventing Reality: The Politics of the Mass Media*. New York: St Martin's Press.

Pasquier, Martial, and Jean-Patrick Villeneuve. 2007. 'Organizational Barriers to Transparency: A Typology and Analysis of Organizational Behaviour Tending to Prevent or Restrict Access to Information', *International Review of Administrative Sciences* 73, 1: 147–62.

Pateman, Carole. 1970. *Participation and Democratic Theory*. Cambridge: Cambridge University Press.

Patton, Carl V., and David S. Sawicki. 1993. *Basic Methods of Policy Analysis and Planning*. Englewood Cliffs, NJ: Prentice-Hall.

Pawson, Ray. 2002. 'Evidence-Based Policy: In Search of a Method?', *Evaluation* 8, 2: 157–81.

———. 2006. *Evidence-Based Policy: A Realist Perspective*. London: Sage.

Payne, John W. 1982. 'Contingent Decision Behaviour', *Psychological Bulletin* 92, 2: 382–402.

———, James R. Bettman, and Eric J. Johnson. 1988. 'Adaptive Strategy Selection in Decision Making', *Journal of Experimental Psychology; Learning, Memory and Cognition* 14, 3: 534–52.

Pedersen, Lene Holm. 2007. 'Ideas Are Transformed as They Transfer: A Comparative Study of Eco-Taxation in Scandinavia', *Journal of European Public Policy* 14, 1: 59–77.

Perl, Anthony. 1991. 'Financing Transport Infrastructure: The Effects of Institutional Durability in French and American Policymaking', *Governance* 4, 4: 365–402.

——— and James A. Dunn Jr. 1997. 'Reinventing Amtrak: The Politics of Survival', *Journal of Policy Analysis and Management* 16, 4: 598–614.

——— and ———. 2007. 'Reframing Automobile Fuel Economy Policy in North America: The Politics of Punctuating a Policy Equilibrium', *Transport Reviews* 27, 1: 1–35.

——— and Donald J. White. 2002. 'The Changing Role of Consultants in Canadian Policy Analysis', *Policy and Society* 21, 1: 49–73.

Perrow, Charles. 1984. *Normal Accidents: Living with High-Risk Technologies*. New York: Basic Books.

Peters, B. Guy. 1984. *The Politics of Bureaucracy: A Comparative Perspective*. New York: Longman.

———. 1992a. 'The Policy Process: An Institutionalist Perspective', *Canadian Public Administration* 35, 2: 160–80.

———. 1992b. 'Government Reorganization: A Theoretical Analysis', *International Political Science Review* 13, 2: 199–218.

———. 1998. 'The Experimenting Society and Policy Design', in William N. Dunn, ed., *The Experimenting Society: Essays in Honour of Donald T. Campbell*. New Brunswick, NJ: Transaction, 125–39.

———. 1999. *Institutional Theory in Political Science: The 'New Institutionalism'*. London: Pinter.

———. 2002. 'The Politics of Tool Choice', in Salamon (2002a: 552–64).

——— and Anthony Barker, eds. 1993. *Advising West European Governments: Inquiries, Expertise and Public Policy*. Edinburgh: Edinburgh University Press.

———, John C. Doughtie, and M. Kathleen McCulloch. 1977. 'Types of Democratic Systems and Types of Public Policy', *Comparative Politics* 9: 327–55.

———, ———, and ———. 1978. 'Do Public Policies Vary in Different Types of Democratic System?', in P.G. Lewis, D.C. Potter, and F.G. Castles, eds, *The Practice of Comparative Politics: A Reader*. London: Longman.

——— and Brian W. Hogwood. 1985a. *The Pathology of Public Policy*. New York: Oxford University Press.

——— and ———. 1985b. 'In Search of the Issue-Attention Cycle', *Journal of Politics* 47, 1: 238–53.

——— and J. Pierre. 2000. 'Citizens versus the New Public Manager: The Problem of Mutual Empowerment', *Administration and Society* 32, 1: 9–28.

———, ———, and Desmond S. King. 2005. 'The Politics of Path Dependency: Political Conflict in Historical Institutionalism', *Journal of Politics* 67, 4: 1275–300.

——— and F.K.M. Van Nispen, eds. 1998. *Public Policy Instruments: Evaluating the Tools of Public Administration*. New York: Edward Elgar.

Peterson, John. 1995. 'Decision-making in the European Union: Towards a Framework for Analysis', *Journal of European Public Policy* 2, 1: 69–93.

Petry, Francois. 1999. 'The Opinion–Policy Relationship in Canada', *Journal of Politics* 61, 2: 540–50.

Phang, Sock-Yong, and Rex S. Toh. 2004. 'Road Congestion Pricing in Singapore: 1975 to 2003', *Transportation Journal* 43, 2: 16–25.

Phidd, Richard W. 1975. 'The Economic Council of Canada: Its Establishment, Structure, and Role in the Canadian Policy-Making System 1963–74', *Canadian Public Administration* 18, 3: 428–73.

———— and G. Bruce Doern. 1983. *Canadian Public Policy: Ideas, Structures, Process.* Toronto: Methuen.

Phillips, Jim, Bruce Chapman, and David Stevens, eds. 2001. *Between State and Market: Essays on Charities, Law and Policy in Canada.* Toronto: University of Toronto Press.

Phillips, Susan D. 1991a. 'How Ottawa Blends: Shifting Government Relationships with Interest Groups', in F. Abele, ed., *How Ottawa Spends 1991–92: The Politics of Fragmentation.* Ottawa: Carleton University Press, 183–228.

————. 1991b. 'Meaning and Structure in Social Movements: Mapping the Network of National Canadian Women's Organizations', *Canadian Journal of Political Science* 24, 4: 755–82.

————. 1998. 'Discourse, Identity, and Voice: Feminist Contributions to Policy Studies', in L. Dobuzinskis, M. Howlett, and D. Laycock, eds, *Policy Studies in Canada: The State of the Art.* Toronto: University of Toronto Press, 242–65.

———— and Karine Levasseur. 2004. 'The Snakes and Ladders of Accountability: Contradictions between Contracting and Collaboration for Canada's Voluntary Sector', *Canadian Public Administration* 47, 4: 451–74.

Pielke, R.A. 2004. 'What Future for the Policy Sciences?', *Policy Sciences* 37: 209–25.

Pierre, J. 1998. 'Public Consultation and Citizen Participation: Dilemmas of Policy Advice', in B.G. Peters and D.J. Savoie, eds, *Taking Stock: Assessing Public Sector Reforms.* Montreal and Kingston: McGill-Queen's Press, 137–63.

Pierson, Paul. 1993. 'When Effect Becomes Cause: Policy Feedback and Political Change', *World Politics* 45: 595–628.

————. 2000a. 'Increasing Returns, Path Dependence, and the Study of Politics', *American Political Science Review* 94, 2: 251–67.

————. 2000b. 'Not Just What, but When: Timing and Sequence in Political Processes', *Studies in American Political Development* 14: 72–92.

————. 2000c. 'The Limits of Design: Explaining Institutional Origins and Change', *Governance* 13, 4: 475–99.

————. 2004. *Politics in Time: History, Institutions, and Social Analysis.* Princeton, NJ: Princeton University Press.

Pigou, A.C. 1932. *The Economics of Welfare*, 4th edn. London: Macmillan.

Pittel, K., and D.T.G. Rubbelke. 2006. 'Private Provision of Public Goods: Incentives for Donations', *Journal of Economic Studies* 33, 6: 497–519.

Poel, Dale H. 1976. 'The Diffusion of Legislation among the Canadian Provinces', *Canadian Journal of Political Science* 9: 605–26.

Pollitt, C. 2001. 'Clarifying Convergence: Striking Similarities and Durable Differences in Public Management Reform', *Public Management Review* 4, 1: 471–92.

Pollock, Philip H., Stuart A. Lilie, and M. Elliot Vittes. 1989. 'Hard Issues, Core Values and Vertical Constraint: The Case of Nuclear Power', *British Journal of Political Science* 23, 1: 29–50.

Polsby, Nelson W. 1963. *Community Power and Political Theory.* New Haven: Yale University Press.

————. 1984. *Political Innovation in America: The Politics of Policy Initiation.* New Haven: Yale University Press.

Porter, T., and K. Ronit. 2006. 'Self-Regulation as Policy Process: The Multiple and Criss-Crossing Stages of Private Rule-Making', *Policy Sciences* 39: 41–72.

Posner, Richard A. 1974. 'Theories of Economic Regulation', *Bell Journal of Economics and Management Science* 5, 2: 335–58.

Potoski, M. 1999. 'Managing Uncertainty through Bureaucratic Design: Administrative Procedures and State Air Pollution Control Agencies', *Journal of Public Administration Research and Theory* 9, 4: 623–39.

Poulantzas, Nicos. 1973a. *Political Power and Social Classes*. London: New Left Books.

———. 1973b. 'On Social Classes', *New Left Review* 78: 27–54.

———. 1978. *State, Power, Socialism*. London: New Left Books.

Powell, Walter W., and Paul J. DiMaggio, eds. 1991. *The New Institutionalism in Organizational Analysis*. Chicago: University of Chicago Press.

Pralle, S.B. 2003. 'Venue Shopping, Political Strategy, and Policy Change: The Internationalization of Canadian Forest Advocacy', *Journal of Public Policy* 23, 3: 233–60.

Pressman, Jeffrey L., and Aaron B. Wildavsky. 1984. *Implementation: How Great Expectations in Washington Are Dashed in Oakland*, 3rd edn. Berkeley: University of California Press.

Presthus, Robert V. 1973. *Elite Accommodation in Canadian Politics*. Cambridge: Cambridge University Press.

Preston, Lee E., and Duane Windsor. 1992. *The Rules of the Game in the Global Economy: Policy Regimes for International Business*. Boston: Kluwer.

Prichard, J. Robert S., ed. 1983. *Crown Corporations in Canada: The Calculus of Instrument Choice*. Toronto: Butterworths.

Priest, Margot, and Aron Wohl. 1980. 'The Growth of Federal and Provincial Regulation of Economic Activity 1867–1978', in W.T. Stanbury, ed., *Government Regulation: Scope, Growth, Process*. Montreal: Institute for Research on Public Policy.

Prince, Michael J. 1979. 'Policy Advisory Groups in Government Departments', in G.B. Doern and P. Aucoin, eds, *Public Policy in Canada: Organization, Process, Management*. Toronto: Gage, 275–300.

Princen, Sebastiaan. 2007. 'Agenda-Setting in the European Union: A Theoretical Exploration and Agenda for Research', *Journal of European Public Policy* 14, 1: 21–38.

Pritchard, David. 1992. 'The News Media and Public Policy Agendas', in Kennamer (1992).

Pross, A. Paul. 1992. *Group Politics and Public Policy*. Toronto: Oxford University Press.

——— and Susan McCorquodale. 1990. 'The State, Interests, and Policy-Making in the East Coast Fishery', in Coleman and Skogstad (1990).

——— and Iain S. Stewart. 1993. 'Lobbying, the Voluntary Sector and the Public Purse', in S.D. Phillips, ed., *How Ottawa Spends 1993–1994: A More Democratic Canada?* Ottawa: Carleton University Press, 109–42.

——— and Kernaghan R. Webb. 2003. 'Embedded Regulation: Advocacy and the Federal Regulation of Public Interest Groups', in Kathy L. Brock, ed., *Delicate Dances: Public Policy and the Nonprofit Sector*. Montreal and Kingston: McGill-Queen's University Press, 63–122.

Pryor, F.L. 1968. *Public Expenditures in Communist and Capitalist Nations*. Homewood, Ill.: R.D. Irwin.

Przeworski, Adam. 1987. 'Methods of Cross-national Research, 1970–83: An Overview', in M. Dierkes, H.N. Weiler, and A.B. Antal, eds, *Comparative Policy Research: Learning from Experience*. Aldershot: Gower, 31–49.

———. 1990. *The State and the Economy under Capitalism*. Chur, Switzerland: Harwood.

——— and Fernando Limongi. 1997. 'Modernization: Theories and Facts', *World Politics* 49: 155–83.

Putnam, Robert D. 1988. 'Diplomacy and Domestic Politics: The Logic of Two-Level Games', *International Organization* 42: 427–60.

———. 1995a. 'Bowling Alone: America's Declining Social Capital', *Journal of Democracy* 6, 1: 65–78.

———. 1995b. 'Tuning In, Tuning Out: The Strange Disappearance of Social Capital in America', *PS: Political Science and Politics* (Dec.): 664–83.

———. 1996. *The Decline of Civil Society: How Come? So What?* Ottawa: Canadian Centre for Management Development.

———. 2000. *Bowling Alone: The Collapse and Revival of American Community.* New York: Simon and Schuster.

———. 2001. 'Social Capital: Measurement and Consequences', *Isuma* 2, 1: 41–52.

Qualter, Terence H. 1985. *Opinion Control in the Democracies.* London: Macmillan.

Quarter, Jack. 1992. *Canada's Social Economy: Co-operatives, Non-Profits, and Other Community Enterprises.* Toronto: James Lorimer.

Raab, Jorg, and Patrick Kenis. 2007. 'Taking Stock of Policy Networks: Do They Matter?', in Frank Fischer, Gerlad J. Miller, and Mara S. Sidney, eds, *Handbook of Public Policy Analysis: Theory, Politics and Methods.* Boca Raton, Fla: CRC Press, 187–200.

Raboy, Marc. 1995. 'Influencing Public Policy on Canadian Broadcasting', *Canadian Public Administration* 38, 3: 411–32.

Radford, K.J. 1977. *Complex Decision Problems: An Integrated Strategy for Resolution.* Reston, Va: Reston Publishing Company.

Radin, Beryl A. 2000. *Beyond Machiavelli: Policy Analysis Comes of Age.* Washington: Georgetown University Press.

Rakoff, Stuart H., and Guenther F. Schaefer. 1970. 'Politics, Policy, and Political Science: Theoretical Alternatives', *Politics and Society* 1, 1: 51–77.

Ramesh, M. 1995. 'Economic Globalization and Policy Choices: Singapore', *Governance* 10, 2: 243–60.

———. 2000. *Welfare Capitalism in Southeast Asia: Social Security, Health, and Education Policies.* London: Macmillan.

——— and Michael Howlett, eds. 2006. *Deregulation and Its Discontents: Rewriting the Rules in Asia.* Cheltenham: Edward Elgar.

Raphael, Dennis. 2008. 'Shaping Public Policy and Population Health in the United States: Why Is the Public Health Community Missing in Action?', *International Journal of Health Services* 38, 1: 63–94.

Ray, James Lee. 2001. 'Integrating Levels of Analysis in World Politics', *Journal of Theoretical Politics* 13, 4: 355–88.

Rayner, J., et al. 2001. 'Privileging the Sub-Sector: Critical Sub-Sectors and Sectoral Relationships in Forest Policy-Making', *Forest Policy and Economics* 2, 3 and 4: 319–32.

Reagan, Michael D. 1987. *Regulation: The Politics of Policy.* Boston: Little, Brown.

Reid, Timothy E. 1979. 'The Failure of PPBS: Real Incentives for the 1980s', *Optimum* 10, 4: 23–37.

Rein, Martin, Gosta Esping-Andersen, and Lee Rainwater, eds. 1987. *Stagnation and Renewal in Social Policy: The Rise and Fall of Policy Regimes.* Armonk, NY: M.E. Sharpe.

——— and Donald Schon. 1996. 'Frame-Critical Policy Analysis and Frame-Reflective Policy Practice', *Knowledge and Policy* 9, 1: 85–105.

Reinicke, Wolfgang H. 1998. *Global Public Policy: Governing without Government?* Washington: Brookings Institution.

Relyea, Harold C. 1977. 'The Provision of Government Information: The Freedom of Information Act Experience', *Canadian Public Administration* 20, 2: 317–41.

Resodihardjo, S.L. 2006. 'Wielding a Double-Edged Sword: The Use of Inquiries at Times of Crisis', *Journal of Contingencies and Crisis Management* 14, 4: 199–206.

Rhodes, R.A.W. 1984. 'Power-Dependence, Policy Communities and Intergovernmental Networks', *Public Administration Bulletin* 49: 4–31.

————. 1996. 'The New Governance: Governing without Government', *Political Studies* 44: 652–67.

————. 1997a. *Understanding Governance: Policy Networks, Governance, Reflexivity, and Accountability*. Buckingham: Open University Press.

————. 1997b. 'From Marketisation to Diplomacy: It's the Mix that Matters', *Australian Journal of Public Administration* 56, 2: 40–54.

———— and David Marsh. 1992. 'New Directions in the Study of Policy Networks', *European Journal of Political Science* 21: 181–205.

Ricci, David. 1993. *The Transformation of American Politics: The New Washington and the Rise of Think Tanks*. New Haven: Yale University Press.

Rich, A. 2004. *Think Tanks, Public Policy, and the Politics of Expertise*. New York: Cambridge University Press.

Richardson, Jeremy J., ed. 1990. *Privatisation and Deregulation in Canada and Britain*. Aldershot: Dartmouth.

————. 1995. 'EU Water Policy: Uncertain Agendas, Shifting Networks and Complex Coalitions', in H. Bressers, L.J. O'Toole, and J. Richardson, eds, *Networks for Water Policy: A Comparative Perspective*. London: Frank Cass, 139–67.

————. 1999. 'Interest Groups, Multi-Arena Politics and Policy Change', in S.S. Nagel, ed., *The Policy Process*. Commack, NY: Nova Science, 65–100.

————. 2000. 'Government, Interest Groups and Policy Change', *Political Studies* 48: 1006–25.

————, Gunnel Gustafsson, and Grant Jordan. 1982. 'The Concept of Policy Style', in Richardson, ed., *Policy Styles in Western Europe*. London: George Allen and Unwin.

———— and A.G. Jordan. 1979. *Governing under Pressure: The Policy Process in a Post-Parliamentary Democracy*. Oxford: Martin Robertson.

————, ————, and R.H. Kimber. 1978. 'Lobbying, Administrative Reform and Policy Styles: The Case of Land Drainage', *Political Studies* 26, 1: 47–64.

Rickenbach, M., and C. Overdevest. 2006. 'More Than Markets: Assessing Forest Stewardship Council (FSC) Certification as a Policy Tool', *Journal of Forestry* 104, 3: 143–7.

Riedel, James A. 1972. 'Citizen Participation: Myths and Realities', *Public Administration Review* (May–June): 211–20.

Riker, William H. 1962. *The Theory of Political Coalitions*. New Haven: Yale University Press.

————. 1983. 'Political Theory and the Art of Heresthetics', in Ada W. Finifter, ed., *Political Science: The State of the Discipline*. Washington: American Political Science Association, 47–67.

————. 1986. *The Art of Political Manipulation*. New Haven: Yale University Press.

———— and Grace A. Franklin. 1980. *Congress, the Bureaucracy, and Public Policy*, 3rd edn. Homewood, Ill.: Dorsey Press.

Risse-Kappen, Thomas. 1995. *Bringing Transnational Relations Back In: Non-State Actors, Domestic Structures and International Institutions*. Cambridge: Cambridge University Press.

Rist, Ray C. 1994. 'The Preconditions for Learning: Lessons from the Public Sector', in F.L. Leeuw, R.C. Rist, and R.C. Sonnischen, eds, *Can Governments Learn: Comparative Perspectives on Evaluation and Organizational Learning*. New Brunswick, NJ: Transaction.

Rittberger, Volker, and Peter Mayer, eds. 1993. *Regime Theory and International Relations*. Oxford: Clarendon Press.

Rittel, Horst W.J., and Melvin M. Webber. 1973. 'Dilemmas in a General Theory of Planning', *Policy Sciences* 4: 155–69.

Robbin, A. 2000. 'Administrative Policy as Symbol System: Political Conflict and the Social Construction of Identity', *Administration and Society* 32, 4: 398–431.

Roberts, Nancy C., and Paula J. King. 1991. 'Policy Entrepreneurs: Their Activity Structure and Function in the Policy Process', *Journal of Public Administration Research and Theory* 1, 2: 147–75.

Robinson, Scott E. 2007. 'Punctuated Equilibrium Models in Organizational Decision Making', in Morçöl (2007: 133–49).

——— and Flou'say Caver. 2006. 'Punctuated Equilibrium and Congressional Budgeting', *Political Research Quarterly* 59, 1: 161–6.

———, ———, Kenneth J. Meier, and Laurence J. O'Toole Jr. 2007. 'Explaining Policy Punctuations: Bureaucratization and Budget Change', *American Journal of Political Science* 51, 1: 140–50.

Rochefort, David A., and Roger W. Cobb. 1993. 'Problem Definition, Agenda Access, and Policy Choice', *Policy Studies Journal* 21, 1: 56–71.

Roe, Emory. 1998. *Taking Complexity Seriously: Policy Analysis, Triangulation and Sustainable Development*. Boston: Kluwer.

———. 2000. 'Poverty, Defense and the Environment: How Policy Optics, Policy Incompleteness, fastthinking.com, Equivalency Paradox, Deliberation Trap, Mailbox Dilemma, the Urban Ecosystem and the End of Problem Solving Recast Difficult Policy Issues', *Administration and Society* 31, 6: 687–725.

Roemer, John, ed. 1986. *Analytical Marxism*. Cambridge: Cambridge University Press.

Rogers, David L., and David A. Whetton, eds. 1982. *Interorganizational Coordination: Theory, Research and Implementation*. Ames: Iowa State University Press.

Rogers, Harry. 1978. 'Management Control in the Public Service', *Optimum* 9, 3: 14–28.

Rogers, H.G., M.A. Ulrick, and K.L. Traversy. 1981. 'Evaluation in Practice: The State of the Art in Canadian Governments', *Canadian Public Administration* 24, 3: 371–86.

Rona-Tas, Akos. 1998. 'Path Dependence and Capital Theory: Sociology of the Post-Communist Economic Transformation', *East European Politics and Societies* 12, 1: 107–31.

Rondinelli, Dennis A. 1976. 'International Assistance Policy and Development Project Administration: The Impact of Imperious Rationality', *International Organization* 30: 573–605.

———. 1983. *Development Projects as Policy Experiments: An Adaptive Approach to Development Administration*. London: Methuen.

Roots, R.I. 2004. 'When Laws Backfire: Unintended Consequences of Public Policy', *American Behavioural Scientist* 47, 11: 1376–94.

Rose, Richard. 1976. 'Models of Change', in Rose, ed., *The Dynamics of Public Policy: A Comparative Analysis*. London: Sage, 7–33.

———. 1980. *Do Parties Make a Difference?* London: Macmillan.

———. 1988. 'Comparative Policy Analysis: The Program Approach', in M. Dogan, ed., *Comparing Pluralist Democracies: Strains on Legitimacy*. Boulder, Colo.: Westview Press, 219–41.

———. 1990. 'Inheritance before Choice in Public Policy', *Journal of Theoretical Politics* 2, 3: 263–91.

———. 1991. 'What Is Lesson-Drawing?', *Journal of Public Policy* 11, 1: 3–30.

———. 1993. *Lesson-Drawing in Public Policy: A Guide to Learning across Time and Space*. Chatham, NJ: Chatham House.

Rosenau, James N. 1969. *Linkage Politics: Essays on the Convergence of National and International Systems*. New York: Collier-Macmillan.

Rosenau, P.V. 1999. 'The Strengths and Weaknesses of Public–Private Policy Partnerships', *American Behavioral Scientist* 43, 1: 10–34.

Rosenbloom, David H. 2007. 'Administrative Law and Regulation', in Jack Rabin, W. Bartley Hildreth, and Gerald J. Miller, eds, *Handbook of Public Administration*. London: CRC Taylor & Francis, 635–96.

———— and R.D. Schwartz. 1994. *Handbook of Regulation and Administrative Law*. New York: Marcel Dekker.

Rosendal, G. Kristin. 2000. 'Overlapping International Regimes: The Case of the Intergovernmental Forum on Forests (IFF) between Climate Change and Biodiversity'. Oslo: Fridtjof Nansen Institute Paper. At: <www.fni.no, 2000>.

Ross, Fiona. 2007. 'Questioning Path Dependency Theory: The Case of the British NHS', *Policy and Politics* 35, 4: 591–610.

Rothmayr, Christine, and Sibylle Hardmeier. 2002. 'Governmental Polling: Use and Impact of Polls in the Policy-Making Process in Switzerland', *International Journal of Public Opinion Research* 14, 2: 123–40.

————, Uwe Serduelt, and Elisabeth Maurer. 1997. 'Policy Instruments: An Analytical Category Revised', paper presented at the ECPR Joint Sessions Workshops, 27 Feb.–4 Mar., Bern.

Rothschild, M.L. 1979. 'Marketing Communications in Non-Business Situations, or Why It's So Hard to Sell Brotherhood Like Soap', *Journal of Marketing* 43: 11–20.

Rousseau, Jean-Jacques. 1973. *The Social Contract and Discourses*. London: J.M. Dent.

Rowley, C.K. 1983. 'The Political Economy of the Public Sector', in R.J.B. Jones, ed., *Perspectives on Political Economy*. London: Pinter.

Ruiter, D.W.P. 2004. 'Types of Institutions as Patterns of Regulated Behaviour', *Res Publica* 10: 207–31.

Russell, Peter H. 1982. 'The Effect of a Charter of Rights on the Policy-Making Role of Canadian Courts', *Canadian Public Administration* 25: 1–33.

Ryan, Phil. 1995. 'Miniature Mila and Flying Geese: Government Advertising and Canadian Democracy', in S.D. Phillips, ed., *How Ottawa Spends 1995–96: Mid-Life Crises*. Ottawa: Carleton University Press, 263–86.

Sabatier, Paul A. 1975. 'Social Movements and Regulatory Agencies: Toward a More Adequate—and Less Pessimistic—Theory of "Clientele Capture"', *Policy Sciences* 6: 301–42.

————. 1977. 'Regulatory Policy-Making: Toward a Framework of Analysis', *Natural Resources Journal* 17, 3: 415–60.

————. 1986. 'Top-Down and Bottom-Up Approaches to Implementation Research: A Critical Analysis and Suggested Synthesis', *Journal of Public Policy* 6: 21–48.

————. 1987. 'Knowledge, Policy-Oriented Learning, and Policy Change', *Knowledge: Creation, Diffusion, Utilization* 8, 4: 649–92.

————. 1988. 'An Advocacy Coalition Framework of Policy Change and the Role of Policy-Oriented Learning Therein', *Policy Sciences* 21, 2 and 3: 129–68.

————. 1992. 'Political Science and Public Policy: An Assessment', in W.N. Dunn and R.M. Kelly, eds, *Advances in Policy Studies Since 1950*. New Brunswick, NJ: Transaction, 27–58.

————. 1993a. 'Top-down and Bottom-up Approaches to Implementation Research', in Hill (1993).

————. 1993b. 'Policy Change over a Decade or More', in Sabatier and Jenkins-Smith (1993a: 13–40).

————, ed. 1999a. *Theories of the Policy Process*. Boulder, Colo.: Westview Press.

————. 1999b. 'The Need for Better Theories', in Sabatier (1999a: 3–17).

———— and Hank C. Jenkins-Smith, eds. 1993a. *Policy Change and Learning: An Advocacy Coalition Approach*. Boulder, Colo.: Westview Press.

—— and ——. 1993b. 'The Advocacy Coalition Framework: Assessment, Revisions, and Implications for Scholars and Practitioners', in Sabatier and Jenkins-Smith (1993a).

—— and D.A. Mazmanian. 1981. *Effective Policy Implementation.* Lexington, Mass.: Lexington Books.

Sager, Tore. 2001. 'Manipulative Features of Planning Styles', *Environment and Planning A* 33: 765–91.

Saint-Martin, Denis. 1998. 'The New Managerialism and the Policy Influence of Consultants in Government: An Historical-Institutionalist Analysis of Britain, Canada and France', *Governance* 11, 3: 319–56.

Salamon, Lester M. 1981. 'Rethinking Public Management: Third-Party Government and the Changing Forms of Government Action', *Public Policy* 29, 3: 255–75.

——. 1987. 'Of Market Failure, Voluntary Failure, and Third-Party Government', in Ostrander and Langton (1987).

——, ed. 1989a. *Beyond Privatization: The Tools of Government Action.* Washington: Urban Institute.

——. 1989b. 'The Changing Tools of Government Action: An Overview', in Salamon (1989a).

——. 1989c. 'Conclusion: Beyond Privatization', in Salamon (1989a).

——. 1995. *Partners in Public Service: Government-Nonprofit Relations in the Modern Welfare State.* Baltimore: Johns Hopkins University Press.

——, ed. 2002a. *The Tools of Government: A Guide to the New Governance.* New York: Oxford University Press.

——. 2002b. 'Economic Regulation', in Salamon (2002a: 117–55).

——. 2002c. 'The New Governance and the Tools of Public Action', in Salamon (2002a: 1–47).

—— and Michael S. Lund. 1989. 'The Tools Approach: Basic Analytics', in Salamon (1989a: 23–50).

Salisbury, Robert H., et al. 1987. 'Who Works with Whom? Interest Group Alliances and Opposition', *American Political Science Review* 81, 4: 1217–34.

Salmon, Charles, ed. 1989a. *Information Campaigns: Managing the Process of Social Change.* Newberry Park, Calif.: Sage.

——. 1989b. 'Campaigns for Social Improvement: An Overview of Values, Rationales, and Impacts', in Salmon (1989a: 1-32).

Salter, Liora. 1981. *Public Inquiries in Canada.* Ottawa: Science Council of Canada.

Sampson, Steven, 1991. 'Is There an Anthropology of Socialism?', *Anthropology Today* 7, 5: 16–19

Samuels, Warren J. 1991. ' "Truth" and "Discourse" in the Social Construction of Economic Reality: An Essay on the Relation of Knowledge to Socioeconomic Policy', *Journal of Post-Keynesian Economics* 13, 4: 511–24.

Sandel, Michael J., ed. 1984. *Liberalism and Its Critics.* Oxford: Blackwell.

Sanderson, Ian. 2002a. 'Evaluation, Policy Learning and Evidence-Based Policy-Making', *Public Administration* 80, 1: 1–22.

——. 2002b. 'Making Sense of What Works: Evidence Based Policymaking as Instrumental Rationality?', *Public Policy and Administration* 17, 3: 61–75.

——. 2006. 'Complexity, "Practical Rationality" and Evidence-Based Policy Making', *Policy and Politics* 34, 1: 115–32.

Sarpkaya, S. 1988. *Lobbying in Canada—Ways and Means.* Don Mills, Ont.: CCH Canadian.

Savas, E.S. 1977. *Alternatives for Delivering Public Services: Toward Improved Performance.* Boulder, Colo.: Westview Press.

——. 1987. *Privatization: The Key to Better Government.* Chatham, NJ: Chatham House.

Savoie, Donald J. 1990. *The Politics of Public Spending in Canada*. Toronto: University of Toronto Press.

———. 1999. *Governing from the Centre: The Concentration of Power in Canadian Politics*. Toronto: University of Toronto Press.

Saward, Michael. 1990. 'Cooption and Power: Who Gets What from Formal Incorporation', *Political Studies* 38: 588–602.

———. 1992. *Co-Optive Politics and State Legitimacy*. Aldershot: Dartmouth.

Schaap, L., and M.J.W. van Twist. 1997. 'The Dynamics of Closedness in Networks', in W.J.M. Kickert, E.-H. Klijn, and J.F.M. Koppenjan, eds, *Managing Complex Networks: Strategies for the Public Sector*. London: Sage, 62–78.

Schaefer, Guenther F. 1974. 'A General Systems Approach to Public Policy', *Policy and Politics* 2, 4: 331–46.

Schafer, A. 2006. 'Resolving Deadlock: Why International Organisations Introduce Soft Law', *European Law Journal* 12, 2: 194–208.

Scharpf, Fritz W. 1990. 'Games Real Actors Could Play: The Problem of Mutual Predictability', *Rationality and Society* 2: 471–94.

———. 1991. 'Political Institutions, Decision Styles, and Policy Choices', in R.M. Czada and A. Windhoff-Heritier, eds, *Political Choice: Institutions, Rules and the Limits of Rationality*. Frankfurt: Campus Verlag, 53–86.

———. 1997. *Games Real Actors Play: Actor-Centered Institutionalism in Policy Research*. Boulder, Colo.: Westview Press.

———. 2000. 'Institutions in Comparative Policy Research', *Comparative Political Studies* 33, 6 and 7: 762–90.

Schattschneider, E.E. 1935. *Politics, Pressures and the Tariff*. New York: Prentice-Hall.

———. 1960. *The Semi-sovereign People: A Realist's View of Democracy in America*. New York: Holt, Rinehart and Winston.

Schelling, T.C. 1971. 'On the Ecology of Micromotives', *The Public Interest* 25 (Fall): 59–98.

Schlager, Edella. 1999. 'A Comparison of Frameworks, Theories, and Models of Policy Processes', in Sabatier (1999a: 233–60).

Schmidt, Vivien A. 2001. 'The Politics of Economic Adjustment in France and Britain: When Does Discourse Matter?', *Journal of European Public Policy* 8, 2: 247–64.

———. 2008. 'Discursive Institutionalism: The Explanatory Power of Ideas and Discourse', *Annual Review of Political Science* 11: 303–26.

——— and C.M. Radaelli. 2005. 'Policy Change and Discourses in Europe: Conceptual and Methodological Issues', in C.M. Radaelli and V.A. Schmidt, eds, *Policy Change and Discourse in Europe*. London: Routledge, 1–28.

Schmitter, Phillipe C. 1977. 'Modes of Interest Intermediation and Models of Societal Change in Western Europe', *Comparative Political Studies* 10, 1: 7–38.

———. 1982. 'Reflections on Where the Theory of Neo-Corporatism Has Gone and Where the Praxis of Neo-Corporatism May Be Going', in G. Lehmbruch and P.C. Schmitter, eds, *Patterns of Corporatist Policy-Making*. London: Sage.

———. 1985. 'Neo-corporatism and the State', in W. Grant, ed., *The Political Economy of Corporatism*. London: Macmillan.

Schneider, Anne, and Helen Ingram. 1988. 'Systematically Pinching Ideas: A Comparative Approach to Policy Design', *Journal of Public Policy* 8, 1: 61–80.

——— and ———. 1990a. 'Behavioural Assumptions of Policy Tools', *Journal of Politics* 52, 2: 510–29.

——— and ———. 1990b. 'Policy Design: Elements, Premises and Strategies', in S.S. Nagel, ed., *Policy Theory and Policy Evaluation: Concepts, Knowledge, Causes and Norms*. New York: Greenwood, 77–102.

—— and ——. 1993. 'Social Construction of Target Populations: Implications for Politics and Policy', *American Political Science Review* 87, 2: 334–47.

—— and ——. 1997. *Policy Design for Democracy*. Lawrence: University Press of Kansas.

Schneider, F., and Bruno S. Frey. 1988. 'Politico-Economic Models of Macroeconomic Policy: A Review of the Empirical Evidence', in Thomas D. Willett, ed., *Political Business Cycles: The Political Economy of Money, Inflation and Unemployment*. Durham, NC: Duke University Press, 239–75.

Schneider, Joseph W. 1985. 'Social Problems Theory: The Constructionist View', *Annual Review of Sociology* 11: 209–29.

Scholz, John T. 1984. 'Cooperation, Deterrence, and the Ecology of Regulatory Enforcement', *Law and Society Review* 18, 2: 179–224.

——. 1991. 'Cooperative Regulatory Enforcement and the Politics of Administrative Effectiveness', *American Political Science Review* 85, 1: 115–36.

Schon, Donald A., and Martin Rein. 1994. *Frame Reflection: Towards the Resolution of Intractable Policy Controversies*. New York: Basic Books.

Schrad, Mark Lawrence. 2007 'Constitutional Blemishes: American Alcohol Prohibition and Repeal as Policy Punctuation', *Policy Studies Journal* 35, 3: 437–63.

Schulman, Paul R. 1988. 'The Politics of "Ideational Policy"', *Journal of Politics* 50: 263–91.

Schultz, Richard, and Alan Alexandroff. 1985. *Economic Regulation and the Federal System*. Toronto: University of Toronto Press.

Schwartz, Bryan. 1997. 'Public Inquiries', *Canadian Public Administration* 40, 1: 72–85.

Sciarini, Pascal. 1986. 'Elaboration of the Swiss Agricultural Policy for the GATT Negotiations: A Network Analysis', *Swiss Journal of Sociology* 22, 1: 85–115.

Scott, Rudy. n.d. 'Empiricism, Rationalism, and Positivism'. At: <www.rudyscott.com/philosophy/phil425/isms.htm>.

Scrase, J.I., and W.R. Sheate. 2002. 'Integration and Integrated Approaches to Assessment: What Do They Mean for the Environment?', *Journal of Environmental Policy and Planning* 4, 1: 275–94.

Searle, J.R. 2005. 'What Is an Institution?', *Journal of Institutional Economics* 1, 1: 1–22.

Seeliger, R. 1996. 'Conceptualizing and Researching Policy Convergence', *Policy Studies Journal* 24, 2: 287–310.

Self, Peter. 1985. *Political Theories of Modern Government: Its Role and Reform*. London: Allen and Unwin.

Sell, S.K., and A. Prakash. 2004. 'Using Ideas Strategically: The Contest between Business and NGO Networks in Intellectual Property Rights', *International Studies Quarterly* 48, 1: 143–75.

Shapiro, Robert Y., and Lawrence R. Jacobs. 1989. 'The Relationship between Public Opinion and Public Policy: A Review', in S. Long, ed., *Political Behaviour Annual*. Boulder, Colo.: Westview Press.

Sharkansky, Ira. 1971. 'Constraints on Innovation in Policy Making: Economic Development and Political Routines', in Frank Marini, ed., *Toward a New Public Administration: The Minnowbrook Perspective*. Scranton, Penn.: Chandler.

——. 1997. *Policy Making in Israel: Routines for Simple Problems and Coping with the Complex*. Pittsburgh: University of Pittsburgh Press.

Sharp, Elaine B. 1994a. 'Paradoxes of National Anti-Drug Policymaking', in David A. Rochefort and Roger W. Cobb, eds, *The Politics of Problem Definition: Shaping the Policy Agenda*. Lawrence: University Press of Kansas, 98–116.

——. 1994b. 'The Dynamics of Issue Expansion: Cases from Disability Rights and Fetal Research Controversy', *Journal of Politics* 56, 4: 919–39.

Sharpe, D. 2001. 'The Canadian Charitable Sector: An Overview', in J. Phillips, B. Chapman, and D. Stevens, eds, *Between State and Market: Essays on Charities Law and Policy in Canada*. Toronto: University of Toronto Press.

Sharpe, L.J. 1975. 'The Social Scientist and Policy-Making: Some Cautionary Thoughts and Transatlantic Reflections', *Policy and Politics* 4, 2: 7–34.

———. 1985. 'Central Coordination and the Policy Network', *Political Studies* 33, 3: 361–81.

Sheingate, Adam D. 2000. 'Agricultural Retrenchment Revisited: Issue Definition and Venue Change in the United States and European Union', *Governance* 13, 3: 335–63.

Sheriff, Peta E. 1983. 'State Theory, Social Science, and Governmental Commissions', *American Behavioural Scientist* 26, 5: 669–80.

Shotland, R. Lance, and Melvin M. Mark. 1985. *Social Science and Social Policy*. Beverly Hills, Calif.: Sage.

Siaroff, Alan. 1999. 'Corporatism in 24 Industrial Democracies: Meaning and Measurement', *European Journal of Political Research* 36: 175–205.

Sieber, Sam D. 1981. *Fatal Remedies: The Ironies of Social Intervention*. New York: Plenum.

Siedschlag, Alexander. 2000. 'Institutionalization and Conflict Management in the New Europe—Path-Shaping for the Better or Worse?', paper presented to the 18th World Congress of the International Political Science Association, Quebec City.

Simeon, Richard. 1976a. 'Studying Public Policy', *Canadian Journal of Political Science* 9, 4: 548–80.

———. 1976b. 'The "Overload Thesis" and Canadian Government', *Canadian Public Policy* 2, 4: 541–52.

Simmons, Robert H., et al. 1974. 'Policy Flow Analysis: A Conceptual Model for Comparative Public Policy Research', *Western Political Quarterly* 27, 3: 457–68.

Simon, Herbert A. 1946. 'The Proverbs of Administration', *Public Administration Review* 6, 1: 53–67.

———. 1955. 'A Behavioral Model of Rational Choice', *Quarterly Journal of Economics* 69, 1: 99–118.

———. 1957a. *Administrative Behavior: A Study of Decision-Making Processes in Administrative Organization*, 2nd edn. New York: Macmillan.

———. 1957b. *Models of Man, Social and Rational: Mathematical Essays on Rational Human Behavior in a Social Setting*. New York: Wiley.

———. 1973. 'The Structure of Ill Structured Problems', *Artificial Intelligence* 4: 181–201.

———. 1991. 'Bounded Rationality and Organizational Learning', *Organization Science* 2, 1: 125–35.

Sinclair, Darren. 1997. 'Self-Regulation versus Command and Control? Beyond False Dichotomies', *Law and Policy* 19, 4: 529–59.

Sinden, J.A., and D.J. Thampapillai. 1995. *Introduction to Benefit Cost Analysis*. Melbourne: Addison-Wesley Longman.

Singer, Otto. 1990. 'Policy Communities and Discourse Coalitions', *Knowledge: Creation, Diffusion, Utilization* 11, 4: 428–58.

Skilling, H.G. 1966. 'Interest Groups and Communist Politics', *World Politics* 18, 3: 435–51.

Skocpol, Theda. 1985. 'Bringing the State Back In: Strategies of Analysis in Current Research', in Evans et al. (1985).

Skogstad, Grace. 1998. 'Ideas, Paradigms and Institutions: Agricultural Exceptionalism in the European Union and the United States', *Governance* 11, 4: 463–90.

———. 2003. 'Legitimacy and/or Policy Effectiveness? Network Governance and GMO Regulation in the European Union', *Journal of European Public Policy* 10, 3: 321–38.

Skok, James E. 1995. 'Policy Issue Networks and the Public Policy Cycle: A Structural-Functional Framework for Public Administration', *Public Administration Review* 55, 4: 325–32.

Skowronek, Stephen. 1982. *Building a New American State: The Expansion of National Administrative Capacities 1877–1920*. Cambridge: Cambridge University Press.

Slovic, Paul, Baruch Fischoff, and Sarah Lichtenstein. 1977. 'Behavioural Decision Theory', *Annual Review of Psychology* 28: 1–39.

———, ———, and ———. 1985. 'Regulation of Risk: A Psychological Perspective', in R.G. Noll, ed., *Regulatory Policy and the Social Sciences*. Berkeley: University of California Press, 241–78.

Smith, Adrian. 2000. 'Policy Networks and Advocacy Coalitions: Explaining Policy Change and Stability in UK Industrial Pollution Policy?', *Environment and Planning C: Government and Policy* 18: 95–114.

Smith, Gilbert, and David May. 1980. 'The Artificial Debate between Rationalist and Incrementalist Models of Decision-Making', *Policy and Politics* 8, 2: 147–61.

Smith, Martin J. 1990. 'Pluralism, Reformed Pluralism and Neopluralism: The Role of Pressure Groups in Policy-Making', *Political Studies* 38 (June): 302–22.

———. 1993. *Pressure, Power and Policy: State Autonomy and Policy Networks in Britain and the United States*. Aldershot: Harvester Wheatsheaf.

———. 1994. 'Policy Networks and State Autonomy', in S. Brooks and A.-G. Gagnon, eds, *The Political Influence of Ideas: Policy Communities and the Social Sciences*. New York: Praeger.

———, David Marsh, and David Richards. 1993. 'Central Government Departments and the Policy Process', *Public Administration* 71 (Winter): 567–94.

Smith, Richard A. 1979. 'Decision Making and Non-Decision Making in Cities: Some Implications for Community Structural Research', *American Sociological Review* 44, 1: 147–61.

Smith, Rogers M. 1997. 'Still Blowing in the Wind: The American Quest for a Democratic, Scientific Political Science', in T. Bender and C.E. Schorske, eds, *American Academic Culture in Transformation: Fifty Years, Four Disciplines*. Princeton, NJ: Princeton University Press, 271–305.

Smith, T. Alexander. 1982. 'A Phenomenology of the Policy Process', *International Journal of Comparative Sociology* 23, 1 and 2: 1–16.

Smith, Thomas B. 1977. 'Advisory Committees in the Public Policy Process', *International Review of Administrative Sciences* 43, 2: 153–66.

———. 1985. 'Evaluating Development Policies and Programmes in the Third World', *Public Administration and Development* 5, 2: 129–44.

Snook, Scott A. 2000. *Friendly Fire: The Accidental Shootdown of U.S. BlackHawks over Northern Iraq*. Princeton, NJ: Princeton University Press.

Snow, David A., and Robert D. Benford. 1992. 'Master Frames and Cycles of Protest', in A.D. Morris and C.M. Mueller, eds, *Frontiers in Social Movement Theory*. New Haven: Yale University Press, 133–55.

Sobeck, J. 2003. 'Comparing Policy Process Frameworks: What Do They Tell Us about Group Membership and Participation for Policy Development?', *Administration and Society* 35, 3: 350–74.

Soroka, Stuart. 2002. *Agenda-Setting Dynamics in Canada*. Vancouver: University of British Columbia Press.

Spector, Malcolm, and John I. Kitsuse. 1987. *Constructing Social Problems*. New York: Aldine de Gruyter.

Speers, Kimberly. 2007. 'The Invisible Public Service: Consultants and Public Policy in Canada', in Dobuzinskis et al. (2007: 220–31).

Spence, David B. 1999. 'Agency Discretion and the Dynamics of Procedural Reform', *Public Administration Review* 59, 5: 425–42.

Spicker, P. 2005. 'Targeting, Residual Welfare and Related Concepts: Modes of Operation in Public Policy', *Public Administration* 83, 2: 345–65.

————. 2006. *Policy Analysis for Practice*. Bristol: Policy Press.

Spitzer, Robert J., ed. 1993. *Media and Public Policy*. Westport, Conn.: Praeger.

Spranca, Mark, Elisa Minsk, and Jonathan Baron. 1991. 'Omission and Commission in Judgement and Choice', *Journal of Experimental Social Psychology* 27: 76–105.

Sproule-Jones, M. 1989. 'Multiple Rules and the "Nesting" of Public Policies', *Journal of Theoretical Politics* 1, 4: 459–77.

————. 1994. 'User Fees', in A.M. Maslove, ed., *Taxes as Instruments of Public Policy*. Toronto: University of Toronto Press, 3–38.

Stanbury, W.T., and Jane Fulton. 1984. 'Suasion as a Governing Instrument', in A. Maslove, ed., *How Ottawa Spends 1984: The New Agenda*. Toronto: James Lorimer.

Stanton, Thomas H. 2002. 'Loans and Loan Guarantees', in Salamon (2002a: 381–409).

———— and Ronald C. Moe. 2002. 'Government Corporations and Government-Sponsored Enterprises', in Salamon (2002a: 80–116).

Stark, Andrew. 1992. '"Political-Discourse" Analysis and the Debate over Canada's Lobbying Legislation', *Canadian Journal of Political Science* 25, 3: 513–34.

Starling, Jay D. 1975. 'The Use of Systems Constructs in Simplifying Organized Social Complexity', in La Porte (1975: 131–72).

Starr, Paul. 1989. 'The Meaning of Privatization', in S.B. Kamerman and A.J. Kahn, eds, *Privatization and the Welfare State*. Princeton, NJ: Princeton University Press, 15–48.

————. 1990a. 'The Limits of Privatization', in D.J. Gayle and J.N. Goodrich, eds, *Privatization and Deregulation in Global Perspective*. New York: Quorum Books.

————. 1990b. 'The New Life of the Liberal State: Privatization and the Restructuring of State–Society Relations', in Suleiman and Waterbury (1990).

Stavins, Robert N. 2001. *Lessons from the American Experiment with Market-Based Environmental Policies*. Washington: Resources for the Future.

Stead, D., and E. Meijers. 2004. 'Policy Integration in Practice: Some Experiences of Integrating Transport, Land-Use Planning and Environmental Politics in Local Government', paper presented at the Berlin Conference on the Human Dimensions of Global Environmental Change: Greening of Policies—Interlinkages and Policy Integration.

Steinberg, Marc W. 1998. 'Tilting the Frame: Considerations on Collective Action Framing from a Discursive Turn', *Theory and Society* 27, 6: 845–72.

Steinberger, Peter J. 1980. 'Typologies of Public Policy: Meaning Construction and the Policy Process', *Social Science Quarterly* 61, 2: 185–97.

Steuerle, C. Eugene, and Eric C. Twombly. 2002. 'Vouchers', in Salamon (2002a: 445–65).

Stevenson, Randolph T. 2001. 'The Economy and Policy Mood: A Fundamental Dynamic of Democratic Politics', *American Journal of Political Science* 45, 3: 620–33.

Stewart, John. 1974. *The Canadian House of Commons*. Montreal and Kingston: McGill-Queen's University Press.

Stigler, George J. 1975. *The Citizen and the State: Essays on Regulation*. Chicago: University of Chicago Press.

Stimson, James A. 1991. *Public Opinion in America: Moods, Cycles and Swings*. Boulder, Colo.: Westview Press.

————, Michael B. Mackuen, and Robert S. Erikson. 1995. 'Dynamic Representation', *American Political Science Review* 89, 3: 543–65.

Stoker, Robert P. 1989. 'A Regime Framework for Implementation Analysis', *Policy Studies Review* 9, 1.

Stokey, Edith, and Richard Zeckhauser. 1978. *A Primer for Policy Analysis*. New York: Norton.

Stokman, F.N., and J. Berveling. 1998. 'Predicting Outcomes of Decision-Making: Five Competing Models of Policy-Making', in M. Fennema, C. Van der Eijk, and H. Schijf, eds, *In Search of Structure: Essays in Social Science and Methodology*. Amsterdam: Het Spinhuis, 147–71.

Stone, Deborah A. 1988. *Policy Paradox and Political Reason*. Glenview, Ill.: Scott, Foresman.
———. 1989. 'Causal Stories and the Formation of Policy Agendas', *Political Science Quarterly* 104, 2: 281–300.
Stone, Diane A. 1996. *Capturing the Political Imagination*. London: Frank Cass.
———. 2007. 'Recycling Bins, Garbage Cans, or Think Tanks? Three Myths Regarding Policy Analysis Institutes', *Public Administration* 85, 2: 259–78.
———, Andrew Denham, and Mark Garnett. 1998. *Think Tanks across Nations: A Comparative Approach*. Manchester: Manchester University Press.
———. 2008. 'Global Public Policy, Transnational Policy Communities, and Their Networks', *Policy Studies Journal* 36, 1: 19–38.
Studlar, Donley T. 2002. *Tobacco Control: Comparative Politics in the United States and Canada*. Peterborough, Ont.: Broadview Press.
———. 2007. 'Ideas, Institutions and Diffusion: What Explains Tobacco Control Policy in Australia, Canada and New Zealand?', *Commonwealth and Comparative Politics* 45, 2: 164–84.
Suchman, Edward A. 1967. *Evaluative Research: Principles and Practices in Public Service and Social Action Programs*. New York: Russell Sage Foundation.
———. 1979. *Social Sciences in Policy-Making*. Paris: OECD.
Suchman, Mark C. 1995. 'Managing Legitimacy: Strategic and Institutional Approaches', *Academy of Management Review* 20, 3: 571–610.
Suedfeld, Peter, and Philip E. Tetlock. 1992. 'Psychological Advice about Political Decision Making: Heuristics, Biases, and Cognitive Defects', in Suedfeld and Tetlock, eds, *Psychology and Social Policy*. New York: Hemisphere Publishing, 51–70.
Suleiman, Ezra N., and John Waterbury, eds. 1990. *Political Economy of Public Sector Reform and Privatization*. Boulder, Colo.: Westview Press.
Sulitzeanu-Kenan, R., and C. Hood. 2005. 'Blame Avoidance with Adjectives? Motivation, Opportunity, Activity and Outcome', paper for ECPR Joint Sessions, Blame Avoidance and Blame Management Workshop 14–20 Apr., Granada, Spain.
Sunnevag, Kjell J. 2000. 'Designing Auctions for Offshore Petroleum Lease Allocation', *Resources Policy* 26: 3–16.
Surel, Yves. 2000. 'The Role of Cognitive and Normative Frames in Policy-Making', *Journal of European Public Policy* 7, 4: 495–512.
Sutherland, Sharon L. 1993. 'The Public Service and Policy Development', in M. Michael Atkinson, ed., *Governing Canada: Institutions and Public Policy*. Toronto: Harcourt Brace Jovanovich.
Suzuki, Motoshi. 1992. 'Political Business Cycles in the Public Mind', *American Political Science Review* 86, 4: 989–96.
Svenson, Ola. 1979. 'Process Descriptions of Decision Making', *Organizational Behaviour and Human Performance* 23: 86–112.
Swank, Duane. 2000. *Diminished Democracy? Global Capital, Political Institutions, and Policy Change in Developed Welfare States*. New York: Cambridge University Press.
Swiss, James E. 1991. *Public Management Systems: Monitoring and Managing Government Performance*. Upper Saddle River, NJ: Prentice-Hall.
Talbert, Jeffrey C., Bryan D. Jones, and Frank R. Baumgartner. 1995. 'Non-legislative Hearings and Policy Change in Congress', *American Journal of Political Science* 39, 2: 383–406.
Tamuz, Michael. 2001. 'Learning Disabilities for Regulators: The Perils of Organizational Learning in the Air Transportation Industry', *Administration and Society* 33, 3: 276–302.
Taylor, Andrew J. 1989. *Trade Unions and Politics: A Comparative Introduction*. Basingstoke: Macmillan.

Teisman, Geert R. 2000. 'Models for Research into Decision-Making Processes: On Phases, Streams and Decision-Making Rounds', *Public Administration* 78, 4: 937–56.

Tenbensel, T. 2004. 'Does More Evidence Lead to Better Policy? The Implications of Explicit Priority-Setting in New Zealand's Health Policy for Evidence-Based Policy', *Policy Studies* 25, 3: 190–207.

Tepper, S.J. 2004. 'Setting Agendas and Designing Alternatives: Policymaking and the Strategic Role of Meetings', *Review of Policy Research* 21, 4: 523–42.

Termeer, C.J.A.M., and J.F.M. Koppenjan. 1997. 'Managing Perceptions in Networks', in W.J.M. Kickert, E.-H. Klijn, and J.F.M. Koppenjan, eds, *Managing Complex Networks: Strategies for the Public Sector*. London: Sage, 79–97.

Thacher, D., and M. Rein. 2004. 'Managing Value Conflict in Public Policy', *Governance* 17, 4: 457–86.

t'Hart, Paul, and Marieka Kleiboer. 1995. 'Policy Controversies in the Negotiatory State', *Knowledge and Policy* 8, 4: 5–26.

——— and Ariadne Vromen. 2008. 'A New Era for Think Tanks in Public Policy? International Trends, Australian Realities', *Australian Journal of Public Administration* 67, 2: 135–48.

Thatcher, Mark. 1998. 'The Development of Policy Network Analysis: From Market Origins to Overarching Frameworks', *Journal of Theoretical Politics* 10, 4: 389–416.

Thelen, Kathleen. 2003. 'How Institutions Evolve: Insights from Comparative Historical Analysis', in J. Mahoney and D. Rueschemeyer, eds, *Comparative Historical Analysis in the Social Sciences*. Cambridge: Cambridge University Press, 208–40.

———. 2004. *How Institutions Evolve: The Political Economy of Skills in Germany, Britain, the United States and Japan*. Cambridge: Cambridge University Press.

——— and S. Steinmo. 1992. 'Historical Institutionalism in Comparative Politics', in Steinmo, Thelen, and F. Longstreth, eds, *Structuring Politics: Historical Institutionalism in Comparative Analysis*. Cambridge: Cambridge University Press.

Therborn, Goran. 1977. 'The Rule of Capital and the Rise of Democracy', *New Left Review* 103: 3–41.

———. 1986. 'Neo-Marxist, Pluralist, Corporatist, Statist Theories and the Welfare State', in A. Kazancigil, ed., *The State in Global Perspective*. Aldershot, UK: Gower.

Thomas, E.V. 2003. 'Sustainable Development, Market Paradigms and Policy Integration', *Journal of Environmental Policy and Planning* 5, 2: 201–16.

Thomas, Gerald B. 1999. 'External Shocks, Conflict and Learning as Interactive Sources of Change in U.S. Security Policy', *Journal of Public Policy* 19, 2: 209–31.

Thomas, H.G. 2001. 'Towards a New Higher Education Law in Lithuania: Reflections on the Process of Policy Formulation', *Higher Education Policy* 14, 3: 213–23.

Thomas, John W., and Merilee S. Grindle. 1990. 'After the Decision: Implementing Policy Reforms in Developing Countries', *World Development* 18, 8: 1163–81.

Thompson, E.P. 1978. *The Poverty of Theory and Other Essays*. London: Merlin Press.

Thompson, G.F. 2003. *Between Hierarchies and Markets: The Logic and Limits of Network Forms of Organization*. Oxford: Oxford University Press.

Thompson, John B. 1990. *Ideology and Modern Culture: Critical Social Theory in the Era of Mass Communication*. Cambridge: Polity Press.

Thompson, W.B. 2001. 'Policy Making through Thick and Thin: Thick Description as a Methodology for Communications and Democracy', *Policy Sciences* 34: 63–77.

Thomson, Robert. 2001. 'The Programme to Policy Linkage: The Fulfilment of Election Pledges on Socio-Economic Policy in the Netherlands, 1986–1998', *European Journal of Political Research* 40: 171–97.

———, Frans N. Stokman, and Rene Torenvlied. 2003. 'Models of Collective Decision-Making: Introduction', *Rationality and Society* 15, 1: 5–14.

Tilly, Charles. 1984. *Big Structures, Large Processes, Huge Comparisons*. New York: Russell Sage Foundation.

Timmermans, Arco. 2001. 'Arenas as Institutional Sites for Policymaking: Patterns and Effects in Comparative Perspective', *Journal of Comparative Policy Analysis* 3: 311–37.

——— and Ivar Bleiklie. 1999. 'Institutional Conditions for Policy Design: Types of Arenas and Rules of the Game', ECPR Joint Sessions of Workshops, Mannheim.

Tocqueville, Alexis de. 1956. *Democracy in America*. New York: New American Library.

Torenvlied, Rene, and A. Akkerman. 2004. 'Theory of "Soft" Policy Implementation in Multilevel Systems with an Application to Social Partnership in the Netherlands', *Acta Politica* 39: 31–58.

Torfing, Jacob. 2001. 'Path-Dependent Danish Welfare Reforms: The Contribution of the New Institutionalisms to Understanding Evolutionary Change', *Scandinavian Political Studies* 24, 4: 277–309.

Torgerson, Douglas. 1983. 'Contextual Orientation in Policy Analysis: The Contribution of Harold D. Lasswell', *Policy Sciences* 18: 240–52.

———. 1986. 'Between Knowledge and Politics: Three Faces of Policy Analysis', *Policy Sciences* 19, 1: 33–59.

———. 1990. 'Origins of the Policy Orientation: The Aesthetic Dimension in Lasswell's Political Vision', *History of Political Thought* 11 (Summer): 340–4.

———. 1996. 'Power and Insight in Policy Discourse: Post-Positivism and Policy Discourse', in L. Dobuzinskis, M. Howlett, and D. Laycock, eds, *Policy Studies in Canada: The State of the Art*. Toronto: University of Toronto Press, 266–98.

Torgler, B. 2004. 'Moral Suasion: An Alternative Tax Policy Strategy? Evidence from a Controlled Field Experiment in Switzerland', *Economics of Governance* 5, 3: 235–53.

Townsend, R.E., J. McColl, and M.D. Young. 2006. 'Design Principles for Individual Transferable Quotas', *Marine Policy* 30: 131–41.

Trebilcock, Michael J., and Douglas G. Hartle. 1982. 'The Choice of Governing Instrument', *International Review of Law and Economics* 2: 29–46.

——— et al. 1982. *The Choice of Governing Instrument*. Ottawa: Canadian Government Publication Centre.

Triantafillou, Peter. 2007. 'Benchmarking in the Public Sector: A Critical Conceptual Framework', *Public Administration* 85, 3: 829–46.

Tribe, Laurence H. 1972. 'Policy Science: Analysis or Ideology?', *Philosophy and Public Affairs* 2, 1: 66–110.

True, James L., Bryan D. Jones, and Frank R. Baumgartner. 1999. 'Punctuated-Equilibrium Theory: Explaining Stability and Change in American Policymaking', in Sabatier (1999a: 97–115).

Truman, David R. 1964. *The Governmental Process: Political Interests and Public Opinion*. New York: Knopf.

Tufte, Edward R. 1978. *Political Control of the Economy*. Princeton, NJ: Princeton University Press.

Tumber, H., and S.R. Waisbord. 2004. 'Political Scandals and Media across Democracies, Volume I', *American Behavioural Scientist* 47, 8: 1031–9.

Tuohy, Caroline. 1992. *Policy and Politics in Canada: Institutionalized Ambivalence*. Philadelphia: Temple University Press.

———. 1999. *Accidental Logics: The Dynamics of Change in the Health Care Arena in the United States, Britain, and Canada*. New York: Oxford University Press.

——— and A.D. Wolfson. 1978. 'Self-Regulation: Who Qualifies?', in P. Slayton and M.J. Trebilcock, eds, *The Professions and Public Policy*. Toronto: University of Toronto Press, 111–22.

Tupper, Allan. 1979. 'The State in Business', *Canadian Public Administration* 22, 1: 124–50.

———— and G.B. Doern. 1981. 'Public Corporations and Public Policy in Canada', in Tupper and Doern, eds, *Public Corporations and Public Policy in Canada*. Montreal: Institute for Research on Public Policy, 1–50.

Tversky, Amos, and Daniel Kahneman. 1981. 'The Framing of Decisions and the Psychology of Choice', *Science* 211 (Jan.): 453–8.

———— and ————. 1982. 'Judgement under Uncertainty: Heuristics and Biases', in Kahneman, P. Slovic, and Tversky, eds, *Judgement under Uncertainty: Heuristics and Biases*. Cambridge: Cambridge University Press, 3–20.

———— and ————. 1986. 'Rational Choice and the Framing of Decisions', *Journal of Business* 59, 4, part 2: S251–79.

Twight, C. 1991. 'From Claiming Credit to Avoiding Blame: The Evolution of Congressional Strategy for Asbestos Management', *Journal of Public Policy* 11, 2: 153–86.

UNCTAD. 2001. *World Investment Report 2001*. New York: United Nations.

Unger, Brigitte, and Frans van Waarden. 1995. 'Introduction: An Interdisciplinary Approach to Convergence', in Unger and van Waarden, eds, *Convergence or Diversity? Internationalization and Economic Policy Response*. Aldershot: Avebury, 1–35.

Utton, M.A. 1986. *The Economics of Regulating Industry*. Oxford: Blackwell.

Uusitalo, Hannu. 1984. 'Comparative Research on the Determinants of the Welfare State: The State of the Art', *European Journal of Political Research* 12, 4: 403–22.

Valkama, Pekka, and Stephen J. Bailey. 2001. 'Vouchers as an Alternative Public Sector Funding System', *Public Policy and Administration* 16, 1: 32–58.

van Bueren, Ellen, Erik-Hans Klijn, and Joop Koppenjan. 2001. 'Network Management as a Linking Mechanism in Complex Policy-Making and Implementation Processes: Analyzing Decision-Making and Learning for an Environmental Issue', paper for the Fifth International Research Symposium in Public Management, Barcelona, 9–11 Apr.

van de Kerkof, Marleen. 2006. 'Making a Difference: On the Constraints of Consensus Building and the Relevance of Deliberation in Stakeholder Dialogues', *Policy Sciences* 39, 3: 279–99.

van der Eijk, Door C., and W.J.P. Kok. 1975. 'Non-decisions Reconsidered', *Acta Politika* 10, 3: 277–301.

Van Kersbergen, K., and F. Van Waarden. 2004. ' "Governance" as a Bridge between Disciplines: Cross-Disciplinary Inspiration Regarding Shifts in Governance and Problems of Governability, Accountability and Legitimacy', *European Journal of Political Research* 43, 2: 143–72.

van Meter, D., and C. van Horn. 1975. 'The Policy Implementation Process: A Conceptual Framework', *Administration and Society* 6, 4: 445–88.

Van Waarden, Frans. 1992. 'Dimensions and Types of Policy Networks', *European Journal of Political Research* 21, 1 and 2: 29–52.

Van Winden, Frans A.A.M. 1988. 'The Economic Theory of Political Decision-Making', in J. van den Broeck, ed., *Public Choice*. Dordrecht: Kluwer.

Varone, Frederic. 2000. 'Le Choix des instruments de l'action publique: Analyse Comparée des politiques energétiques en Europe et en Amérique du Nord', *Revue Internationale de Politique Comparée* 7, 1: 167–201.

———— and Rejean Landry. 1997. 'The Choice of Policy Tools: In Search of Deductive Theory', paper presented at the European Consortium for Political Research Joint Sessions, Bern, Switzerland, 27 Feb.–4 Mar.

Vaughan, Diane. 1996. *The Challenger Launch Decision: Risky Technology, Culture and Deviance at NASA*. Chicago: University of Chicago Press.

Vedung, Evert, and Frans C.J. van der Doelen. 1998. 'The Sermon: Information Programs in the Public Policy Process—Choice, Effects and Evaluation', in Bemelmans-Videc et al. (1998: 103–28).

Verheijen, T. 1999. *Civil Service Systems in Central and Eastern Europe*. Cheltenham: Edward Elgar.

Vertzberger, Yaacov Y.I. 1998. *Risk Taking and Decision-making: Foreign Military Intervention Decisions*. Stanford, Calif.: Stanford University Press.

Vining, Aidan R., A.E. Boardman, and F. Poschmann. 2005. 'Public–Private Partnerships in the US and Canada: "There Are No Free Lunches"', *Journal of Comparative Policy Analysis* 7, 3: 199–220.

———— and David L. Weimer. 1990. 'Government Supply and Government Production Failure: A Framework Based on Contestability', *Journal of Public Policy* 10, 1: 1–22.

Vogel, David. 1986. *National Styles of Regulation: Environmental Policy in Great Britain and the United States*. Ithaca, NY: Cornell University Press.

Vogel, Steven K. 1996. *Freer Markets, More Rules: Regulatory Reform in Advanced Industrial Countries*. Ithaca, NY: Cornell University Press.

von Beyme, Klaus. 1983. 'Neo-Corporatism: A New Nut in an Old Shell?', *International Political Science Review* 4, 2: 173–96.

————. 1984. 'Do Parties Matter? The Impact of Parties on the Key Decisions in the Political System', *Government and Opposition* 19, 1: 5–29.

Voss, James F. 1998. 'On the Representation of Problems: An Information-Processing Approach to Foreign Policy Decision Making', in D.A. Sylvan and J.F. Voss, eds, *Problem Representation in Foreign Policy Decision Making*. Cambridge: Cambridge University Press, 8–26.

———— and Timothy A. Post. 1988. 'On the Solving of Ill-Structured Problems', in M.T.H. Chi, R. Glaser, and M.J. Farr, eds, *The Nature of Expertise*. Hillsdale, NJ: Lawrence Erlbaum Associates, 261–85.

Wade, H.W.R. 1965. 'Anglo-American Administrative Law: Some Reflections', *Law Quarterly Review* 81: 357–79.

————. 1966. 'Anglo-American Administrative Law: More Reflections', *Law Quarterly Review* 82: 226–52.

Wagle, Udaya. 2000. 'The Policy Science of Democracy: The Issues of Methodology and Citizen Participation', *Policy Sciences* 33: 207–23.

Wagner, Peter, et al. 1991. 'The Policy Orientation: Legacy and Promise', in Wagner, Bjorn Wittrock, and Helmut Wollman, eds, *Social Sciences and Modern States: National Experiences and Theoretical Crossroads*. Cambridge: Cambridge University Press, 2–27.

Wagner, Richard K. 1991. 'Managerial Problem Solving', in R.J. Sternberg and P.A. French, eds, *Complex Problem Solving: Principles and Mechanisms*. Hillsdale, NJ: Lawrence Erlbaum Associates, 159–83.

Wagschal, Uwe. 1997. 'Direct Democracy and Public Policy-Making', *Journal of Public Policy* 17, 2: 223–46.

Walker, Jack L. 1974. 'The Diffusion of Knowledge and Policy Change: Toward a Theory of Agenda Setting', paper presented to the annual meeting of the American Political Science Association, Chicago.

————. 1977. 'Setting the Agenda in the U.S. Senate: A Theory of Problem Selection', *British Journal of Political Science* 7: 423–45.

————. 1981. 'The Diffusion of Knowledge, Policy Communities and Agenda-Setting: The Relationship of Knowledge and Power', in John E. Tropman, M. Dluhy, and R. Lind, eds, *New Strategic Perspectives on Social Policy*. New York: Pergamon Press, 75–96.

————. 1991. *Mobilizing Interest Groups in America: Patrons, Professions and Social Movements*. Ann Arbor: University of Michigan Press.

Walker, W.E., and V.A.W.J. Marchau. 2004. 'Dealing with Uncertainty in Policy Analysis and Policymaking', *Integrated Assessment* 4, 1: 1–4.

Walsh, Annmarie Hauck. 1978. *The Public's Business: The Politics and Practices of Government Corporations*. Cambridge, Mass.: MIT Press.

Walsh, C. 1987. 'Individual Irrationality and Public Policy: In Search of Merit/Demerit Policies', *Journal of Public Policy* 7, 2: 103–34.

Walsh, James I. 1994. 'Institutional Constraints and Domestic Choices: Economic Convergence and Exchange Rate Policy in France and Italy', *Political Studies* 42: 243–58.

Warwick, Paul V. 2000. 'Policy Horizons in West European Parliamentary Systems', *European Journal of Political Research* 38: 37–61.

Weaver, R. Kent. 1986. 'The Politics of Blame Avoidance', *Journal of Public Policy* 6, 4: 371–98.

———. 1988. *Automatic Government: The Politics of Indexation*. Washington: Brookings Institution.

———. 1989. 'The Changing World of Think Tanks', *PS: Political Science and Politics* 22: 563–78.

——— and Bert A. Rockman, eds. 1993a. *Do Institutions Matter? Government Capabilities in the United States and Abroad*. Washington: Brookings Institution.

——— and ———. 1993b. 'When and How Do Institutions Matter?', in Weaver and Rockman (1993a).

——— and ———. 1993c. 'Assessing the Effects of Institutions', in Weaver and Rockman (1993a).

Webber, David J. 1986. 'Analyzing Political Feasibility: Political Scientists' Unique Contribution to Policy Analysis', *Policy Studies Journal* 14, 4: 545–54.

———. 1992. 'The Distribution and Use of Policy Knowledge in the Policy Process', in W.N. Dunn and R.M. Kelly, eds, *Advances in Policy Studies Since 1950*. New Brunswick, NJ: Transaction.

Weber, Max. 1978. *Economy and Society: An Outline of Interpretive Sociology*. Berkeley: University of California Press.

Weber, Ronald E., and William R. Shaffer. 1972. 'Public Opinion and American State Policy-Making', *Midwest Journal of Political Science* 16: 683–99.

Wedel, J.R., C. Shore, G. Feldman, and S. Lathrop. 2005. 'Toward an Anthropology of Public Policy', *Annals, American Academy of Political and Social Science* 600: 30–51.

Weick, Karl E. 1976. 'Educational Organizations as Loosely Coupled Systems', *Administrative Science Quarterly* 21: 1–19.

Weimer, David L., and Aidan R. Vining. 1992. *Policy Analysis: Concepts and Practice*, 2nd edn. Englewood Cliffs, NJ: Prentice-Hall.

——— and ———. 1999. *Policy Analysis: Concepts and Practice*, 3rd edn. Englewood Cliffs, NJ: Prentice-Hall.

Weir, Margaret. 1992. 'Ideas and the Politics of Bounded Innovation', in Sven Steinmo, Kathleen Thelen, and Frank Longstreth, eds, *Structuring Politics: Historical Institutionalism in Comparative Analysis*. Cambridge: Cambridge University Press, 188–216.

Weiss, Andrew, and Edward Woodhouse. 1992. 'Reframing Incrementalism: A Constructive Response to Critics', *Policy Sciences* 25, 3: 255–73.

Weiss, Carol H. 1972. *Evaluation Research: Methods of Assessing Program Effectiveness*. Englewood Cliffs, NJ: Prentice-Hall.

———. 1977a. *Using Social Research in Public Policy Making*. Lexington, Mass.: Lexington Books.

———. 1977b. 'Research for Policy's Sake: The Enlightenment Function of Social Science Research', *Policy Analysis* 3, 4: 531–45.

———. 1980. 'Knowledge Creep and Decision Accretion', *Knowledge: Creation, Diffusion, Utilization* 1, 3: 381–404.

————. 1983. 'Ideology, Interests, and Information', in Daniel Callahan and Bruce Jennings, eds, *Ethics, the Social Sciences, and Policy Analysis*. New York: Plenum Press, 213–45.

Weiss, Janet A. 1982. 'Coping with Complexity: An Experimental Study of Public Policy Decision-Making', *Journal of Policy Analysis and Management* 2, 1: 66–87.

———— and Mary Tschirhart. 1994. 'Public Information Campaigns as Policy Instruments', *Journal of Policy Analysis and Management* 13, 1: 82–119.

Weiss, Linda. 1999. 'Globalization and National Governance: Autonomy or Inter-dependence', *Review of International Studies* 25 (supp.): 59–88.

———— and John M. Hobson. 1995. *States and Economic Development: A Comparative Historical Analysis*. Cambridge: Polity Press.

Werner, Jann, and Kai Wegrich. 2007. 'Theories of the Policy Cycle', in Frank Fischer, Gerald J. Miller, and Mara S. Sidney, eds, *Handbook of Public Policy Analysis: Theory, Politics and Methods*. Boca Raton, Fla: CRC Press, 43–62.

West, W. 2005. 'Administrative Rulemaking: An Old and Emerging Literature', *Public Administration Review* 65, 6: 655–68.

Weyland, K. 2005. 'Theories of Policy Diffusion—Lessons from Latin American Pension Reform', *World Politics* 57, 2: 262–95.

Whalen, Thomas. 1987. 'Introduction to Decision-Making under Various Kinds of Uncertainty', in J. Kacprzyk and S.A. Orlovski, eds, *Optimization Models Using Fuzzy Sets and Possibility Theory*. Dordrecht: D. Reidel, 27–49.

Whitley, Edgar A., Ian R. Hosein, Ian O. Angell, and Simon Davies. 2007. 'Reflections on the Academic Policy Analysis Process and the UK Identity Cards Scheme', *The Information Society* 23: 51–8.

Wildavsky, Aaron. 1962. 'The Analysis of Issue-Contexts in the Study of Decision-Making', *Journal of Politics* 24, 4: 717–32.

————. 1969. 'Rescuing Policy Analysis from PPBS', *Public Administration Review* (Mar.–Apr.): 189–202.

————. 1979. *Speaking Truth to Power: The Art and Craft of Policy Analysis*. Boston: Little, Brown.

Wilensky, Harold L. 1975. *The Welfare State and Equality: Structural and Ideological Roots of Public Expenditures*. Berkeley: University of California Press.

———— et al. 1985. *Comparative Social Policy: Theories, Methods, Findings*. Berkeley: Institute of International Studies.

———— and Lowell Turner. 1987. *Democratic Corporatism and Policy Linkages: The Interdependence of Industrial, Labor-Market, Incomes, and Social Policies in Eight Countries*. Berkeley: University of California International & Area Studies.

Wilks, Stephen, and Maurice Wright. 1987. 'Conclusion: Comparing Government–Industry Relations: States, Sectors, and Networks', in Wilks and Wright, eds, *Comparative Government–Industry Relations: Western Europe, the United States, and Japan*. Oxford: Clarendon Press, 274–313.

Williamson, Oliver E. 1985. *The Economic Institutions of Capitalism: Firms, Markets, Relational Contracting*. New York: Free Press.

————. 1996. 'Transaction Cost Economics and Organization Theory', in Williamson, ed., *The Mechanisms of Governance*. New York: Oxford University Press, 219–49.

Wilsford, David. 1985. 'The *Conjoncture* of Ideas and Interests', *Comparative Political Studies* 18, 3: 357–72.

————. 1994. 'Path Dependency, or Why History Makes It Difficult but Not Impossible to Reform Health Care Systems in a Big Way', *Journal of Public Policy* 14, 3: 251–84.

Wilson, Carter A. 2000. 'Policy Regimes and Policy Change', *Journal of Public Policy* 20, 3: 247–71.

Wilson, Graham K. 1990a. *Business and Politics: A Comparative Introduction*, 2nd edn. London: Macmillan.

———. 1990b. *Interest Groups*. Oxford: Blackwell.

Wilson, James Q. 1974. 'The Politics of Regulation', in J.W. McKie, ed., *Social Responsibility and the Business Predicament*. Washington: Brookings Institution, 135–68.

Wilson, V. Seymour. 1971. 'The Role of Royal Commissions and Task Forces', in Doern and Aucoin (1971: 113–29).

Wilson, Woodrow. 1887. 'The Study of Administration', *Political Science Quarterly* 2, 2: 197–222.

Winkler, J.T. 1976. 'Corporatism', *European Journal of Sociology* 17, 1: 100–36.

Woerdman, Edwin. 2000. 'Organizing Emissions Trading: The Barrier of Domestic Permit Allocation', *Energy Policy* 28: 613–23.

Wolf, Charles, Jr. 1979. 'A Theory of Nonmarket Failure: Framework for Implementation Analysis', *Journal of Law and Economics* 22, 1: 107–39.

———. 1987. 'Markets and Non-Market Failures: Comparison and Assessment', *Journal of Public Policy* 7, 1: 43–70.

———. 1988. *Markets or Governments: Choosing between Imperfect Alternatives*. Cambridge, Mass.: MIT Press.

Wolfe, Joel D. 1989. 'Democracy and Economic Adjustment: A Comparative Analysis of Political Change', in R.E. Foglesong and J.D. Wolfe, eds, *The Politics of Economic Adjustment*. New York: Greenwood Press.

Woll, Cornelia. 2007. 'Leading the Dance? Power and Political Resources of Business Lobbyists', *Journal of Public Policy* 27, 1: 57–78.

Wood, B. Dan, and A. Doan. 2003. 'The Politics of Problem Definition: Applying and Testing Threshold Models', *American Journal of Political Science* 47, 4: 640–53.

——— and Jeffrey S. Peake. 1998. 'The Dynamics of Foreign Policy Agenda-Setting', *American Political Science Review* 92, 1: 173–84.

Wood, R.S. 2006. 'The Dynamics of Incrementalism: Subsystems, Politics and Public Lands', *Policy Studies Journal* 34, 1: 1–16.

Woodside, K. 1983. 'The Political Economy of Policy Instruments: Tax Expenditures and Subsidies', in M. Atkinson and M. Chandler, eds, *The Politics of Canadian Public Policy*. Toronto: University of Toronto Press, 173–97.

———. 1986. 'Policy Instruments and the Study of Public Policy', *Canadian Journal of Political Science* 19, 4: 775–93.

Woodward, Richard. 2004. 'The Organisation for Economic Cooperation and Development', *New Political Economy* 9, 1: 113–27.

Wraith, R.E., and G.B. Lamb. 1971. *Public Inquiries as an Instrument of Government*. London: George Allen and Unwin.

Wright, P. 1974. 'The Harassed Decision Maker: Time Pressures, Distraction and the Use of Evidence', *Journal of Applied Psychology* 59, 5: 555–61.

Wuthnow, Robert, ed. 1991. *Between States and Markets: The Voluntary Sector in Comparative Perspective*. Princeton, NJ: Princeton University Press.

Yanow, Dvora. 1992. 'Silences in Public Policy Discourse: Organizational and Policy Myths', *Journal of Public Administration Research and Theory* 2, 4: 399–423.

———. 1999. *Conducting Interpretive Policy Analysis*. Thousand Oaks, Calif.: Sage.

———. 2007. 'Interpretation in Policy Analysis: On Methods and Practice', *Critical Policy Analysis* 1, 1: 110–22.

Yarbrough, Beth V., and Robert M. Yarbrough. 1990. 'International Institutions and the New Economics of Organization', *International Organization* 44, 2: 235–59.

Yates, J. Frank, and Lisa G. Zukowski. 1976. 'Characterization of Ambiguity in Decision-Making', *Behavioural Science* 21: 19–25.

Ye, Min. 2007. 'Poliheuristic Theory, Bargaining, and Crisis Decision Making', *Foreign Policy Analysis* 3: 317–44.

Yee, Albert S. 1996. 'The Causal Effects of Ideas on Policies', *International Organizations* 50, 1: 69–108.

Yishai, Yael. 1993. 'Public Ideas and Public Policy', *Comparative Politics* 25, 2: 207–28.

Young, L., and J. Everitt. 2004. *Advocacy Groups*. Vancouver: University of British Columbia Press.

Young, Oran R. 1980. 'International Regimes: Problems of Concept Formation', *World Politics* 32: 331–56.

Zahariadis, N. 1995. *Markets, States, and Public Policy: Privatization in Britain and France*. Ann Arbor: University of Michigan Press.

——— and Christopher S. Allen. 1995. 'Ideas, Networks, and Policy Streams: Privatization in Britain and Germany', *Policy Studies Review* 14, 1 and 2: 71–98.

Zarco-Iasso, Hugo. 2005. 'Public–Private Partnerships: A Multidimensional Model for Contracting', *International Journal of Public Policy* 1, 1 and 2. 22–40.

Zarkin, Michael J. 2008. 'Organisational Learning in Novel Policy Situations: Two Cases of United States Communications Regulation', *Policy Studies* 29, 1: 87–100.

Zeckhauser, Richard. 1975. 'Procedures for Valuing Lives', *Public Policy* 23, 4: 419–64.

———. 1981. 'Preferred Policies When There Is a Concern for Probability of Adoption', *Journal of Environmental Economics and Management* 8: 215–37.

——— and Elmer Schaefer. 1968. 'Public Policy and Normative Economic Theory', in R.A. Bauer and K.J. Gergen, eds, *The Study of Policy Formation*. New York: Free Press, 27–102.

Zeigler, L. Harmon. 1964. *Interest Groups in American Society*. Englewood Cliffs, NJ: Prentice-Hall.

Zelditch, Morris, Jr, and Joan Butler Ford. 1994. 'Uncertainty, Potential Power and Nondecisions', *Social Psychology Quarterly* 57, 1: 64–76.

———, William Harris, George M. Thomas, and Henry A. Walker. 1983. 'Decisions, Nondecisions and Metadecisions', *Research in Social Movements, Conflict and Change* 5: 1–32.

Zerbe, Richard O., and Howard E. McCurdy. 1999. 'The Failure of Market Failure', *Journal of Policy Analysis and Management* 18, 4: 558–78.

Zey, Mary. 1992. 'Criticisms of Rational Choice Models', in Zey, ed., *Decision Making: Alternatives to Rational Choice Models*. Newbury Park, Calif.: Sage, 10–31.

Zijlstra, Gerrit Jan. 1978–9. 'Networks in Public Policy: Nuclear Energy in the Netherlands', *Social Networks* 1: 359–89.

Ziller, J. 2005. 'Public Law: A Tool for Modern Management, Not an Impediment to Reform', *International Review of Administrative Sciences* 71, 2: 267–77.

Zucker, Lynne G. 1988. 'Where Do Institutional Patterns Come From? Organizations as Actors in Social Systems', in Zucker, ed., *Institutional Patterns and Organizations: Culture and Environment*. Cambridge, Mass.: Ballinger, 23–49.

Zweifel, Thomas D., and Patricio Navia. 2000. 'Democracy, Dictatorship, and Infant Mortality', *Journal of Democracy* 11, 2: 99.

Zysman, John. 1983. *Governments, Markets and Growth*. Ithaca, NY: Cornell University Press.

———. 1994. 'How Institutions Create Historically Rooted Trajectories of Growth', *Industrial and Corporate Change* 3, 1: 243–83.

Index